Reanalyzing Program Evaluations

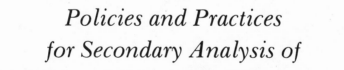

*Policies and Practices
for Secondary Analysis of
Social and Educational Programs*

Robert F. Boruch

Paul M. Wortman

David S. Cordray

and Associates

Reanalyzing Program Evaluations

Jossey-Bass Publishers

San Francisco • Washington • London • 1981

074613

REANALYZING PROGRAM EVALUATIONS
Policies and Practices for Secondary Analysis of
Social and Educational Programs
  by Robert F. Boruch, Paul M. Wortman,
  David S. Cordray, and Associates

Copyright © 1981 by: Jossey-Bass Inc., Publishers
  433 California Street
  San Francisco, California 94104

&

  Jossey-Bass Limited
  28 Banner Street
  London EC1Y 8QE

Library of Congress Cataloging in Publication Data
Main entry under title:

Reanalyzing program evaluations.

  Includes bibliographies and indexes.
  1. Evaluation research (Social action programs) —
Addresses, essays, lectures. I. Boruch, Robert F.
II. Wortman, Paul M. III. Cordray, David S.
IV. Title
H61.R36   361.6'1'072   81-2841
ISBN 0-87589-495-X   AACR2

H
61
· R36
1981

Manufactured in the United States of America

JACKET DESIGN BY WILLI BAUM

FIRST EDITION

Code 8109

The Jossey-Bass
Social and Behavioral Science Series

Special Adviser
Methodology of Social and
Behavioral Research
DONALD W. FISKE
University of Chicago

Preface

Secondary analysis here refers to the reanalysis of data generated in evaluations of social programs and in surveys bearing on these programs. The relevant programs include special efforts to create and improve educational processes, training labor, health services, criminal justice, and law enforcement. The general purposes of secondary analysis are to verify the credibility of earlier findings, develop and test new methods of analysis and new theories, and clarify the inferences that may be drawn from the data.

This volume is a descendant of two earlier monographs on applied social research to which we have contributed. The progenitor, *Social Experimentation* (New York: Academic Press, 1974), identifies secondary analysis as an arena for serious intellectual attention, partly on the grounds that data used in policy development ought to be open to criticism. The second, *Assuring the Confidentiality of Social Research Data* (Philadelphia: University of Pennsylvania Press, 1979), examines methods to protect the privacy of survey respondents while satisfying the scholar's need to examine the quality of evidence generated in surveys and social experiments. The renewed interest among social scientists in policy-relevant synthesis or meta-analysis, which is discussed in Chapter One, also informs the present volume.

The majority of the chapters collected here were written for the book, although several are adapted from sources not often reviewed by social scientists and two are based extensively on unpublished reports. The topical coverage is reasonably broad, covering policy on secondary analysis, rules and practices, and illustrations from different disciplines. The chapters on the character of secondary analysis respond to persistent old problems, such as difficulty in gaining access to data, and new ones. We believe the case studies help to reiterate the catholicity of applied social research; they are almost invariably interdisciplinary.

Our intended audience is the researcher who must capitalize on existing data by applying his or her findings in the interest of advancing science and policy. This audience includes the academic scholar and graduate student who recognize that most scientific research advances in small steps and that several steps might be taken with any particular data set. It includes the governmental or private sponsor of research who, using independent sources and competing analyses, tries to assure that data are well analyzed and that they contribute to our knowledge of social programs. Finally, the contractor or grantee who is occasionally responsible for secondary analysis will find valuable information here.

Development of this book has been facilitated by grants from the National Institute of Education, NIE-C-74-0115 and NIE-G-79-0128. Part of David Cordray's work on the book was supported by a National Institute of Mental Health grant 5T32MH15113-01. We are indebted to Daniel Antonoplos and Charles Stalford of the National Institute of Education for their encouragement and for their criticism of earlier work on the topic. Agency support does not, of course, imply agency or agency staff agreement with the opinions registered in this volume.

Finally, we have had the benefit of conscientious amanuenses. Lucina Gallagher, Ethelyn Bond, and Jean Holther performed with skill, unreasonable patience, and good humor. We are grateful to them for each virtue.

July 1981   ROBERT F. BORUCH
Evanston, Illinois

PAUL M. WORTMAN
Ann Arbor, Michigan

DAVID S. CORDRAY
Evanston, Illinois

Contents

Preface   ix

Contributors   xiv

1. Secondary Analysis: Why, How, and When   1
    Robert F. Boruch, David S. Cordray, Paul M. Wortman

    Part One: Policies of Key Agencies and Data Resources

2. Federal Statistical System: Access and Dissemination   21
    President's Reorganization Project

3. National Archives: Data Transfer and Storage   34
    Charles M. Dollar, Bruce I. Ambacher

4. National Institute of Justice: Access and Secondary   43
   Analysis
     Joel Garner

5. U.S. General Accounting Office: Role of   50
   Reanalysis in an Oversight Agency
     Harry S. Havens

6. Resources for Locating Public and Private Data   57
     William M. K. Trochim

Part Two: Documentation of Evaluations

7. Need for Better Documentation: Problems in a   68
   Reanalysis of Teacher Bias
     Joan A. W. Linsenmeier, Paul M. Wortman,
     Michael Hendricks

8. Technical Guidelines for Preparing and   84
   Documenting Data
     Alice Robbin

Part Three: Improving Reanalyses of Evaluations

9. Data Analysis in the Absence of Randomization   144
     Melvin R. Novick

10. Structural Equation Models in Analysis of   163
    Nonexperimental Data
      David M. Rindskopf

11. Regression-Based Analyses of Multilevel   194
    Education Data
      Leigh Burstein, M. David Miller

12. Empirical Bases for Estimating Effect Size   212
      Lee Sechrest, William H. Yeaton

13. Using the Results of Randomized Experiments   225
    to Construct Social Programs
      David B. Pillemer, Richard J . Light

Contents

Part Four: Diverse Aims and Methods: Case Studies

14. Capital Punishment as Deterrent: Challenging   237
    Isaac Ehrlich's Research
        William J. Bowers, Glenn L. Pierce

15. Capital Punishment as Deterrent: Challenging   262
    the Reanalysis
        Isaac Ehrlich

16. Reevaluating Educational Effects in the   283
    Cali Experiment
        Hernando Gomez

17. Assessing Educational and Nutritional Findings   294
    in the Cali Experiment
        Isaac I. Bejar, Victor Rezmovic

18. Reanalyzing Studies of Races Differences in   309
    Intelligence: Scale Dependent Mistakes
        Leroy Wolins

19. Reassessing the Impact of School Desegregation   322
        Joel M. Moskowitz, Paul M. Wortman

20. Rethinking the Results of a Negative Income   341
    Tax Experiment
        Margaret E. Boeckmann

21. Examining Potential Bias in Manpower   356
    Training Evaluations
        Steven M. Director

22. Research Uses of Longitudinal Survey Data on Women   364
        Clifford B. Hawley, William T. Bielby

Name Index   387

Subject Index   395

Contributors

ROBERT F. BORUCH is professor of psychology and education and director of the Program on Methodology and Evaluation Research at Northwestern University. He is also affiliated with Northwestern's Center for Urban Affairs and Policy Research, the Center for Statistics and Applied Probability, the Center for Health Services Policy Research, and the Applied Anthropology Program. Boruch was awarded the B.E. degree in metallurgical engineering from Stevens Institute of Technology (1964) and the Ph.D. degree in psychology from Iowa State University (1968).

Boruch has served as a member of various committees and panels of the National Academy of Sciences and has chaired the Committee on Program Evaluation for the Social Science Research Council. He has also acted as a consultant to government agencies in the United States, Europe, Africa, and South America.

Boruch's interests are in problems of applied social research and policy analysis, particularly methodology, social experimentation, policy, measurement, and legal and ethical problems in social research.

He is the author of numerous journal articles and is coauthor and coeditor of several books, including *Assuring the Confidentiality of Social Research Data* (with J. Cecil, 1979), *Social Experimentation: A Method for Planning and Evaluating Social Interventions* (with H. Riecken and others, 1974), and *An Appraisal of Educational Program Evaluations: Federal, State, and Local Agencies* (with D. S. Cordray, 1980).

PAUL M. WORTMAN is associate professor of public health and program director in the Center for Research on the Utilization of Scientific Knowledge, Institute of Social Research, University of Michigan. Prior to joining the faculty at Michigan, he served as a senior research associate and codirector of the Division of Methodology and Evaluation Research at Northwestern University and as assistant professor of psychology at Duke University. He was awarded the B.A. degree in mathematics from Yale University (1962), the M.S. degree in psychology and industrial administration from the Carnegie Institute of Technology (1965), and the Ph.D. degree in psychology from Carnegie-Mellon University (1967).

In addition to his academic activities, Wortman has been a consultant for the National Center for Health Services Research, National Institute of Education, and has been a member of the Psychology Training Review Committee for the National Institute of Mental Health (NIMH) and National Review Panel on School Desegregation.

Wortman has published an array of articles on methodology, program planning, secondary analysis, training in evaluation research, and evaluation practices in the educational, health, and mental health sectors. These articles have appeared in such journals as *American Psychologist, Evaluation Review, Professional Psychology,* and *Review of Educational Research.* Besides serving on editorial boards for professional journals, among them *Evaluation and the Health Professions* and *Evaluation and Program Planning,* he has recently edited *Methods for Evaluating Health Services* (1981).

DAVID S. CORDRAY is assistant professor of psychology and associate director of the Program on Methodology and Evaluation Research at Northwestern University. He is associated with Northwestern's Center for Health Services and Policy Research (as co-chair of the evaluation task force) and is also a faculty affiliate with the School of Education at Northwestern. Cordray was awarded the B.A. and M.A. degrees in experimental social psychology from California State University, Northridge (1972 and 1974, respectively), the Ph.D. degree in social and environmental psychology from Claremont Graduate School (1979), and a NIMH postdoctoral fellowship at Northwestern University.

Cordray's research interests encompass evaluation in education, criminal justice, and health; developing methods for improving causal inference in qualitative and quantitative field research; and establishing methods for secondary analysis and meta-analysis. He has published articles on these topics in *Evaluation Review, New Directions for Program Evaluation, Educational Researcher,* and *Educational Evaluation and Policy Analysis* and has also edited *An Appraisal of Educational Program Evaluations: Federal, State, and Local Agencies* (with R. F. Boruch, 1980).

BRUCE I. AMBACHER is archivist, Machine-Readable Archives Division, National Archives and Records Service.

ISAAC I. BEJAR is research scientist, Educational Testing Service, Princeton, New Jersey.

WILLIAM T. BIELBY is assistant professor of sociology, University of California, Santa Barbara.

MARGARET E. BOECKMANN is research associate, Urban Institute.

WILLIAM J. BOWERS is director, Center for Applied Social Research, Northeastern University.

LEIGH BURSTEIN is associate professor of education, University of California, Los Angeles.

STEVEN M. DIRECTOR is associate professor, Institute of Management and Labor Relations, Rutgers University.

CHARLES M. DOLLAR is director, Machine-Readable Archives Division, National Archives and Records Service.

ISAAC EHRLICH is professor of economics, State University of New York, Buffalo.

JOEL GARNER is social scientist, Office of Research and Evaluation Methods, National Institute of Justice.

HERNANDO GOMEZ is director of research, Human Ecology Research Foundation, Cali, Colombia.

HARRY S. HAVENS is assistant comptroller general, U.S. General Accounting Office.

CLIFFORD B. HAWLEY is assistant professor of economics, West Virginia University.

MICHAEL HENDRICKS is program analyst, U.S. Department of Health and Health Services.

RICHARD J. LIGHT is professor of education, Harvard University.

JOAN A. W. LINSENMEIER is research associate, Department of Psychology, Stanford University.

M. DAVID MILLER is research associate, School of Education, University of California, Los Angeles.

JOEL M. MOSKOWITZ is director of research, Napa Project, Pacific Institute for Research and Evaluation.

MELVIN R. NOVICK is professor of education and statistics, University of Iowa.

GLENN L. PIERCE is assistant director, Center for Applied Social Research, Northeastern University.

DAVID B. PILLEMER is assistant professor of psychology, Wellesley College.

VICTOR REZMOVIC is evaluation specialist, Office of Policy, Planning, and Evaluation, Food and Nutrition Service, U.S. Department of Agriculture.

DAVID M. RINDSKOPF is assistant professor, Department of Educational Psychology, Graduate Center, City University of New York.

ALICE ROBBIN is director, Data and Program Library Service, University of Wisconsin, Madison.

LEE SECHREST is director, Center for Research on the Utilization of Scientific Knowledge, Institute for Social Research, University of Michigan.

WILLIAM M. K. TROCHIM is assistant professor, Department of Human Services Studies, Cornell University.

LEROY WOLINS is professor of psychology and statistics, Iowa State University.

WILLIAM H. YEATON is research investigator, Center for Research on the Utilization of Social Knowledge, Institute for Social Research, University of Michigan.

Reanalyzing Program Evaluations

Policies and Practices
for Secondary Analysis of
Social and Educational Programs

Robert F. Boruch
David S. Cordray
Paul M. Wortman

1

Secondary Analysis:
Why, How, and When

A recent argument over the integrity of evidence on the effects of diabetes control methods bore more similarity to a war than to a scholarly exchange of views. Decisions, based on the University Group Diabetes Program data, were made before the analysis had been critiqued much less corroborated. Opposition groups emerged from universities and colleges to join forces with members of the pharmaceutical industry to assault the trials. Others mustered to the defense. Still others, the neutral estates, were appointed to poke through the rubble and establish the legitimacy of claims. The dissemination of data for reanalysis was blocked, in *Forsham* v. *Califano*, in the interest of territorial rights—the proprietary rights of the investigator—and probably also the wish not to succor the enemy. The bitter argument has been durable, having been waged for some ten years.

Not all arguments about the meaning of data are so grim. Scientists would not have time for much else if that were the case. This volume reflects a less combative posture. We focus on the secondary analysis of applied social research, especially evaluative research, and consider remedies to some problems it engenders.

Secondary analysis is the analysis of evaluative and policy-relevant data usually in ways other than those used in the original analysis; for example, testing new theories or hypotheses on data generated from the evaluation of social programs, testing new methods of analysis on data that are well understood, and verifying the credibility of original findings through the reanalysis of microdata. At its most intensive, secondary analysis may involve the reanalysis of individual records and the collection of information to increase the original records' interpretability and usefulness. At its simplest, it may involve critique—not a mean task when the objective is balance and the pressures for imbalance are substantial.

The instances of each type of secondary analysis that have appeared in recent years should not be taken as evidence that these analyses are easily or routinely undertaken. Recent experience suggests that these efforts, particularly those requiring access to microdata, are often hampered by technical, political, and institutional constraints. This volume focuses partly on ways to relax these restrictions.

This volume contains four major parts. The first three describe ways to increase the feasibility of secondary analyses, and the fourth contains illustrative case studies. The chapters appearing in Part One address issues related to institutional policy on access and dissemination of data, especially data that were generated under federal sponsorship. Part Two covers standards and guidelines for documentation of data files and analyses. Methodological issues pertinent to applied research in general and to secondary analysis in particular are discussed in Part Three. Part Four contains reports of actual reanalyses, covering a variety of substantive areas. They illustrate the diverse reasons why secondary analysis is conducted and the varied approaches to the task. We confine attention here to the social sciences, including psychology, education, economics, and sociology, although problems similar to those we discuss occur in other disciplines, including engineering and the physical sciences.

Rationale for Secondary Analysis

This volume is a descendant of other books on social experimentation to which we have contributed. The antecedents include the Social Science Research Council's Committee on Social Experiments which produced monographs on the use of randomized field experiments as a device for estimating the effects of social programs (see Riecken and others, 1974). Subsequent monographs, such as Boruch and Cecil (1979) and the present volume, attempted to better our understanding of major problems identified in the earlier work.

Other efforts, more directly linked to the subject at hand, include the demonstration by Campbell and Erlebacher (1970) that the Westinghouse-Ohio study of Head Start could have been mistaken in employing conventional statistical methods to analyze data that did not meet the requirements of those methods. Other precedents include the U.S. Office of Education's reviews of the quality of data generated by local program evaluations at the school district level. They also include a good many other studies of program evaluation efforts during the middle 1960s which suggested that many evaluations' designs were so flawed as to be useless for judging the effectiveness of programs.

The financial support for our research on secondary analysis and our preparation of this monograph on the topic stems partly from the National Institute of Education's interest in the issue. The institute has responsibility for advancing the methodology of educational research and development, which includes improving methods of collecting evidence, appraising its quality, and enhancing its utility. This mission derives from a tradition that views the quality of evidence as an important focus of attention, a necessary part of efforts to improve educational and social programs.

The rationale for secondary analysis and the forms it may take have been clarified over the past five years, partly because of actual secondary analysis of major program evaluations. These include the reassessment of data from evaluations of programs: Sesame Street by Cook and others (1975), Head Start by Magidson (1977) and Barnow and Cain (1977), the Equal Educational Opportunity Surveys by Mosteller and Moynihan (1972) and by Cain and Watts (1970), Follow Through by House and others (1978), desegregation appraisals by Jackson (1975) and Linsenmeier and Wortman (1978), and Voucher projects by Wortman, Reichardt, and St. Pierre (1978).

The general justifications for such reassessment are not much different in the governmental and scientific arenas. Political pressures to draw particular conclusions are persistent, and if one espouses the Jeffersonian view that free government is founded on jealousy, not confidence, the idea of competing analysis is natural. Especially if we adopt the position, as Cronbach and Suppes (1969) do, that, to be most effective, internal evaluators should be benign skeptics, the need for external analysts who are (if not less benign) benign in different ways is justified in local operations as well. To the extent that independent review is visible and conscientious, it may also impede diminution of the credibility of evaluation, a problem that affected early assessments of compensatory education programs.

Secondary analysis is also a constructive activity whose goals are fundamental to science: the verification of the quality of information and analysis. That analysts sometimes readily identify egregious errors is evident from the reexamination of early Follow Through evaluations in compensatory education (U.S. General Accounting Office, 1975). Among other errors, the original analysis failed to recognize chance variation, contained no statistical tests, and ignored the mislabeling of nonparticipating students as program participants. Not even "simple" research is immune from the problem if we judge by errors in scientific journals. Similar problems appear in law: witness Borchard's (1932) seminal work on eyewitness testimony and Loftus' (1979) remarkable illustrations of jury decisions based on beggarly evidence. In the physical sciences, the matter ranges from the mundane to the historically spectacular, if we may judge from Galileo's arguments with the Aristotelians, Watson and Crick's concerns about the adequacy of available data in their search for the structure of proteins, and other incidents.

Secondary analysis is an economical activity in that an expensive data set is used for several purposes, as illustrated by analysts' use of the Head Start data as part of university training, in justifying better evaluation design in government, and in understanding how difficult it is to produce and detect an effect of ameliorative action in the field (Datta, 1976). It is a new laboratory for the social sciences, created with marginal additions to the investments in the original research. It should be a catholic strategy; analysts must recognize both legislative intent and history of program activity, but neither intentions nor history may be clear. Further, the pedagogical justification is as pertinent in educational program evaluation as it is in such arenas as cancer research that are regarded by some as dramatic. Neither the student nor the professional analyst can learn to improve analyses effectively unless recent evaluations are routinely analyzed to identify their strengths and weaknesses.

Finally, interest in secondary analysis accompanies the emergence of another major area in applied social research—meta-analysis, defined by Glass (1976) as the reviewing of the results of different studies and the combining of statistical estimates of program effects to obtain a composite view of the effect of planned interventions. Smith and Glass (1977) illustrate the application of meta-analysis to psychotherapy research, Glass and Smith (1979) use meta-analysis to report on class size and achievement, and Light and Smith (1971) describe procedures for resolving conflicts among different studies. Glass is careful to recognize that secondary analysis is a crucial prerequisite to the aggregation of statistical estimates necessary for meaningful meta-analysis.

We do not mean to imply that all secondary analysis at the microdata level yields worthwhile results. The effort one may choose to exert ranges from simple review, through systematic and comprehensive assessment of the contents of reports, to full-blown reanalysis of data, internal reports, and any other product of the original exercise, including oral history, that the analyst can obtain. The poorest of evaluations can, we believe, be identified easily in less zealous review. More generally, the expertise and time required to handle intensive reanalysis warrants a stepwise approach to assessment: one begins with the simplest method and stops when the exercise no longer proves illuminating.

Nor will all secondary analyses produce new findings. Indeed, merely certifying that original estimates of program effect are reasonable may be quite sufficient. And a secondary analysis may be no less ambiguous than the original one. Such ambiguity is useful, despite the confusion it may engender, because it may help to verify that things are indeed as untidy as they seem to be.

Contemporary Problems

Although emphasis on the routine reanalysis of contemporary program evaluations is relatively new, the general idea of secondary analysis dates back to Madison's arguments with Congress about the quality and utility of information collected in the first censuses. The theme was evident prior to and during the Civil War with the American Statistical Association's (ASA) secondary analyses of data, which had been interpreted as showing the genetic inferiority of blacks.

As one ought to expect, three specific contemporary problems also have historical origins. One is the difficulty of obtaining the data needed for secondary analysis from the agencies or individuals who generated an evaluation. To illustrate, Rindskopf (1976) requested from a federal agency twenty evaluation reports cited by the agency in its annual report to the Congress. He successfully elicited only half the reports, and it is likely that he would have obtained only about a third of the actual data sets. Such problems may be more crucial at the local level of government. For example, when we attempted to obtain data generated in a training experiment in the Los Angeles Police Department, we were told that the data were "sufficiently well analyzed already" and "needed no further analysis." The problem is not a new one, of course. Demographic history, for example, tells us that the Massachusetts Bay Colony vigorously resisted efforts to obtain data about its mortality rates, fearing such analyses might discourage potential investors. Nor is this problem confined to the social sector. *For-*

sham v. *Califano* gives judicial support to the contention that even statistical health data can be legally withheld from the secondary analysts under certain conditions.

A second contemporary difficulty concerns data processing and analysis. Record keeping in the United States does not have a strong tradition: Records are often sloppy and record keeping is often not regarded as a professional exercise. Since research contractors and scholars receive no encouragement to produce good documentation, data are often poorly documented. That this problem is not a new one is quite clear. Alexander Graham Bell's efforts to establish the linkages between heredity and deafness by using census records were frustrated, among other things, by the fact that census interview protocols were scattered in a basement rather than being stored in an orderly way for ready access. Similar mishandling is often accorded prison records (Rossi, Berk, and Lenihan, 1980), crime records (Chelimsky, 1977), medical records (Roos and others, 1979), and tax and social security records (Del Bene and Scheuren, 1979).

A third problem is one fundamental to scientific research: The problem of identifying plausible explanations, especially estimating program effects, based on imperfect data. In principle, this problem is identical to that encountered by James Watson and Francis Crick, whose examination of the structure of DNA involved matching flawed and incomplete data to a model for the acid. Although history provides examples of this problem in the physical sciences, the history of plausible rival hypotheses and competing explanations in the social sciences is not particularly well documented. A simple example can, however, be found in the medieval rabbinical history: In debates about the allegedly different rates of in utero development of males and females, the learned men availed themselves of natural experiments. Maidservants who had been condemned to death were impregnated and then sent to prison. Postmortem examination revealed no sex differences in rate of development, even though impregnation had presumably occurred at the same time. The dissenting opinion by Rabbi Ismael identifies a rival explanation for the "tie" as absence of a guardian for lust—a guard might have had his way with one of the miscreants.

The Decision to Reanalyze Data

The nature of the decision to perform a secondary analysis of a program evaluation and the administrative mechanisms to assist that decision have not been well explored. Put simply, the factors that ought to be taken into account before one reanalyzes have not often been made explicit.

In a recent report to Congress on educational program evaluation, we made an explicit recommendation that all major program evaluations be subjected to an independent, objective critique and to reanalysis when necessary. We also recommended that a sample of federally sponsored local program evaluations be subjected to critique. The following remarks are based on that report (Boruch and Cordray, 1980) and extend the recommendation.

Four questions ought to be addressed in deciding to undertake a secondary analysis: (1) Why perform the secondary analysis and who would it serve? (2) At what level should it be undertaken? (3) Are the data accessible? and (4) Is the quality of data sufficient to sustain reanalysis?

The first question is probably the most difficult to answer. We pose it because it is fundamental and it shapes responses to subsequent questions. In justifying our recommendations to Congress, we emphasized that, although evaluations are used to develop policy, to make decisions, and to shape perspective on education at the national level, there is no formal mechanism for balanced, independent review of major evaluations. We argue that critique and secondary analysis can help the federal program manager to anticipate legitimate criticism of evaluations and to respond to incompetent criticism. For Congress and the manager, secondary analysis can illuminate the evaluation's strengths and weaknesses and inform decisions about future policy. It can complement the efforts of oversight agencies such as the General Accounting Office (GAO), and, indeed, should inform the GAO's own efforts. The Congressional Budget Office's staff members stress that they consider the quality of evaluations when they develop recommendations, and independent secondary analysis should make easier the task of assessing quality. The results can be exploited in congressional hearings on the evaluation itself if the secondary analysis parallels the primary evaluation.

Our rationale for recommending the periodic critique of a sample of local evaluations reflects our interest in fostering good practice. That practices are sometimes poor is evident from our review of local program evaluations. No federal agency routinely examines their quality; indeed, there is no real review in some areas. We did not recommend routine reanalysis of local data simply because we could see no justification for the expense such a process might engender.

The arguments against secondary analysis include redundancy. In brief, why should the government pay for a critique when most major evaluation contracts are subject to intensive review, competent monitoring, and the attention of good, critical advisory boards? It is possible that these procedures are quite sufficient. Our argument to both the Department of Education and to Congress, however, is that verifying their sufficiency is necessary. We believe, moreover, that such criticism ought to be competent rather than rhetorical, and that competent critiques must be encouraged. The rhetorical assaults need no encouragement when politically controversial programs are at issue. To minimize redundancy analysts must choose the appropriate level of secondary analysis.

A second argument against critique and reanalysis is that the activity may divert resources that can be better used elsewhere. Alternative activities include, for example, extensions of the original research to provide better documentation of nonsampling errors—a topic that is rarely given thorough treatment in evaluations—and the design of field replications of the earlier evaluation. We can offer no specific advice here, partly because experience in making such choices is so meager. We believe, however, that the recognition of these choices is warranted.

At what level should a secondary analysis be performed? That depends partly on the importance and complexity of the original evaluation. In some cases, simple critique is sufficient to highlight weaknesses, for example, the National Institute of Education's recent criticism of the American Institutes for Research evaluation of bilingual education. But that critique would have been more helpful had it included estimates of program effects based on secondary analysis of raw statistical records. As a practical matter, the importance of a program could be defined by how much was spent on the program, how many people will be affected by policy based on the original evaluation, and how durable the resulting policy will be.

Complexity of the evaluation is a natural standard here but it is no easier to define than importance. Most large-scale evaluations are complex and often some components are weak. Secondary analysis may help improve the product, perhaps by focusing on strong evidence and constructing new views of the data and their implications, or by evaluating the level of confidence the evidence inspires. Some analyses, for instance, are satisfactory to both primary and secondary analysts. A more intricate analysis of the same data will generate more cautious agreement, perhaps more qualification. Other analyses generated in the same study will be argued and debated. The specification of such agreements and disagreements is important for the policy makers, and in the long run, for applied social science.

If the data are not accessible, of course, decisions on reanalysis are moot. In our work, for instance, we have easily obtained some data to explore the use of evaluation designs required by Title I programs. We are unlikely to have the same luck with evaluations of bilingual programs—the field is too new and politically controversial to have attracted many conscientious methodologists and record keepers. The data from large-scale programs are often available from the National Archives and the various academic data banks, but local and state data may not be so accessible. It seems sensible to assure that samples of evaluations are available for reanalysis, and current regulations requiring the maintenance of data facilitate the task.

To assay the quality of data, we may use simple guidelines proposed by the statistical and evaluation communities. Information on sample design, sample size, response rate, and measurement error is essential for judging quality. If such information exists and points to either very high or very low quality, the analyst's decision is easy. The quality of most data falls between the two extremes, of course, which may argue for a mixture of critique based partly on review of documents and partly on reanalysis of subsets of the data. If the quality of the data is unknown, establishing the level of quality might be regarded as the only goal of secondary analysis.

Plan of the Book

If secondary analysis is to achieve its potential, some improvements in practice are warranted: the development of explicit policy regarding access, storage, and dissemination of data produced under government sponsorship; the formulation of standards for documenting the data; the development of new analytic methods; and the construction of case studies that illustrate the products of secondary analysis. The chapters in this volume are organized around these topics.

Part One: Policies of Key Agencies and Data Resources. Only a few government agencies have explicit written policy on secondary analysis. The Social Security Administration's Office of Research and the U.S. Bureau of the Census, for instance, have a sturdy tradition of making statistical data available to the public. Of the agencies with major responsibility for program evaluation, only one had a written policy on the disclosure of research data at this writing—the National Institute of Justice. Informal policy does exist elsewhere. Both the National Institute of Education and the U.S. Department of Education's evaluation unit, for example, have encouraged the reanalysis of data by providing financial support and by fostering a de facto tradition of access to evaluative research data. The National Center for Health Services Research has encouraged reanalysis by aiding the development of a policy-data archive on long-term care experiments at Michigan State University, among other projects (Katz and others, 1979).

These informal policies are admirable. But for several reasons, it seems sensible to develop formal policy. First, critique and secondary analysis are susceptible to pressure just as original analyses are. Access to data can be impeded by politicians, bureaucrats, and scientists. In the absence of formal policy, the occasional refusals to release data will continue. One may also reasonably expect that explicit policy will serve as a partial prophylactic for intemperate adherence to proprietary rights in the academic sector. Furthermore, normal turnover of staff of agencies, contractors, and advisory boards does affect access to data, and we believe policy can have a stabilizing influence. In the long run, policy should also foster development of better methods and better secondary analyses—it is a legitimate part of scientific policy.

Chapter Two is an excerpt from the Federal Statistical System Project Report, a product of the President's Reorganization Project. It focuses on how federal statistical activities could be better organized to facilitate access to federal data. This discussion provides a broad view of the federal statistical system in the United States, pointing out the major weaknesses in the current organization that impede access. The project's recommendations, generated under the direction of James Bonnen, recognize the need for a centralized policy on statistical activities in order to ensure high quality and accessible data across agencies. The merits and costs of developing a central statistical office, a federal data locator service, and other access mechanisms are described.

The remaining chapters in Part One examine policy and resources in specific organizations. In Chapter Three, Charles Dollar and Bruce Ambacher present the National Archives' position, explain the types of data that are stored, and describe the duration of storage and the standards for judging if a data set is valuable enough to warrant permanent storage. The National Archives' relationship to other federal agencies, user services, and clearinghouse function are also discussed. The National Archives is an important agent in making available to outside analysts the data sets generated in research supported by the federal government. Dollar and Ambacher make it clear, however, that other institutions should be involved, for example, the federal agency sponsoring the research. Their argument is based on the large volume of data generated in research, evaluation, and development projects; the variety of clients for such data; and the need for quality control and dissemination devices that meet different clients' interests.

In Chapter Four, Joel Garner describes the access policy developed by the National Institute of Justice (NIJ). The institute's policy is remarkable for its attention to the details of assuring access and for its early appearance, in 1976. The initial policy, developed by LEAA staff, covers issues pertinent to privacy and security of data, makes provision for professional storage of the data, prohibits third-party agreements that hinder access by others—clearly establishing federal agency authority for release—and attends to the researchers' proprietary rights to the data until the project has been completed. The institute's experience is likely to be useful to other agencies that attempt to devise policies on access and secondary analyses.

In general, policy on these topics has not been well articulated by private foundations. The research unit of the Police Foundation, under Joseph Lewis's leadership, had a formal commitment to competing reanalysis. A few other private foundations have provided support for independent secondary analysis, though they do not have a formal policy on the reanalysis of the primary data that they generate. The Russell Sage Foundation, for instance, was instrumental in the critique and reanalysis of evaluations of Sesame Street. The Carnegie Corporation supported major reanalyses of the 1966 Study of Equality of Educational Opportunity.

Interest in secondary analysis is not confined to the executive agencies of government but extends to Congressional support staff. For example, the GAO has responsibility, under the Budget Control Act of 1970, to oversee the quality of social program evaluations. It has taken that mission seriously, as can be judged from the development of the Program Analysis Division and the more recent creation of an Institute for Program Evaluation. In Chapter Five, Harry Havens, assistant comptroller general for program evaluation, describes secondary analysis in such forms as review and reanalysis of microdata as a fundamental vehicle for meeting the responsibility of the GAO. The process is a dynamic one: the GAO reanalyzes and synthesizes evidence from previous studies. To foster a balanced perspective, it subjects its reanalysis to criticism by others in the field, publishes the competing views as part of its report to Congress, and makes explicit the rationale for its interpretation of the evidence or choice among competing views.

One of the first problems a secondary analyst encounters is locating data for reanalysis. Research is decentralized; it is carried out by individuals through contracts, grants, or other arrangements and disseminated to others through written and oral reports and professional journals. Partly as a consequence of this decentralization, professional organizations have been formed to consolidate the interests of information users. For example, the Association of Public Data Users (APDU), based in the United States, is dedicated to assuring that large-scale data files become available to academic institutions for reanalysis. The International Association for Social Science Information Service and Technology, the Council for European Social Science Data Archives, the International Federation of Data Organizations, and other international groups are interested in developing standards and in making sure data are readily available. Most of these organizations build on a traditional interest in social survey research. We know of no professional organization of evaluators with formal parallel interests, but this is probably due more to the youth of evaluation research than to disinterest. Although there are no major differences between the methods of analyzing social survey research data and evaluation research data, the focuses are different.

It is also a consequence of decentralization that compendia of evaluations such as those produced by the GAO and the Department of Health, Education, and Welfare are valuable. William Trochim, in Chapter Six, reviews the contents of major resources, such as the GAO's sourcebook, the data holdings of various organizations like APDU, and other resources that assist analysts in locating data sets. Trochim identifies national, international, public, and private sources and describes some of the salient features of the data search process, including bibliographical entries and services.

Part Two: Documentation of Evaluations. Formal policy can stimulate interest in secondary analysis. But openness, which is supposed to underpin the scientific exchange of information, is constrained by a variety of factors. These include the difficulties analysts encounter in learning about the availability of data; technical considerations such as documentation of the data and of analyses; and questions about the proprietary rights of the researcher, confidentiality of the data, and privacy of the respondent. Secondary analysis is still a new field, and such necessary support mechanisms as locator services and technical standards are still being developed.

Successful reanalysis depends on the quality of information about data. But only recently have coherent standards for documenting social science data been developed. That such documentation is problematic is exemplified in Joan Linsenmeier, Paul Wortman, and Michael Hendricks' report (Chapter Seven) of their attempt to reanalyze aspects of the Riverside School Desegregation Project, originally conducted by Gerard and Miller (1975). They describe the delays and difficulties they encountered even with a data base that was considered to be well documented, professionally maintained, and easily obtainable. They urge that primary analyses be better documented to ensure successful reanalysis.

In Chapter Eight, Alice Robbin provides us with detailed technical guidelines on all phases of the documentation, access, storage, and dissemination of machine-readable data files. The guidelines stress documentation as part of the planning process. Robbin directs attention to the roles and responsibilities of the federal agency and the researcher for the production and preservation of high-quality machine-readable data files.

oving Reanalysis of Evaluation. There is, of
hematical difference between primary and
e analyses differ in that often more time and
ᵜ secondary efforts. Reanalyses undertaken in
often innovative because of the luxuries of
⸻ exchanges among scholars on the meaning of
tne data, and freedom from the major management problems that
primary evaluators face. These innovations include new ways of estimating the effects of social programs.

We believe that lack of clear opportunity for reanalysis impedes
the development of better methodology, hampers the identification of
poorly implemented evaluations, and obscures the important methodological problems that must be resolved to design better evaluations
and develop better programs. The purpose of Part Three is to highlight
salient methodological issues pertinent to secondary and primary
analysts.

The first chapter in this part discusses the chronic problem of
analyzing data from evaluations based on observational data. In Chapter Nine, Melvin Novick illustrates Simpson's paradox—the classic
demonstration of the equivocality inherent in causal statements
derived from observational data. This paradox is a major aspect of
what is now known as the model misspecification problem, a problem
that plagues most quasi-experimental research designs. Briefly, in the
absence of randomization, there is always the possibility of identifying
one or more factors that can turn a positive effect to negative, or vice
versa. In the absence of strong theory or specific information about
how individuals are assigned to the program and to comparison conditions, there is no satisfying means of estimating program effects. Novick's approach depends on strong theory and his paper illustrates its
role in statistical analysis.

Recent technical developments in data analysis have built
on earlier attempts to understand the effects of interventions. One such
development, structural equation modeling, recognizes and attempts to
accommodate model misspecification and measurement error. David
Rindskopf, in Chapter Ten, provides an overview of the rudiments of
structural models, rules for writing models, and practical guidelines
for interpreting the analyses. Using data from the original Westinghouse-Ohio evaluation of Head Start, Rindskopf illustrates two structural modeling techniques, each of which produces results different
from the original analysis. Structural equation modeling is a considerable improvement over other strategies, notably those given in conventional texts that merely advise covariance analysis or matching. But it

is complicated and it too may lead to ambiguous conclusions. kopf is careful to note its limitations as well as its strengths.

Most large-scale evaluations can involve different levels of unit of analysis—individuals, individuals within groups, groups within institutions. The unit chosen for analysis has important consequences. Cronbach (1976), for instance, has argued, as others have, that the choice of a particular unit of analysis in an evaluation may conceal more than it reveals. In this volume, Leigh Burstein and Michael Miller (Chapter Eleven) discuss the mathematical issues pertaining to such choices and the consequences of choices for making inferences about program effects and processes. For example, they argue that examining intergroup differences alone can hide important differences occurring within groups and pertaining to the distribution of effects. Like Rindskopf, Burstein and Miller discuss the advantages of performing competing analyses and the criteria for deciding which analysis to perform. They also provide empirical support for the use of alternative statistical indices of program effects.

The last two chapters in this part concern the interpretation of results generated by evaluative studies. In Chapter Twelve, Lee Sechrest and William Yeaton argue that conventional estimates of program effect, based on the probability that the effect could have occurred by chance alone, are insufficient for deciding the clinical, educational, or practical significance of findings. They argue that to interpret evidence from evaluative research one must consider the integrity of the treatment and size of the effect. They describe the advantages and disadvantages of relative, absolute, and cost-benefit assessments of effect size in judging social interventions. Sechrest and Yeaton's chapter has a focus different from the other chapters in this volume; it represents that branch of social research devoted to understanding how to interpret findings from individual and multiple evaluative studies.

Also important to our understanding of the strengths and limitations of program evaluations are the issues raised by David Pillemer and Richard Light. In Chapter Thirteen, adapted from *Evaluation Studies Review Annual* (1979), they describe three factors that potentially limit the generalizability of findings from evaluations. Further, these factors provide a basis for resolving apparent inconsistencies among studies that purport to test the same intervention. Readers may also consult Light and Smith (1971), Glass (1977) and Rosenthal (1978) on analytic strategies for summarizing evidence across multiple studies. As the number of evaluation studies increases, knowledge of these topics will become more important to researchers and policy makers.

Part Four: Diverse Aims and Methods: Case Studies. Earlier, we identified a variety of activities that fall under the rubric of secondary analysis. At least a half dozen taxonomies have been developed to map this terrain, the most thorough being that of Cook and Gruder (1978). However, because many secondary analyses have several purposes, it is difficult to exploit neat classification schemes. Part Four provides nine illustrations of secondary analysis that exemplify the diversity in function, type, and form of secondary analysis.

One of the more obvious functions of secondary analysis is to assure the credibility of original conclusions. This function is consistent with scientific enterprise in that evidence must be verifiable in order for science to proceed. It is consistent with policy because decision makers need to know how much confidence they can place in the data. This function is demonstrated by William Bowers and Glenn Pierce in Chapter Fourteen; adapted from their paper in the *Yale Law Journal.* They reanalyze Ehrlich's (1975) assessment of the effect of capital punishment on homicide rates. They claim Ehrlich's conclusions are untenable because his data and statistical procedures are inadequate. Bowers and Pierce replicate Ehrlich's original analysis, identify what they believe to be rival explanations for his conclusions, execute alternative analyses, offer extensive discussion of the strengths and weaknesses of their interpretations, and draw upon other evidence in support of their conclusion. Beyond its substantive contribution, the chapter by Bowers and Pierce serves a useful pedagogical function. Remarkable for its thoroughness, it is an exemplary secondary analysis.

By no means does the secondary analyst have the final word. Isaac Ehrlich's rejoinder to Bowers and Pierce in Chapter Fifteen, adapted from a paper in the *Yale Law Journal,* discusses flaws in the reanalyses by Bowers and Pierce and by Baldus and Cole (1975). He argues that Bowers and Pierce's replication of his results, which used slightly different measures of constructs, strengthens his case. He identifies flaws in the supporting evidence and shows the compatibility of his results with theory—concluding that his critics are in error. Such debate is not uncommon. For instance, Magidson (1977, 1978) and Bentler and Woodward (1978) have joined in robust debate over the interpretation of Magidson's reanalysis of the Head Start data. Reanalyses of data from the University Group Diabetes Project and argument over their implications have been vigorous for ten years—though Kilo, Miller, and Williamson (1980) believe they have finally identified the critical weaknesses of the study.

These controversies are at times disruptive, even embarrassing or unpleasant. But they serve to clarify the issues and the underlying assumptions and theoretical premises of analysts. Researchers, policy makers, and the public are well served by such debate.

Making data available for secondary analysis has been justified as an opportunity for conducting methodological studies and a means of examining theoretical issues. These justifications are represented in the reanalyses by Hernando Gomez (Chapter Sixteen) and by Isaac Bejar and Victor Rezmovic (Chapter Seventeen). All used the data generated during experimental field tests of a nutritional and educational enrichment program in Cali, Colombia. Gomez reanalyzes the data to ascertain whether more sophisticated methods of estimating children's abilities, notably Rasch models, will alter estimates of the program's effects. Bejar and Rezmovic assay the credibility of the original findings and explore the nutritional component of the program more extensively than the original analysts. Both reanalyses are also pertinent to theory. They show that the factor structure of cognitive ability stays relatively stable within experimental and control groups over the five-year study and that the factor structures do not differ much across groups. The two reanalyses show the Cali results to be robust to analytic strategies that make different assumptions about the data.

Large-scale evaluations generally have the resources to secure competent statistical advice and, at least in some agencies, there is considerable pressure to do so. The researcher who works on a smaller scale may be handicapped by insufficient resources or may fail to take advantage of available experts. In Chapter Eighteen, Leroy Wolins discusses one group of this sort—scholars who publish in regular academic journals. He reanalyzes published tables to illustrate errors in analysis and suggests corrections. His work is based partly on reanalysis of microdata and focuses on a class of errors of inference, termed scale dependent mistakes, found in studies that examine race differences in IQ. The chapter is an excerpt from Wolins' (1981) draft monograph on statistical errors in social science literature.

Secondary analysis has been promoted as a means of producing better primary level evaluation studies by Boruch and Wortman (1978), Cook (1974), and Cook and Gruder (1978). This goal can be achieved by developing better evaluation strategies, identifying stereotypical problems in analysis, and conscientiously applying conventional research principles. The reanalysis by Joel Moskowitz and Paul Wortman in Chapter Nineteen illustrates the latter. They reexamine Gerard and Miller's (1975) assessment of the effect of school desegration on the intellectual and personality development of Mexican-American pupils. They show that examining rival hypotheses, such as differential attrition and using multiple estimation procedures and cohort analysis, yields a more informed assessment of the impact of desegregation. Margaret Boeckmann, in Chapter Twenty, demonstrates the effect of differential attrition in the New Jersey Negative Income Tax Experiment. The problem of attrition in social experiments is chronic and Boeckmann's illustration is a useful lesson on how attrition affects the inferences one draws from data.

The last two case studies in this part concern manpower research and evaluation of manpower training programs. Stephen Director's task in Chapter Twenty-One is to understand how estimates of the effects of manpower programs based on observational data are susceptible to analytic biases. His reanalyses introduce multiple competing estimates of parameters that are plausible influences on the results, and he shows that the original analyses were probably in error due to a methodological artifact. Clifford Hawley and William Bielby's discussion of secondary analysis of multipurpose manpower data files, Chapter Twenty-Two, is instructive in showing the broad range of ways in which longitudinal research has been used in universities and in government. They also specify areas that have not been well examined and methodological issues that should be addressed in order to maximize the utility of the files to the secondary analyst.

References

Baldus, D. C., and Cole, J. W. L. "A Comparison of the Work of Thorsten Sellin and Isaac Ehrlich on the Deterrent Effect of Capital Punishment." *Yale Law Journal*, 1975, *85*, 170–186.

Barnow, B. S., and Cain, G. G. "A Reanalysis of the Effect of Head Start on Cognitive Development: Methodological and Empirical Findings." *Journal of Human Resources*, 1977, *12*, 177–197.

Bentler, P. M., and Woodward, J. A. "A Head Start Reevaluation: Positive Effects Are Not Yet Demonstrable." *Evaluation Quarterly*, 1978, *2*(3), 493–510.

Borchard, E.M. *Convicting the Innocent: Errors of Criminal Justice.* New Haven, Conn.: Yale University Press, 1932.

Boruch, R. F., and Cecil, J. S. *Assuring the Confidentiality of Social Research Data.* Philadelphia, Pa: University of Pennsylvania Press, 1979.

Boruch, R. F., and Cordray, D. S. (Eds.). *An Appraisal of Educational Program Evaluations: Federal, State, and Local Agencies.* Washington, D.C.: U.S. Department of Education, 1980. (ERIC No. ED 192466.)

Boruch, R. F., and Rindskopf, D. "Experiments, Quasi-Experiments, and Data Analysis." In L. Rutman (Ed.), *Evaluation Research Methods.* Beverly Hills, Calif.: Sage, 1977.

Boruch, R. F., and Wortman, P. M. "An Illustrative Project on

Secondary Analysis." In R. F. Boruch (Ed.), *New Directions for Program Evaluation: Secondary Analysis,* no. 4. San Francisco: Jossey-Bass, 1978.

Cain, G. G., and Watts, H. W. "Problems in Making Policy Inferences from the Coleman Report." *American Sociological Review,* 1970, *35,* 228-242.

Campbell, D. T., and Erlebacher, A. "How Regression Artifacts in Quasi-Experimental Evaluations Can Mistakenly Make Compensatory Education Look Harmful." In J. Hellmuth (Ed.), *Compensatory Education: A National Debate.* New York: Brunner/Mazel, 1970.

Chelimsky, E. "The Need for Better Data to Support Crime Control Policy." *Evaluation Quarterly,* 1977, *1*(3), 439-474.

Cook, T. D. "The Potential and Limitations of Secondary Evaluation." In M. W. Apple, M. J. Subkoviak, and H. S. Lufler, Jr. (Eds.), *Educational Evaluation: Analysis and Responsibility.* Berkeley, Calif.: McCutchan, 1974.

Cook, T. D., and Gruder, C. L. "Metaevalutation Research." *Evaluation Quarterly,* 1978, *2*(1), 5-52.

Cook, T. D., and others. *Sesame Street Revisited.* New York: Russell Sage Foundation, 1975.

Cronbach, L. J. *Research on Classrooms and Schools: Formalization of Questions, Design, and Analyses.* Occasional Paper, Stanford Evaluation Consortium. Stanford, Calif.: Stanford University, 1976.

Cronbach, L. J., and Suppes, P. (Eds.). *Research for Tomorrow's Schools: Disciplined Inquiry for Education.* New York: Macmillan, 1969.

Datta, L. "The Impact of the Westinghouse/Ohio Evaluation on the Development of Project Head Start." In C. C. Abt (Ed.), *The Evaluation of Social Programs.* Beverly Hills, Calif.: Sage, 1976.

Del Bene, L., and Scheuren, F. (Eds.). *Statistical Uses of Administrative Records with Emphasis on Mortality and Disability Research.* Washington, D.C.: Social Security Administration, 1979.

Ehrlich, I. "The Deterrent Effect of Capital Punishment: A Question of Life or Death" *American Economic Review,* 1975, *65,* 397-417.

Gerard, H. B., and Miller, N. *School Desegregation.* New York: Plenum, 1975.

Glass, G. V., "Primary, Secondary, and Meta-Analysis of Research." *Educational Researcher,* 1976, *5*(10), 3-8.

Glass, G. V. "Integrating Findings: The Meta-Analysis of Research." *Review of Research in Education,* 1977, *5,* 351-379.

Glass, G. V., and Smith, M. L. "Meta-Analysis of Research on Class Size and Achievement." *Educational Evaluation and Policy Analysis,* 1979, *1,* 2–16.

House, E. R., and others. "No Simple Answer: Critique of the Follow Through Evaluation." *Harvard Educational Review,* 1978, *48,* 128–160.

Jackson, G. "Reanalysis of Coleman's 'Recent Trends in School Integration'." *Educational Researcher,* 1975, *9*(10), 21–25.

Katz, S., Hedrick, S. C., and Henderson, N. "The Measurement of Long-Term Care Needs and Impact." *Health and Medical Care Services Review,* 1979, *2*(1), 1–21.

Kilo, C., Miller, J. P., and Williamson, J. R. "The Achilles Heel of the University Group Diabetes Program." *New England Journal of Medicine,* 1980, *243*(5), 450–457.

Light, R. J., and Smith, P. V. "Accumulating Evidence: Procedures for Resolving Contradictions Among Different Research Studies." *Harvard Educational Review,* 1971, *41,* 429–471.

Linsenmeier, J. A. W., and Wortman, P. M. "The Riverside School Study of Desegregation: A Re-Examination." *Research Review of Equal Education,* 1978, *2*(2), 1–40.

Loftus, E. F. *Eyewitness Testimony.* Cambridge, Mass.: Harvard University Press, 1979.

McLaughlin, M. W. *Evaluation and Reform: The Elementary and Secondary Education Act of 1965/Title I.* Cambridge, Mass.: Ballinger, 1975.

Magidson, J. "Toward a Causal Model Approach for Adjusting for Preexisting Differences in the Nonequivalent Control Group Situation." *Evaluation Quarterly,* 1977, *1*(3), 399–420.

Magidson, J. "Reply to Bentler and Woodward: The .05 Significance Level Is Not All-Powerful." *Evaluation Quarterly,* 1978, *2*(3), 511–520.

Mosteller, F., and Moynihan, D. P. (Eds.). *On Equality of Educational Opportunity.* New York: Vintage, 1972.

Pillemer, D. L., and Light, R. J. "Using the Results of Randomized Experiments to Construct Social Programs: Three Caveats." *Evaluation Studies Review Annual,* 1979, *4,* 717–726.

Riecken, H. W., and others. *Social Experimentation.* New York: Academic Press, 1974.

Rindskopf, D. "Memo on Acquisition of Evaluation Data From 20 Studies Supported by the U.S. Office of Education in 1974." Unpublished memo, Department of Psychology, Northwestern University, 1976.

Roos, L. L., and others. "Using Administrative Data Banks for Research and Evaluation." *Evaluation Quarterly*, 1979, *3*(2), 236–255.

Rosenthal, R. "Combining Results of Independent Studies." *Psychological Bulletin*, 1978, *85*, 185–193.

Rossi, P. H., Berk, R. A., and Lenihan, K. J., *Money, Work, and Crime.* New York: Academic Press, 1980.

Smith, M. L., and Glass, G. V. "Meta-Analysis of Psychotherapy Outcome Studies." *American Psychologist*, 1977, *32*, 752–760.

U.S. General Accounting Office. *Follow Through: Lessons Learned From Its Evaluation and the Need to Improve Its Administration.* MWD–75–34. Washington, D.C.: U.S. General Accounting Office, 1975.

U.S. General Accounting Office. *Assessing Social Program Impact Evaluations: A Checklist Approach.* PAD–76–9. Washington, D.C.: U.S. General Accounting Office, 1978.

Wolins, L. *Mistakes in Statistics.* Ames: Psychology Department, Iowa State University, 1981.

Wortman, P. M., Reichardt, C. S., and St. Pierre, R. G. "The First Year of the Education Voucher Demonstration: A Secondary Analysis of Student Achievement Test Scores." *Evaluation Quarterly*, 1978, *2*, 193–214.

2 *President's Reorganization Project*

Federal Statistical System:
Access and Dissemination

Editors' Note: The President's Reorganization Project was undertaken to summarize earlier administrative research and to explore options and solutions to problems in complex areas of federal administration. Operating as part of this general effort, the Federal Statistical System Project (1978) focused on the ways in which federal statistical activities could be better organized, improved in quality, and made more efficient. Their final report considers the quality of data and the integrity of data production, the reduction of respondent burden including privacy and confidentiality matters, and the policy relevance of information generated by the system, as well as data access.

The following remarks, from chapter 8 of the project's complete report, review broad objectives of statistical activity, and describe problems encountered in properly meeting those objectives. Considerable

Note: James T. Bonnen was executive director of the Federal Statistical Systems Project; staff included Larry K. Roberson, Theodore Clemence, Ivan Fellegi, Thomas Jabine, Ronald Kutscher, and Charles Waite. The task force group with responsibility for considering access to data consisted of Lois Alexander, William Smith, Peter Yates, and Paul Zeisset (chairman).

attention is given to elaborating solutions to access problems, notably inventory, inquiry services, and distribution of data. The final section of the paper provides explicit policy recommendations and options that are likely to affect future federally sponsored or funded applied research activities.

One of the major recommendations calls for the establishment of a Central Statistical Office charged with setting overall policy for federal agencies.

Introduction

The prime objective of statistical activity is to place statistical information in the public domain—subject to confidentiality constraints. Thus access, as discussed here, refers to making information available in such a way that it is useful to researchers but cannot be related to a specific individual.

Adequate data access can be characterized along a number of dimensions; these include the ease with which relevant information sources can be located and retrieved, the availability of information about the nature and limitations of the data or statistics, the timeliness of the acquisition process, and the minimum costs to the researcher for its acquisition. Good data access has far-reaching benefits. It facilitates the policy responsiveness of the statistical system by enabling analysts to shed light on policy issues from existing data sources. Similarly, it contributes to better decision making outside the government and a better informed public. Further, the use of existing data, rather than instituting new data collection, keeps the burden to respond at a minimum.

Since the initial purpose of collection is of secondary interest to the user, the scope for coordinating access mechanisms for statistical purposes should be broad. It should encompass all data of potential statistical interest.

Current Problems

Many potential users of the statistical system, we may assume, do not know precisely the location of the data they need. This will be particularly true of researchers with data needs transcending single data sources—for example, analysts dealing with crosscutting issues. Such a user would have to be assisted, first of all, in finding the available relevant data sources, including their characteristics and limitations, and second, having found the right data sources, he would have to accomplish the access (retrieval) itself. The present section is accordingly organized into two subsections dealing respectively with access aids and access proper. For our purposes, all federal statistical data sources are considered to be included—whether the data can be obtained from files that were initially created for statistical, administrative, or regulatory purposes.

Access Aids. Facilitating access to complex data can be very difficult. Some of the vehicles which can be and have been adopted to facilitate the process are discussed here.

Publicity and Marketing. Publicity, generally defined, is an act or device designed to attract public interest. It is not enough to make the statistical product available. Attention must be called to its existence in terms which are relevant for its users. Unlike most other products, the objective of marketing of data is not to increase profits but to bring the available statistical information to bear on public and private decision making and research.

The tools of publicity for data products are also generally different from those used in relation to other products. Paid advertising is of less use compared to press releases, articles in journals, trade papers, professional meetings, displays at conventions, direct mailing to special groups, publication of thoughtful case studies showing how statistics can be utilized in particular types of decision problems, and training of potential secondary disseminators. The latter include librarians, local dissemination centers, state and local government officials, and college teachers.

There is no timely, comprehensive publication covering the recent releases of the entire federal statistical system. Nor is there a publication of selective analytical highlights of particular interest or importance. One recent study conducted by the Institute for Social Research, University of Michigan, indicated that when high-level federal administrators used social science knowledge in formulating policy decisions, an overwhelming proportion of the source surveys were either conducted or funded by their own agencies (Caplan, Morrison, and Stambaugh, 1975). The lack of current systemwide publications clearly inhibits interagency data utilization.

Inquiry Service. A user with a vaguely defined need for information, although with a possibly well-defined problem, needs assistance to formulate his information needs. No satisfactory federal statistical inquiry service exists—in Washington, D.C. or regionally. Some inquiry services exist in some regional offices, but they are either fragmented along agency lines (for example, separate Bureau of the Census and Bureau of Labor Statistics regional offices) or their statistical mission (hence knowledge of data sources) is secondary at best (industry and trade associations, offices of commerce, federal information centers). It is not suggested that a single inquiry center could ever hope to be directly responsive to the full variety of data needs. It could, however, answer more routine inquiries and, in more complex cases, direct the inquirer to the appropriate contacts.

The *Federal Statistical Directory* is issued by the Office of Statistical Policy Standards biennially and it can be of assistance in locating the "right" persons. Its usefulness for this purpose is somewhat limited by the fact that it is oriented to organizations, as opposed to subject matter, and tends to restrict its coverage largely to management personnel. The *Telephone Contacts for Data Users*, published by the Bureau of the Census, and, separately, by the Bureau of Labor Statistics, are excellent examples of subject-oriented telephone directories. Their scope is, however, restricted to their respective organizations. The National Technical Information Service (NTIS) recently introduced a so-called Statistical Reference Service which undertakes to identify available statistical data sources for a fee—ranging from $45 to $75. The level of inquiry service within agencies (more generally, internal support of users) is highly variable: ranging from the excellent support of the Bureau of the Census to the practically nonexistent.

Tools for Locating Needed Data. A variety of catalogues exist in printed form, each with its definite utility as well as limitations. The *Statistical Abstract of the U.S.*, although often used as an aid to locate data, is not really a catalogue. It is a sample of available data. The *American Statistics Index* is an abstract of available publications. The *Directory of Computerized Data Files*, published by NTIS in cooperation with the National Archives and Records Service, covers only machine-readable public use files, and the *Directory of Federal Statistics for Local Areas* (Bureau of the Census) is an infrequently updated directory of published statistics containing substate level data.

All of these tools have, for purposes of locating data, limitations which derive primarily from three factors. They do not use a consistent subject classification (and/or key words). They are restricted to published aggregates and the relatively few machine-readable public use files. And their coverage generally excludes administrative and regulatory data sources.

The Commission on Federal Paperwork recommended the establishment of a Federal Information Locator Service, referred to in the present report as Federal Data Locator Service, or FDLS. Essentially, what is needed is a subject-oriented, easily accessible reference of all federal data holdings of potential statistical interest (excluding perhaps some very special data sources). The FDLS would not be restricted to published aggregates, but rather it would be designed to provide information about data holdings for which aggregate statistical information can be potentially retrieved. For the FDLS to be workable, there would have to exist an administrative mechanism to keep the information content up to date.

Documentation of Data Sources. Before a user can effectively use statistical information, in fact even before the user can decide whether a data set is of interest, he or she has to be able to assess the data source. The following are some of the key aspects of documentation: definition of concepts used, the way the concepts were applied in the collection operation, reference dates, population or subgroups covered, frequency of collection, survey design, sample size (if applicable), measured errors or factors affecting the quality of data (for example, response rates), geographical coverage and detail, and access mechanisms.

The level of documentation of U.S. statistical data sources is highly variable, ranging from the generally excellent documentation of decennial census data to quite unacceptable or missing documentation. Directive No. 2 of the Office of Federal Statistical Policy and Standards of the U.S. Department of Commerce (1978) establishes standards of documentation for the publication of statistics. Perhaps as a result of this directive, and other efforts, noticeable improvements occurred in the last few years. While this is laudable, the improvement is not uniform. There is no mechanism to monitor adherence to this directive and to enforce it. Furthermore, it applies only to statistical publications: the status of statistical extracts from administrative or regulatory data sources is unclear, and it does not cover primary data sources, for example, microdata files from which statistics can be retrieved.

Data Access. Having identified their data needs, users may access statistical data through at least five different media: printed copy, microform (microfilm or microfiche), tapes, through on-line access, and through a custom-made retrieval from the agencies' microdata files. Each of these forms of dissemination has different advantages and disadvantages, from the points of view of both users and producers. The salient feature of the current situation is a lack of coherent and comprehensive guidelines for the appropriate mix of these media under different circumstances. Furthermore, policy has to be flexible to accommodate the impact of the extremely fast-developing technology.

Printed Copy. Printed publications are the most accessible to the largest number of users, partly because no expensive equipment is needed to read them and partly because of the existence of a well-developed network of "retailers" such as bookstores and libraries. However, printed publications are expensive to prepare, involve significant time delays, and contain data that are necessarily subject to rather severe preselection and are relatively difficult to manipulate.

Printed publication was the only dissemination vehicle available to statistical offices until about twenty years ago. Because of its ease of access by a large segment of the population, it will probably always be a major method of dissemination. However, its relative price is increasing and serious users (that is, those interested in great detail) increasingly prefer machine-readable data. Thus an evaluation of the detail which publications should contain is overdue.

Some very specific problems were identified with respect to the role of the Government Printing Office (GPO). The GPO has been identified as the source of long delays in printing and in filling orders of customers. Moreover, its marketing restrictions apparently prevent users from obtaining the most up-to-date publications: advance orders cannot be placed (in fact, pricing information is withheld until a report is printed), and it does not provide an invoicing service (billing after mailing the publication). All these factors, and others, combine to render the GPO monopoly a major bottleneck to statistical timeliness.

Microform. Next to printed paper, the most readily accessible form of output is microfilm or microfiche: most libraries have the necessary reading (and reproduction) equipment. It is considerably cheaper to prepare and requires less storage space. However, it is subject to the same problems of preselection and difficulty of manipulation as the printed publication.

There is some duplication in the dissemination of statistics on microform. NTIS is probably the government's largest microfiche disseminator, but some agencies disseminate their own products (for example, the Bureau of the Census). Also, the Congressional Information Service copies virtually all federal statistical publications on microfiche.

Computer Tapes. For users with access to computers, statistical output on tape is potentially the most useful form of output. Two types of product must be distinguished under this heading: the so-called summary tapes (aggregate data) and public use tapes (fully disaggregated microdata, with identification of individual respondents removed).

Summary tapes are particularly useful when a very large volume of aggregate data is to be disseminated and when the data are likely to be the subject of subsequent manipulation by users (often in the form of "building blocks" for reaggregation by users). Like printed publications, summary tapes are subject to preselection. Public use tapes, on the other hand, provide the greatest flexibility for the most sophisticated users. Once the microdata themselves are disseminated, users can prepare their own summaries from them, although certain analyses are predicated on access to microdata. Confidentiality constraints limit the utilization of public use tapes as a medium of dissemination to surveys of persons or households. For example, businesses, even with identification removed, are too easily identifiable. Even then the level of coding detail must often be reduced compared to what is available on in-house files.

The extent to which tapes are used as dissemination vehicles by different statistical agencies and, indeed, by agencies supplying statistics from administrative or regulatory data sources is highly variable. Even more variable is the extent to which they support this product—through good documentation, user advisory service, or software. With few exceptions, tapes appear to be regarded as afterthoughts, as opposed to being planned products of the processing activity. At least, the timeliness of output on tape generally lags far behind that of other forms. No policy exists across agencies, or even within agencies, regarding standardization. In effect, a user has to learn the particular organization and conventions adopted for each data tape. This further delays its effective utilization.

On-Line Access to Aggregate Data. On-line access presupposes the existence of archives containing regularly updated data. For users with more than a passing interest in statistics, this is one of the potentially most useful forms of access. Apart from the limitation of preselection inherently involved in any aggregate statistical output, on-line access permits great flexibility of manipulation. If the data banks are updated as part of the statistical production process, they also can provide quite timely information. Moreover, telecommunications networks allow simultaneous access across the nation. Built-in software can make utilization very simple, compared to the use of tapes. The data banks can be linked with graphic display systems, such as the Domestic Information Display System, for ease of analysis and overview. The major disadvantage of on-line aggregate data banks is cost: storage and updating for the agency maintaining them, and retrieval and manipulation for the user. However, both of these costs have been declining along with the costs of hardware and storage devices.

The Bureau of Labor Statistics (BLS) has developed, initially for its own internal use, an on-line data bank of aggregates containing its data products (LABSTAT). The major limitation of LABSTAT is, of course, its limited coverage: restricted to BLS data. There is a real risk that, without overall coordination, fragmented, agency-oriented aggregate data banks might be developed—to the great inconvenience of users. However, LABSTAT is a worthy model on which an interagency effort can be built.

Custom-Made Retrievals. With the exception of data which lend themselves to output in the form of public use tapes, all other outputs are subject to preselection, that is, a decision by the producers as to which of the astronomical number of potential aggregates to include in the output. When the utilization of public use tapes is difficult or impossible, for whatever reasons, the producing agencies should be able to retrieve directly from their internal microdata files the particular output desired by users. Few agencies appear to give high priority to the development of such a capacity.

It must be emphasized that such capacity does not simply represent an investment of resources. It requires almost a change in the philosophy with which data are regarded. The traditional view was that data were collected to produce a publication, after which they lost their value. Viewing microdata as capital which can be drawn upon repeatedly and long after the issuance of publications has far-reaching consequences: for the maintenance of the internal data bases, the way they are stored, the needed integrity of data at the microlevel, their security, their documentation, their compatibility with easy-to-use generalized retrieval and manipulation software. No systemwide policy, and hence standards, exist in this area—resulting in generally long delays and high costs for users wishing to request a custom-made output. As a result, users generally try to avoid this service, if at all possible.

Not only external users but also internal ones (analysts) are handicapped by the low level of this form of service. Knowing that custom-made output will be very expensive and subject to great delays, they tend to require as standard output a very wide variety of possibly useful aggregates: almost all aggregates that they believe they might need later. This, in turn, results in unnecessarily expensive production runs, delays, and considerable wasted output. Moreover, it translates itself, rather naturally, into very detailed and, as a consequence, overly expensive publications that appear long after the reference date.

Lack of interagency standards for microdata management also inhibits record linkage applications—even when the confidentiality problems can be resolved. This, in turn, inhibits certain kinds of cross-cutting analyses, that is, those which depend on linked microdata from different surveys.

Options and Recommendations

Option 1. Locate a data access policy function in a Central Statistical Office (CSO). This activity would establish an overall dissemination policy for the federal statistical system, including guidelines for the conditions under which different media of dissemination should be used, as well as for the nature and extent of internal user support that should exist in all agencies involved in disseminating statistical information. It could seek and employ a proper balance of private sector participation in the task of distributing federal statistics, while guarding against both predatory commercial practices as well as the right of the federal government to provide the data it collects to internal (government) and external users. The CSO would also establish standards for user documentation and file design, for the development of internal data storage methods for the fully processed, "clean" microdata. It would represent multiagency and public user interests both in relation to individual agencies (interceding in some cases as an "ombudsman" for the data user), and in the budgetary decision making at the agency, department, and presidential levels. It would assign to individual agencies specific systemwide responsibilities (for example, development of overall directories).

This plan addresses the interests of users who need to utilize the output of several agencies. As such, it would contribute to the responsiveness of the statistical system to the needs of analysts involved in crosscutting issues (policy responsiveness). It would take a broad view of the impact of technology on current access and dissemination practices; it would attempt to foster the exploitation of effective new techniques to the benefit of users; and it would prevent the development of incompatible agency-level access policies and dissemination mechanisms. It would thus minimize the need for extremely expensive future remedial actions.

The presence of a CSO would foster the exchange of experience among agencies. This is quite important in light of the fast-changing technology and the highly variable agency capacities in this field. It would also provide technical assistance to agencies which are weaker in this field. The fact that additional resources would be involved in the CSO is an argument against this option.

Option 2. Under option 2, in addition to the policy activity described in option 1, the Federal Data Locator Service (FDLS) would also be established in the CSO, together with a central data user inquiry service. Both services would relate to the entire statistical output of the federal system, including administrative and regulatory data sources.

Depending on the approach taken, the implementation of FDLS can be a very expensive undertaking. It would appear, however, that at least an initial implementation could be tied to the clearance process with rather modest expenditures. If all federal data collection forms were registered with the clearance process, including those not under Office of Management and Budget clearance authority, and if the clearance form was suitably amended, including an indication of all subjects covered, this information would provide the basis for a modest start on the FDLS program. A potential user interested in data about a subject or combination of subjects would readily identify through the FDLS the forms or questionnaires that contain data on those subjects. A copy of the forms involved would provide additional detail to the potential user about the information content of the data file. Assuming that the substantive review which precedes clearance ensures that adequate documentation on other aspects of the collection are filed with the FDLS (for example, population covered, methodology used, known limitations of data, contact officer's name), a very useful service could be initiated. Combined with an inquiry service, it would provide an entry point for potential users to most of the federal statistical information base, with very few exceptions.

This option would do more than any other alternative action to ease the burden on users of having to deal with a multitude of agencies for their data needs. User confusion about where to go for what would be reduced. In effect, a single entry point for the statistical system (broadly interpreted) would be created.

The FDLS would have other benefits not related to access: it would be a tool to control response burden, for example, avoiding duplication of data collection. While this option would locate the FDLS in the CSO, the latter would maintain the system on behalf of the entire federal government. Thus the question of the location of ultimate policy control of response burden is not prejudged by this option.

Another benefit of FDLS, also not directly related to access, is that it would be a central location of information about all data collection activities in related subject matter areas, together with documentation of the concepts used and other relevant information. This would serve as invaluable raw material for the integration function of the CSO—to establish, where applicable, common definitions of concepts and to monitor adherence to them.

In the fourth quarter of the twentieth century, it is stating the obvious to say that the CSO could not carry out its mandate effectively without coordinating the automatic data processing (ADP) aspects of agencies' work—subject to governmentwide guidelines. Yet coordination requires ADP expertise which can best be acquired and maintained with a degree of actual involvement in ADP work. The FDLS would provide the concrete setting for such involvement. The central inquiry service would also provide the agencies with a record of the frequency of different types of inquiries (market intelligence).

Assuming that a FDLS service, so strongly recommended by the Commission on Federal Paperwork, is established somewhere in the federal government, arguments may exist for locating it somewhere else. The central inquiry service might be viewed by agencies as establishing some distance between them and their users. This should not be the case: The inquiry service would directly handle only routine inquiries, referring the more complex requests for data to the agencies concerned.

Option 3. In addition to the actions involved in options 1 and 2, responsibility for the establishment and maintenance of a federal statistical data bank of aggregates would also be located in the CSO under option 3. This would not necessarily mean housing such a data bank in a computer owned or rented by the CSO. The bank, containing non-confidential data, may well be housed in the private sector, with national access guaranteed to it.

The CSO would not necessarily undertake the direct updating of all data series in the bank. Instead, it would mandate the provisions of machine-readable updates by the agencies, either directly or through the CSO, and it would monitor adherence. The CSO would be the prime contractor with the private sector, it would be the focal point for users of the system, it would determine what series and with what level of disaggregation would be maintained in the bank, and it would be the initiator of any necessary developments to enhance user services. Moreover, the bank could be directly interfaced with the Domestic Information Policy Display System to provide the latter with all the necessary data inputs.

The existence of an on-line bank of aggregates, covering all of the most widely used (or usable) federal statistical series, would be a liberating influence for all analysts, particularly those dealing with crosscutting issues. The CSO could use this data bank for a variety of important purposes: to carry out broad analytical work; to monitor the sequence of changes in important series from "preliminary" to "revised" to "final"; and to prepare, directly from the bank, print-ready publication tapes.

The agencies themselves could use the bank to prepare their own publication-ready tapes directly from it. This could be the source of considerable efficiencies for regular publications. Such a data bank could be the federal government's baseline system for application of consistent and equitable distribution policies, especially as regards the interface with private-sector statistical purveyors. The bank, through its network of users, could be utilized as a vehicle for nationwide press releases or other important statistical news. This option would require some extra resources both in the CSO and in the data producing agencies.

Recommendation 1. The CSO would undertake to publish a daily statistical bulletin, as well as a weekly or biweekly statistical highlights publication containing brief statistical analyses of topics of current interest. The daily bulletin would typically contain one descriptive paragraph for each listing, and a few paragraphs with perhaps a summary table for key series. The scope of the bulletin should be as broad as practicable. The substantive review by the CSO of all data collection forms could provide the information necessary to define its scope pragmatically.

Recommendation 2. In order to enhance the timeliness of their publications and their distribution to users, statistical agencies should be permitted to meet their publication requirements through direct contracting with the private sector and they should be allowed to handle their publication distribution programs in-house, subject to Government Printing Office oversight.

Organizing Principles

In order for the CSO to undertake the access and dissemination activities outlined in the previous section, it would have to acquire the necessary resources. When the CSO is reestablished with its new mandate, the mandate should spell out the preferred options with respect to access and dissemination. Given the mandate, resources required might be assigned explicitly to the CSO. Alternatively, the CSO itself, in its capacity as "manager" of the federal statistical system, might be asked to reassign resources within the system in order to get the chosen overall access and dissemination activities underway.

Should the CSO be given responsibility to identify and allocate the resources required for the central function, then clearly the more authority it has over budgets, the more it is able to do. Furthermore, line control over the agencies involved in the consolidation would enable the chief statistician to extend the scope of best practices within each of the component agencies to the entire consolidated agency (for example, the strong data base technology of the BLS and its LABSTAT program, and the strong user support activity of the Bureau of the Census).

References

Caplan, N., Morrison, A., and Stambaugh, R. *The Use of Social Knowledge in Policy Decisions at the National Level.* Ann Arbor: Institute for Social Research, University of Michigan, 1975.

Federal Statistical System Project, President's Reorganization Project. "Issues and Options." Reproduced report, Office of Management and Budget, Washington, D.C., 1978.

U.S. Department of Commerce, Office of Federal Statistical Policy and Standards. *A Framework for Planning U.S. Federal Statistics.* Washington D.C.: U.S. Department of Commerce, 1978.

Charles M. Dollar
Bruce I. Ambacher

3

National Archives:

Data Transfer and Storage

The benefits of secondary analysis of machine-readable data are well known. They include economy of money, time, and manpower; minimization of instrusions into personal privacy; and more comprehensive, definitive research. Secondary analysis of federal machine-readable data can, however, be difficult. Identification and location of the data and the person responsible for the data present problems. Also, federal agencies have different interpretations of their missions and responsibilities regarding the documentation and dissemination of data they have collected. The procedures for release of the data, and the corresponding pricing structure, are similarly varied. Some agencies will not support such dissemination since they cannot retain the fees received. Many agencies have no systematic procedures for receiving and maintaining data collected under contract or research grant. (The access problems that have emerged in secondary analysis of data from federal program evaluations are described by Bryant and Wortman, 1978, and by Hedrick, Boruch, and Ross, 1978.)

To perform a secondary analysis, the researcher must know that the data set exists, that documentation for using the file is adequate and sufficiently standardized for use by others, and that the data set available contains the microlevel data collected. Open access to federal data will permit cross-examination of that data, eliminate the cost of replicating the data, and promote better oversight of projects and policy.

The National Archives and Records Service

Since its creation in 1934, the National Archives and Records Services (NARS) has fostered research and analysis of federal records through the preservation and administration of the nation's permanently valuable records. NARS has promoted the fullest possible public use of records in its custody while protecting personal, restricted, or classified records against unauthorized disclosure. (For the history of NARS, see Jones, 1969, and McCoy, 1978.) The National Archives retains noncurrent records for the protection of both public and private rights, and for research use. Records created to serve the routine administrative and policy needs of numerous federal agencies have been centrally located in the National Archives, where they may be consulted. The nature of these records and the types of information they contain confine their use, for the most part, to traditional primary research in history, political science, and public policy.

The kind of records preserved and their uses have changed over the years, reflecting an evolution in the role of the federal government as a data collector and data disseminator. Statistics and longitudinal survey data, especially multipurpose and large-scale statistical programs collected to permit federal agencies to perform mandated responsibilities, have a wide range of possible uses in secondary analysis. The Federal Records Act of 1950, as amended in 1976, defines federal records as "all books, papers, maps, photographs, or other documentary materials, regardless of physical form or characteristics, made or received by any agency of the United States government in pursuance of federal law or in connection with the transaction of public business" (57 Stat. 380–383; 59 Stat. 434). Under this act, no federal record may be destroyed without the authorization of the archivist of the United States.

Through the General Records Disposition Schedules and specific records schedules prepared by the federal agencies, an estimated 5 percent of all federal records having permanent historical or informational value are identified, transferred, and preserved. In most instances, textual records of permanent value are twenty to twenty-five years old when they are accessioned into the National Archives, while computerized records suitable for secondary analysis are acquired as soon as possible. The National Archives currently retains approximately 900,000 cubic feet of permanent records.

Machine-Readable Archives Division

Since 1969, NARS has had its own special unit concerned solely with the "identification, preservation, and dissemination of permanently valuable machine-readable data files created by the federal government" (Heddesheimer, 1978, p. 1146). The Machine-Readable Archives Division (MRAD) preserves machine-readable records of permanent value and makes them publicly available for research and analysis. The division prefers to archive data at the microlevel—that is, information maintained in its original form before aggregation or summarization. Given the limitations of contemporary computer storage devices, the division attempts to acquire data as soon as an agency releases them, to ensure proper maintenance, environment, and security.

Most machine-readable data are accessioned within three to five years after creation, although this delay sometimes conflicts with an agency's concept of active records and the life cycle of records. In order to avoid such problems, division staff members work with agency personnel to ensure the earliest possible transfer of permanent data to the archives. Agencies have been encouraged to acquire and archive primary data derived from grants and contracts and to release them for secondary analysis after the reports are published. After a few years, they are requested to submit their data to NARS for appraisal and possible accessioning.

Records are appraised by MRAD in terms of their legal, evidential, or informational value. (For discussions of appraisal criteria, see Dollar, 1978, and Fishbein, 1972.) Most data are preserved for their informational value and their potential use by other researchers. Documentation sufficient to understand and use the data is created and compiled. The data are maintained in a software-independent format compatible with current technology. While the division manually validates several records in each file, ascertains that the layout and all coding are correct and within the prescribed range, and compiles the necessary documentation, it makes no effort to correct, amend, or alter the file. The file's creator defines the project, establishes its parameters, ensures the accuracy of the data encoded, and "cleans" the data by checking for out-of-range responses and other errors. NARS maintains the data "as received" from the sponsoring agency. This policy does not preclude reformatting or conversion to a software-independent format. This policy conforms to accepted archival standards.

The division creates a documentation package that includes an introduction giving some background on the file and its use by the agency, any technical problems that may be present, record layouts and codes necessary to interpret the data, and sample printouts of the data. Any known instances of bias or data imputation are also included in this documentation package. The division also attempts to clarify any problems discovered by previous users and maintains disclosure-free versions of the data whenever necessary to guarantee individual privacy.

The MRAD is currently cooperating with a variety of organizations to improve and enhance the standardization, descriptive procedures, and dissemination of machine-readable data. Staff members are working with the International Association for Social Science Information Service and Technology and the Society of American Archivists Committee on Automation and Data Records. They are compiling a directory of data archives and developing a guide to the establishment and operation of a data archive. Other staff members are actively involved in a federal ad hoc committee on abstracting and cataloguing federal statistical machine-readable data files. The division has also provided staff assistance and information for certain facets of *A Framework for Planning U.S. Federal Statistics for the 1980s,* coordinated by the Office of Federal Statistical Policy and Standards (1978).

The absence of clear guidelines regarding the creation, format, retention, preservation, and dissemination of data created under a federal grant or contract also complicates the dissemination and use of federal data. In the past, many federal grants and contracts did not contain any clause calling for the delivery of the data base along with the final report or other specified product; grantees and contractors were not required to maintain the data collected or to provide them to the sponsoring federal agency. Some grants and contracts do contain a clause stating that the data are considered a record of the sponsoring federal agency.

Given the wide range of grants and contracts let by the federal government, it is virtually impossible, and probably unwise, to arbitrarily declare all such data to be federal records deliverable to the sponsoring federal agency. Various federal agencies, including NARS, the Department of Health, Education and Welfare, and the National Science Foundation, are working in this area to ensure that greater amounts of this type of data are transferred to the agencies and considered for permanent retention by NARS. The MRAD works with agencies to ensure the preservation of such data for archiving when the sponsoring agency has not done so. Some records created some years ago under contract for the National Commission on Marijuana and Drug Abuse were made available to NARS only recently. In other instances, records appear to have been permanently lost.

Privacy and Information Storage

A small but significant portion of the permanently valuable machine-readable records contain personal information and is subject to the Privacy Act of 1974 and other guidelines designed to protect the individual and to prevent deductive disclosure. Long before privacy became a national issue, the archivist of the United States exercised authority, under 44 U.S.C. 2104, to impose restrictions on the access and use of records containing personal information. Prior to the enactment of the Privacy Act of 1974, the National Archives' policy was to restrict access for seventy-five years to records containing information about the physical and mental health, medical and psychiatric care and treatment, and investigation of individuals. Individually identifiable records are available to qualified researchers who provide NARS with written assurance that confidentiality will be maintained.

Archival records in the permanent custody of NARS containing personal information are exempt from those aspects of the Privacy Act of 1974 that permit record amendment or correction. While archival records are open to public inspection, they cannot be amended or corrected. Archival records are not part of an agency's system of records because they are not under the legal control of the originating agency and researchers are not restricted to the identifiers used by the agency.

Since a machine-readable record consists of defined individual data elements, and since each record in a file can be examined to determine whether it contains personal information, it is relatively easy to provide a disclosure-free version of the records by deleting or not defining certain elements or by creating a summary version of the records. Privacy restrictions imposed on the Equal Employment Opportunity Surveys conducted by the Equal Employment Opportunity Commission, for example, specify that disclosure-free aggregations that can be made available to researchers shall consist of no fewer than three employers, that no one employer shall contribute more than 50 percent of the aggregate, and that no two employers shall contribute more than 75 percent of the aggregate. In other instances, disclosure-free versions can be created by deleting personal identifiers. When the U.S. Commission on Civil Rights conducted its School Superintendents' Survey in 1976 to collect factual and attitudinal data on the recent experience with school desegregation, it pledged confidentiality to the responding superintendents. When the records were acquired, it was determined that the deletion of the Office for Civil Rights' school district identification number would provide a disclosure-free version fulfilling that pledge.

Research Data

In addition to those records that are permanently valuable and those that are disposable, there are records that have current research use but may not have permanent value. In the past, such data have remained in the sponsoring agency's custody until NARS could make a determination of their archival value. Public access to the data was limited, and researchers could not fully explore the data. To facilitate public access to this type of data, NARS created the Center for Machine-Readable Records, which accepts machine-readable data of uncertain archival value and serves as a liaison for such federal agencies as the Civil Aeronautics Board (CAB) and the Departments of Education and Health and Human Services. The center, operated by MRAD, accepts the records, assembles adequate documentation, maintains the records, informs the research community of their availability, disseminates them to researchers, and consults with users when necessary. The sponsoring agency retains legal custody. Center data files are initially available for five years. If the files continue to have current research value and demand, this period is extended or the files are appraised as having permanent value and are accessioned by NARS. All records having permanent value are indefinitely preserved and disseminated.

The major data files in the center include several types of CAB surveys of airline traffic, origin and destination studies, financial information, and route usage statistics; extracts from the 1970 census created for the U.S. Commission on Civil Rights; national surveys, conducted in 1963 and 1970, of trends in health service utilization and expenditures; and several files containing information on financial institutions and securities transactions. A catalogue system facilitates access (National Archives and Records Service, 1977, 1981).

NARS currently stores a variety of information developed from formal research efforts in education and other social sciences. It is now the principal archival repository and disseminator of federally produced education data and has more information relating to education than any other federal agency. This information includes data files developed from special studies such as the President's Commission on Campus Unrest, 1967–1970; the National Commission on the Financing of Postsecondary Education, 1972; and the 1976 School Superintendents' Survey on desegregation. It also includes large-scale, general surveys, such as the Higher Education General Information Surveys, 1971–1973; the College Locator Services Study, 1971–1972; the Survey of Postsecondary Career Schools, 1973; The Vocational Education Directory Survey, 1970–1971; and the Elementary and Secondary School Civil Rights Survey, 1968–1972. Some recent acquisitions are from large-scale evaluative studies and surveys supported by the federal government. These include the evaluation of the Performance Contracting Experiments supported by the Office of Economic Opportunity, 1970–1972; the Safe Schools surveys of crime and vandalism, 1977; the Beginning Teacher Evaluation Study, 1972–1978, and the Education Voucher Demonstration—both supported by the National Institute of Education.

Other studies in the social sciences include the Commission to Determine the National Policy Toward Gambling, 1974–1976; the Equal Employment Opportunity Surveys, 1966–1977; the Longitudinal Retirement History Study, 1969–1975; the Regional Economic Information System, 1929–1974; the National Longitudinal Surveys (Employment and Training), 1966–1976; the 1976 Survey of Income and Education conducted jointly by the Department of Health, Education, and Welfare and the Bureau of the Census; surveys of the Characteristics of Households Receiving Food Stamps, 1975–1976; and surveys conducted by the Department of Housing and Urban Development as part of the Experimental Housing Allowance Program, 1972–1976.

The division's holdings also include a large number of domestic and foreign public opinion polls. Several national commissions conducted such polls to assist them in shaping policy recommendations. These include surveys on Population Growth and the American Future, 1971; Campus Unrest, 1967–1970; Drug Use and Abuse, 1971–1972; and Violence in America, 1968. Over 200 surveys conducted by the International Communication Agency since 1972 in more than seventy-five nations are now being received. The topics include international radio broadcast listenership, media studies, the foreign image of America, international strength and security, political and economic issues, and information content analyses (National Archives and Records Service, 1977, 1981).

NARS is the only official repository of permanently valuable federal records. The Federal Records Act of 1950, as amended, mandates NARS to permanently preserve and disseminate these records. Other repositories may acquire copies of these and other federal data files, but they are under no obligation to retain them. While federal agencies have designated institutions to be the repository for specific kinds of data files and provided grants to underwrite their efforts, at some point the National Archives must be consulted regarding their disposition.

The MRAD has arranged with other repositories to acquire and store federal data files that do not meet its criteria for permanent retention and which complement the collections of these other archives. Certain of the data files in the Coleman study on desegregation were sent to the Interuniversity Consortium for Political and Social Research at the University of Michigan and some data files from the American Revolution Bicentennial Commission were transferred to the University of Virginia under this type of arrangement. While NARS supports broad dissemination of federal data, it does not believe that public funds should be used to maintain files whose permanent archival value is questionable.

The MRAD is seeking to identify new research communities that are not familiar with its records and to acquaint them with the holdings. Traditional major research communities are historians, political scientists, genealogists, federal agency personnel, and students of public policy. The newer types of records, especially the machine-readable data files, appeal not only to these traditional users but also to social and physical scientists, businessmen, and other commercial users. The division is informing these potential users through direct mailings, personal contacts at association meetings, and special interest brochures.

The MRAD is also prepared to facilitate secondary analysis of machine-readable data by functioning as a clearinghouse for information on the existence, location, and availability of data created by federal agencies. The division can respond to requests for specific data, for general types of data, or for data compatible with those currently being used by a researcher. Division staff members have a general knowledge of data currently held by federal agencies, and they know whom to contact in those agencies to obtain more detailed information about those data or about current and future data collection plans. Information concerning data created and maintained under federal contract will also be available. In addition, the division is prepared to coordinate the dissemination of federal data for those agencies. Finally, NARS has recommended that all primary evaluation research data created under government auspices be submitted to the sponsoring agency as a requirement of funding.

References

Bryant, F. B., and Wortman, P. M. "Secondary Analysis: The Case for Data Archives." *American Psychologist,* 1978, *33,* 381–387.

Dollar, C. M. "Appraising Machine-Readable Records." *American Archivist,* 1978, *41,* (4), 423–430.

Fishbein, M. "Appraising Information in Machine Language Form." *American Archivist*, 1972, *35*, (1), 35–43.

Heddesheimer, W. J. "Information on Data Archives." *American Psychologist*, 1978, *33*, 1146.

Hedrick, T. E., Boruch, R. F., and Ross, J. "On Ensuring the Availability of Evaluative Data for Secondary Analysis." *Policy Sciences*, 1978, *9*, 259–280.

Jones, H. G. *The Records of a Nation: Their Management, Preservation, and Use.* New York: Atheneum, 1969.

McCoy, D. R. *The National Archives: America's Ministry of Documents, 1934–1969.* Chapel Hill: University of North Carolina Press, 1978.

National Archives and Records Service. *Catalog of Machine-Readable Records in the National Archives of the U.S.: 1977.* Washington, D.C.: National Archives and Records Service, 1977.

National Archives and Records Service. *Catalog of Machine-Readable Records in the National Archives of the U.S.: 1979.* Washington, D.C.: National Archives and Records Service, 1981.

Office of Federal Statistical Policy and Standards. A *Framework for Planning U.S. Federal Statistics for the 1980s.* Washington, D.C.: U.S. Government Printing Office, 1978.

4

Joel Garner

National Institute of Justice:
Access and
Secondary Analysis

The National Institute of Justice (NIJ), as a research institute within an action-oriented agency, has long appreciated the importance of disseminating the results of its projects for use by researchers and practitioners. Of course, our efforts in this area have emphasized the production and dissemination of printed materials reporting the findings and conclusions of research we have supported. However, as it became clear that several projects we had initiated were producing extensive machine-readable data sets, the institute in 1976 set about establishing a policy to provide specific guidance to our grantees and contractors about data accessibility and documentation.

The access policy is stated in a special condition added to all grants at the time of award. It reads: "Upon grant termination, grantee agrees that computer-readable copies and adequate documentation of all data bases and programs developed or acquired in connection with the analysis in this project will be submitted to NIJ, at no additional costs. These may be used by the government, or disseminated to others for their use, for any purposes deemed appropriate by NIJ, without further compensation to the grantee. The grantee shall make no guarantee that the data collected will not be transferred or released without the prior approval of the institute. Consistent with 28 C.F.R., Part 22, the grantee must remove individual identifiers from any data bases and programs prior to submission to NIJ."

The policy has four components. First, researchers are entitled to retain the data sets until the completion of their project. This gives the data collectors the advantage of first use but provides for public availability after that time. The cost of reproducing one copy of the data sets is expected to be a normal cost of the original grant and not subject to additional billings. Given that most of our awards exceed $100,000, our expectation that grantees absorb the cost (usually no more than $50) for a data tape seems reasonable.

Second, the policy speaks clearly to the question of dissemination and secondary use. This decision is solely the prerogative of NIJ, not the grantees or other institutions involved in obtaining the data. Furthermore, the grantee is prohibited from making agreements that restrict the institute's ability to disseminate any of the data utilized in research it sponsors. Third, the special condition explicitly includes the privacy and security requirements (Law Enforcement Assistance Administration, 1978).

The fourth component of our policy is the establishment of a criminal justice archive and information network at the University of Michigan's Institute for Social Research. To establish a full-access policy would be meaningless unless we provide for an efficient mechanism to properly store and disseminate machine-readable data.

This policy evolved from a number of archiving and internal grant management concerns and, to my knowledge, did not stem from any specific request for data or from interest expressed by the research community outside of NIJ. In September 1975, the institute awarded a grant to Richard Roistacher at the University of Illinois to assess the storage needs for criminal justice research ("A Cooperative Program in Law and Society," 75-NI-99-0077). At about the same time, the institute's staff were updating the requirements that were attached to grants. While grantees were required to provide twenty-five copies of a camera-ready report with an executive summary, the staff noted that there were no provisions for the receipt of machine-readable data. As a result, administrative staff within the director's office conferred with research staff within the institute to devise a data access policy. No outside consultants were involved in developing this policy; nor were any inquiries for data from researchers influential in stimulating our action. The prohibition against grantees' making agreements with third parties was added as the direct result of one grantee making such an arrangement with another federal agency.

The access policy was developed in conjunction with the institute's grant monitors and with the Bureau of Justice Statistics (BJS), a sister office within the U.S. Department of Justice. Because BJS has a much larger role in compiling statistics on criminal justice operations, it has taken the lead in developing privacy and security regulations and in financially supporting the data archive. The institute's staff, however, are responsible for ensuring that the grantees are fully informed about the institute's policy and, upon the project's completion, for obtaining a copy of all data sets used in the project's research.

The National Academy of Sciences, in their assessment of NIJ's research program (White and Krislow, 1977), supported the establishment of a data archive and our policy of making machine-readable data available to the research community. That support, while certainly welcome, came after the policy had been adopted and implemented. The adoption of this policy, then, stemmed primarily from the internal considerations of NIJ and were developed in a fairly routine manner by institute staff.

In 1979 BJS established technical standards for the submission of machine-readable data sets. These standards offer guidance to NIJ staff and grantees on tape characteristics, data types, file organization, data codes, and documentation. Some of these standards are stated as requirements, others are suggestions providing general advice (Law Enforcement Assistance Association, 1979). In 1980 the Bureau of Justice Statistics published additional information on the preferred format for codebooks, data files, and bibliographic references (Bureau of Justice Statistics, 1980). These documents are not limited to criminal justice applications and represent standards that are appropriate for virtually all data storage and secondary uses.

These published standards are expected to increase the availability of well-documented research data sets. To date, relatively few data sets exist which meet the Category I standards established by the Interuniversity Consortium for Political and Social Research. Numerous other data sets are presently available in less desirable form, and we are constantly adding sets as they are produced by NIJ grantees and the research community. (The Appendix includes a current list of those sets that the Consortium judges to have met its standards for cleanliness and documentation.)

The institute has sought to encourage secondary analyses in several areas. In a report for us on deterrence and incapacitation, the

National Academy of Sciences (Blumstein, Cohen, and Nagin, 1978) includes several articles that involve the reanalysis of Isaac Ehrlich's seminal work on the deterrent effect of capital punishment (see Chapters Fourteen and Fifteen). Perhaps the best-known of our efforts is the PROMIS research project, from which two extensive data sets on over 34,000 criminal cases from the District of Columbia are now available. Researchers on the PROMIS project have produced numerous monographs based on the 1974 and 1975 public use tapes; these monographs are available from the Institute for Law and Social Research, Washington, D.C. With NIJ support, the University of Southern California is constructing an extensive set of socioeconomic and criminal justice data for census tracts in Los Angeles. Their explicit purpose is to encourage secondary analyses ("The Analysis of Interorganizational Networks in the Delivery of Criminal and Juvenile Justice Services," 78-NI-AX-0009).

The institute's interest in data accessibility is an expression of its desire to improve the quality of criminal justice research and the resulting public policy analysis. Our access policy will succeed only if the research community uses the data we have made available. As criminal justice research becomes more expensive, we will look to secondary analyses as an economical and a scientifically desirable way to increase knowledge about the causes of crime and the operation of the criminal justice system.

APPENDIX

Data Available from the Criminal Justice Archive and Information Network (as of July 1979). The archive is a unit of the Interuniversity Consortium for Political and Social Research (ICPSR) at the University of Michigan, and is being developed under the auspices of the Institute for Social Research at the University of Michigan, Ann Arbor. The consortium has been funded by the Law Enforcement Assistance Administration (LEAA) to develop the Criminal Justice Archive and Information Network.

Data sets available from ICPSR are divided into four classes. Class I data sets have been checked for errors, corrected if necessary or documented if this is impossible, and formatted to ICPSR specifications. The data are also recoded and reorganized in consultation with the original investigator to maximize their utilization and accessibility. A computer-readable codebook is usually available, which fully documents the data and includes descriptive statistics such as frequencies or other summary measures.

Class II studies have been checked and formatted to ICPSR standards. All nonnumeric codes have been removed. The studies in this class are available in a variety of technical formats. The documentation consists of either a machine-readable codebook, or a multilithed draft version, or a photocopy of the investigator's codebook. Any peculiarities in the data are indicated in the documentation even if they cannot be corrected or remedied.

Class III studies have been checked by the ICPSR staff for the appropriate number of cards per case and accurate data locations as specified by the investigator's codebook. Often frequency checks or other measures of distributional properties of the variables are made. Known data discrepancies and other problems, if any, will be communicated to the user at the time the data are requested.

Class IV studies are distributed in the form received by the ICPSR from the original investigator. The documentation for class IV studies is reproduced from the materials originally received. A few studies in this category are available only on cards because they contain multiple punches.

Currently Available Data

- Association of the Bar of New York. *New York Drug Evaluation Project* (six data sets, class IV).
- Blumenthal, M., Kahn, R., and Andrews, F. *Justifying Violence: Attitudes of American Men* (class I).
- Champagne, A. S., and Nagel, S. S. *Legal Services Agencies, 1970* (class II).
- Ehrlich, I. *Deterrence Data* (class IV).
- Gold, M. *1967 Survey of Youth* (class IV) and *1972 Survey of Youth* (class IV).
- Law Enforcement Assistance Administration:
  Expenditure and Employment Data for the Criminal Justice System: Longitudinal File, 1971–1977 (class II).
  Expenditure and Employment Data for the Criminal Justice System: Annual Files, 1971–1977 (seven data sets, class II).
  Juvenile Detention and Correctional Facility Census, 1971, 1973–1975 (class II).
  National Crime Surveys: National Complete Sample (eighteen collection quarters in 1973–1977, class I).
  National Crime Surveys: Cities Complete Sample (thirty-nine files from 1972–1975, class I).
  National Crime Surveys: Attitude Subsamples (thirty-nine files from 1972–1975, class I).

National Jail Census, 1970 (class II).

National Manpower Survey (class IV).

National Survey of Court Organizations, 1971–1972 (two data sets, class II).

Prosecutor's Management Information System: District of Columbia, 1974 and 1975 (class II).

State and Local Probation and Parole Agencies (class II).

State and Local Prosecution and Legal Attorney Systems (class II).

Survey of Inmates of Local Jails: Inmate Data, 1972 (class II).

Survey of Inmates of Local Jails: Institutional Data, 1972 (class II).

- Loftin, C. *Merged UCR and City/County Data* (class IV).
- Monkonnen, E. *Historical Police and Arrest Data* (three data sets, class IV).
- Nagel, S. S. *Federal Court Cases, 1962–1963* (class IV).
- Nagel, S. S. *Judicial Characteristics and Judicial Decision-Making Study, 1955* (class IV).
- Nagel, S. S. *Search and Seizure Data, 1963* (class IV).
- Nagel, S. S., and Champagne, A. *Legal Representation Data, 1970* (class IV).
- Nagel, S. S., Eimermann, T., and Reinbolt, K. *Free Press, Fair Trial Data, 1970* (class IV).
- Nagel, S. S., Wice, P., and Neef, M. *Pretrial Release Data* (class IV).
- National Center for Health Statistics. *Mortality Detail Files, 1972–1976* (five annual files, class I).
- National Center for State Courts. *Public Image of the Courts: General Public File* (class IV) and *Public Image of the Courts: Special Public File* (class IV).
- Silverstein, L., and Nagel, S. S. *American Bar Foundation: State Criminal Court Cases, 1962* (class IV).
- Skogan, W., and Klecka, W. *SETUPS: The Fear of Crime.*

Data in Process

- Block, M. *Uniform Crime Report Data, 1967–1976* (class II).
- Law Enforcement Assistance Administration. *National Crime Survey: First Two Collection Quarters, 1977* and *All Four Collection Quarters, Incident Level, 1977* (class I). Additional data to follow continuously.
- University of Pittsburgh. *Criminal Justice Archive Data Sets* (class II).
- Wolfgang, M. *Birth Cohort Study* (class II).

Data Being Acquired

- Akers, R., and Haner, N. *Comparative Prisonization Data* (class II).
- Klecka, W., and Tuchfarber, A. *Cincinnati Random Digit Dialing Experiment* (class II).
- Knudten, R. *Milwaukee Reinterview Survey* (class II).
- Kobrin, S., and Scheuerman, L. *Los Angeles Indicators Project* (class IV).
- Koch, G., and Feinberg, S. *Alaska Plea Bargaining Study* (class IV).
- Law Enforcement Assistance Administration. *National Jail Census, 1978* (class II).
- Mednick, S. A. *Study of Twins* (class II).
- Miller, W. B. *Data from the Study of Boston Gangs* (class IV).
- National Center for State Courts. *Pretrial Delay Data* (class II).
- Police Foundation. *Kansas City Patrol Experiment* (class II).
- RAND Corporation. *Study of Career Criminals* (class II).
- San Diego Police Department. *Calls for Service* (class IV).

References

Blumstein, A., Cohen, J., and Nagin, D. (Eds.) *Deterrence and Incapacitation: Estimating the Effects of Criminal Sanctions on Crime Rates.* Washington, D.C.: National Academy of Sciences, 1978.

Bureau of Justice Statistics. *A Style Manual for Machine-Readable Data Files and Their Documentation.* Washington, D.C.: Bureau of Justice Statistics, 1980.

Law Enforcement Assistance Administration. *Confidentiality of Research and Statistical Data.* Washington, D.C.: Law Enforcement Assistance Administration, 1978.

Law Enforcement Assistance Administration. *Technical Standards for Machine-Readable Data Supplied to the Law Enforcement Assistance Administration.* Washington, D.C.: Law Enforcement Assistance Administration, 1979.

White, S., and Krislow, S. (Eds.). *Understanding Crime: An Evaluation of the National Institute of Law Enforcement and Criminal Justice.* Washington, D.C.: National Academy of Sciences, 1977.

5

Harry S. Havens

U.S. General Accounting Office:
Role of Reanalysis
in an Oversight Agency

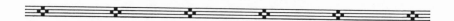

The time has long passed since the work of the U.S. General Accounting Office (GAO) was limited to the audit of financial operations, audits of compliance with applicable laws and regulations, and audits to determine if resources are being used economically and efficiently. A large and growing part of our work (a third or more) now consists of projects called "program results auditing" or "reviews of program effectiveness." These reviews involve evaluating programs and analyzing evaluations performed by others (see General Accounting Office, 1978c). Such analysis is based, in large measure, on the idea that if better information is made available to the decision maker, decisions will be better. Our evaluation work is becoming increasingly sophisticated as we try (or are asked by Congress) to answer increasingly difficult questions about increasingly complicated problems or programs.

Added impetus for such evaluation was provided by the congressional Budget and Impoundment Control Act of 1974. Title VII of that act amends Section 204 of the Legislative Reorganization Act of 1970 in several ways. It authorizes congressional committees to carry out their own evaluation studies, to contract for such studies, or to require them from government agencies. It requires the GAO to review and evaluate government programs carried on under existing law, to develop and recommend methods for reviewing and evaluating these programs, to assist in developing statements of legislative objectives and goals, and to develop methods for assessing and reporting actual program performance. However, we are interested in improving evaluation processes and products not only because we have been told to do so, but also because of our long-standing belief that evaluation is important.

Our concern with secondary analysis is not difficult to understand: Secondary analysis appears to offer significant potential for improving the quality of evaluative information. While we respect researchers whose sole objective is to increase the world's store of knowledge, our primary objective is not knowledge for the sake of knowledge. Rather, we seek information that is relevant to governmental decision processes, particularly those of Congress. We are constantly looking for ways to improve the quality, reliability, and timeliness of the information available to Congress.

For the purpose of the immediate discussion, I would like to use a broad definition of secondary analysis. If an analyst reexamines the hypotheses, data, assumptions, and methodology developed by another analyst for the purpose of confirming or modifying the primary analyst's conclusions, that reexamination constitutes a secondary analysis. The GAO staff members act in each role and we switch roles regularly.

The multiple roles of an agency such as GAO are illustrated by the following example. The GAO was asked by Congress to review a study, conducted by the Army, of a new approach to training called One Station Unit Training (OSUT). Based on a review of several pilot projects, the Army concluded that OSUT could substantially improve the efficiency of certain training processes and proposed to invest in the facilities needed to implement the new approach. The GAO was to review the Army study and establish whether it was a sufficient basis for the investment decision.

The GAO's review (1977a) of the Army study represents one fairly typical type of secondary analysis. It includes a critical review of both documents and data sets collected by the Army and a reanalysis of their content. This review reports a number of deficiencies, including weaknesses in the study design—such as inadequate randomization—and errors in carrying out the design. The review concludes that the Army's conclusion that OSUT would produce greater efficiency is not well founded. Some of the indicated efficiencies in the OSUT pilot testing might have been caused by conditions or activities that could not be maintained in a full implementation of the new approach. Moreover, in reexamining the data, the GAO concludes that other changes in the training process—changes that would not require the investment necessary to implement OSUT—might well provide substantial increases in efficiency and might, therefore, be preferable to OSUT, even if the claimed results of OSUT were confirmed. During meetings with Army officials responsible for the study, the weaknesses in design and implementation were discussed, but the Army chose not to make any changes. GAO advised congressional staff members of the study's shortcoming. Congress then directed the Army to take actions to provide information not contained in the Army's original study but necessary to the decision-making process.

The GAO's conclusions were written up in a "draft report." At this point, the roles switch as the GAO's draft report itself becomes the subject of secondary analysis. Except in unusual circumstances, a GAO draft report is sent to the affected agency for review and comment. That is, the GAO requests a secondary analysis of its findings and conclusions. When a GAO study involves particularly complex, difficult, or controversial matters, GAO often submits the draft for review and comment to several outside experts, who may be asked to respond either individually or may be organized into review panels.

The GAO routinely invites critical review of its draft reports to ensure, insofar as is possible, that GAO's final report is both objective and complete. Thus GAO not only performs secondary analysis, but subjects its own work to secondary analysis by outside experts. Their criticism usually prompts some revision of the draft report, but does not guarantee that all differences will be reconciled. To ensure that any important differences in opinion are available to decision makers, the opinions are regularly published in the GAO's final report. For an illustration, see the U.S. General Accounting Office's (1978b) review of the Experimental Housing Allowance Program.

The GAO's institutional structure and role require us to regularly perform secondary analysis and regularly invite others to reanalyze our work. GAO's most important institutional relationship is with Congress, and our reports are intended to inform Congress in making decisions about particular problems or issues. Although the GAO is by no means the only source of information or advice available to Congress, on any given issue GAO must act as the primary source because relatively few other organizations have an incentive for balanced, indepth, objective presentation of information. Most of them (and there are obvious exceptions) are primarily interested in supporting a particular line of policy or point of view. To a degree, the dialectical approach of argument between such competing interests can lead to a balanced presentation of information, particularly if each side has the opportunity to perform secondary analysis of its opponent's presentation. But this opportunity does not always arise and, at best, such an approach is unreliable.

For example, several years ago the Senate was considering legislation to control the use of toxic chemicals in various manufacturing processes. The proposed bill (the Toxic Substances Control Act) would require the testing of new chemical substances for toxicity before they could be used in manufacturing. The bill granted the Environmental Protection Agency authority to ban unduly hazardous chemicals. One of the major issues in the debate was the likely cost of the testing procedures and the resulting effect on the chemical industry and the process of innovation.

In this case, there were several widely divergent estimates of the cost to the industry of compliance with the proposed bill. The Senate committee that was considering the bill asked the GAO to review the various estimates and determine which was the most reliable. The GAO (U.S. General Accounting Office, 1975) quickly established that one of the three principal estimates of costs was clearly outside the range of probability. The difference between the other two estimates was more difficult to resolve. In each case, the GAO found minor faults with the methodology, but these were marginal.

The fundamental difference lay in the assumptions that were made about the way the proposed law would be implemented. The analysts made greatly differing assumptions about the number of tests that would be required and the extent of the testing process. Since one of the estimates had been made by the agency authorized to implement the bill, the GAO concluded that the assumptions underlying that estimate were probably derived from a realistic view of how the bill would be implemented. In general, however, the GAO concluded from its secondary analysis that it was impossible to reliably estimate the costs. Thus, the GAO study included a strong recommendation that provision be made for careful evaluation of the program's direct costs and benefits and potential hidden costs, such as reduced incentives for innovation and the social costs of the delayed introduction of new products.

In this case, a dialectical approach might have led to the same conclusion, but having a group of independent analysts identify the nature of the differences appears to have facilitated the process. In the case of the Army study discussed earlier, a dialectical approach would have failed because the issue simply was not one that attracted wide public attention. If the GAO had not reanalyzed the study, it is highly unlikely that anyone else would have done so. These two examples of secondary analysis by the GAO illustrate the principal characteristics of our procedures. In neither case was the GAO seeking knowledge because of its intrinsic value. The information was valuable solely because of its relevance to a decision that Congress had to make.

The critical review of social program evaluations presents some distinctive problems for the secondary analyst. The assessment itself often cannot be clearcut, and standards for evaluating an evaluation may be ambiguous, unspecified, or remarkably different from those used in the design of the evaluation. Because social program evaluation is new as a formal discipline, the language, techniques, and standards are evolving, and changes, though necessary, complicate the review process.

The GAO has undertaken some concerted efforts to avoid problems in this area; for example, we obtain the advice of interdisciplinary councils in resolving special problems. The Social Science Research Council's Committee on Evaluation Research, for example, has assisted in the development of guidelines to clarify problems and identify solutions in conflicts between the GAO's need for access to data for assuring quality and the evaluator's or researcher's need to assure confidentiality of reports from research participants (U.S. General Accounting Office, 1977b). GAO has also developed guidelines to clarify the language, perspective, and terminology in the area (U.S. General Accounting Office, 1976), and to ensure that GAO's standards for review of complex evaluations are clear (1978a). The spirit of this work on the new topic of large-scale applied social research is consistent with efforts in more traditional audit and review activities, for example, the GAO's standards for the auditing of governmental organizations (1972).

As we have seen, secondary analysis can be critically important when the object of the reanalysis is research or information needed by decision makers. Government officials need the best possible information; they cannot base their decisions on a plethora of conflicting information of uncertain value or on a set of data from a single source whose objectivity is uncertain. Decision makers must be assured of the relevance, reliability, and completeness of the information given them. Secondary analysis can help provide such assurance.

Secondary analysis performed to inform decision making, however, must meet standards in addition to that of quality. If the analysis is not available when the decision is to be made, its value may well be nil, no matter what rigorous standards of quality it meets. In the political decision process, timeliness can be such a critical factor that the analyst must sometimes compromise other considerations such as precision and confidence levels.

Secondary analysis in the decision-making arena must also meet the standard of completeness. In some cases, decision makers require only a reanalysis of a single study; for example, the GAO reviewed the results of the OSUT pilot test. In other cases, the decision makers need to reconcile several studies that offer contradictory conclusions on a crucial point. The cost estimates on controlling toxic substances is an example of this more complex situation. In an increasing number of cases, however, we find the decision makers asking a much broader question. In effect, they say, "Tell me what I need to know about this subject and what I should do about it." If the subject happens to be one that people have been concerned about, secondary analysis often represents the most efficient approach to answering the question, because much of the information has already been collected. It is likely, however, that the information is to be found in bits and pieces, scattered through a large body of prior research. To answer the question, the analyst cannot merely report the results of that research. To provide useful synthesis of this information, the analyst must reanalyze the data and methodology, thereby establishing the validity and relevance of the results and reconciling the conflicts that inevitably appear.

While secondary analysis is a crucial tool in synthesizing previous research, it is unfortunately not a panacea. In most cases, we discover that the prior research—valuable though it may be—does not completely cover the subject. If timing is not critical (an unusual luxury), the analyst can undertake additional research. More commonly, however, the analyst will have to supply appropriately qualified informed judgments or leave these to the decision maker.

Although gaps in existing research are inevitable, secondary analysis can provide a coherent body of knowledge on which to base decisions. This focus on the need to make decisions affects the character of the GAO's use of secondary analysis. In scholarly research, secondary analysis is valuable because it can confirm or modify findings and thus lead to further steps in the search for knowledge. In decision-oriented research, secondary analysis is valuable because it can facilitate better decisions.

References

U.S. General Accounting Office. *Standards for Audit of Government Organizations, Programs, Activities and Functions.* Washington, D.C.: U.S. General Accounting Office, 1972.

U.S. General Accounting Office. *A Comparison of Three Estimates of Costs of the Proposed Toxic Substances Control Act.* OPA 76-6. Washington, D.C.: U.S. General Accounting Office, 1975.

U.S. General Accounting Office. *Evaluation and Analysis to Support Decision-Making.* Washington, D.C.: U.S. General Accounting Office, 1976.

U.S. General Accounting Office. *The Army's Test of One Station Unit Training: Adequacy and Value.* FPCD 76-100. Washington, D.C.: U.S. General Accounting Office, 1977a.

U.S. General Accounting Office, Program Analysis Division. *Background Paper for Use by the SSRC Committee on Evaluation Research on the Need for Access by GAO Auditors in the Audit of Social Research and Experiments.* Washington, D.C.: U.S. General Accounting Office, 1977b.

U.S. General Accounting Office. *The Concorde: Results of a Supersonic Aircraft's Entry into the United States.* CED-77-131. Washington, D.C.: U.S. General Accounting Office, 1977c.

U.S. General Accounting Office. *Finding Out How Programs Are Working: Suggestions for Congressional Oversight.* PAD-78-3. Washington, D.C.: U.S. General Accounting Office, 1977d.

U.S. General Accounting Office. *Assessing Social Program Impact Evaluations: A Checklist Approach.* PAD-79-2. Washington, D.C.: U.S. Government Printing Office, 1978a.

U.S. General Accounting Office. *An Assessment of the Department of Housing and Urban Development's Experimental Housing Allowance Program.* CED-78-29. Washington, D.C.: U.S. General Accounting Office, 1978b.

U.S. General Accounting Office. *Federal Program Evaluations.* 1977 Congressional Sourcebook Series. PAD-78-27. Washington, D.C.: U.S. Government Printing Office, 1978c.

U.S. General Accounting Office. *Report Manual of the U.S. General Accounting Office.* Washington D.C.: U.S. General Accounting Office, 1978d.

6 *William M. K. Trochim*

Resources for Locating Public and Private Data

Samuel Johnson said, "Knowledge is of two kinds: we know a subject ourselves, or we know where we can find information upon it." This paper is concerned with the latter of these kinds of knowledge. Because data archives and individual researchers routinely store data, often in machine-readable form, the first task for the secondary analyst is to locate these resources. Extensive documentation on the existence of data sources is already available and the following enumeration should be valuable to secondary analysts. While one's awareness of the existence of data archives makes secondary analysis an attractive prospect, we will see that this attractiveness needs to be balanced against some of the difficulties inherent in the search and acquisition processes.

Data Archives: Issues and Sources

Many of the troublesome issues in using data archives have been discussed in the literature. Questions of accessibility, confidentiality, and the use of such data for secondary analysis have been raised by Boruch and Reis (1980), Hedrick, Boruch, and Ross (1978), and

Schoenfeldt (1970), among others. The federal government offers discussions of data archiving and access in work such as the Federal Statistical System Project (1978; see Chapter Two), and in the many publications of such groups as the Office of Federal Statistical Policy and Standards, the General Accounting Office, the National Technical Information Service, and the National Archives. Organizations of data users such as the Federal Statistics Users' Conference and the International Association for Social Science Information Service and Technology (IASSIST) also discuss these problems.

One of the major decisions facing the secondary analyst is how narrowly to define the search strategy. While overspecifying the topic in the early stages of a search may reduce wasted time, less restrictive specification allows one to discover unexpected but relevant data sources. Even when a researcher knows of a specific data base, a general search for related sources may yield separate indicators of the same phenomenon or data that can be used to supplement or check the validity of the major analyses. Cordray (1978) and Lipsey, Cordray, and Berger (in press) provide examples of how archival data can be used in this way. For example, if one is studying the effect of a compensatory education program within a local school system, one could search for data from other school systems in order to determine the importance of such factors as local idiosyncracies, historical forces, and developmental growth patterns. However, such broader specification of the data needed may predispose the researcher to alter the research question to fit the data that are available (Schoenfeldt, 1970). While researchers cannot always determine in advance how narrowly they should define their search, researchers must attempt to use the data archive rather than be used by it.

To use available archives, researchers need to understand the characteristics of various data bases. For example, some data archives contain actual data, while others simply have information that leads one to data sources. Bibliographical data files usually contain abstracts of publications or information about research project reports. If one suspects that needed data may be available from an individual researcher or report, a search of bibliographical data bases might be the quickest way to locate the data. Nonbibliographical data bases hold actual data, usually in machine-readable form. Archives also differ in the following characteristics: originator (government, research institute, private organization); duration of collection (continuing data collection, individual studies); restrictions on the accessibility of the data; provisions for preserving the confidentiality of respondents and the proprietary rights of the data collector; adequacy of documentation; and cost of use.

Given the wealth of data that are available from a wide variety of sources, no single search is likely to discover all the available data on a particular topic for secondary analysis. The following guidelines for a search should be tailored to fit the individual researcher's needs.

Specification of Needs. Often, the only way to discover where data are located is through various subject indexes that describe data archives and their holdings. For example, one might begin a search for data on electricity pricing by looking under the keywords *energy, electricity, prices,* and so on. During the search, the researcher may discover that the keywords *prices* and *energy* are too broad, while *utilities, peak-load pricing,* and others are more directly relevant. Through trial and error, one's search becomes more narrowly focused.

Initial Familiarization. Using the list of keywords, one begins to search the guides, catalogues, and lists of data archives and organizations that may hold appropriate data. While these sources may indicate the potential usefulness of a given archive, they will seldom supply information that is detailed enough to determine whether specific data are available.

Initial Contacts. Once one has identified likely sources of data, one needs to determine if the data file is truly appropriate for the specific analysis. At this stage, the most effective strategy is to contact individuals who are familiar with the archive in question. They should be able to provide information about specific data holdings, the form of storage, acquisition procedures, and the availability of other relevant data. Some files have restricted access or are available in specific formats. A government department or a private research firm may allow only their own employees to use the archive. Such restrictions can be readily determined by a simple phone call.

Secondary Contacts. Once it appears that an individual or archive holds appropriate data, one should seek additional information before attempting to acquire the data file. Helpful information includes: more detailed documentation of the desired data, considerations of the mode of transfer (punched card, magnetic tape, or computer listing), and the institutional capabilities. Magnetic tape files differ in the number of tracks and bits per inch appropriate for the tape. These and other matters are sometimes covered in catalogue description of archives, but should nevertheless be verified prior to making the acquisition request.

Accessibility Problems. Acquiring the data by no means ensures a successful analysis. Inevitable difficulties arise in setting up tapes, writing or using programs to access them, and so on. As with all phases of archive retrieval, it is useful to develop personal contacts with people who have experience using the data.

Analysis and Supplemental Analyses. As the analysis proceeds, one sometimes discovers that additional data are needed. Analysts' knowledge of the availability of related data and their personal contacts should improve their ability to gather additional data quickly and efficiently. For example, if the research question requires the use of an indicator of poverty, but the analysis reveals potential inadequacies in the index due to contamination, changes in reporting practices, and the like, the original list of archives or personal contacts may reveal other measures that could be substituted or used to validate the integrity of the initial measure.

General Sources and Guides

Probably the most difficult steps in the process we have described are the first two. Once specific data sources have been located, one is increasingly able to rely on the expertise of individuals who know the data. Because it is often difficult to initially locate sources of data, we devote the remainder of this chapter to a discussion of general guides and catalogues. While our listing is by no means completely comprehensive, it does provide sufficient information for a good general data search.

Two types of resources are generally available to one who is beginning a search for data. First, there are printed catalogues, guides, and directories of archives and data bases. These vary in quality and scope. However, knowledge of the major ones will greatly reduce search time. Second, a number of organizations and user groups are able to aid researchers who are trying to acquire data.

One of the most general, accessible catalogues of archives is the *Encyclopedia of Information Systems and Services* (Kruzas, 1978). It lists over two thousand archives and data bases, bibliographical and nonbibliographical, covering all types of archives including federal, independent, and foreign. For each archive, the *Encyclopedia* includes the address, phone number, name and title of director, number of staff, related organizations, description of system or service, scope or subject matter, input sources, holdings and storage media, publications, microform products and services, other services, clientele and availability, projected publications and services, remarks and addenda, and the name of a person to contact. The volume also contains eighteen indexes including an index of data base producers and publishers, a listing of data collection and analysis centers, a publications index, and geographical subject indexes. It can be used to locate individual researchers who may have relevant data (through bibliographical data bases), organizations that will perform data searches, and data archives themselves. Because it attempts to be comprehensive and is updated periodically, the *Encyclopedia* is probably a good starting point for a general data search.

Another general guide for locating data for secondary analysis is *Statistics Sources* (Wasserman and Paskar, 1977). This volume is a subject guide to data on industry, business, social conditions, education, finance, and other topics; it covers the United States and the international community. The volume is divided into two sections and primarily references data stored in printed form in government documents, periodicals, and trade journals. The first section is a selected bibliography of key statistical sources including guides, almanacs, U.S. governmental publications, census guides and publications, the statistical abstract of the U.S., yearbooks, and international sources. It describes many of the sources mentioned in this chapter as well as many more subject-specific guides and catalogues. The second and major portion of the book contains listings of specific sources by subject. For example, under the heading "France—unemployment" are two listings: the *Labour Force Statistics* of the Organization for Economic Cooperation and Development and the *Statistical Yearbook* of the Statistical Office of the United Nations. Similarly, the heading "Children—orphans" lists the *Social Security Bulletin* of the U.S. Social Security Administration as a data source.

Much of the data stored in archives are collected by nongovernmental research organizations, many of which retain a copy of the data as part of their own archival system. While few, if any, nongovernmental organizations have a formal policy of making data available to the public, they can direct the secondary analyst to appropriate data files or evaluation studies. Two general catalogues list nongovernmental research groups. The *Research Centers Directory* (Palmer, 1979) contains 6,268 listings of nonprofit and university-related research institutes, centers, foundations, laboratories, bureaus, and other research groups. The directory is organized into sixteen basic subject areas and includes an institutional index, an index of research centers, and a detailed subject index. The *Consultants and Consulting Organizations Directory* (Wasserman and McLean, 1976) offers information on over 5,000 for-profit firms and individuals engaged in consultation for business and industry. The entries are arranged alphabetically and the volume contains a subject key, index by state, and an enumeration of principal persons in each organization. Using the subject indexes of these two directories one could, for a given topic, locate nonprofit groups and for-profit firms that are or have been engaged in work related to the secondary analyst's area of interest.

Agencies within the federal government are major producers, either directly or through contracted research, of statistical data. Several guides describe data systems within the federal government. Although not intended as a reference tool, *A Framework for Planning U.S. Federal Statistics* (U.S. Department of Commerce, Office of Federal Statistical Policy and Standards, 1978) provides a description of the federal statistical system and the data bases held by various agencies. It does not describe in great detail the specific data holdings of each agency but does explain the general categories of the agencies' holdings. In addition, it covers each of eighteen substantive areas (for example, criminal justice, education, energy, health, housing and community development, income maintenance and welfare), describes the agencies holding data on these topics, comments on the quality of the data, and recommends future data collection policy. The *Framework* is especially useful in limiting the number of federal agencies within which one needs to search. More specific information on the data that are held must be obtained directly from the agencies.

Four other sources, spanning the entire federal system, document some of the available resources—including evaluation studies, longitudinal surveys, and ongoing demographic and economic data collection efforts. The National Technical Information Service publishes the *Directory of Computerized Data Files and Related Software* (U.S. Department of Commerce, National Technical Information Service, 1978). This document describes machine-readable data bases and computer programs and indicates how they can be acquired. The *Directory* is divided into forty-six subject fields and includes a detailed subject and agency index. The National Archives publishes the *Catalog of Machine-Readable Records in the National Archives of the United States* (U.S. National Archives and Record Service, 1977), which describes ninety-nine files created by a wide variety of federal agencies. While neither the National Archives nor the National Technical Information Service comprehensively index federal holdings, they are both likely to become major depositories in the future. The General Accounting Office (GAO) issues *Federal Information Sources and Systems: A Directory for the Congress* (U.S. General Accounting Office, 1976), which covers automated information systems, catalogues, and listings issued by over sixty federal agencies. This directory emphasizes information for administrative rather than research use. It includes, for example, an on-line literature search system for medicine (MEDLARS and MEDLINE) and various departmental management information systems. Although most data banks containing purely statistical information apparently fall outside the information resources designated by the GAO, the directory is nonetheless a vehicle for primary and secondary analysis of administrative information. In addition, the Congressional Information Service publishes the *American Statistics Index* (Congressional Information Service, annual), which is intended as a master guide and index to all the statistical publications of the federal government. It consists of an index to and abstracts of any governmental reports that present statistics. Its major usefulness for secondary analysis is in providing access to tables and charts that can be analyzed or cited and in directing the analyst to persons or agencies that hold the data discussed in reports.

In addition to these federal guides, there are catalogues that describe the holdings of a particular agency or agencies. These include: *Selected Federal Computer-Based Information Systems* (Herner and Vellucci, 1972), *Standardized Microdata Tape Transcripts* (U.S. Department of Health, Education, and Welfare, National Center for Health Statistics, 1976), *Some Statistical Research Resources Available at the Social Security Administration* (U.S. Department of Health, Education, and Welfare, 1979), *Research Microdata Files* (U.S. Department of Health, Education, and Welfare, Social Security Administration, 1978), the *Directory of Federal Agency Education Tapes* (U.S. Department of Health, Education, and Welfare, National Center for Education Statistics, 1976), the *Directory of Automatic Data Processing Systems in the Public Health Service* (U.S. Department of Health, Education, and Welfare, Public Health Service, annual), and the *BLS Data Bank Files and Statistical Routines* (U.S. Department of Labor, periodical), among others. Most agencies involved in government archives issue some type of catalogue of their holdings. For example, the Bureau of the Census, by far the largest data collector, issues a wide variety of documents on holdings and suggestions for access.

Numerous federal agencies publish periodicals that discuss statistical systems, including the *Vital and Health Statistics Publications Series* of the National Center for Health Statistics, the *Review of Public Data Use* of the National Technical Information Service, the *Bureau of the Census Catalog* of the Bureau of the Census, and the *Statistical Reporter* published by the Office of Federal Statistical Policy and Standards. In addition, an external agency, the Federal Statistics Users' Conference, publishes a *Newsletter*. The problem, at least within the federal government, is not a lack of information, but rather, how to locate the appropriate sources. The best approach is to locate the appropriate agencies and then contact them or the regional office for further information on sources. A helpful document in this regard is the *Federal Statistical Directory* (U.S. Office of Management and Budget, 1974)—a telephone directory of persons engaged in statistical programs and related activities of the federal government.

Outside the federal system there are few sources (excepting the aforementioned *Encyclopedia of Information Systems and Services)* that provide comprehensive calatogues of data archives. Almost every archive issues its own catalogue and, once the researcher has identified likely sources, individual catalogues may be obtained. For example, the Data Library at the University of British Columbia published a basic catalogue in 1974 and updates it annually; the Interuniversity Consortium for Political and Social Research annually publishes a complete *Guide to Resources and Services.* Similarly, once appropriate profit and nonprofit research firms have been located through some of the sources listed earlier, their annual reports and bulletins can be acquired and checked for pertinent information. In addition, the Association of Public Data Users publishes the *Data File Directory* (Association of Public Data Users, 1977), which describes a large number of independent data sources and archives. However, these are available only to association members. Finally, the United Nations publishes a catalogue of its data holdings entitled the *Directory of International Statistics* (United Nations, 1975).

A number of organizations either will provide information about available archives or will conduct a data search. The National Technical Information Service has set up an Information Documentation Center with an independent firm, DUALabs, Inc. DUALabs will, for a fee, search the federal statistical system for data sources, usually within five days of the request. Because of the complexity of the decentralized federal statistics system, a search of this type by experienced people is often advisable. DUALabs issues a report for each search as well as giving names of persons to contact within the federal government.

Four major user groups are likely to have useful information for those seeking data. These are the Data Clearinghouse for the Social Sciences, in Canada, and in Europe, the International Federation of Data Organizations for the Social Sciences, the European Association of Scientific Information Dissemination Centers, and the International Association for Social Science Information Service and Technology. Each group publishes a bulletin and holds regular meetings. The addresses for the associations and user groups mentioned in this chapter are listed in the Appendix.

As the technology of data archives becomes more sophisticated, the field continues to change rapidly; archives combine into new networks, gather additional data, and revise their acquisition and transfer policies. Because a researcher alone seldom has the capacity to stay abreast of recent developments, use of the documents, catalogues, and guides described here provides a way for the individual to discover appropriate data sources with a minimum of effort.

APPENDIX

- Association of Public Data Users (APDU)
  Box 9287 Rosslyn Station
  Arlington, Va. 22209

- Data Clearinghouse for the Social Sciences
  151 Slater
  Ottawa, ON
  Canada KIP 5NI

- DUALabs, Inc.
  Information Documentation Center
  1601 N. Kent St.
  Suite 900
  Arlington, Va. 22209

- European Association of Scientific Information Dissemination
  Centers (EUSIDIC)
  P.O. Box 1776
  The Hague
  Netherlands

- Federal Statistics Users' Conference
  1030 Fifteenth St., N.W.
  Washington, D.C. 20005

- International Association for Social Science Information Service
  and Technology (IASSIST)
  Judith S. Rowe, United States Secretariat
  Princeton University Computer Center
  87 Prospect Avenue
  Princeton, N.J. 08540

- International Federation of Data Organizations for the Social
  Sciences (IFDO)
  Guido Martinotti, President
  Archivio Datie Programmi Per Le Scienze Sociali (ADPSS)
  Via G. Cantoni
  4 - Milano
  Italy

References

Association of Public Data Users. *Data File Directory*. Arlington, Va.:
  Association of Public Data Users, 1977.

Boruch, R. F., and Reis, J. "The Student, Evaluative Data, and Secondary Analysis." In L. Sechrest (Ed.), *New Directions in Program Evaluation: Training Program Evaluators,* no. 8. San Francisco: Jossey-Bass, 1980.

Congressional Information Service. *American Statistics Index.* Washington, D.C.: Congressional Information Service, (annual).

Cordray, D. S. "Making the Case for the Use of Patchwork Analyses in Quasi-Experimental Evaluation Research." Unpublished doctoral dissertation, Department of Psychology, Claremont Graduate School, 1978.

Federal Statistical System Project, President's Reorganization Project. *"Issues and Options."* Reproduced report, Office of Management and Budget, Washington, D.C., 1978.

Hedrick, T. E., Boruch, R. F., and Ross, J. "On Ensuring the Availability of Evaluative Data for Secondary Analysis." *Policy Sciences,* 1978, *9,* 259–280.

Herner, S., and Velluci, M. J. (Eds.). *Selected Federal Computer-Based Information Systems.* Washington, D.C.: Information Resources Press, 1972.

Kruzas, A. T. (Ed.). *Encyclopedia of Information Systems and Services.* (3rd ed.) Detroit: Gale Research, 1978.

Lipsey, M. W., Cordray, D. S., and Berger, D. E. "The Use of Multiple Lines of Evidence to Evaluate a Juvenile Diversion Program." *Evaluation Review,* in press.

Palmer, A. M. (Ed.). *Research Centers Directory.* (6th ed.) Detroit: Gale Research, 1979.

Schoenfeldt, L. F. "Data Archives as Resources for Research, Instruction, and Policy Planning." *American Psychologist,* 1970, *25,* (7), 609–616.

United Nations. *Directory of International Statistics.* Statistical Papers, Series M., No. 56. New York: United Nations Publications, 1975.

U.S. Department of Commerce, National Technical Information Service. *Directory of Computerized Data Files and Related Software.* Washington, D.C.: U.S. Department of Commerce, 1978.

U.S. Department of Commerce, Office of Federal Statistical Policy and Standards. *A Framework for Planning U.S. Federal Statistics.* Washington, D.C.: U.S. Department of Commerce, 1978.

U.S. Department of Health, Education, and Welfare, National Center for Education Statistics. *Directory of Federal Agency Education Tapes.* Washington, D.C.: U.S. Department of Health, Education, and Welfare, 1976.

U.S. Department of Health, Education, and Welfare, National Center for Health Statistics. *Standardized Microdata Tape Transcripts.*

Washington, D.C.: U.S. Department of Health, Education, and Welfare, 1976.

U.S. Department of Health, Education, and Welfare, Public Health Service. *Directory of Automatic Data Processing Systems in the Public Health Service.* Washington, D.C.: U.S. Department of Health, Education, and Welfare, annual.

U.S. Department of Health, Education, and Welfare. *Some Statistical Research Resources Available at the Social Security Administration.* Washington, D.C.: U.S. Department of Health, Education, and Welfare, 1979.

U.S. Department of Health, Education, and Welfare, Social Security Administration. *Research Microdata Files.* Washington, D.C.: U.S. Department of Health, Education, and Welfare, 1978.

U.S. Department of Labor, Bureau of Labor Statistics. *BLS Data Bank Files and Statistical Routines.* Washington, D.C.: U.S. Department of Labor, periodical.

U.S. General Accounting Office. *Federal Information Sources and Systems: A Directory for the Congress.* Congressional Sourcebook Series. Washington, D.C.: U.S. General Accounting Office, 1976.

U.S. National Archives and Records Service. *Catalog of Machine-Readable Records in the National Archives of the United States.* Washington, D.C.: U.S. National Archives and Record Service, 1977.

U.S. Office of Management and Budget, Statistical Policy Division. *Federal Statistical Directory.* (24th ed.) Washington, D.C.: U.S. Office of Management and Budget, 1974.

Wasserman, P., and McLean, J. (Eds.). *Consultants and Consulting Organizations Directory.* (3rd ed.) Detroit: Gale Research, 1976.

Wasserman, P., and Paskar, J. (Eds.). *Statistics Sources.* (5th ed.) Detroit: Gale Research, 1977.

Joan A. W. Linsenmeier
Paul M. Wortman
Michael Hendricks

7

Need for Better Documentation:
Problems in a Reanalysis of Teacher Bias

This chapter does not report any new findings uncovered in our secondary analysis. Indeed, our preliminary work with the data led us to decide that further analyses should not be done. Much of this chapter is devoted to explaining the reasoning behind this decision.

Our example involves data from the Riverside School Study of desegregation (RSS). This study of how school desegregation affects children has been hailed as "the most thorough to date" (Useem, 1977, p. 71) and "the most long-term, completely documented, and widely noted" (St. John, 1975, p. 25). The study has also received attention from the media (see Lofton, 1976; Miller and Gerard, 1976) and is

Note: The authors thank Herb Nickles and Bruce Foster for their invaluable assistance in handling and managing the data. The work on this manuscript was supported in part by Contract No. C-74-10015 from the National Institute of Education.

important because of its potential effect on national policy. Statutes and court actions are continuing to order the desegregation of the nation's schools (Henderson, 1978). It is important, therefore, to try to understand how to minimize any harmful effects of this process.

The RSS project was a five-year examination of the effects of school desegregation on white, Mexican-American, and black elementary school children in Riverside, California. Data were collected from the children (school and racial attitudes, sociometrics, classroom grades, and achievement test scores), their parents (economic and occupation information, racial attitudes, and family values), and their classroom teachers (background, teaching philosophy, and evaluations of the children). The study team included Harold Gerard and Norman Miller, of the University of California at Riverside, when the study was initiated. The results and conclusions drawn from the research are reported in a book edited by Gerard and Miller (1975). The study is generally viewed as finding no real benefits of desegregation and few significant predictors of "successful" desegregation. It also provides suggestive evidence that racially biased teachers can negatively affect minority students' performance.

Our reexamination of the Riverside data focused on this relationship between teachers' racial biases and their students' performance, a feature of the study that was highlighted by the media. For example, when *Psychology Today* published an article on the Riverside study of desegregation, in June 1976, the synopsis on the contents page stated that "Ten years of large-scale busing brought no great benefits to black and Chicano children. And bigoted teachers did a lot of damage." The researchers, too, have sometimes emphasized this aspect of their findings in speeches, interviews, and testimony (see the interview with Gerard by Sage, 1978). The findings that teachers' attitudes are important is coherent with results of the growing research on the effects of teachers' expectations (Brophy and Good, 1974). Furthermore, St. John (1975), in reviewing the literature on how school desegregation affects children, suggests that desegregation will benefit minority children only if accompanied by an increase in the expectations of their teachers and their parents. Thus, it seemed important to reexamine the RSS conclusion that teachers' racial attitudes have a sizable effect on children's performance and to see if the data would yield findings about the effects of teachers' expectations.

The situation we encountered in our attempt to perform a secondary analysis of the Riverside data was in many ways quite favorable. We encountered no great obstacles in our attempt to access the data, and a primary investigator was supportive and helpful throughout. The data were much more thoroughly documented than most

(Hedrick, Boruch, and Ross, 1978). Nevertheless, the process did not go smoothly, and took considerable time.

Obtaining the Data

Members of the Project on Secondary Analysis at Northwestern University first became interested in reanalyzing the data from the Riverside desegregation study in May 1975. Early that month Norman Miller, one of the principal investigators on the Riverside study, visited Northwestern and gave a colloquium at which he reported some of the preliminary findings. We were especially intrigued by his comments on the importance of teachers' attitudes in determining how students respond to education in desegregated classrooms.

Miller was receptive to our conducting a secondary analysis. Enthusiastic support of the original research investigators, while generally necessary, is often not sufficient for obtaining data for secondary analysis because investigators do not always have the authority to release the data. In the case of the Riverside School Study, that authority lay with a special committee, the Executive Committee of the Riverside Joint Research Study, composed of staff members of the Board of Education and University of California-Riverside and chaired by the superintendent of schools of the Riverside Unified School District. While Gerard was a voting member of this committee, Miller, our principal contact, was not.

Miller's subsequent letter to Donald T. Campbell was passed on to Paul Wortman, who responded with a description of the aims of the Project on Secondary Analysis and also affirmed our interest in reanalyzing the Riverside data. Miller, at that time a visiting professor at the University of Iowa, replied that he would work out the necessary arrangements when he returned to Los Angeles in June. Later, he wrote a letter on our behalf to Riverside's superintendent of schools and was informed that we would have to submit a formal proposal to the dean of research at the University of California-Riverside. Our proposal would be circulated to all members of the executive committee, who would then meet to decide whether or not to grant our request. We had assumed that our informal communications with Miller and his intercession with committee members would result in our receiving permission to use RSS data. Only at this time did we realize that a more formal procedure was required.

We then prepared an official proposal, including a review of relevant literature, an outline of our plans for reanalyzing the data, and a detailed specification of which data we expected to use. We explained that we would focus on the role of the classroom teacher in influencing pupils' behavior. We also stressed our intention to preserve the confidentiality of the data, an important concern to primary analysts who have assured confidentiality to research participants (see Bryant and Wortman, 1978; Hedrick, Boruch, and Ross, 1978). Our proposal was submitted to the university's dean of research in October 1975.

At this point, the decision about whether to grant us access to the Riverside data rested with the executive committee, which could have denied access for policy, practical, or political reasons. The original investigators had no special monopoly on the data, however. Indeed, the bylaws of the executive committee stated that, subject to certain restrictions, all data generated by the study would be made available to secondary analysts three years after collection. A month after receiving our proposal, the executive committee voted to release to us all the data that we requested.

In November two of us met with Jane Mercer, a faculty member at Riverside and a member of the original RSS team. Since neither Gerard nor Miller were still in Riverside, Mercer had assumed the responsibility for maintaining the study's data files. We learned from her that the files were more extensive than we had supposed. The researchers had accumulated twenty-six computer data tapes and these files were extremely well documented. Detailed codebooks for each tape listed all variables stored on it, the meaning of each possible value of each variable, the tape location of each datum, and the format in which each item of data was stored. The Riverside researchers had also retained a staff person to manage the archive. The bylaws of the executive committee indicated that the project team should include a data processing coordinator to maintain project data and documentation so that information would be readily retrievable from the data files. The coordinator's expertise facilitated our obtaining the precise items of information that we wanted.

Following our meeting with Mercer, we read through the codebooks to locate the data we wanted and selected data from nineteen tapes. We then met with the coordinator, who assured us that he would create new files for us containing the data needed. We agreed to pay for the time, computer services, and materials expended on this task.

While waiting for the data tapes to arrive, we conducted a review of the literature on school desegregation, which convinced us of the importance of examining the role of classroom teachers in desegregated schools. The wait for the data was longer than expected. Instead of arriving before the end of 1975, the four computer tapes containing the data we had requested arrived in March 1976. We then learned that tapes produced on Riverside's IBM computer system are not compatible with the CDC system at Northwestern. Our computer staff member transformed the tapes from Riverside into data files that could be manipulated and analyzed on our computer system and also created a duplicate set of files. We felt that back-up files were a necessary precaution in light of the effort involved in obtaining the initial data set.

A preliminary look at the data indicated that we had failed to request certain data vital to the analyses we had in mind. Our request for supplementary data was quickly fulfilled. By the summer of 1976— one year after our initial request—we had all our data and were ready to proceed with our analyses.

Replicating the Primary Analyses

We first tried to replicate the Riverside researchers' own analysis of the effects of teacher bias on student achievement. Replicating the original analysis of data before proceeding to one's own secondary analyses is advisable for a number of reasons. First, it gives one a feel for the data set, a knowledge of how different variables are coded and how they can be accessed and manipulated. The replication can also reveal problems with the data set: large quantities of missing data; entries that are outside an acceptable range (for example, elementary school children who are twenty-five years old, or responses of "8" on an attitude scale from 1 to 5); and inconsistencies among data entries. As an example of this last problem, consider McSweeney and Wortman's (1979) reanalysis of data used to evaluate the effectiveness of community mental health centers. They discovered that the number of days individuals had supposedly been hospitalized in private facilities added to the number of days they had supposedly been hospitalized in public ones did not always equal the total number of hospitalized days. Some discrepancies were small, but others were substantial, for example 50 compared to 110 days. Such problems cast doubts on the quality of the data used by the primary analysts.

Replicating the original analyses may also reveal problems with those analyses, as opposed to problems with the data. Smith (1969), for instance, noted that the researchers involved with the influential Coleman report (Coleman and others, 1966) had inadvertently failed to use the intended index of socioeconomic status. The replication of primary analyses may also reveal errors in published reports of results, such as incorrect entries in tables and figures due to carelessness in typing, proofreading, and the like. Replication may also indicate that published reports provide insufficient information on the computations performed by the original research team. Our attempt to replicate the original Riverside findings indicated important ambiguities about the conduct of the original analyses.

The data files provided by the RSS team contained information on 1,779 children. The team's report, however, indicated that 1,731 children participated in the study (Redfearn and Gerard, 1975). Therefore, we began by attempting to determine which children listed on our data file were included in the study and which were omitted at its start. One variable stored on the tapes was labeled "status in study" and one value of this variable was labeled "still in study." We thought that we could determine which children were included by seeing which were identified as "still in study" during the first year of data collection. However, this approach yielded neither the reported total of 1,731 children nor the reported subtotals for ethnic groups and school grades. When we consulted members of the RSS team, we learned that "status in study" only indicated whether children were in the study's jurisdiction at the start of the school year. The RSS team apparently had no documentation of the criteria used to decide which children were included in different analyses.

We then examined the data record for each child and discovered that four children's records were missing information about critical variables such as race and grade in school, three children were whites initially enrolled in predominantly minority schools, and forty-one children were mentally retarded. By eliminating these forty-eight students, we achieved the proper ethnicity and grade breakdowns. Thus we decided that we had probably discovered the proper criteria for eliminating subjects. We then applied these and similar criteria to data files from subsequent years of the Riverside project. After much guessing, arithmetic, and rearranging, we were able to obtain the total number of students reported by Redfearn and Gerard (1975) for each year, although several small discrepancies in subsample sizes remained (for example, 143 compared to 140 sixth-grade students for the 1966–67 school year).

We then wrote to Miller and described our problems in trying to match the original sample sizes. He agreed that our figures were close enough to warrant our proceeding with our reanalysis. The identification of the children actually included in the research was then considered complete. This was accomplished by the end of the summer of 1976, a little over a year after we had requested certain files from the RSS team, and about four months after we actually received the data tapes.

We thought it would now be fairly easy to replicate the Riverside group's analysis of the effects of teacher bias before proceeding to our own analyses. As it turned out, this was not the case. But before discussing the problems we encountered, let us briefly describe the information we had on how the original investigators looked at teacher bias effects.

According to the report by Johnson, Gerard, and Miller (1975), teachers involved in the study annually rated the children on a fifty-five-item semantic differential scale. Factor analysis of the first year's rating yielded two factors: the "discipline" factor concerned how well behaved a child was and the "brightness" factor indexed the child's academic talent and motivation. The researchers created a measure of the teacher's evaluation of each child's brightness by summing the ratings given to the child on each of the thirteen items loading on the brightness factor. They then standardized these sums by grade and sex to "eliminate sources of extraneous variation" (p. 246).

For each teacher with at least one white and one minority student in the 1966–67 sample, the researchers calculated the ratio of the average standardized brightness score given whites to the average standardized brightness score given minority students. Then, to correct for actual performance differences, they divided this brightness ratio by the ratio of average performances on achievement tests during the previous year, again standardized by grade and sex. This yielded a bias index that was to indicate the degree to which ethnic differences in achievement were overestimated or underestimated by classroom teachers. The calculation of the bias index thus may be summarized as follows:

1. Record 1965–66 verbal achievement test score for each child (X_{ach}).
2. Record 1966–67 perceived brightness score for each child. This is the sum of the ratings made of him or her on thirteen scales (X_{br}).
3. Standardize verbal achievement and perceived brightness within each grade and sex (Z_{ach}, Z_{br}).
4. Find average scores for white and minority sample kids in each 1966–67 classroom ($\bar{Z}_{ach\text{-}w}$, $\bar{Z}_{ach\text{-}m}$; $\bar{Z}_{br\text{-}w}$, $\bar{Z}_{br\text{-}m}$).
5. Find ratio of average perceived brightness scores within each classroom. Brightness ratio = $\bar{Z}_{br\text{-}w}/\bar{Z}_{br\text{-}m}$.
6. Correct for actual differences by dividing by ratio of average achievement scores. Bias index = $(\bar{Z}_{br\text{-}w}/\bar{Z}_{br\text{-}m})/(\bar{Z}_{ach\text{-}w}/\bar{Z}_{ach\text{-}m})$

The effects of teacher bias, as assessed by this index, on student achievement were then examined in two ways. First, the researchers calculated the correlation of the teacher bias index with the change in the achievement gap between white and minority students in each teacher's classroom. Second, they classified children with respect to their ethnic group (white, Mexican-American, or black), their initial verbal achievement as assessed by performance on the previous year's achievement tests (relatively high or low), and their teacher's racial bias, (relatively high or low), as assessed by the teacher bias index.

Using analysis of variance, they looked at the effects of these three variables on changes in children's verbal achievement between the year preceding wide-scale desegregation (1965–66) and the 1966–67 school year. Their description of the specific analytic procedures used is quite detailed and explicit; frequently, the published report of a study contains much less information on the methodology.

Since the original analyses involved only teachers whose classes included both white and minority students in the study in 1966–67, our next step was to identify those teachers. Johnson, Gerard, and Miller (1975) state that there were 145 teachers. Reviewing data, we discovered 180. Six of these were eliminated for good reasons; for example, some were listed as teaching in two different schools, in neither of which they worked with both minority and white sample children. But we still had 174 teachers who fit the reported criteria.

Since we found more teachers who met the criteria for inclusion than Johnson, Gerard, and Miller (1975) report having used, we were not surprised to find more sample students enrolled in the classrooms of these teachers. We were, however, surprised at the size of the discrepancy. The original investigators, using data from 145 classrooms, included 452 children in their analysis. The 174 teachers we found eligible for inclusion were teaching 936 children from the RSS sample, over twice the number whose achievement was supposedly analyzed.

Rereading the chapter on teacher bias in Gerard and Miller, we focused on the statement that "data will be presented for a subsample of children in the first year of desegregation for whom predesegregation data existed and who entered classrooms containing at least one Anglo and one minority child from the original Riverside sample" (p. 245). We thought initially that the word *subsample* referred to children with both 1965 and 1966 data and in a 1966–67 classroom containing white and minority sample children. We now wondered if data from only a subset of the children fitting this description were used. Our next task, then, was to figure out what determined whether a child was in that subset. We considered several possible decision rules, such as eliminating children missing particular bits of data or dropping all those in classrooms in which the number of white children in the sample did not equal the number from minority backgrounds. None of these approaches yielded a subset near in size to the subset included in the original analysis.

When we described this problem to Miller, he was eager to help. Unfortunately, the individual who had carried out this particular step in the original analysis had left the project and was not available to assist us. A graduate student currently involved in the project tried to find information on the criteria used for inclusion, but could not. She could only suggest that the analyst might have utilized a computer program that selected subsamples. She also reported that he had a reputation for eliminating extreme scores. Since neither we nor our contact in California could recreate the reported sample of 452 children, we decided to replicate the original method of analysis using the 936 children whom we condisered to be eligible.

Since the original teacher bias analysis involved classifying teachers as high or low in bias, our next step was to calculate each teacher's bias index. To do this, we needed the 1966–67 brightness ratings and the 1965–66 achievement scores of each child. Each child took several achievement tests annually, but Gerard and Miller (1975) do not specify which achievement scores were used in deriving the bias index. However, earlier documents indicated that only verbal achievement scores were involved, although mathematics scores were also available for most children. Our graduate student contact told us which tests were probably used for children in kindergarten through third grade. She was not sure, though, whether the "verbal scores" of older children were their reading scores on the Sequential Tests of Educational Progress, their scores on the verbal portion of the School and College Achievement Test, or some composite of these two.

We did know what measures were used to form the brightness score assigned to each child—the ratings given to the child on thirteen items in the fifty-five-item questionnaire that loaded on the brightness factor. Johnson, Gerard, and Miller (1975) report that the brightness score was simply the sum of these thirteen scores. To determine which thirteen items formed the brightness factor, we simply replicated Gerard and Miller's factor analysis of the 1966 ratings. Considering all the children together and using a principal components analysis with varimax rotation, we found thirteen items loading on what could be described as a brightness factor. However, separate factor analyses of the ratings of white, Mexican-American, and black children (not performed by Gerard and Miller) revealed different factor structures for each ethnic group. We were unable to factor analyze the ratings using a maximum likelihood procedure (Jöreskog, 1968). The correlations between items on the fifty-five-item scale were apparently too high for this model to be appropriate, possibly indicating that certain factors were inadvertently built into the rating instrument through the inclusion of items whose meanings were nearly identical.

Thus we found that we could not identify the teachers and children included in the original investigators' analysis of the effects of teacher bias on student achievement; nor could we confidently recreate the original measure of teacher bias. Furthermore, since neither we nor our California contacts could specify the original methodology, we came to have serious doubts about the reported findings. While we had spent nearly a year trying to replicate the analysis carried out by the RSS team, we now decided to abandon that task and to pursue other approaches to assess the influence of teacher bias.

Additional Analyses

While replication is useful for gaining familiarity with a set of data and assessing its quality, it is not an essential step in secondary analysis (see Wortman and St. Pierre, 1977). However, a number of questions besides those concerning statistical techniques must be answered before reanalysis can be performed. For the Riverside data, these questions concerned the determination of appropriate samples and the operationalization of theoretical constructs. Unfortunately, there seemed to be no perfect answers to many of these questions and no satisfactory solution to at least one crucial problem.

Among the questions we explored were: Which children should we include in our analyses? How shall we assess student achievement? How shall we assess ethnic bias in teachers? Of course, these questions are not unique to secondary analysts. Obviously, primary analysts, too, must decide whom to study and how to measure the variables of interest to them. However, the original investigators can consider these questions while designing their study (that is, before subjects have been sampled and attributes have been measured). Secondary analysts, in contrast, must decide how best to explore problems and test hypotheses using data already collected.

The question concerning the operationalization of teacher bias illustrates an unusual problem. Teacher attitudes and their effects were not a major focus of the Riverside study; the original investigators seem to have become interested in this issue only as an alternative to a number of other explanatory theories. Thus in considering the topic, they apparently had to rely on data that they had collected for other purposes. They had to derive a complex and unique indicator of teacher bias to investigate this construct. Such extensions of the basic design of a study often require additional data or entirely new data sets (Cook and Gruder, 1978; Wortman, Reichardt, and St. Pierre, 1978). We therefore felt that the original measure of teacher bias should be carefully examined before performing any further analyses.

We have already discussed some of the problems with the manner in which the Riverside team assessed teacher bias. As we have seen, the original index involved a ratio of the ratios of scores for brightness and scores for achievement—a measure of unknown reliability generated from unspecifiable populations and measures. We were not sure about the appropriateness of the factor analysis of the fifty-five-item scale on which teachers rated students. We also questioned the stability of an index often based on evaluations of only two or three children and involving a small proportion of the items on which students were rated. The index completely ignored the discipline factor, which accounted for the greatest proportion of variance on the fifty-five-item scale, and also other ratings obtained from teachers but not a part of this questionnaire (for example, ratings of how much difficulty children have in learning school subjects). In addition, performance on the prior year's verbal achievement tests is undoubtedly a less than perfect reflection of actual classroom performance. Furthermore, the Riverside group's teacher bias index treats bias against Mexican-Americans and bias against blacks as a single variable (see Linsenmeier and Wortman, 1978).

Consequently, we sought to derive measures superior to the teacher bias index. The Riverside School Study involved the collection of data on a wide range of variables that might be expected to reflect teacher bias. Teachers judged many attributes of their students, reported how their students reacted to them, and indicated their feelings about racial integration. If teachers' attitudes toward students are reflected in students' attitudes toward teachers, then students' and parents' ratings of how much students enjoy school are relevant. We also saw several possible approaches to correcting for true differences among students, using different ways of measuring actual performance and different ways of comparing white and minority children. But no single variable nor any combination of variables seemed an accurate measure of how teachers felt about different ethnic groups. The available indices of teacher bias were less than satisfactory, and exploratory analyses revealed that these different indices often had little empirical relationship to one another. Given the discouraging results of our initial analyses, we doubted it was possible or fruitful to conduct additional tests of the effects of teacher bias using the RSS data. Thus, we reluctantly decided to abandon our plans for further secondary analysis of teacher bias in the RSS data set.

Conclusions and Recommendations

Although we decided not to proceed with our analyses, we do not feel that our efforts on this project were wasted. Secondary analyses of other portions of the Riverside data by Northwestern personnel have been more fruitful (see Chapter Nineteen), and other researchers interested in this data set (Hawley and Levin, 1978) have reportedly benefited from our thinking about its complexities. We conclude this chapter with some recommendations based on our experiences. Some are directed to primary investigators who want to assure that the data they have collected can be reanalyzed by others. Other suggestions are for researchers interested in conducting a reanalysis.

Our first recommendation concerns the need for documentation. Let us distinguish two types of documentation: documentation of a data set and documentation of the method of analyzing the data. The former type of documentation comprises information on what variables were measured, how they were measured, what values each variable can take, and how the values are stored on tapes and cards. The latter type comprises information on how missing data and extreme scores were handled, how variables were combined to form indices, which computer programs were run, and so forth.

The RSS team's documentation of data was generally good. Funds were available not only for storing the data but also for employing a management information specialist familiar with the data archive. We believe that funding for both these activities should routinely be available for large research projects. Fortunately, institutions are now recognizing the need for such archives and are beginning to provide appropriate resources (see Chapter Three).

The documentation of the analyses performed on the Riverside data, unlike the documentation of the data, was relatively weak. We suspect that this pattern is a common one. Primary analysts document their data files to facilitate their own access to them. When conducting specific analyses, however, they are likely to document only their findings and to be less specific about how they obtained the findings.

The documentation of analyses is often incomplete because researchers feel that certain steps in their analyses have no real effect on the results (see Hendricks, 1977). In analyzing any set of data, and especially a large one, one makes many decisions: Should one combine males and females or analyze them separately? Should subjects with missing entries be omitted or assigned mean responses? Which factor analysis procedure should be used? Many researchers have habitual, idiosyncratic ways of answering such questions and feel that their answers, although not clearly better than others, are no worse either. They then employ these personal decision rules and neglect to record them. Without these rules, others cannot reconstruct the analyses. For example, we could not ascertain the criteria used for including students in the RSS analyses of teacher effects and, therefore, were unable to replicate them.

In any large-scale research project in which subjects are included in some analyses but not others, the data file for each subject should indicate if the subject was included or excluded. A variable called "day dropped from study" for each subject or lists of individuals eliminated or included at each point would suffice. Routine filing of such information makes it easier for primary analysts to check their own work and for secondary analysts to assess the original research and conduct their own analyses.

Others (for example Deutscher, 1977; Stufflebeam, 1973) have mentioned the need for detailed process information on the characteristics of a program that is being evaluated. Needed also is more process information on how data are collected and how they are manipulated. This information facilitates replications of the original analyses as well as decisions about additional approaches to be explored.

Two additional comments are relevant here. First, in any large research project, there are subprojects in which the project directors are not intimately involved. Thus, even if the analyst has the full cooperation of the original project's director, he or she will not necessarily be able to consult with the individuals who have information about the subprojects. While personnel ideally should document their activities throughout the project, it is especially important that persons provide such information before leaving the project. If individuals leave insufficient documentation of their experiences and decisions, valuable information may be irretrievably lost.

In a related vein, researchers may use only a portion of the data available to them and thus fail to record alternative data that other analysts might prefer. Obviously, researchers should not put much effort into collecting and recording information they intend to ignore. Still, if certain information were readily available, the data could be used by other researchers. For example, consider the recording of scores on standardized tests. Even if researchers plan to use only derived scores such as grade-equivalents or stanines, they should also record the raw scores from which these variations are derived. The recording of unadjusted test scores allows secondary analysts to use a preferred score type or to compare different adjustments.

Yet secondary analysts who propose to use derived measures should keep in mind the considerable limitations this choice imposes. While multiple, alternative analyses of the original derived measures are usually possible, the converse—multiple, alternative measures that are examined using the original analytic approach—are not. It is easy to ignore this subtle distinction or to assume that what is true for analyses holds for measures. As our discussion of the teacher bias index indicates, this assumption is unwarranted. The problem with derived measures is exacerbated if the measure in question was not a focal point of the original study, as happened to be the case in the Riverside investigation. As Miller (1975) noted, the focus on the child's personality was not the only model that could have been chosen to guide the design of the Riverside study: "An alternative that we considered, and perhaps mistakenly rejected . . . focused primarily on the structural variables within the school and classroom setting, . . . the degree of isolation of minority students because of individual differences in teachers' attitudes and behavior" (p. 279). As we have seen, under this additional constraint, we found secondary analysis untenable.

Finally, we should say something about the time required for secondary analysis. One main argument for secondary analysis is that it requires less time and expense than the collection of original data. It clearly places a smaller burden on the population being studied than does the collection of additional data sets. But even if acquiring another's data takes less time than collecting one's own, it can still take quite a while. One must discover the proper procedure for obtaining the data, work with the committees involved in the process, and arrange one's schedule to accommodate people whose services and expertise are needed. In addition, one may have a long wait between the initial request and the arrival of the data.

The analysis of the data is also time consuming. Data manipulations that seem to be described in great detail in project documents may be more ambiguous on closer inspection. Preliminary analyses may indicate that plans for subsequent analyses must be modified. Certain portions of the data set may be weaker or less complete than supposed. Furthermore, if one's analyses are aimed at exploring hypotheses not considered by the original research team, one must make complex decisions that require additional time and work.

In conclusion, one must ask whether secondary analysis is worth the time, effort, and expense. Two substantive and methodological reasons for answering in the affirmative are utlimately persuasive to us. First, it is often impossible to replicate a research study using an improved theoretical and methodological approach. This is certainly the case with the Riverside study; the cost of reproducing it is prohibitive. Second, one must consider the significance of a data set and the original findings. The Riverside study is a recent study that experts generally hold in high regard, and it has figured prominently in the debate over the merits of busing to achieve school desegregation. Coleman (1978), for example, cites it to support his claims that black achievement has not benefited from mandatory desegregation. In addition, it is the only data set we know of that examines the effects of desegregation on Hispanic students—a significant minority that is increasingly demanding public recognition. Finally, it is a rich data set that contains many measures collected over a number of years and thus can serve as a proving ground for new methods of analysis. For all these reasons, the Riverside data set is an important one that warrants continued examination.

References

Boruch, R. F., and Wortman, P. M. "An Illustrative Project on Secondary Analysis." In R. F. Boruch (Ed.), *New Directions for Program Evaluation: Secondary Analysis*, no. 4. San Francisco: Jossey-Bass, 1978.

Brophy, J., and Good, T. L. *Teacher-Student Relationships: Causes and Consequences.* New York: Holt, Rinehart and Winston, 1974.

Bryant, F. B., and Wortman, P. M. "Secondary Analysis: The Case for Data Archives." *American Psychologist*, 1978, *33*, 381–387.

Coleman, J. S. "Can We Integrate Our Public Schools Without Busing?" *Chicago Tribune*, Sept. 17, 1978, sec. C, 1.

Coleman, J. S. and others. *Equality of Educational Opportunity.* Washington, D.C.: U.S. Government Printing Office, 1966.

Cook, T. D. "The Potential and Limitations of Secondary Evaluations." In M. W. Apple, M. J. Subkoviak, and H. S. Lufler, Jr. (Eds.), *Educational Evaluation: Analysis and Responsibility.* Berkeley, Calif.: McCutchan, 1974.

Cook, T. D., and Gruder, C. L. "Metaevaluation Research." *Evaluation Quarterly*, 1978, *2*, 5–51.

Deutscher, I. "Toward Avoiding the Goal Trap in Evaluation Research." In F. G. Caro (Ed.), *Readings in Evaluation Research.* (2nd ed.). New York: Russell Sage Foundation, 1977.

Dollar, C. M., and Ambacher, B. I. "The National Archives and Secondary Analysis." In R. F. Boruch (Ed.), *New Directions for Program Evaluation: Secondary Analysis*, no. 4. San Francisco: Jossey-Bass, 1978.

Gerard, H. B., and Miller, N. (Eds.). *School Desegregation.* New York: Plenum Press, 1975.

Hawley, W. D., and Levin, B. " 'Wayward' Coverage of School Desegregation." *The Washington Post*, Oct. 14, 1978, p. 17.

Hedrick, T. E., Boruch, R. F., and Ross, J. "On Ensuring the Availability of Evaluative Data for Secondary Analysis." *Policy Sciences*, 1978, *9*, 259–280.

Henderson, R. D. *A Citizen's Guide to School Desegregation Law.* Washington, D.C.: National Institute of Education, 1978.

Hendricks, M. "Debatable Decisions in Analyzing Data: The Best Justification for Secondary Analysis?" *Proceedings of the 85th Annual Convention of the American Psychological Association.* Washington, D.C.: American Psychological Association, 1977.

Johnson, E. B., Gerard, H. B., and Miller, N. "Teacher Influences in the Desegregated Classroom." In H. B. Gerard and N. Miller (Eds.), *School Desegregation*. New York: Plenum Press, 1975.

Jöreskog, K. G. "A General Approach to Confirmatory Maximum Likelihood Factor Analysis." *Psychometrika*, 1968, *34*, 183-202.

Linsenmeier, J. A. W., and Wortman, P. M. "The Riverside School Study of Desegregation: A Reexamination." *Research Review of Equal Education*, 1978, *2*(2), 1-40.

Lofton, J.D., Jr. "Forced Busing a Flop." *Manchester* (N. H.) *Union Leader*, June 23, 1976.

McSweeney, A. J., and Wortman, P. M. "Two Regional Mental Health Treatment Facilities: A Reanalysis of Evaluation of Services." *Evaluation Quarterly*, 1979, *3*, 537-556.

Miller, N. "Summary and Conclusions." In H. B. Gerard and N. Miller (Eds.), *School Desegregation*. New York: Plenum Press, 1975.

Miller, N., and Gerard, H. B. "How Busing Failed in Riverside." *Psychology Today*, June 1976, pp. 66-70, 100.

Redfearn, D., and Gerard, H. B. "The Overall Research Design and Some Methodological Considerations." In H. B. Gerard and N. Miller (Eds.), *School Desegregation*. New York: Plenum Press, 1975.

Sage, W. "The Loaded School Bus." *Human Behavior*, 1978, *7*, 18-23.

St. John, N. H. *School Desegregation: Outcomes for Children*. New York: Wiley, 1975.

Smith, C. P. "The Origin and Expression of Achievement-Related Motives in Children." In C. P. Smith (Ed.), *Achievement-Related Motives in Children*." New York: Russell Sage Foundation, 1969.

Stufflebeam, D. L. "An Introduction to the PDK Book *Educational Evaluation in Decision Making*." In B. R. Worthen and J. R. Sanders (Eds.), *Educational Evaluation: Theory and Practice*. Belmont, Calif.: Wadsworth, 1973.

Useem, E. "Review of School Desegregation by H. B. Gerard and N. Miller." *Harvard Educational Review*, 1977, *47*, 71-74.

Wortman, P. M., Reichardt, C. S., and St. Pierre, R. G. "The First Year of the Educational Voucher Demonstration: A Secondary Analysis of Student Achievement Test Scores." *Evaluation Quarterly*, 1978, *2*, 193-214.

Wortman, P. M., and St. Pierre, R. G. "The Educational Voucher Demonstration: A Secondary Analysis." *Education and Urban Society*, 1977, *9*, 471-492.

8

Alice Robbin

Technical Guidelines for Preparing and Documenting Data

For almost two centuries, social researchers have used governmental statistics to examine a wide range of social phenomena on individuals and social structures and to offer competing analyses of social research and policy. Technological advances have made possible the recording

An earlier draft of these guidelines is found in Robbin (1978). In preparing this version and the earlier chapter, the author acknowledges a special debt of gratitude to S. A. Dodd, University of North Carolina at Chapel Hill, for her contributions in the development of guidelines for producing title pages, cataloguing machine-readable data files, and for the ideas she has shared which led to the guidelines for writing a data abstract. Another debt of gratitude is owed to Richard C. Roistacher, Bureau of Social Science Research, Washington, D.C., who has freely and unstintingly shared ideas and enthusiasm. Without his support, parts of this chapter would not have been written. Some of the current discussion is drawn directly from his work (Roistacher and others, (1980). Not all their reactions and criticism have been accommodated; the author alone bears responsibility for interpretations of their work.

of these statistics in machine-readable form, the collection of new types of data, and increased use of governmental records. Computer technology has radically altered record collection methods and management practices and made available new tools for the analysis of data; it has greatly facilitated the collection, storage, management, and use of detailed information on individual characterstics, human transactions, and organizational processes. The computer has become a powerful tool for implementing programs and policies that require long-term maintenance of records (Robbin, 1979).

Over the last twenty years, there has been a notable expansion of information recorded by the federal government, primarily for administrative purposes, but also for research, policy, and evaluation activities. Federal legislation mandates the collection of this information as a prerequisite for allocating federal resources to state and local governments. This information is used for planning, auditing, and evaluating the distribution of resources to ensure an adequate understanding of human needs and an equitable delivery of benefits to citizens of the state (Duncan, 1978). These statistical data are used as authoritative instruments for understanding social problems, executing solutions, and making rational policy decisions.

While a substantial portion of these data are probably not useful for reanalysis, a great body of data is potentially useful for research related to policy analysis, planning, and evaluation. Some of the data have been transferred to specific agencies (for example, the National Archives) whose major functions are to preserve, describe, and disseminate this information. But most of these potentially rich sources of information remain outside the public domain and are limited in their use because they have not been subjected to the traditional scientific standards of quality (Schmandt, 1978) or the government's audit procedures, nor have they had appropriate funding, preparation, and description.

Among the many reasons for the generally poor condition of data and their documentation is the absence of standards or guidelines for quality control of data collection, processing, and description. Consequently, nonstandard data design, collection, and processing are the norm rather than the exception. Limited value has been placed on these secondary data sources for scientific research and public policy planning, so that analysts prefer to collect their own data rather than rely on data collected by others. Only recently has the federal government recognized that, as a primary producer of data, it has an important responsibility to monitor the quality of its collection, processing, and documenting procedures and to assist in developing standards.

The federal government provides little guidance to its contractors and agencies about quality control procedures for data. Yet, quality assurance is fundamental to careful scientific investigation and to the analysis of public policy alternatives. The development of criteria that define quality represents a significant step forward and is essential to the dissemination of primary and secondary data.

As public policy makers become increasingly dependent on statistical data, it is critical that standards for data quality be established. Such standards must reflect the principle that statistical data represent objective and verifiable evidence that is unambiguously described, so that analysis or evaluation based upon this evidence can be effectively reviewed, criticized, and replicated. Such standards would ensure that data producers and analysts can make maximal use of machine-readable data files.

To this end, we propose a set of guidelines for machine-readable data files. The guidelines reflect the concerns of a variety of users, including analysts, computer programmers, librarians, archivists, and sponsors of the data collection. Analysts need high-quality data and a documented history of the decisions regarding the design, collection, encoding, processing, and reduction of data. Computer programmers need information on the data and decisions about computer processing that affected the file. Librarians are concerned about the bibliographical procedures that identify, describe, and locate the files. Archivists need sufficient information to identify, arrange, and describe records. Sponsors need guidelines to inform their judgments about ways to organize, fund, and maintain the quality of data files and their documentation.

Part One of this chapter describes guidelines for creating a well-documented data file. We place great importance on documentation because access to data is dependent on it. Our experiences with secondary analysis show that the quality and amount of descriptive information about machine-readable records vary greatly from file to file. Analysts need to know how and why a data file was created, the physical structure of the file, and how the data were written. Efforts to create documentation after the data collection and processing or completion of the project, when staff members have disbanded and memories have faded, are expensive and quite often unsuccessful. Formal documentation should be created when the data file itself is created; in this way, the data can be used by researchers who are not associated with the original data collection. Proper documentation will also facilitate the primary analyst and project staff's own data analysis.

Part Two describes guidelines for assuring the quality of recorded data. Many data files are poorly constructed and processed or improperly edited and corrected, resulting in numerous errors. Our guidelines address the identification of elements within each data field, the coding format for each element, and the enumeration of data values (including explicit identification of missing values and nonstandard codes). Adherence to these guidelines in the construction of files should enhance the quality of the analyst's results.

Part Three introduces guidelines on bibliographical practice to ensure access to information about the data file once it is available for release. Experience suggests that one of the greatest problems facing the secondary analyst is locating a file. We have found that standard bibliographical practices carried out by authors, publishers, libraries, and archives for printed materials have not been used by data producers. Good bibliographical practices facilitate access to information about machine-readable data files.

Finally, Part Four describes guidelines for the sponsor and researcher to ensure the quality of data and documentation and to facilitate access. Data files that are created by insufficiently experienced grantees or contractors may be minimally useful to other analysts. Unfortunately, many sponsors show little interest in the quality of the data products and related documentation, and too many data collections are carried out with insufficient funding for preserving the data. Statistical data are a national resource, and proper arrangements must be made to fund, organize, and manage data gathering and dissemination. Further, just as quality control, reliability assurance, secondary analyses, and evaluation criteria are applied to other governmental activities, these same criteria need to be developed for statistical data and documentation. Thus, our guidelines are suggested to improve the quality of data collection and documentation activities carried out by primary analysts under government sponsorship.

Readers will note that not every guideline is relevant to a particular data file. Readers should also realize that although this chapter represents the experience of a great many analysts, computer scientists, and archivists, it is one of the first attempts to set down formal guidelines for data files and their documentation. The guidelines have had only limited testing, under highly favorable conditions, in a data library at the University of Wisconsin-Madison. As yet, they have not been applied by researchers, government contractors, research agencies, and the like. We recommend that these guidelines be tested over the next few years, modified, and then considered for adoption by data producers and oversight agencies such as the General Accounting Office.

Part One: Technical Standards for Documentation

A machine-readable data file (MRDF) must be accompanied by a written history of its development and contents. Documentation describes the purpose for which the data file was created and the conceptual framework of the file's creators. Such documentation facilitates effective communication among data processing staffs during data collection and anlysis, provides an historical record of the work performed on the file, informs potential users of the data file who were not involved in its creation, and reports the results of statistical analysis performed on the file and the means used to attain the results (Robbin, 1975). Thus, documentation is an integrated set of information that identifies, describes, clarifies, and provides access to the data so that they may be evaluated, analyzed (or reanalyzed), and archived.

Documentation is essential to a preliminary, informed appraisal of a data file. Without sufficient or adequate documentation, the contents of the machine-readable record cannot be known and the record has no value. Documentation is critical to the archivist's accessioning process because it "supplies information on the provenance of the file, is an equivalent for the conventional archival inventory, and supplies information for other bibliographical access tools" (Johnson, 1977, p. 2). Documentation is critical to librarians because it provides bibliographical control and user access to MRDFs. In other words, documentation is the user's guide to organizing, synthesizing, understanding, and locating the data file.

Zeisset (1974) notes that documentation should be comprehensive and inclusive—that it should anticipate "all the normal questions a user is going to have about the data file" (p. 5). Adequate documentation is rarely brief, and if the project has involved a number of substudies that have complex file structures, extensive documentation is required. Leinwand Associates (1979b), for example, note that "documentation on each individual data file written as a separate entity [does] not convey the relationships between the various data files. Clearly, overview documentation [is] needed to provide an overall introduction to the research project, its data files, and their relationships" (p. 1). Thus, the length of documentation of an MRDF can exceed 500 or 600 pages if data files require extensive treatment of all phases of the research process. Nevertheless, quality and completeness are primary considerations, and it is critical that sufficient resources be provided to produce documentation for an MRDF.

Components of Documentation

Documentation consists of five major parts: (1) a general study overview, (2) a history of the project (or study) which produced the MRDF, (3) a summary of the MRDF's data processing history, (4) a listing of the data items in the file (often called a *codebook, data dictionary,* or *tape,* or *record lay-out*), and (5) a set of appendices or additional volumes (containing glossaries, error listing, publications, and the like) that explain the construction and use of the data file. The first four components of the documentation should be concise and information should be easily accessible. Details are more appropriately placed in the appendices or accompanying volumes. Each of the major components of MRDF documentation has numerous subcomponents. Figure 1 shows the ordering of the components and indicates which guidelines are associated with each component and subcomponents.

To facilitate an appreciation for constructing documentation, we adapted the example of the Featherman and Hauser documentation. Throughout the discussion, references are made to aspects of this example. When possible, guideline numbers are used to indicate specific examples of the requirements of a specific recommendation. In other cases specific examples are provided following the guideline under consideration. Bibliographical entries for the file documentation used in the examples appear in the Appendix. The examples are keyed to these entries by a number enclosed within a pair of brackets. To facilitate location of specific guidelines, a subject index appears at the end of this chapter.

Study Overview

The study overview is composed of a *title page, data acknowledgments statement, abstract,* and *table of contents.* This component of documentation provides bibliographical control of the MRDF. Specifically, the title page is used by the library cataloguer to create a catalogue entry. Dodd (1979a) notes that "with the cataloguing of MRDFs according to existing international standards for bibliographic representation, we can anticipate that information [about the data file] will be extended to any user of a library resource" (p. 77). The importance of this information to secondary analysts is quite apparent. Analysts' initial access to many social science numeric data files is through cited reference in the research literature. Dodd (1979a) also notes that rules for title pages ensure that the primary analysts (who are often the data producers) receive proper credit and recognition for their contribution to research, policy, and program evaluation. The data acknowledgments statement provides additional information when the title page is insufficient and is typically employed by a data archive (distributor) to provide a more complete reference to the MRDF. The abstract provides summary information about the contents of the MRDF and if standardized can be incorporated in an automated system of bibliographical records about MRDFs. The table of contents for the documentation is the primary means of access to the contents of the entire document. The

Figure 1. Overview of the Components of MRDF Documentation: Sequence and Specification of Relevant Guidelines for Each Component

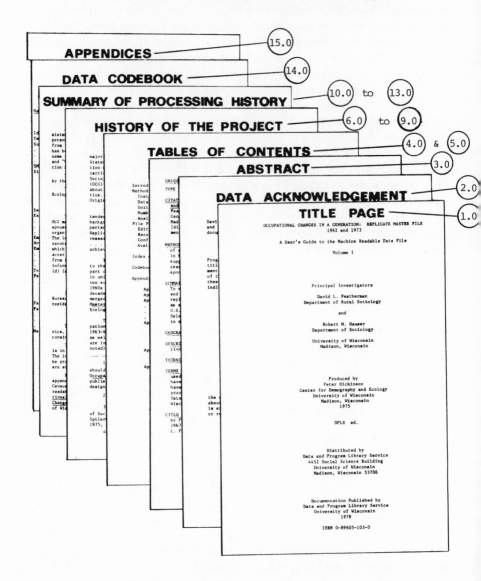

Source: Figures 1–4 and 6 adapted from Featherman and Hauser, 1975.

table of contents of the variables is an item-level description of the data file. This table of contents provides additional information for a bibliographical record in an automated bibliographical data base (see Settel, 1977.)

The Title Page

The title page is the major source of bibliographical information for any published or unpublished informational source. But in most cases, MRDF documentation contains an inadequately specified title page (or none at all), making it very difficult for the secondary analyst to locate a data file. Figure 2a provides a complete example of the contents and format of the title page. The title is important for proper citation, cataloguing, and national union lists, which are critical library access tools. Dodd makes an important point about the wording of the title: "Producers of MRDF should be aware that descriptive words contained in a title take on added significance with the existing technology for keyword or full-text retrieval. For example, the only subject approach to *Social Science Citation Index* (whether it be by the printed reference work or by the on-line search capability) is via the descriptive words contained in the respective titles." (1977, p. 13).

Guideline 1.0 Provide a title page for every data file.

For example, see Figure 2a.

Title pages compiled as part of the MRDF's documentation must identify the documentation, the specific version of the file being documented, and the institutional origins of both (Roistacher and others, 1980, p. 6). (For a detailed discussion of title pages, see Roistacher and others, 1980.)

Guideline 1.1 Use a qualifying subtitle if it is necessary to indicate relationship of the documentation to the MRDF.

It is helpful to the cataloguer to differentiate between the title of the MRDF and the statement, "User's Guide to the Machine-Readable Data File." In Figure 2a, for example, the name of the MRDF is clearly distinguished from the "User's Guide" statement, and the latter is dropped down more than one line.

One of the major problems associated with titles for MRDFs is the inadequate description of the subject contents.

Guideline 1.2 Write a fully descriptive title of the subject contents. Use a consistent title when the MRDF is part of an ongoing series, occurring at definite time intervals. Use a subtitle to more fully identify the

Figure 2a. Illustration of the Entries for the Title Page

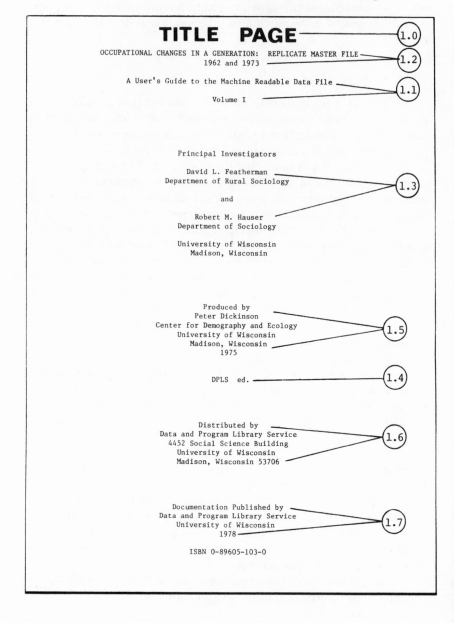

TITLE PAGE ──────── (1.0)

OCCUPATIONAL CHANGES IN A GENERATION: REPLICATE MASTER FILE ── (1.2)
1962 and 1973 ──────

A User's Guide to the Machine Readable Data File ── (1.1)

Volume I ──────

Principal Investigators

David L. Featherman
Department of Rural Sociology ── (1.3)

and

Robert M. Hauser
Department of Sociology

University of Wisconsin
Madison, Wisconsin

Produced by
Peter Dickinson
Center for Demography and Ecology ── (1.5)
University of Wisconsin
Madison, Wisconsin
1975

DPLS ed. ──────── (1.4)

Distributed by
Data and Program Library Service ── (1.6)
4452 Social Science Building
University of Wisconsin
Madison, Wisconsin 53706

Documentation Published by
Data and Program Library Service ── (1.7)
University of Wisconsin
1978

ISBN 0-89605-103-0

title. Include the geographical focus if unique. Include a precise date if there is more than one data collection (or administrative statistical program) a year; the month or season should become part of the title.

For example: *Social Role Study: High School Students' Values, Role Definitions, and Fertility Orientations, Spring 1972 [2]; Higher Education General Information Survey (HEGIS): Earned Degrees Conferred Fall 1969–70 through Fall 1973–74 Academic Year [3]*.

Guideline 1.2.1 Choose a more general title if the MRDF has many different topics.

For example: *Survey Research Center Spring Omnibus Study, 1973 [4]*.

Guideline 1.2.2 Provide the (a) organizational name of the producer, (b) geographical focus (if unique), (c) descriptive content phrase, (d) series or study number (if the MRDF is part of an ongoing series and at unpredictable intervals and with varying focuses), and (e) chronological date of data collection,

For example: *California Poll Berkeley Public Opinion Survey No. 2546, September 1977 [5]*.

Guideline 1.2.3 Avoid beginning a title with articles, numerics, acronyms, or data set names. If acronyms are used, spell out their meaning and enclose the acronym in brackets.

Title pages of an MRDF should resemble, to the extent possible, title pages of other informational sources. Thus, authorship, edition, producer or publisher, and distributor statements must be included.

Guideline 1.3 Provide the full name of the individual (principal investigator) or corporate body (survey organization or federal agency) responsible for the design of the instrument or content.

Guideline 1.3.1 Indicate the relationship of the work to the individual or corporate body that otherwise would not be known.

For example: Conducted for the Division on Aging of the Wisconsin Department of Health and Social Services, 1979.

Guideline 1.4 Use an edition statement only when substantive changes have been made since the MRDF's creation. (Separate revisions or subsequent printings of the documentation independent of changes in the MRDF do *not* constitute a new edition of the data file.) A new edition occurs when one of the following criteria is met by the primary analyst, data producer, or designated archive: (1) Any deletions or additions of the original machine-readable data; (2) any deletions or additions of data elements or variables; (3) any recoding or reformatting of the file; (4) any change in the number of logical records; and (5) any change in the programming language.

Efforts have been made, particularly by the cataloguing committee for MRDFs established by the American Library Association (1979), to make MRDF bibliographical definitions parallel to those designed for other print media. Dodd (1979b) points out that "in terms of cataloguing procedures, the publisher field (as normally associated with books) has evolved into the producer and distributor fields for MRDF. However, the roles of each are not always clear and a more accurate parallel might be to equate the current definition of *producer* with that of *printer* and substitute *distributor* for *publisher*. The importance of the roles played both by the producer and distributor highlights the major differences between the process of book production and MRDF creation" (p. 5). This difference leads Dodd to propose a more realistic definition of the term *producer* than that offered by the American Library Association (1979, chap. 9). Her definition clarifies the difference between the author's and producer's responsibilities. Thus, she defines a *producer* as: "that person or organization with the financial or administrative responsibility for producing a computerized file. Such responsibility may include the various tasks associated with collecting data or information and converting the information into a computerized format. These tasks may be contracted out or be performed by more than one party. Financial responsibility alone does not qualify one to become an MRDF producer; and if the tasks associated with MRDF production are contracted or carried out by more than one party, the identity and circumstances should be cited in the file's documentation. If corporate bodies or individuals have been identified as having the primary responsibility for the intellectual content of the file, it is assumed that the producer has carried out this function" (Roistacher and others, 1980, p. 9).

Dodd (1979b) defines the production date for the MRDF as the date the file became operational in a computerized form and available for analysis, processing, and release to the public. In many cases, the MRDF may be produced in one year, analyzed and reported in another, and released to the public several years later by a party other than the producer (see Guideline 1.6 regarding citation of the distributor). If the correct production date is unknown, use the date of data collection as a point of reference.

Guideline 1.5 Include a producer statement that describes the person or organization with financial or general administrative responsibility for producing the data file. Include the name and location of the organization (or person) and date of production.

For example, see Figure 2a.

Dodd also offers a revised definition of distributor; a distributor is that "organization which has been designated by the author or producer to generate copies of a particular file, including any necessary editions or revisions. If a distributor is not cited, then it is assumed that the author or producer fulfills this function" (in Roistacher and others, 1980, p. 9). Dodd (1979b) defines the distribution date as the year the file became available for distribution to the public, usually through an established agency.

Guideline 1.6 Include a distributor statement that describes the organization responsible for generating and disseminating copies of the MRDF, including subsequent editions or revisions. Include the distributor's name, location (or address), and date of distribution.

Authorship and publication responsibilities for the documentation may differ from these responsibilities for the MRDF. If so, it is necessary to cite authorship, publication, edition date, and responsibilities for the documentation.

Guideline 1.7 Distinguish the edition statement for the MRDF from the edition statement for the published documentation. Place the publisher's (of the *documentation*) name and publication date at the bottom of the title page. For clarity, place "published by" or "prepared by" before the name of the publisher of the documentation.

Note the difference between an edition statement for an MRDF and the edition statement for the documentation:

Edition statement for MRDF: LEAA rev. 1975 ed.

Edition statement for MRDF documentation: LEAA User's Guide rev. 1975 ed.

The production and edition dates for the MRDF should be placed close to the producer and edition statements for the MRDF to distinguish them from the publisher and publication date for the documentation, which should appear at the bottom of the title page.

Additional elements can be incorporated in a title page, but they may clutter or confuse responsibilities. These elements include a series title, archival study number, a special order number used to identify an information medium (for example, all traditional print materials include ISSN or ISBN numbers), funding sources, and a public law source or agency (Roistacher and others, 1980). Simplicity is preferred. A series title and special order number are better placed on the verso of the title page (or on the page facing the title page). An internal or archival study number on the title page creates confusion in the title entry. Funding sources and public law sources or agency codes are better placed in the data acknowledgments statement (see Guideline 2.0) and described in the section devoted to the history of the project.

Data Acknowledgments

In some cases, neither the title page nor the history of the project provides sufficient guidance as to the origins of the MRDF and it is necessary to incorporate a data acknowledgments statement to assist the secondary analyst in citing the MRDF and data distributor. A complete example of this component appears as Figure 2b.

Guideline 2.0 Supply a data acknowledgments statement if the information supplied on the title page is insufficient for proper citation or if

Figure 2b. Illustration of Entries for the Data Acknowledgment

DATA ACKNOWLEDGEMENT

These data have been deposited at DPLS for public distribution by David L. Featherman and Robert M. Hauser of the Departments of Rural Sociology and Sociology, respectively, University of Wisconsin-Madison. The text documentation has been prepared by the Data and Program Library Service (DPLS).

ACKNOWLEDGEMENT OF ASSISTANCE

All manuscripts utilizing data made available through the Data and Program Library Service should acknowledge that fact as well as cite the title of the study as indicated on the title page and sample catalog statement and identify the original collector of the data. DPLS urges all users of these data to follow some adaptation of this statement with the parentheses indicating items to be completed or deleted appropriately by the individual analyst.

The data (and tabulations) utilized in this (publication) were made available (in part) by the Data and Program Library Service at the University of Wisconsin-Madison. The data for Occupational Changes in a Generation: Replicate Master File, 1962 and 1973 were originally collected by the U.S. Bureau of the Census under grants from the National Science Foundation to Peter M. Blau and Otis Dudley Duncan at the University of Chicago and to David L. Featherman and Robert M. Hauser at the University of Wisconsin-Madison. The 1962 data were reprocessed and released in unit record form by the Bureau of the Census under NSF grant numbers GI-31604 and GL-44336 to David L. Featherman and Robert M. Hauser. The Bureau of the Census, National Science Foundation, principal investigators, and DPLS do not bear any responsibility for the analyses or interpretations presented here.

In order to provide funding agencies with essential information about the use of archival resources and to facilitate the exchange of information about DPLS participants' research activities, each user of the DPLS facilities is expected to send two copies of each completed manuscript, thesis abstract, or reprint to DPLS.

the specification of further information is desirable.

The Abstract

The abstract has assumed increasing importance for the quick and accurate identification of primary literature, given the increase in the volume of publications, the need for timely access to information, and the value of abstracts in computerized full-text searches. Abstracts offer the most efficient means of access to information about the contents of an MRDF and can be used with existing information storage and retrieval software and communication technology to maximize the transfer of information about MRDFs (just as the on-line bibliographical data bases for documents do). Borko and Bernier (1975) point out that abstracts facilitate selection, reduce search time, improve indexing efficiency, aid in the preparation of reviews and bibliographies, and promote current awareness. There are many different types of abstracts and formats (see American National Standards Institute, 1971). Guideline 3.0 suggests a standardized structure and contents for an abstract describing the machine-readable data file. Figure 2c provides an example of the structure, format, and content of an abstract.

Guideline 3.0 Provide an abstract that includes (1) a unique identification number of the MRDF, (2) type of file, (3) bibliograhical citation, (4) methodology, (5) summary of contents, (6) geographical coverage, (7) descriptors, (8) technical notes, (9) terms of availability, and (10) cited references.

Guideline 3.1 Include a unique identification number for the abstract of the MRDF if appropriate.

Guideline 3.2 Describe the type of file (for example, text, representational, software, numeric).

Guideline 3.3 Provide a bibliographical citation. Include authorship, title, and statement of responsibility; edition statement; statement of edition responsibility (if appropriate); place, organizaton, and date of production; place, organization, and date of distribution (if different from production). Follow title of MRDF with material designator in brackets: [machine-readable data file]. Follow producer and distributor statements with producer and distributor in brackets: [producer], [distributor]. Notes may be used to amplify the citation (for example, units of analysis; number of files, logical records, or variables; restrictions on access; hardware or software dependency or intended audience.

Guideline 3.4 Describe the methodology employed in the study, and include (a) sources of information, (b) chronological coverage of data

Figure 2c. Illustration of the Contents of the Abstract

ABSTRACT

(3.1) UNIQUE IDENTIFICATION NUMBER (S): Accession number SB-001-002-USA-DPLS-1962-1

(3.2) TYPE ON FILE: numeric

(3.3) CITATION: Occupational Changes in a Generation: Replicate Master File, 1962
and 1973 [machine readable data file]. Principal investigators, David L.
Featherman and Robert M. Hauser. DPLS ed. Madison, WI: Peter Dickinson,
Center for Demography and Ecology, University of Wisconsin [producer], 1975.
Madison, WI: University of Wisconsin Data and Program Library Service
[distributor]. 1 data file (62,651 logical records), plus accompanying documentation (755 pages). The study was supported by ... under ...

(3.4) METHODOLOGY: The Current Population Survey (CPS) design provided the basic sample
of eligible respondents in a stratified multi-stage cluster sample in March 1962.
In March 1973, the basic CPS design was expanded to include black and Spanish
supplements to the sample. The target population in 1962 was males 20 to 64
years ... The Replicate Master File encompasses only... The number of respondents in 1962 is 24,687; in 1973, 37,964.

(3.5) SUMMARY OF CONTENTS: This study focuses on social mobility in the United States.
To measure changes in the process of social stratification, the Peter M. Blau
and Otis Dudley Duncan study, Occupational Changes in a Generation (OCG-I) was
replicated and extended in 1973. Both the 1962 and 1973 surveys were carried out
as supplements to the March Current Population Surveys (CPS) conducted by the
U.S. Bureau of the Census, to elicit data about socioeconomic origins...
Selected data from the two surveys were merged to permit examination of changes
in social mobility... There are 136 variables in the file.

(3.6) GEOGRAPHIC COVERAGE: United States

(3.7) DESCRIPTORS: social mobility, status attainment, social stratification, occupational mobility, inequality of opportunity, educational mobility.

(3.8) TECHNICAL NOTES: (a) rectangular file structure, (b) file size: 62,651

(3.9) TERMS OF AVAILABILITY: (a) Edit checks have been made on only selected variables
used in analyses and publications; a number of inconsistencies between variables
have been noted, (b) Information on geographic location of the respondents
have been deleted following Bureau of the Census confidentiality-preserving
procedures, (c) Copies of the documentation and data can be obtained from the
Data and Program Library Service, 4452 Social Science Building, University of
Wisconsin-Madison, Madison, Wisconsin 53706, USA; telephone number (608)-262-7962.

(3.10) CITED REFERENCES: Principal monographs include The American Occupational Structure
by Peter M. Blau and Otis Dudley Duncan (New York: John Wiley and Sons, Inc.,
1967). Socioeconomic Background and Achievement by Otis Dudley Duncan, David
L. Featherman, and Beverly Duncan (New York: Seminar Press, 1972). ...

(if survey data), (c) universe description or target population characteristics, (d) type of sample, (e) characteristics of instrumentation, (f) date
or dates of data collection.

Guideline 3.5 Summarize the major contents and include (a) purpose
or scope of the file, (b) special characteristics of the file, (c) subject
matter, (d) number of variables.

Guideline 3.6 Describe the geographical coverage in the following
order: (a) country, (b) region within country, (c) state, province, or
department, (d) standard metropolitan statistical area (SMSA), (e)
county or other small units (city, township, enumeration district), (e)
other.

Guideline 3.7 Supply meaningful terms that express an idea or concept or phenomenon not covered in the body of the abstract. Use terms
that summarize the underlying conceptual framework of the study.

Guideline 3.8 Describe (a) file structure, (rectangular, hierarchical,
variable length), (b) file size, (c) special formats (SPSS, OSIRIS, SAS),
(d) computer or software dependence.

Guideline 3.9 Describe terms of availability and include (a) condition
of data (for example, statements that edit checks have been made), (b)
restrictions (if any), (c) contact person (complete address and telephone
number).

Guideline 3.10 Provide cited references for reports based on these data
that provide additional information for the potential user. If substantial, cite only major works.

Guideline 4.0 Supply a table of contents for all sections of the
document.
See Figure 2d for a complete example of Guidelines 4.0 and 5.0.

Guideline 5.0 Supply a table of contents for the variables contained in
the data file, together with headings for sections of variables. A variant
of this table of contents is a variable index by subject type, useful if the
data items are not arranged in any logical order in the file and facilitates a search for variables of a particular record type.

History of the Project

The documentation of an MRDF should include a short history
of the data collection effort, the rationale for the project, the reason for

Figure 2d. Excerpts of the Entries for the Table of Contents

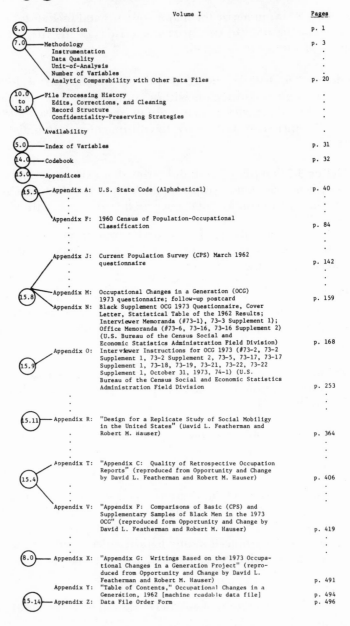

4.0 & 5.0 ——— TABLES OF CONTENTS

Volume I   Pages

6.0 —— Introduction   p. 1

7.0 —— Methodology   p. 3
     Instrumentation
     Data Quality   .
     Unit-of-Analysis   .
     Number of Variables
     Analytic Comparability with Other Data Files   p. 20

10.0 to 12.0 —— File Processing History
     Edits, Corrections, and Cleaning   .
     Record Structure   .
     Confidentiality-Preserving Strategies   .

     Availability   .

5.0 —— Index of Variables   p. 31

14.0 —— Codebook   p. 32

15.0 —— Appendices

15.5 —— Appendix A: U.S. State Code (Alphabetical)   p. 40
     .
     .

     Appendix F: 1960 Census of Population-Occupational
                  Classification   p. 84
     .
     .
     .

     Appendix J: Current Population Survey (CPS) March 1962
                  questionnaire   p. 142
     .
     .

15.8 —— Appendix M: Occupational Changes in a Generation (OCG)
                  1973 questionnaire; follow-up postcard   p. 159
     Appendix N: Black Supplement OCG 1973 Questionnaire, Cover
                  Letter, Statistical Table of the 1962 Results;
                  Interviewer Memoranda (#73-1), 73-3 Supplement 1);
                  Office Memoranda (#73-6, 73-16, 73-16 Supplement 2)
                  (U.S. Bureau of the Census Social and
                  Economic Statistics Administration Field Division)   p. 168
     Appendix O: Interviewer Instructions for OCG 1973 (#73-2, 73-2
                  Supplement 1, 73-2 Supplement 2, 73-5, 73-17, 73-17
15.9   Supplement 1, 73-18, 73-19, 73-21, 73-22, 73-22
                  Supplement 1, October 31, 1973, 74-1) (U.S.
                  Bureau of the Census Social and Economic Statistics
                  Administration Field Division)   p. 253
     .
     .

15.11 —— Appendix R: "Design for a Replicate Study of Social Mobiligy
                  in the United States" (David L. Featherman and
                  Robert M. Hauser)   p. 364
     .
     .

     Appendix T: "Appendix C: Quality of Retrospective Occupation
                  Reports" (reproduced from Opportunity and Change
15.4   by David L. Featherman and Robert M. Hauser)   p. 406
     .
     .

     Appendix V: "Appendix F: Comparisons of Basic (CPS) and
                  Supplementary Samples of Black Men in the 1973
                  OCG" (reproduced form Opportunity and Change by
                  David L. Featherman and Robert M. Hauser)   p. 419
     .
     .

8.0 —— Appendix X: "Appendix G: Writings Based on the 1973 Occupa-
                  tional Changes in a Generation Project" (repro-
                  duced from Opportunity and Change by David L.
                  Featherman and Robert M. Hauser)   p. 491
     Appendix Y: "Table of Contents," Occupational Changes in a
                  Generation, 1962 [machine readable data file]   p. 494
15.14 —— Appendix Z: Data File Order Form   p. 496

collecting the particular data, and, if appropriate, the statutory or executive authority (Roistacher and others, 1980). Thus, the section devoted to the history of the project describes the evolution of the data from the original design of the study to the conversion of the data into machine-readable form. The following items are included in this section: scope of data collected (population for which the data were collected and sampling frame), information on the period covered by the survey or the waves of a panel survey, instrumentation, interviewers' instructions, coding instructions, and manual editing procedures. A bibliography for the project and a description of other documents relevant to the history of the project might be included in this section. A complete example of the contents of the history of the project appears as Figure 3.

Guideline 6.0 Provide a short history of the data collection effort: the rationale for the project, the reason for collecting these particular data, and, if appropriate, the statutory or executive authority.

Guideline 7.0 Describe the instrumentation process (how information about the phenomenon was translated into numeric or coded form).

Roistacher and others (1980) suggest that the history include the answers to six questions. (1) What type of phenomena were measured? Provide an explicit description to explain that the data represent, for example, verbal responses, or barometric pressures, or geographical coordinates. (2) Where, over what area, when, and over what period were the phenomena measured? This account of instrumentation should include a discussion of the populations and sampling, if appropriate. (3) What type of measurement or collection instrument was used? If hardware instruments were used, give manufacturers, types, and model numbers. Give names, editions, and form numbers or versions of published or standard paper instruments and questionnaires. (4) How did the instrument operate? Describe options and procedures specific to the study, including threshold and sensitivity settings for hardware, and probing instructions for interviewers. (5) How was the quality of the data monitored at the time they were collected? (6) What was done to correct data found to be in error?

Guideline 8.0 Provide a bibliography for the project history and a description of other documents relevant to the history of the project. If the bibliography and other relevant information are extensive, place them in an appendix.

Figure 3. Illustration of the Section on History of the Project

---

HISTORY OF THE PROJECT

(6.0)————————————————— ORIGINS

   In the early 1960s, Peter M. Blau and Otis Dudley Duncan proposed a
major study to ascertain the pattern of occupational mobility in the United
States, specifically, to estimate the extent of intergenerational occupation mobility . . .This project was to be one in a series which was being
carried out in various countries under the auspices of the International
Sociological Association. Entitled, "Occupational Changes in a Generation"
(OCG) . . .The two page mail-back questionnaire included supplementary details
about socioeconomic origins, residential background, and spouse characteristics. . .The Bureau of the Census collected and tabulated the data . . .
Original funding support was provided by the National Science Foundation.[1]

   In 1973, David L. Featherman and Robert M. Hauser replicated and extended the Blau and Duncan study to explore the effects that peoples'
backgrounds, schooling, training in the military, and their early work experiences have on their work careers.[2] As they noted in a "Design for a
Replicate Study of Social Mobility in the United States" the value of the
research lies in its potential contributions--substantive and methodological
. . . and . . . in improving the measurement of processes of social and economic
achievement.[3]

   The U.S. Bureau of the Census conducted the 1973 survey as a supplement
to the March 1973 <u>Current Population Survey Annual Demographic File</u>.[4] As
part of the Featherman and Hauser project, the Bureau reprocessed and placed
in unit record form the original 1962 OCG data. Selected data items from the
two surveys were merged to permit examination of changes between the early
1960s and early 1970s, and to help document trends and shifts over several
decades of the 20th century for cohorts born between 1897 and 1951. This
merged data file is entitled, <u>Occupational Changes in a Generation-Replicate
Master File, 1962 and 1973</u>. Peter Dickinson, Center for Demography and
Ecology.

   The data include. . . number of siblings and paternal education, occupation . . . The data file includes the National Opinion Research Center (NORC)
1963-65 Occupational Prestige Scores and the Duncan Socio-Economic Index (SEI)
as well as . . . Bureau of the Census codes for states and foreign countries
are included for both years (in some cases, codes have changed, and these are
noted).

(8.0)————— [1]A great many publications have resulted from this study. Readers
should see, in particular: The bibliography to the machine readable file,
<u>Occupational Changes in a Generation</u>, 1962, contains full references to
published sources. The documentation for this data file describes sample
design, measurement and . . .

   [2]Funding support was provided by the National Science Foundation . . .

   [3]David L. Featherman and Robert M. Hauser. "Design for a Replicate Study
of Social Mobility in the United States." In Kenneth C. Land and Seymour
Spilerman (eds.), <u>Social Indicator Models</u>. New York: Russell Sage Foundation,
1975, 219-251.

   [4]Demographic Surveys Division was responsible for the data gathering. . .

Guideline 9.0 If the data have been produced under executive or legislative mandate, include all relevant government accounting codes and
identification established for reporting purposes.

Figure 3 (continued)

METHODOLOGY

The target population in 1962 was males 20 to 64 years old . . . The Current Population Survey design, a stratified, multi-stage cluster sample, included more than 35,000 occupied dwelling units or households which contained about 25,000 eligible males. The response rate was 83%.

The target population in 1973 was males 20 to 65 years old in the civilian noninstitutional population. The Current Population Survey (CPS) sample was expanded to include over 48,000 household interviews, yielding an average of 0.73 eligible OCG respondents per household. More than 33,600 completed supplements (88%) were returned. A supplement sample of black males was drawn, based on households headed by a black in October 1972. Of the nearly 4,300 households headed by a black in October 1972, nearly half were eliminated because of noninterviews on the CPS questionnaire or because of the absence of an eligible OCG male. In the remaining cases, a response rate of about 93% yielded approximately 2,200 supplemental black males. The 1973 March CPS was also supplemented by households identified as having a head of Spanish origin in October 1972. . . . A comparison of the basic (CPS) and supplementary samples of black men in the 1973 OCG is contained in the appendix to the User's Guide (Appendix F of Opportunity and Change, pp. 541-544, has been reproduced).

Each sample case in 1962 represents about 2,200 men; in 1973, about 1600 men. Populations of reference total nearly 45 million men in 1962 and nearly 53 million in 1973.

The population of the Replicate Master File encompasses the . . . details on population coverage, weighting, and sampling variability in the 1962 and 1973 OCG surveys are contained in the appendix to the User's Guide (Appendix B of Opportunity and Change, pp. 507-514, has been reproduced).

(7.0)————————————————— INSTRUMENTATION

The CPS interviewers in March 1962 left behind a two-page OCG supplement questionnaire for each eligible male. (See Occupational Changes in a Generation, 1962 [machine readable data file] for information on interviewer instructions.) The OCG 1973 supplement items were ascertained by means of an eight-page mailout-mailback questionnaire in August-November 1973. Nonrespondents were followed up by a combination of mailings (1973 only), telephone calls, and personal interviews. (See appendix to the User's Guide for office memoranda, interviewer, and field instructions issued by the U.S. Bureau of the Census.) . . . All supplemental black males were interviewed by a household visit rather than by telephone. (See the appendix to the User's Guide for office memoranda, interviewer and field instructions issued by the U.S. Bureau of the Census.)

Items common to both the 1962 and 1973 OCG studies are identically worded. However, even with the same wording, a deliberate change in question context made the data on first full-time civilian jobs incomparable between the 1962 and 1973 surveys.

File Processing History

The file processing history describes how the originating project or organization responsible for distributing the MRDF edited the data into an archival (microlevel or public use) file. This section should clearly specify what processing, checking, and editing procedures were

Figure 3 (continued)

DATA QUALITY

   Both the 1962 and 1973 surveys were subject to standard error and
edit checks carried out by the U.S. Bureau of the Census. The analyst is
referred to detailed descriptions of the methodology of the Current
Population Survey in the Bureau of the Census Technical Reports Nos. 7 and
40, The Current Population Survey: A Report on Methodology (1963) and
Design and Methodology (1978); Evaluation and Research Program of the U.S.
Censuses of Population and Housing, 1960: Effects of Coders (Series ER 60,
No. 9, 1972); and Coding Performance in the 1970 Census (PHC(E)-8). Two
items in the 1962 and 1973 supplement (father's occupation and son's first
full-time occupation) were subjected to a field edit, and the entire supplement was reviewed when the response to either of these items was deficient.

   . . . Limited efforts were made to measure the reliability or validity
of retrospective reports in the 1962 and 1973 surveys. For the 1962 data,
see Peter M. Blau and Otis Dudley Duncan, The American Occupational Structure (New York: John Wiley and Sons, Inc., 1967), Appendix D ("Chicago
Pretest Matching Study") . . . and William T. Bielby, "The Specification
of Measurement Error in Models of the Socioeconomic Achievement Process"
(unpublished dissertation, University of Wisconsin-Madison; also available
in limited distribution, as Center for Demography and Ecology Working
Paper 76-26) . . .

   The replicate variables in the OCG-Replicate Master File were recoded
into identical classifications. The reader is referred to the appendix
. . . for full details.

   Occupation, industry, and class of worker descriptions were coded
using materials from the 1960 Census in the 1962 OCG survey, and using
materials from the 1960 and 1970 Census in the 1973 OCG survey. Only
the 1960-basis Census codes are included in the OCG-Replicate Master File
. . .

   Data cannot be used without the appropriate weights. Use of the
file without the weight variable will produce results which are not
comparable with other published results. Three weights are assigned to
each OCG respondent: the CPS weight (WGTCPS), OCG weight (WGTPRM), and
an alternate OCG weight (WGTALT) or 1973 only . . . The alternate weight
pertains only to OCG respondents in the target population (i.e., not the
black supplement). The Bureau of the Census modified the CPS weights to
take account of nonresponse in the OCG surveys. Basically, the CPS
weights for the OCG respondents were adjusted to sum to age specific
population counts for the black, Spanish, and majority populations.
(See . . . and "Appendix B: Population Coverage, Weighting, and Sampling
Variability in the 1962 and 1973 OCG Surveys" from Opportunity and Change
[both are reproduced in the appendix of the User's Guide]) . . . Please
note that Volume II of the User's Guide (frequency counts for selected
variables) provides distributions for the unweighted sample only).

   There are some inconsistencies in the data. For example, inconsistencies are contained in the marital reports data in the CPS and OCG

performed on the data. Lansing and Morgan (1971) suggest that the
"presentation of such materials in survey reports should not only
improve the understanding of each report, but provide the base on
which to improve the processing of future surveys" (p. 243). Records of
processing prevent problems like the following, described by Lansing
and Morgan (p. 244):

Figure 3 (continued)

---

segments. In addition, there are suspicious illegal values (e.g., age at first job, age at first marriage). It is recommended that the analyst not use the income allocation data for 1962.

UNIT OF ANALYSIS

The unit of anlaysis is civilian noninstitutional males in the OCG target population. In 1962, the N is 24,687 (22,208 Whites, 2,231 Blacks, 248 Others). In 1973, the N is 37,964 (32,329 Whites, 5,216 Blacks, 419 Others). In 1962, the OCG target population is N of 20,329; in 1973, N of 33,613. The total combined N in the release file is 62,651.

NUMBER OF VARIABLES

There are 106 variables in the release file. Note that these variables represent only a selected subset of the variables in the Occupational Changes in a Generation, 1962 and Occupational Changes in a Generation, 1973.

Discovery of errors after variables had been used to create other variables or had been transferred to other decks or tapes, requiring multiple corrections, and redoing of later steps.

Creation of a sequence of data tapes, each altering the tape location and variable number of each variable, [without having first created] a new code for each or maintaining in the variable name a reference to its original code location, so that locating the code detail requires translating through several transformation lists—those lists not with the codes but buried in piles of machine output.

Failure to date the completion of each step, so that one cannot tell whether an analysis run was done before or after certain corrections or changes in variables.

Regressions or other least squares analyses run with variables containing extreme cases, because the distribution had not been examined in advance.

Guideline 10.0 Describe general editing strategies rather than corrections made to particular data items.

For example, see Figure 4.

For example, Roistacher and others (1980) report that analysts working with the Law Enforcement Assistance Administration

**Figure 4. Illustration of the Processing History
Component of the Documentation**

SUMMARY OF PROCESSING HISTORY

(10.0)————————— FILE PROCESSING HISTORY: EDITS, CORRECTIONS, AND CLEANING

    All items included in the Replicate Master File were subject to edit and con-
sistency checks. Selected items were corrected in the recoding process. The
person-record identifier is constructed from the 1962 serial and line numbers and
from the 1973 random cluster codes, segment, serial, and line number. Each variable
has been assigned a unique character name: the last character(s) of the variable
name is "X" for the OCG respondent; "W" for spouse; "F" for respondent's father;
and "WF" for spouse's father. See the appendix to the User's Guide. "OCG Tabulation Specification No. 5," for full details.

(12.0)——The processing of these data was carried out using utility programs developed
by the project staff.

    These data were processed on an IBM 370/135 at the Center for Demography and
Ecology, University of Wisconsin-Madison.

(11.0)————————————————— LOGICAL RECORD STRUCTURE

    The record length is fixed, containing (for the OCG target male) CPS male data,
OCG male data (for OCG interview cases only, filler (9s) for non-interviews), OCG
spouse data (if married OCG target male, otherwise filled with 9s). Records are
organized to represent male records, including spouse data or blanks as appropriate.
The logical order of information is as follows: (a) household geographic and person-
record identifiers (character locations 1-45); (b) male's OCG and CPS information
which overlaps with present spouse's (order of items identical in (b) and (d) (character locations 46-131); (c) male's unique data (i.e., not reported by or for female)
from the OCG and CPS (character locations 132-213); and (d) female's OCG and CPS
information overlapping with present-spouse's (order of items identical in (b) and
(d) (character locations 214-300).

(13.0)——————————————— CONFIDENTIALITY PRESERVING STRATEGIES

    In order to assure anonymity of the data subjects, in conformity with U.S.
Bureau of the Census regulations, all identification numbers, state of current
residence, SMSA or current residence items have been coded with 9s.

(15.13)——————————————— AVAILABILITY

    The data and documentation are available from the Data and Program Library Ser-
vice, 4452 Social Science Building, University of Wisconsin-Madison (Madison, Wisconsin, 53706 USA).

    The archival file consists of one file stored on magnetic tape. All information
is in character format; EBCDIC mode, unlabelled, odd parity, nine channel, 1600 BPI.
The logical record size is 300 characters; block size is 7,200 characters. Data can
be provided in ASCII, BCD, or Univac SDF format to meet user requirements. The data
are software and hardware independent. Number of logical records is 62,651.

    For publications based on analyses of these data, see the bibliography in the
appendix to this User's Guide. See also key publications of the U.S. Bureau of the
Census which discuss design and methodology of the Current Population Surveys machine
readable data file. Also, Peter M. Blau and Otis Dudley Duncan, The American Occupational Structure (New York: John Wiley and Sons, Inc., 1967) . . . and Occupational
Changes in a Generation, 1962 [machine readable data file] (Madison, WI: University
of Wisconsin Data and Program Library Service, 1977).

(LEAA) Data Archive ran frequency distributions for categorical variables and for minima and maxima for continuous variables in order to determine undefined or unreasonable values. Two-way cross-tabulations were run on the Bureau of the Census identification variables and identification variables from the questionnaire where the variables seemed to represent the same information. In this way known errors could be corrected.

Examples of editing include changing missing data values to numeric values and the elimination of unused values or precoded values for expected responses. Such editing is necessary for items that were closed-ended questions, in which certain responses were expected but were not given; or for previously defined codes that were unused, and later assigned higher-order field widths.

The file processing history also provides a detailed description of the machine-readable dictionary and data files, including the data management system, type of organization, number of records, number of variables, and record lengths of each file. The number of reels of tape required to distribute the data in various formats and recording densities should also be provided to alert the potential analyst or programmer assisting the analyst to the operating system, management, analysis software, and computer hardware appropriate to the data's physical and logical structures.

Guideline 11.0 Provide a detailed description of the machine-readable dictionary (if created) and data files, including the type of organizaiton, number of records, number of variables, and record lengths of each file.

For example, see Figure 4.

Guideline 12.0 Describe the software used to process the data file and create the data dictionary.

For example: "The data and dictionary files were prepared using the OSIRIS III data management and analysis programs developed at the Center for Political Studies at the University of Michigan. The text in the *User's Guide* was formatted and printed using FORMAT, an implementation of FMT—A Documentation Program, written by Bill Webb at the University of British Columbia. In addition to the OSIRIS III system, for which the dictionary and data files were designed, they can be used directly with SPSS, SAS, and MIDAS. The data can also be read into many other statistical packages or into programs on computers of many different makes" (Roistacher and others, 1980, p. 20).

A full description of the confidentiality procedures should contain an account of the assurances made to respondents concerning confidentiality and the steps the project staff took to ensure confidentiality. Roistacher and others recommend that standards for the documentation of encryption procedures be included: "The security of a procedure should not depend on maintaining the secrecy of the procedure itself. If the procedure itself is secret, it is impossible for users of the data to estimate the procedure's statistical effect on the data. Also, it is far easier to compromise a secret procedure than a secret list of keys for individual records in a particular file" (1980, p. 24).

Guideline 13.0 Provide a list of all variables that were deleted to preserve respondent confidentiality. If random values were added to variables, disclose the distribution functions and statistical parameters of the random values. Provide an explicit statement of the intent of the confidentiality procedures to (perhaps) inhibit the publication of results that violate assurances of confidentiality.

Data Dictionary (Codebook)

A data dictionary describes the characteristics of each variable. The informational elements for each variable include working as close as possible to the original data collection instrument: an address (variable name or number); a reference number that maintains continuity in the variable's identity if its name or number changes; text label to identify the variable on printed output; explanatory text to describe either a group of variables or a group of code values; a response text consisting of a numeric code value, a short response category label, an optional extended response text item, and an optional frequency count; and a universe definition. Thus the data dictionary represents a set of annotated entries with detailed notes showing the function of each element (see also Roistacher and others, 1980, chap. 7, the source of the present discussion.)

Guideline 14.0 Include all information required for an understanding of the variable. Always include the sequence of questions that elicited the values for the attribute (variable).

For example, see Figure 5.

Guideline 14.1 Maintain a codebook entry or series of entries of original information as close as possible to the original data collection instrument. If necessary the wording of the entry can be shortened. If the original wording is extensive and pertains to a block of questions, place the original text at the beginning of the series of entries.

Figure 5. Example of the Format and Content for the Documentation of Each Variable in the MRDF

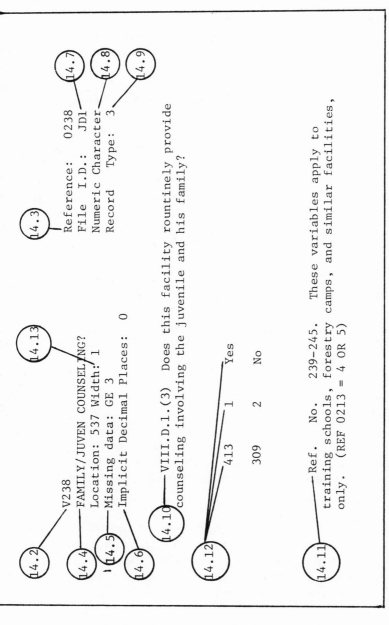

Source: Adapted from Roistacher and others, 1980, p. 39.

Guideline 14.2 Supply variable names or numbers that are not only identifiers, but addresses.

Guideline 14.3 Supply permanent reference numbers that do not change when the original archival file is subsetted, rearranged, or merged with another file.

Guideline 14.4 Supply a variable label that is a text other than variable name or number and is used to identify the variable on printed output. The variable labels are restricted in length and character set. Variable labels are helpful additions to variable identification when creating system files and performing analysis.

Guideline 14.5 Designate missing data. Many data management and analysis packages require that certain types of data that are usually excluded from analysis be designated as "missing data"—for example, inappropriate, unascertained, unascertainable, or ambiguous data.

Guideline 14.6 Describe the number of decimal places that are implicit in the variables if variables contain implicit decimal places.

Guideline 14.7 Create a unique identification number for this data file. The file identification and the reference number together should implicitly identify the variable in any context.

Guideline 14.8 Describe the storage mode (numeric, alphabetic) of the variable.

Guideline 14.9 Identify the record type and universe definition for any variable not applicable to all observations. It is helpful for the variable to carry a logical expression that defines the observations for which the variable is applicable.

Guideline 14.10 Supply an unabbreviated variable label or variable text, for example, the text of a question in a survey instrument. Make an effort to maintain the same vocabulary and to retain the meaning of the original phrasing. The dependency and contingency of a variable are indicated here if appropriate.

Guideline 14.11 Supply an explanatory text that describes either a group of variables or a group of code values in order to condense repetitive responses or to classify a subset of responses.

Guideline 14.12 Provide a response text that consists of a numeric code value, a short response category label, an optional extended response text item, and an optional frequency count. (The abbreviated response text is used by several statistical systems to label printed output.) If the original full text of the response must be shortened to fit the category label, the full response should be included as additional text following the category label.

Guideline 14.13 Supply the location and width of each variable.

Not every data producer has the resources to create a data dictionary that meets these standards. Nevertheless, even a minimal codebook must contain (1) a reference number, (2) an unambiguous name for the item, (3) a textual description of the item, or the text of the question (if from a questionnaire), (4) starting location, width, location of implicit decimal point, or scale factor, (5) missing data codes and their meanings, (6) mode in which the variable is represented (numeric character, alphanumeric string, floating point binary), (7) a list of the valid values for categorial items and valid ranges for continuous items.

Appendices

If possible, describe the full set of information in the body of the documentation text. The complexity of some data files, data processing information, coding schemes, data management software descriptions, may demand appendices or supporting volumes. The body of the documentation should then highlight the relevant information about a data file, not submerge the reader in massive amounts of detail. Roistacher and others (1980) note that "the use of appendices for bulky ancillary material makes it possible to split the source documentation into two volumes, one of which contains the heavily used dictionary listing" (p. 40).

Guideline 15.0 Include an appendix or appendices if ancillary material is too detailed or bulky to include in the body of the documentation.

Guideline 15.1 Include an appendix of definitions (or glossary) if the subject matter includes unusual terminology, or if terms have special definitions relevant to the data. Include acronyms, abbreviations, and special terms referring to government agencies, research consortia, or research organization; enabling legislation, administrative units, and program administration; study variables; data analysis models; and other concepts.

Guideline 15.2 Describe data items obtained during data collection but deleted from the public use file.

Guideline 15.3 List known errors for individual cases if they cannot be corrected.

Hedrick, Boruch, and Ross (1978) and Watts (1972) recommend including anecdotal information ("unwritten communication"), which may be critical for an analyst who needs to know what data items "really" mean and what errors were located but not formally reported. While many investigators do not include this information in their data documentation, its inclusion seems useful.

Guideline 15.4 Describe the known limitations of the data.

As Roistacher and others (1980) note; those using the documentation should not be required to thumb through the data dictionary in order to locate all the response categories for a complex variable.

Guideline 15.5 For variables having a very large number of response options or categories, place a full listing of the response categories in the appendix. Such variables include geographical, occupational, and college codes.

Guideline 15.6 If a data file has gone through several editions or is part of a longitudinal data file (or series of data files), include cross references that indicate the use of different numbers of variables. Follow the same principle to show changes in sample size and design.

Sometimes the primary analyst creates measurement variables and indexes based on the raw data. As Lansing and Morgan (1971) report, "[I]n panel studies, the process of variable generation is a great deal more complicated [than in cross-sectional studies] because one generates a set of variables for each year, but when the next wave comes along a very large number of possibilities open up for generating variables which reflect changes from one year to the next, either absolute differences or percentage changes" (p. 241).

Guideline 15.7 Provide sufficient information on the generation of measurement variables and indexes.

It is essential that the original data collection instrument be included. A copy of this instrument allows analysts to understand the construction of the data file, evaluate biases in response sets, understand the branching of questions, and anticipate unexpected outcomes when filtering observations or variables. The original instrument also helps users identify which data items in the MRDF were constructed from original responses. Oftentimes, variables constructed for editing or analysis are maintained in an archival or public use file and are rarely documented. Secondary analysts who intend to replicate or verify published findings often find no description of the construction of the derived items other than that derived from an inspection of items contained in the original instrument.

Guideline 15.8 Provide a copy of the original data collection instrument.

Interviewers' instructions provide important insights into how the data were obtained. Often the wording of a question determines particular responses.

Guideline 15.9 Include a complete copy of the field or laboratory procedures to provide information on the data collection activity; if procedures are lengthy, provide a sample. Include a sample of the office memorandums if relevant.

Coding involves arbitrary decisions. These decisions must be documented.

Guideline 15.10 Provide a copy of the coding instructions and conventions.

Special methodological and design problems reported in short articles or exerpted from larger texts are often essential to the understanding of a data file.

Guideline 15.11 Supply articles or reports on special methodological and design problems if they are not readily accessible in the published literature. Request written permission from the holder of the copyright before reproducing the article or report.

Helpful, but optional, is a complete format description of the machine-readable dictionary. This description will become more important as more documentation is created in machine-readable form.

Guideline 15.12 Supply a complete format description of the machine-readable dictionary.

A description of the physical structure of the data file is important because it describes the file and its accompanying documentation as shipped by the data supplier. Many file management and statistical analysis packages or computers are not designed to accept large records or blocks of information. With the increasing size of longitudinal data files, many researchers will not be able to use them unless they have access to a large computing facility.

Guideline 15.13 Supply a description of the physical structure of the file and its accompanying documentation. Describe available formats, specifying structure, types of software that may be used, number of bytes for each respondent, total number of respondents, and similar characteristics.

An order form, appended to the documentation, helps analysts who wish to obtain copies of the data. Of course, if special extracts or subsets of a study are available and a complex cost structure governs their purchase, a simple order form may be inadequate.

Guideline 15.14 Supply an order form. This form should include space for the specification of: mode, track, parity, density, labels, blocking limitations, and special instructions.

Organization and Format of Documentation

The organization of the documentation about MRDFs plays an important role in information retrieval processes (Robbin, 1978). If the documentation cannot be located by the usual methods of bibliographical search and retrieval, if it is poorly identified or out of logical order, users will be unable to locate the information. If the documentation is improperly indexed or not organized by subject content, or if elements of information are not located in the relevant section of the documentation, users will be unable to locate needed information and will make judgments based on incomplete information or possibly err in some part of their statistical analysis. Complete, organized documentation serves as a minimal information system that describes the intellectual and technical processes of data creation (David, Gates, and Miller 1974; Robbin, 1975).

Guideline 16.0 Describe the historical process of the data's creation. Careful design and packaging of documentation enhances its utility and motivates the user to make successful and creative use of the product (Zeisset, 1974).

Guideline 16.1 Provide documentation that is legible, literate, and well designed. Make the descriptive prose understandable to individuals in a variety of disciplines.

Documentation in Machine-Readable Form

Most documentation is now produced in hard-copy form. The increasing complexity, length, and costs of documentation (including rising paper and postage expenses) suggest that in the future, documentation will be generated directly in machine-readable form during data collection and file creation. Thus, it will be available in such nonprint media as microfiche and magnetic tape.

Documentation in machine-readable form introduces new problems because the user must have equipment to read the documentation and produce hard copy (should it be preferred). Microfiche requires a fiche reader, usually available at libraries, but often entailing some delays if immediate review is desired. Magnetic tape requires the user to understand tape specifications and the physical structure of the file and to have access to software for retrieval of the file or printing of the documentation. Roistacher's (1978) comments about self-described data files are relevant for documentation in machine-readable form: "Even though self-described files make life easier for the user of a particular data management system, they complicate matters for the data archivist, or for the person who wishes to transmit data to someone who uses a different data management system. Most self-described files have been designed to maximize processing efficiency in their 'home' systems. In many cases, data are stored in a nonprinting internal form, with a high degree of machine and program dependence (p. 3)."

Sometimes it is necessary to develop software to print the machine-readable documentation file. In other cases, it is necessary to return the file to the data supplier for a hard copy. Most of the documentation produced in machine-readable form is not easily accessible by microfiche because fiche lack indexes, thereby making it difficult for a user to locate specific items. Users bear the expensive cost of producing their own print or fiche copy. Whereas users may act independently in retrieving information contained in printed documents, they may require specialized personnel to assist in obtaining machine-readable documentation long before they have even seen the data.

Despite these inconveniences, more documentation will be produced in machine-readable form. Data management systems permit retrieval of documentation along with data, reducing errors in extracting or subsetting the desired variables. More people are using on-line systems and computer networks to transfer information. As computer transmission costs decrease, documentation will be transferred on-line.

Guideline 17.0 Produce machine-readable documentation that describes the contents of the machine-readable file and the data management system used to create the documentation file

Guideline 17.1 Produce machine-readable documentation in a format that can be accessed with a standard (utility) print program. Create the documentation in card-image form so that no additional software needs to be written to reformat the file to fit the software and hardware specifications of a user's equipment.

Guideline 17.2 Produce a documentation file that does not contain any special characters that cannot be interpreted by a user's computer. Write the documentation file entirely in character form.

Guideline 17.3 Separate the documentation file from the statistical data file so that each can be used as a single file.

Roistacher (1978), discussing data interchange files, lists the advantages of using a free format: "The use of a free format for recording missing data information, variable, and category labels allows both greater ease of file creation, and greater flexibility in adapting to the characteristics of new statistical systems as they appear on the scene . . . . [Free format] information is probably easier reading for the person who must interpret the dictionary manually" (p. 7).

Guideline 17.4 Produce the documentation file in free format.

Minimal Documentation

Creating a well-documented data file requires not only a commitment to writing a historical record of the process of data collection and management but also access to the original project records and sufficient funds and time to write the record. These prerequisites are not always available. Nevertheless, standards can be established for minimal documentation, that is, descriptive material that provides the potential analyst with sufficient information to carry out preliminary investigations of the data and to perform analyses that do not require detailed knowledge of the file's processing history.

Guideline 18.0 Provide minimal documentation consisting of (1) bibliographical information that identifies the data file, principal investigator or corporate body, producer and date(s) of production, and source of funding (grant number); (2) original collection instrument(s), including survey questionnaires and interview schedules; (3) editing and coding instructions used for creating the data file; (4) codebook or data dictionary; (5) printout of a sample of the first and last records in the data file to provide a visual description of the data and to assist in a manual editing check; (6) a description of the number of files, blocks, logical records, character format, and computer used to write the data; and (7) if possible, a frequency distribution for each categorical variable and mean, standard deviation, range, and number of cases of continuous variables. Optional, but very helpful, are a tape volume table of contents and an octal or hexadecimal (internal format) listing of the sample of records.

Part Two: Technical Standards for Quality Data

Access to data is facilitated by the preparation of high-quality empirical evidence that represents as faithfully as possible the information recorded during interviews or other means of data collection. The task of data reduction is especially significant for any planned primary or secondary statistical analysis because before coded data can be analyzed, they must be stored for easy retrieval and tabulation (Warwick and Lininger, 1975). In this section, we set forth some recommendations for good practice in organizing a data file, identifying record types and data items, describing missing data, employing standardized coding schemes, maintaining data at their lowest level of aggregation, and recording standards for the transfer of data files from one computer to another.

Record and Data Item Identification

It is important that each record and all record types in files containing more than one record type be identified. Roistacher and others (1980) recommend that a different record type be used whenever there is a "significant change in any of the procedures used to generate that record [and when] coding instructions or code values are changed. Otherwise, analysts may not properly interpret the presence or absence of variables which do not occur in all types of records" (p. 56). If records in a file represent a hierarchy or tree, each record should carry a unique identification that identifies it and its position in the hierarchy.

This identification will permit the analyst to sort and subset the file without the use of special software.

Guideline 19.0 Include an explicit and unique identifier for each record. Assign a sequence number if the data subjects have not been assigned a unique identification number.

Guideline 20.0 Identify each record type uniquely if a data file contains more than one record (for example, a hierarchical file that contains household, family, and individual records).

Guideline 20.1 Include an explicit type identifier even if each record in the file has a different length.

Guideline 21.0 Identify and document all data items.

One problem facing a secondary analyst is the extraction of data items (in variable length records, in particular) when the same item is not located in the same field in all (logical) records.

Guideline 22.0 Place every data item in the same field in every logical record to facilitate data extraction with standard software.

A data file should not contain irrelevant fields, but the width of a variable should be "sufficient to accommodate the entire range of variation which may be expected of the item" (Roistacher and others, 1980, p. 56). Some researchers recommend that in planning for the widest field space possible, an extra character be provided. All too often a variable turns out to contain values of a higher order than originally anticipated. Field width can always be reduced after the coding process is completed. However, as Roistacher and others (1980) note, "fields need be no wider than is required to accommodate the maximum expected value of a variable" (p. 56).

Guideline 23.0 Delete irrelevant fields. Maintain fields no wider than required.

David, Gates, and Miller (1974) warn that "it is bad practice to code values in tens of dollars for over-the-field cases and in units for the remaining population" (p. 2). He suggests that "a consistent decimal across all observations be used . . . by allowing excess space for data capture and subsequent reduction in the size of fields following analysis of maximum and minimum values" (p. 2).

Guideline 23.1 Allow for over-the-field amounts, refusals, not ascertained, and inappropriate, in addition to a range of values including negative and positive items.

For example:

Code	Description of Code Values
–xxxx	Negative amount of income in dollars (x)
–9999	Negative less than $9,998
00000	Zero income
xxxxx	Amount of income in dollars (x) if less than $88,887
88888	Inappropriate, income questions not asked for this respondent
88887	Income in excess of $88,886
99999	Income not ascertained, refused

One problem confronting the analyst is ascertaining which time period (year, month, or day) is represented by a data file that is part of an ongoing series of data collections. If a file is one of a series of identically structured fields, the date must be included as a unique record identifier. Sorting by date is facilitated within a file that is updated on a regular basis. The date of a data collection may be indicated simply by stating the year, month, and day as a six-digit variable (yy-mm-dd).

Guideline 24.0 If the data file is part of an ongoing series of data collections, represent the full date (yy-mm-dd) and specify the location of this variable in the documentation.

Data files are often revised, corrected, or updated. Logical records and variables may be added or deleted, and files may be reformatted into "system" formats. Substantial cleaning and correction, such as recoding or removing multiple and wild punches, are often undertaken. To identify revisions or editions of the data file once it has been distributed, it is useful to establish a field that describes the edition or version of the data file.

Guideline 25.0 Identify the edition of a data file and create a data item to identify either the date of the edition (see Guideline 24.0 for format) or the edition number (1 = first edition, 2 = second edition). Place this data item at the beginning or end of the record and describe this field in the file documentation (codebook).

Oftentimes, a data file is part of a collection of files in an archive or part of an ongoing series of studies. In these cases, it is helpful to identify uniquely the data file by imbedding (representing) the file number in the study to tie the data file to other parts of the collection.

Guideline 26.0 Imbed a study number of a data file and create a data item to identify this study number. Place this data item at the beginning of the record and describe this field in the file documentation (codebook).

Data Types

Many data producers imbed alphabetic characters in data files or document zone punches (+, –) as alphabetic characters, "X" or "Y," which are then interpreted as alphabetic values. Such practices create problems for the analyst who must transform the alphabetic and zone punches to numeric characters in order to use standard statistical packages. All nonnumeric and zone punch characters should be eliminated.

Guideline 27.0 Create entirely alphanumeric EBCDIC or ASCII character data files. Computational items should be numeric and contain the characters 0–9, +, and −. Decimal points are legal characters.

Roistacher and others (1980) note an exception to this general rule for imbedding data. If "D"- or "E"-format floating point data are represented, it is acceptable to represent floating point data in integer format (with implicit decimal places noted in the documentation). While in principle, scientific notation is the most efficient way to transfer data, not all computing installations have software that accept these data.

Guideline 27.1 Avoid storing data in floating point to facilitate the transfer of data from one computer site to another.

In general, decimal points create problems for the secondary analyst if the documentation does not describe whether the decimal point has been physically encoded in the field. Although a visual check of the data will immediately inform the analyst of the presence of a decimal point, such a check should not be necessary.

Guideline 27.2 Describe all uses of a decimal point or an implied decimal point.

Data files that contain fields with items that are not right-justified, blanks (either documented or undocumented), signs that are not left-justified, or signed zeros create significant problems. For example, blanks are interpreted differently by various statistical software; some treat them as valid characters and others as missing data. Roistacher and others (1980) note that "fields containing only a signed zero are unacceptable, since some computers cannot represent a signed zero" (p. 55).

Guideline 27.3 Right-justify computational items by placing zeros to the left.

Guideline 27.4 Eliminate blanks in the field.

Guideline 27.5 Immediately precede the left-most numeric character with the sign if a computational field is signed.

Missing Data

The values used to represent missing data must be explicitly identified; if unidentified, they are assumed by the analyst and the statistical software to be nonexistent. They should occur in the same field as the variable to which they refer and "in no case should the alternate value be carried in the base variable, with an explanation code in another variable. [The meaning of a variable should be] determinable without reference to a second variable" (Roistacher and others, 1980, p. 54).

Roistacher and others (1980) also note that "if an alternative value is to be used in place of a missing data value, the base item should carry an appropriate missing data code, while the alternative value is shown in a separate data item which has been declared for that purpose. . . . If the true value of a variable has been suppressed or modified, then the value of the data item should indicate such suppression or modification. If an alternative value is to be offered in such cases, the appropriate data item in the record can then be read if the analyst so wishes" (p. 54).

Guideline 28.0 Describe explicitly the values used to represent missing data. Indicate suppression or modification if the true value of a variable has been suppressed or modified. Place missing data values in the same field as the variable to which they refer.

A corollary of the problem of missing data values is the coding of an attribute such that missing data values are logically outside the range of the variable. The missing data value should not be imbedded in the range of legal values; for example, if a variable ranges from 0 to

99, do not use 34 to represent a missing value. Nor should attributes that can assume negative and positive values, such as income, carry missing data values in the form of a negative number; this practice is misleading and risks later misinterpretation, particularly in an analysis program (David, Gates, and Miller, 1979). Missing data values should be appropriate to the attribute measured.

Guideline 28.1 Code missing data values for an attribute so that the value is logically outside the range of the variable.

Guideline 28.2 Do not code attributes that can assume negative or positive values with a missing data value in the form of a negative number.

Standardization of Data Codes

Federal statistical offices and other established national and international agencies (for example, the Organization for Economic Cooperation and Development and the International Standards Organization) have developed standards for data elements and representations to be used in automated federal data systems and among national governments (see U.S. Department of Commerce, 1978). For example, the National Bureau of Standards of the U.S. Department of Commerce provides Federal Information Processing Standards (FIPS) codes for data elements and develops standards in areas that do not fall under other agencies' jurisdiction. These standards include: calendar dates; country, state, and county abbreviations and codes; federal administrative regions; standard metropolitan statistical areas (SMSAs); industrial classifications of establishments and enterprises; occupational and payroll codes for employment reports; ethnicity; and various standards for the fields of science and engineering. Other federal agencies have developed standards for their particular statistical reporting systems; for example, the Office of Education for school districts. Researchers long involved in a particular discipline have developed useful classification schemes (see Van Dusen and Zill, 1975). When possible, these standard data coding schemes should be used and ad hoc coding schemes avoided. Researchers collecting standard data items, such as work histories, should use established classification schemes that provide for comparability across data files.

Guideline 29.0 Whenever possible, apply standard codes to facilitate comparisons with other data files and merging of data. Consult with the central statistics office of a national government for statistical coding standards.

Aggregation

Watts (1972), in a discussion of the uses of microdata, suggests that "different analyses are likely to apply to different decision units or even different versions of what is nominally the same unit. Thus, the choices of definition have to be made, and the questions of how units are to be matched, put together, and followed from survey to survey, depend on these choices" (p. 184). When data are aggregated to a level higher than their original state, significant distortions and biases may be introduced into the file. Aggregation may also limit the ability of analysts to use the data for different types of analyses or replication of the primary analyst's results (see Hedrick, Boruch, and Ross, 1978). While confidentiality rules may preclude access to some data, it is imperative that they be preserved in their original microlevel form.

Guideline 30.0 Maintain data at their lowest level of aggregation. Maintain item-level responses in their original form.

Data Transfer

Access to data is inhibited by incomplete descriptions of the format of data in a particular medium and nonstandard file exchange formats. Until computer networking permits ready access and rapid transfer of large amounts of information, data will continue to be transferred by magnetic tape. Thus, standards of good practice regarding data dissemination through magentic-tape processing should be followed and standard exchange formats should be used. To the extent possible, information describing the physical characteristics of the file and the logical composition of each record type should be stored on the magnetic tape for retrieval by a standard utility print program. The first file should consist of a tape table of contents, a program that also verifies the readibility of the tape. The second file should consist of bibliographical information in the form of a citation to the machine-readable data file that follows it. Standard IBM or ANSI volume and file labels should be used if the operating system accepts them. User header and trailer labels (which are ignored by the operating system but can be printed out with a utility program) can be used to carry the bibliographical information for the MRDF.

Guideline 31.0 Write data in either external EBCDIC or ASCII character code. Write data at seven or nine track, preferably at nine track, at a density of 800, 1600, or 6250 bpi. (Note that phase encoding [used at 1600 bpi] is more reliable than nonreturn to zero encoding [used at 800 bpi]; and group encoding [used at 6250 bpi] is more reliable than either.) Prepare a magnetic tape with IBM or ANSI volume and file labels.

Guideline 32.0 Provide a description of the physical characteristics of the file and logical composition of each record type. Supply the information in machine-readable form (if possible) and hard-copy form. Provide information on the number of files, block and record size, number of records for each record type, and number of reels. Accompany the data file with a tape table of contents that includes information from the volume and file labels.

Guideline 33.0 Incorporate the American National Standard magnetic tape labels for information interchange to provide a comprehensive tape labeling facility. Use this standard to create a user header label (UHL) to represent a facsimile of a bibliographical citation for the MRDF (or its documentation, if the documentation is in machine-readable form on the magnetic tape).

For an example of the use of user header labels, see Guideline 37.1. Note that if the MRDF *documentation* is a file on the magnetic tape, the title of the documentation should so indicate. For example: *Occupational Changes in a Generation: Replicate Master File 1962 and 1973: A User's Guide to the Machine-Readable Data File* [machine-readable data file].

The growing complexity of today's statistical data files makes it increasingly difficult to maintain fixed record lengths; but most standard statistical packages require rectangular files and logical records that are not "split" between physical blocks. Although variable-length records are to be avoided, if they are present, users should be able to specify which format (fixed or variable) they prefer.

Guideline 34.0 If the data contain more than one record type and the record lengths for each record type are variable, allow the user to specify whether variable-length records are to be placed in a fixed format the length of the longest record.

Many computing sites cannot accept blocks larger than 2,000 characters in length. The data supplier should be sensitive to other analysts' computing constraints and should make data available in physical structures and formats that are compatible with typical computer systems.

Guideline 35.0 Block the data in the size most efficient for the computer systems on which they are likely to be used.

Guideline 35.1 Put blocks of information in fixed format since most computer systems do not have the software to handle variable-length blocks.

Part Three: Providing Access to Information
About Machine-Readable Data Files

Access to machine-readable data files requires techniques and mechanisms that allow efficient information management and dissemination. Access is facilitated by the circulation of information about a data file's existence and availability; the filing of such information in library, scientific, and technical information systems; and the establishment of archives to ensure the preservation and future availability of data. In this part, we address these issues.

Standards of good bibliographical practice permit information to reach the public. Just as authors follow standard rules for identifying their articles, books, or reports, and publishers follow standard publishing practices for identifying their publications, data producers should follow accepted bibliographical practices for describing their data files.

Guideline 36.0 Do not take the title for an MRDF from a publication based on the data file. Such duplication may constitute a violation of copyright laws cause problems with international coding schemes or conflicts within automated bibliographical systems.

An internal file label (which precedes a statistical data file on a magnetic tape) represents one of the best forms for describing the data file that follows.

Guideline 37.0 Incorporate the American National Standard magnetic tape labels for information interchange to provide a comprehensive tape labeling facility.

Dodd (1979b) recommends that User Header Labels (UHL) be used to represent a facsimile of a title page for the MRDF documentation: "Upon receiving a data file or program stored on magnetic tape, the user would arrange for the contents of the tape's labels to be printed out. The resulting printout of the tape's UHL would reveal the file's bibliographical identity. . . . The advantage of an internal title page for

MRDF is that it is *totally file-specific* (describing only the information recorded on the magnetic tape) and would not be lost or separated from the file it is describing" (p. 6).

Guideline 37.1 Use a user header label (UHL) to represent a facsimile of a title page for the MRDF documentation.

For example:

UHL1 General Social Surveys, 1972–1978: Cumulative Data (machine-
UHL2 readable data file). Principal investigator, James A. Davis. Con-
UHL3 ducted for the National Data Program for the Social Sciences at
UHL4 the National Opinion Research Center. Chicago: National Opin-
UHL5 Research Center (producer), 1978. New Haven, Conn: Roper
UHL6 Public Opinion Research Center, Yale University (distributor).

Guideline 38.0 Identify the data file by a standard library classification number (International Standard Series Number [ISSN] if the data file is part of an ongoing series; or International Standard Book Number [ISBN]). [The ISSN can be obtained through the Library of Congress; the ISBN through R. R. Bowker, 1180 Avenue of the Americas, New York, N.Y. 10036.]

Guideline 39.0 Identify a data file produced under federal contract or grant by its Office of Management and Budget and General Accounting Office reporting codes.

Guideline 40.0 Copyright a data file and documentation whenever relevant or permissible as recognition of the intellectual contribution of its author(s). [Copyright information may be obtained from the Copyright Office of the Library of Congress.]

Guideline 41.0 Produce a catalogue entry to identify the data file. Identify the catalogue entry with the statement "cataloguing during production."

A "cataloguing during production" statement is analogous to the book publisher's activity of "cataloguing in publication." Information on cataloguing may be obtained from the Library of Congress. In order to produce a standard catalogue entry for an MRDF, seek the assistance of a professional librarian. The American Library Association (1979) has formal rules for cataloguing MRDFs.

Guideline 41.1 Produce a catalogue entry to identify the documentation for the machine-readable data file. This entry will not carry a medium designator statement (machine-readable data file) unless the documentation is produced in machine-readable form.

Using Information Channels

Just as book publishers announce the release of new books, data producers should use existing information channels to report the availability of data to their potential user community. Announcements may be sent to relevant government publications and reports, the Government Printing Office, the National Technical Information Service, the National Archives and Records Service, scholarly journals and newsletters, and centers for the dissemination of data.

Guideline 42.0 Publicize the availability of the data file when it is ready for release. Briefly describe the contents of the file and note any relevant publications based on analysis of the data. Describe release conditions, conditions of the data, file structure, and file exchange information. Supply the name, address, and telephone number of a contact person.

For example, see Figure 6.

Any publications based on the analysis of an MRDF should refer to the data file.

Guideline 43.0 Explicitly identify the data file used in a publication by a bibliographical citation or a data acknowledgement statement.

Guideline 43.1 Press releases or other types of publicity about the publication should include a short description of the MRDF.

Archival Facilities

Most producers of machine-readable data files do not have the resources or expertise to preserve, maintain, and distribute their data. They do not have established procedures for easy access to and inexpensive use of their data by potential users. Few data producers can supply their users with adequate support services related to teaching, research, coordination of multiple research projects, computation, and general information services related to MRDFs, which are often by-products of large data-gathering projects. In general, the gathering, encoding, processing, and documentation of data are expensive.

**Figure 6. Illustration of the Contents and Format of a
Data Availability Announcement**

New Data File Now Available

Data which examine changes in social mobility in the period between
the early 1960s and early 1970s, and help document trends and shifts over
several decades of the twentieth century for cohorts born between 1897 and
1951 are now available.

In 1973, the U.S. Bureau of the Census conducted a survey on behalf
of David L. Featherman and Robert M. Hauser to explore the effects that
peoples' backgrounds, schooling, training in the military, and their early
work experiences have on their careers. The study was a replicate and
extension of the 1962 Occupational Changes in a Generation survey conducted by the U.S. Bureau of the Census on behalf of Peter M. Blau and
Otis Dudley Duncan to examine the extent and sources of social mobility
in the United States.

The independent, cross-sectional surveys were conducted as supplements
to the 1962 and 1973 March Current Population Surveys. Selected data items
from the surveys were merged to create the data file, Occupational Changes
in a Generation: Replicate Master File, 1962 and 1973. The data include
education, occupation, industry and earnings for men aged 20 to 64 years
and their wives; number of siblings and paternal education, occupation,
and industry for men and their wives; and additional social background and
work-history variables for men. The recently published monograph by Featherman and Hauser, Opportunity and Change (Academic Press, 1978), reports analyses of these data.

The Occupational Changes in a Generation-Replicate Master File, 1962
and 1973 data file and two volume set of documentation (755 p.), A User's
Guide to the Machine Readable Data File and Tabulations for Selected Variables (Unweighted Counts) are now available. The data file and documentation can be obtained for about $150; documentation alone, $80. The cost
includes xeroxing, staff time, magnetic tape, computer time, postage, and
a small DPLS overhead. The data file can be written in BCD, EBCDIC, or
ASCll to meet a user's computer needs. For further information, contact
the Data and Program Library Service, 4452 Social Science Building, University
of Wisconsin-Madison, Madison, WI 53706 (tel. no.: 262-7962).

Data archives or libraries offer data producers the best means for
preserving their data and documentation. Data repositories provide
established distribution channels for data and information. Data centers maintain procedures for easy and relatively inexpensive access to
data and documentation, providing users with such services as copying
data and documentation, explanation of the contents and structure of a
data file, and consultation on data use and computation. Further, data
centers can provide users of a data file with reports and publications
related to research that has used the data and information on modifications, updates, and errors in the data file.

Guideline 44.0 Deposit an archival quality public use version and the original microlevel data file in a data archive. Follow recommended technical guidelines for producing material of archival quality.

Guideline 44.1 Deposit one copy of any data file created under federal grant or contract with the National Archives and Records Service, Machine Readable Archives Division. Deposit one copy of the public use version in an academic data archive to facilitate access to the data by students and scholars.

Guideline 44.2 Arrange for the deposit of the MRDF with appropriate archives as the research project is being planned and funded to ensure good practices for data and documentation preparation, minimal delays in transfer and data preparation for future users, and timely access to the data when associated publications appear.

Although most libraries do not have the resources to provide full services for machine-readable data files, they are the most appropriate place for an MRDF documentation reference collection. With the newly formalized rules for cataloguing MRDFs, libraries are now prepared to accept the MRDF documentation as another information resource and to integrate the documentation in their collection.

Guideline 45.0 Send one copy of the MRDF documentation to the cataloguing department of a library or information center to ensure that the published document will become part of a library collection and available to a wide community of users.

Part Four: Roles of the Researcher, Sponsor, and Government Agencies

Well-documented data files, quality data, and information channels that facilitate access to the products of social research potentially enhance our understanding of social problems and advance general scientific knowledge. A policy that promotes well-documented, high-quality data and open access to these products needs to be supported by all constituencies of the social scientific research enterprise. As has been repeatedly noted, most research projects that involve data gathering do not receive funding sufficient for the documentation and preservation of research data. Both researchers and sponsors share responsibility for this situation. The following guidelines highlight the inherent interdependencies (with respect to responsibility for ensuring high-quality data collection, description and dissemination) among government agencies, sponsors of research, and grantees. The ensuing guidelines have been generated so as to encompass each phase of the research process. Thus, guidelines relevant to the production of useful data begin with the planning and submission of proposals and conclude with storage and dissemination of the data.

Planning: The Researcher's Role

While researchers often underestimate the cost of data processing and file documentation, sponsors of research are responsible for not providing adequate funding for well-documented and clean data files. When researchers do request funds for these activities, sponsors often eliminate or substantially reduce funds earmarked for the production of high-quality data and their documentation. Researchers who understand the need for adequate data processing and documentation have had to conceal these funds in their total budget request. Further, few research proposals include a detailed description of the procedures for the entry, processing, documentation, and dissemination of data. Obviously, sponsors are reluctant to authorize funds for activities only vaguely outlined in a research proposal.

Guideline 46.0 Write a budget that fully describes the anticipated cost of processing the data and producing the documentation. Present an itemized budget for data cleaning, processing, documentation, and dissemination; consolidate these costs with those for computer time and supplies.

Guideline 46.1 Request funds for personnel skilled in file architecture, processing, and documentation.

Guideline 46.2 Request funds to hire individuals during the initial planning of the project to be responsible for archival activities, documentation, and data base management.

Guideline 46.2.1 Designate a specialist to be responsible for maintaining the records of the data collection, processing, and documentation; for supervising the data entry staff in creating the data documentation; for designing (with project directors and the data management specialist) the data documentation; for coordinating the work of analysts and other users of the data during the life of the project.

Guideline 46.2.2 Designate a specialist to be responsible for designing the data base structure, designing or supervising the development of software, supervising the production of the data base, producing files for primary or secondary analysts, and preparing public use versions.

Researchers should plan to consult with experts in the areas of data base management, file architecture, data documentation, software and hardware, processing, and archival activities on a regular basis during the life of the project.

Guideline 46.3 Request funds for consultants if these experts are not members of the project staff.

Developing a budget for data processing and documentation is one of the hardest aspects of preparing a budget proposal because it is difficult to estimate the quality of the data before processing and analysis. One rule of thumb is to estimate the cost and then double that estimate.

Guideline 47.0 Consult programming and information management specialists for estimates of the costs of preparing quality data and documentation.

Guideline 48.0 Recognize that after the cost of data collection, the greatest costs of primary or secondary data analysis are the processing and preparing of the data for analysis, not the cost of performing the analysis itself.

Researchers planning large-scale data gathering should consider acquiring inexpensive data entry terminals with CRT screens and off-line data editing and storage capabilities. Such peripheral data processing equipment provides an efficient way to enter, edit, and correct documentation and data; all researchers should investigate whether automated processing of materials is economical for their project. While software can be elegantly written to document every aspect of the editing process, simple and inexpensive software can be developed and integrated with the editing capabilities of these off-line data entry terminals. The researcher should consult with computing center personnel to learn about the various types of available peripheral data entry equipment and terminals.

Guideline 49.0 Investigate the use of inexpensive CRT terminals with editing capabilities for data entry and text documentation.

All too often, only after the data files are created and the analysis is initiated do researchers discover that changes must be made in the data structure because the software or computer cannot be used efficiently or the data do not reflect the project's intended design. Pilot tests designed to assay the adequacy of the instrument are part of every research design. Similarly, pilot tests that assay the adequacy of the data base structure for efficient analysis seem desirable. Testing the data base structure for a sample of data files will indicate the need for changes in coding procedures, software, or data structure.

Guideline 50.0 Request sufficient funds to produce a pilot test of the data base structure, data documentation, and data management software.

Planning and Monitoring: The Sponsor's Role

Experts in file architecture, data documentation, and archival activities are too rarely consulted by agencies that are developing specifications for requests for proposals. Many potential problems can be avoided if these individuals are consulted by the sponsoring agency before a program announcement is publicized.

Guideline 51.0 Sponsors of large-scale data gathering projects should consult with governmental and nongovernmental advisory boards and consultants in file architecture, data documentation, and archiving.

Effective project monitors must have expertise in research and in information management. But the monitoring of the implementation of a project requires the expertise of a number of individuals; project monitors cannot possibly be expected to have skills to evaluate data structures, processing, and documentation.

Guideline 52.0 Use advisory boards and consultants to share the responsibilities of monitoring and evaluating the gathering, processing, documentation, and preservation of data.

Federal agencies need to develop a diversified and professional staff to evaluate the quality of research design, data collection, and data processing. This group would evaluate the sponsored projects' budget, personnel, operational setting, performance, and statistical products. The General Accounting Office can also play a useful role in overseeing and monitoring federally sponsored projects (Social Science Research Council, 1978). In addition, federal sponsors should profit from the experience and expertise of the Office of Management and Budget and the Office of Federal Statistical Policy and Standards, Department of Commerce.

Guideline 53.0 Consider the creation of an agency or divisionwide group responsible for monitoring the implementation of a data gathering project (collection, processing, and documentation).

Guideline 54.0 Encourage the General Accounting Office to develop manuals and guidelines for activities related to data gathering, processing, and documentation. Guidelines for evaluating the quality of data and documentation should be developed for project monitors, consultants, review boards, projects staffs, auditors, and evaluators.

Audits and quality control procedures can promote high standards for the creation of data. Files have been created by nongovernmental organizations that lack expertise in producing clean, well-documented data files. Better monitoring of data gathering projects is necessary.

Guideline 55.0 Consider audit and evaluation as integral parts of the project. Design the audit during the implementation stages to assist the staff in its processing of the data. Include in the final project evaluation an assessment of the quality of the data and related information products.

Providing Support for Continued and Future Use

Large, longitudinal studies and complex data files may require user support services and facilities for access and retrieval of selected samples and variables for special analyses. Oftentimes, special software is required to access these large complex files and this software cannot be transported easily. In many instances, the data structures are complex and require programming efforts more sophisticated than those available to most researchers. In these cases, the sponsor should not terminate funding at the completion of the project but should provide adequate, continued support for user services to ensure and facilitate access to the data files. Admirable precedents were established by the funding of the Institute for Research on Poverty Data Center (University of Wisconsin) and the National Election Studies of the Center for Political Studies (University of Michigan). Both centers have a user services facility that provides specially tailored extracts of MRDFs. For example, to facilitate dissemination of the data from the New Jersey Maintenance Project study (University of Wisconsin), special software was developed and users are charged only the direct costs of preparing special extracts. Data from the National Election Studies (University of Michigan) are deposited in the Interuniversity Consortium for Political and Social Research and are available to consortium members and at low cost to nonmembers.

Guideline 56.0 Sponsors should provide funds for user support services and for continued archival support to maintain the data files if data structures are complex or if long-term data collection is part of the funding proposal.

Microlevel Data and Public Use Files

Microlevel data are often unavailable. Usual practice has been to preclude any access to microlevel data or to aggregate them to a higher level, which reduces their potential utility.

Guideline 57.0 Draw up guidelines for the availability of the microlevel data before the project is funded. Include strategies to ensure that confidentiality of data on subjects is maintained. If necessary, include funds for a consultant who can advise about strategies to maintain confidentiality.

Guideline 57.1 Place the original microlevel data and a public use version and their accompanying documentation in the archives of an established data repository. Designate the National Archives and Records Service, Machine Readable Archives Division, as the federal repository if the project has been carried out under federal sponsorship.

Guideline 57.2 Provide adequate funds in the budget for the creation of public use files. Produce several public use versions if the data structures are complex and the data are of sufficient interdisciplinary interest.

Guideline 57.2.1 Include raw data from the dependent variables (test scores, scales). If confidentiality of data subjects must be assured, inadvertent disclosure can be protected by other means.

The data file and documentation should be deposited in an established data repository. These plans should be established prior to funding and not after completion of the project.

Dissemination

Reports based on reanalyses of the data, dissemination of information about a specific project, and availability of the data products are important components of the scientific process.

Guideline 58.0 Include funds for dissemination of reports based on reanalysis of the data as a line item in the budget.

Guideline 59.0 Disseminate findings through yearly reports of the General Accounting Office (GAO). Use the GAO's compendium on federal program evaluation to assist in documenting data availability.

Guideline 60.0 Disseminate data products and reports through the National Technical Information Service.

Guideline 61.0 Deposit data products and documentation in the National Archives and Records Service, Machine Readable Archives Division.

Federal Support for Data Archive Centers

Although agencies in the federal government are charged with preserving and maintaining federally produced data, their staffs are not as experienced in problems of data access as those at data services and archives in academic institutions, which have been servicing a broad clientele since the early 1960s. These data centers are more experienced in producing good data and documentation than are contractors in the private sector.

Guideline 62.0 Provide federal funding for data archive centers to produce usable data and documentation for those files originally underwritten by federal funds, if the data archives can demonstrate the research and instructional value and use of particular secondary data collections.

Guideline 63.0 Designate data archives outside the federal government as a national resource.

Guideline 63.1 Fund data archive centers (rather than the producers of data) to provide extended and experienced user support facilities.

Guideline 63.2 Facilitate access to data by maintaining support for a system of distributive data archives. Support a national information system comprising libraries that serve a variety of user communities.

Concluding Remarks

Federal agency administrative reporting requirements have motivated the collection of vast amounts of data in the form of special purpose surveys. Most of these complex and expensive primary data resources have been used for one-time statistical reporting and description of social and economic phenomena, with little or no subsequent analyses of them. Many of these data resources have never been extensively analyzed or made available to researchers; they have been forgotten, or are unavailable, or are stored in a form too intractable for reanalysis. Yet, these data could be used by administrators and researchers to assess, in a rigorous and analytical fashion, technical, administrative, cost, and policy issues.

We acknowledge the initial high cost of producing, documenting, and maintaining quality statistical data. The cost of well-documented and high-quality data, however, should be weighed in relation to the benefits of such information to the scientific and political communities. The guidelines proposed in this chapter need not be routinely applied to all statistical data. Small-scale projects, projects with small budgets, and projects with narrow focuses do not require complex systems of documentation, maintenance, access, and preservation. Nevertheless, designers of small projects should incorporate minimal standards in their planning to provide systematic evidence and record keeping, to allow for the verification of claims of successful or unsucessful program outcomes, and to permit reanalysis of program success and performance. Such prior planning institutionalizes a foundation for the process of producing high-quality evidence and accumulating good evidence to be used in policy development and analysis. To the extent that data are well documented, of high quality, and accessible through a variety of information channels, improved primary analysis and independent secondary analysis are facilitated.

In this chapter, we have in effect plotted the flow of information from its generation to its final disposition. We have suggested scientific and institutional mechanisms for the gathering of data relevant to methodological, technical, and policy issues that rely on empirical data for understanding human behavior. These mechanisms play an important role in the processes of innovation, dissemination, and information transfer. Analysts, data producers, and archivists play important roles in a complex intellectual system that includes scientific research, methods, products, and services (see Havelock, 1969). We have suggested various means by which primary and secondary analysts can facilitate the dissemination of information, using the formal information channels that provide the infrastructure for information transfer.

Our guidelines also suggest that government should play an intelligent, informed, and active role in the effective dissemination of information. Here, we recommend that the government support, monitor, facilitate, and coordinate linkage activities so that the total information system (of which statistical data are an increasingly important part) can function more effectively. Government's stake in quality data is indisputable: Accountability, policy and program development, and democratic ideals promote an increase in the federal government's involvement in facilitating access to statistical data, integrating the myriad pieces of research, and institutionalizing the mechanisms of dissemination.

Our discussion of the process by which statistical data are described, prepared, and disseminated has presented these processes as a set of information transfer activities. While useful, this perspective is somewhat limiting. In the final analysis, and perhaps more important, these activities represent a means of recording, in some permanent way, aspects of human behavior. Thus, the obligation to produce well-documented and high-quality data develops from researchers' and analysts' involvement in recording and preserving historical events and the resultant duty to provide evidence of the events in which they participated.

APPENDIX
Citations for the MRDFs Used as
Illustrations for Selected Guidelines

1. *Occupational Changes in a Generation, 1962* (machine-readable data file). Principal investigators, Peter M. Blau and Otis Dudley Duncan. DPLS ed. Madison, Wis.: David L. Featherman and Robert M. Hauser, University of Wisconsin (producer), 1975. Madison, Wis.: Peter Dickinson, Center for Demography and Ecology, University of Wisconsin Data and Program Library Service (distributor).
2. *Social Role Study: High School Students' Values, Role Definitions, and Fertility Orientations, Spring 1972* (machine-readable data file). Principal investigators, Edgar F. Borgatta and Patricia W. Cautley. DPLS ed. Prepared by Katherine Unertl, Data and Program Library Service. Madison, Wis.: Katherine Unertl (producer), 1978. Madison, Wis.: University of Wisconsin Data and Program Library Service (distributor).
3. *Higher Education General Information Survey (HEGIS): Earned Degrees Conferred—Fall 1969–70 Through Fall 1973–74 Academic Year* (machine-readable data file). National Center for Education Statistics. NCES ed. Washington, D.C.: National Center for Education Statistics (producer and distributor).
4. *Survey Research Center Spring Omnibus Study, 1973* (machine-readable data file). Conducted by the Survey Research Center, University of Michigan. ICPSR ed. Ann Arbor, Mich.; University of

Michigan Survey Research Center (producer), 1973. Ann Arbor, Mich.; Interuniversity Consortium for Political and Social Research (distributor).

5. *California Poll Berkeley Public Opinion Survey No. 2546, September 1977*(machine-readable data file). Conducted by Field Corporation. SRC ed. San Francisco: Field Corporation, Inc. (producer) 1977. Berkeley, Calif.: Survey Research Center, University of California at Berkeley (distributor).

Index to the Guidelines

This is a subject index to the guidelines in this chapter. Guidelines that contain more than one concept have been cross-referenced.

Abstract, components, 3.0–3.10
Advisory boards and consultants for monitoring and evaluating, 52.0
Agency responsibility, monitoring the data gathering, 53.0
Aggregation of data items, 30.0
Appendices, components, 15.0–15.14
Archival facilities
    support for, 56.0, 62.0, 63.00–63.2
    use, 44.0–44.2, 56.0, 57.1, 61.0
Audit checks and evaluation of data gathering, 55.0
Availability of the machine-readable data file, 42.0, 43.0, 43.1
Bibliographical citation
    in an abstract, 3.3
    for the machine-readable data file, 33.0
Bibliographical practice
    catalogue entry, 41.0
    cataloguing during production, 41.0
    conflicts with international coding schemes, 36.0
Bibliography of the project, 8.0
Blanks in data items, 27.3
Budget
    for capital equipment, 49.0
    for computer time for data processing and preparation, 48.0
    for nongovernmental advisory boards and consultants, 51.0, 57.0
    for pilot version of data, 50.0

for reporting results, 58.0
for personnel, 46.1
for public use files, 57.2
writing a, 46.2.1
Catalogue entry
    for the documentation, 41.1
    for the machine-readable data file, 41.0
Cataloguing during production, as a bibliographical practice, 41.0
Codebook. *See* Data dictionary
Coding
    of date, 24.0
    of edition, 25.0
    of missing data, 28.0–28.2
    of study number, 26.0
    use of standard statistical classification codes, 29.0
Coding instructions and conventions, copy, 15.10
Computation items, in the data file, 27.3
Confidential data, raw data, 57.2.1
Confidentiality
    description of deletion of variables to ensure, 13.0
    description of procedures, 13.0
    of data subjects, guidelines for ensuring the, 57.0
Copyright
    avoiding violations, 36.0
    of a data file or documentation, 40.0

Cross references, 15.6
Data acknowledgments, rationale, 2.0
Data archive centers, federal support
for, 62.0–63.2
Data collection instrument, copy, 15.8
Data dictionary, description, components, 14.0–14.13
Data file
identification when produced
under government contract, 39.0
organization, record, and item
identification, 19.0–26.0
producers and distributors, 1.5, 1.6
Data item
deleted from a public use file, 15.2
identification of field location,
22.0
Data type, coding, 27.0
Date(s), coding, 24.0
Decimal places
described in the data dictionary,
14.6
described in the documentation,
27.2
as legal characters in data type,
27.0
Definitions relevant to the data, 15.1
Deletions of variables, in the appendix, 15.2
Depositing. *See also* Archival facilities; National Archives and Records Service.
a data file, arrangements for, 44.2
documentation in a library, 45.0
Dissemination
of findings through the General
Accounting Office, 59.0
of reports about data, 58.0–61.0
through the National Archives
and Records Service, 61.0
throught the National Technical
Information Service, 60.0
Distributive data archives, support,
63.2
Documentation
in machine-readable form,
17.0–17.4
minimal components, 18.0
organization and format, 16.0, 16.1
study overview, 1.0–5.0
Editing strategies, description, 10.0

Edition. *See also* Title page
coding, 25.0
cross references, 15.6
Ensuring access to confidential data,
guidelines for their availability,
57.0
Errors known for individual cases,
15.3
Explanatory text of the variables in
the data dictionary, 14.11
Field procedures, copy or description,
15.9
Field width, size, 23.0, 23.1
File processing history, components,
10.0–13.0
General Accounting Office, role, 54.0
Glossary, in the documentation ap-
pendix, 15.1
Government accounting codes, de-
scribed in the project history, 9.0
History of the project, components,
6.0–9.0
Implicit decimal places. *See* Decimal
place
Information channels, use, 42.0
Instrument, copy, 15.8
Instrumentation description, 7.0
International Standard Book Number
(ISBN), 38.0
International Standards Series Num-
ber (ISSN), 38.0
Interviewer instructions, copy, 15.9
Laboratory procedures, copy or de-
scription, 15.9
Library, use of documentation, 45.0
Library classification schemes for
good bibliographical practice,
38.0
Limitations of the data, 15.4
Location and width of variables in
the data dictionary, 14.13
Long-term support services for data
access, 56.0
Machine-readable dictionary
description, 11.0
format, 15.12
Machine-readable documentation,
17.0–17.4
Measurement variables and indexes,
description, 15.7

Methodological and design articles,
  copy, 15.11
Microlevel data. *See also* Confidential
  data; Confidentiality
  availability, 57.0
  deposit, 57.1
  ensuring preservation, 57.0–57.2.1
Missing data
  coding, 28.1
  placement in the data file, 28.0
National Archives and Records Services, Machine Readable Archives
  Division
  as a depository, 57.1
  for data files created under federal
    contract, 44.1
Nongovernmental advisory boards
  and consultants, use, 51.0
Office memorandums, sample, 15.9
Order form, copy, 15.14
Personnel, 46.2, 46.3
Physical structure, description of the
  file and accompanying documentation, 15.13
Planning
  computer equiment, 49.0
  consulting specialists, 47.0
  estimating costs, 47.0, 48.0
  data gathering, processing, and
    documentation, 46.0–51.0
  personnel, 46.2–46.2.2
  pilot tests for data, 50.0
Public use file
  budgeting, 57.2
  creation, 57.0
Publicity for the data file, 42.0–43.1
Record identification, explicit and
  unique identifier, 19.0–20.1
Record type identification in the data
  dictionary, 14.9
Reference number in the data dictionary, 14.3
Reporting results
  through the General Accounting
    Office, 59.0
  through the National Technical
    Information Service, 60.0
Response categories, description, 15.5
Response text described in the data
  dictionary, 14.12

Role of the sponsor, planning and
  monitoring, 51.0–55.0
Sample size, changes described in the
  documentation, 15.6
Sign, in a computational field, 27.5
Software, used to create the data file,
  12.0
Sponsor activities for monitoring the
  data project, 53.0
Standardization of codes, 29.0
Storage mode, description in the data
  dictionary, 14.8
Study number, coding, 26.0
Study overview, components, 1.0–5.0
Table of contents
  for the data items, 5.0
  for the documentation, 4.0
Tape labeling, 33.0, 37.0, 37.1
Title
  avoiding publication problems,
    36.0
  qualifying subtitle for the docu-
    mentation, 1.1
  writing a descriptive title, 1.2–1.2.3
Title page
  components, 1.0–1.7
  data file responsibility, 1.3, 1.3.1
  distributor statement, 1.6
  documentation responsibility
    statement, 1.7
  edition responsibility statement,
    1.7
  edition statement for the machine-
    readable file, 1.4.0, 1.4.1
  producer statement, 1.5
  writing a title, 1.1–1.2.3
Transfer of data
  American National Standard mag-
    netic tape labels, 33.0, 37.0
  description of the physical struc-
    ture, 32.0
  floating point storage, 27.1
  meeting user needs, 34.0–35.1
  writing data for, 31.0, 32.0
Unique identification number for a
  data file, 14.7
Universe definition, identified in the
  data dictionary, 14.9
User header label for the data file, 37.1
User support services, sponsor support for, 56.0

Variable. *See* Data item
Variable label
  in the data dictionary, 14.4
  unabbreviated in the data dic-
    tionary, 14.10
Variable name, short, 14.2
Variable name or number in the data
  dictionary, 14.2

References

American Library Association. *Anglo-American Cataloging Rules.* (2nd ed.). Chicago: American Library Association, 1979.

American National Standards Institute. *American National Standards for Writing Abstracts.* (ANSI Z39.14.1971), New York: American National Standards Institute, 1971.

Borko, H., and Bernier, L. *Abstracting Concepts and Methods.* New York: Academic Press, 1975.

David, M., Gates, W., and Miller, R. *Linkage and Retrieval of Microeconomic Data: A Strategy for Data Development and Use.* Lexington, Mass.: Heath, 1974.

Dodd, S. A. "Titles: The Emerging Priority in Bringing Bibliographical Control to Social Science Machine-Readable Data Files (MRDF)." *IASSIST Newsletter,* 1977, *1*(4), 11–18.

Dodd, S. A. "Bibliographical References for Numeric Social Science Data Files: Suggested Guidelines." *Journal of the American Society for Information Science,* 1979a, *30*(2), 77–82.

Dodd, S. A. *Notes to the MARC Subcommittee on Editions and Dates.* Chapel Hill, N.C.: Institute for Research in Social Science, 1979b.

Dodd, S. A. *Cataloguing Machine-Readable Data Files: An Interpretive Manual,* in press.

Duncan, J. W. "The Demand for Regional and Local-Area Statistics: Issues Concerning the National Response." *Statistical Reporter,* 1978, *78,*97–100.

Havelock, R. G. *Planning for Innovation through Dissemination and Utilization of Knowledge.* Ann Arbor: Center for Research on Utilization of Scientific Knowledge, Institute for Social Research, University of Michigan, 1969.

Hedrick, T., Boruch, R. F., and Ross, J. "On Ensuring the Availability of Evaluative Data for Secondary Analysis." *Policy Sciences,* 1978, *9*, 259–280.

Johnson, D. "File Documentation as a Key to the Appraisal of Machine-Readable Data Sets." Unpublished report, University of Wisconsin, Madison, 1977.

Lansing, J. B., and Morgan, J. N. *Economic Survey Methods.* Ann Arbor: Survey Research Center for the Institute for Social Research, University of Michigan, 1971.

Leinwand Associates. "File-Level Documentation Standard." Unpublished report, Federal Judicial Center, Washington, D.C., 1979a.

Leinwand Associates. "The Hierarchical Documentation Standard Project-Level Documentation." Unpublished report, National Institute of Education, Washington, D.C., 1979b.

Robbin, A. "Managing Information Access Through Documentation of the Data Base: Characterizing Social Science Data Base Text Documentation as a Minimal Information System." *SIGSOC Newsletter,* Fall/Winter 1975, *6*(2,3), 56–68.

Robbin, A. "The Data Archive Perspective on Machine-Readable Data for Secondary Analysis: Technical Standards for Text Documentation, Quality Data, and Improving Access to Information." Paper presented at the Alternative Designs Conference, National Institute of Education, Washington, D.C., October 30–31, 1978.

Robbin, A., "Understanding the Machine-Readable Numeric Record: Archival Challenges, with Some Comments on Appraisal Guidelines." *Midwest Archivist,* 1979, *4*(1).

Roistacher, R. C. "A General Consistency Check Procedure for Machine-Readable Data." *Sociological Methods and Research,* 1976, *4*(3), 301–320.

Roistacher, R. C. "The Data Interchange File: Progress toward Design and Implementation." Paper presented at 11th annual Conference on the Interface, Raleigh, N.C., 1978.

Roistacher, R. C., and others. *A Style Manual for Machine-Readable Data Files and Their Documentation.* Washington, D.C.: U.S. Department of Justice, 1980.

Schmandt, J. 'Scientific Research and Policy Analysis." *Science,* 1978, *201,* 869.

Settel, B. (Ed.) *Subject Description of Books: A Manual of Proceedings for Augmenting Subject Descriptions in Library Catalogues.* Syracuse, N.Y.: Syracuse University School of Information Studies, 1977.

Social Science Research Council, Committee on Evaluation Research. *Audits and Social Experiments.* New York: Social Science Research Council, 1978.

Subject Access Project. *Books Are for Use, Final Report of the Subject Access Project to the Council on Library Resources.* Syracuse, N.Y.: Syracuse University School of Information Studies, 1978.

U.S. Department of Commerce, Office of Federal Statistical Policy and Standards. *Statistical Policy Handbook.* Washington, D.C.: U.S. Government Printing Office, 1978.

U.S. Department of Commerce, Office of Federal Statistical Policy and Standards. "Federal Statistics, 1979." *Statistical Reporter,* February 1980, no. 80–85, 81–115.

Van Dusen, R. A., and Zill, N. (Eds.). *Basic Background Items for U.S. Household Surveys.* Washington, D.C.: Social Science Research Council, 1975.

Warwick, P., and Lininger, A. *The Sample Survey: Theory and Practice.* New York: McGraw-Hill, 1975.

Watts, H. "Microdata: Lessons from the SEO and the Graduate Work Incentive Experiment." *Annals of Economic and Social Measurement,* 1972, *1*(2), 185–191.

Zeisset, P. T. 'Some Views on Good Documentation." Paper presented at National Bureau of Economic Research Conference, New York, April 18–20, 1974.

9

Melvin R. Novick

Data Analysis
in the Absence
of Randomization

A recent conference in Washington, D.C. on ethical and legal dilemmas in social research prompted some thoughts on the effect of labeling in science and the law. The discussion led me to consider evidence in adversarial proceedings that involve allegations of discrimination in employee selection or other questions pertinent to applied

Note: This chapter is the second revised text of a paper read at the Northwestern University Conference on Solutions to Ethical and Legal Problems in Social Research, Washington, D.C., February 25, 1978, and distributed in the proceedings of that conference. The conference was supported by National Science Foundation Grant DAR-7820374. A first revised text was published in *Socialwissenschaftliche Annalen [Social Science Annals]*, Band 2, 1978, Secte 77–91 (Vienna: Physica-Verlag). I am indebted to William Buss of the College of Law of the University of Iowa for some brief comments on an early version of this paper but more generally for the rich experience I enjoyed collaborating with him on issues related to the case of the National Testing Organization, which in turn made my work on this paper possible.

social science. In turn, this topic leads us to consider the methodology for drawing inferences in situations in which data are acquired by means other than random sampling. These situations are typical in social science and economic research, but have been largely ignored in the standard statistical literature. The approach we offer is based on the ideas of Lindley and Novick (1981) and the earlier work of de Finetti (1974) and Zeisel (1968). We present some concrete examples that bear directly on the analysis and secondary analysis of data from non-randomized studies.

Consider Table 1. We are attempting to predict a performance or criterion score Y from a predictor variable x. For simplicity, we assume

Table 1. The Effects of Labeling on Prediction

$$\hat{Y} \times rx + (1 - r) M_Y \tag{1}$$

		Sex			
		S_1	S_2		
Ethnicity	E_1	480	440	460	
	E_2	560	520	540	
		520	480	500	Group Means

Predicted Values

	$r = .5$			$r = .8$			
x =	480	500	520	480	500	520	
E_1	470	480	490	476	492	508	460
E_2	510	520	530	492	508	524	540
S_1	500	510	520	488	504	520	520
S_2	480	490	500	480	496	512	480

I am most grateful to D. C. Baldus for comments on an earlier draft of this paper that helped me to articulate my position more carefully. Differences in our positions on issues discussed here remain at present, but the gap narrows as we each refine our thinking as a result of discussion. I have used Baldus and Cole (1977) as an example. In their more recent book (*Statistical Proof of Discrimination*, New York: McGraw-Hill, 1980), Baldus and Cole's analytic perspective is closer to my point of view. The area under discussion is not one in which any professional consensus exists, and I believe that my own position will need to be further refined.

that the predictor has been scaled so that it has the same mean and variance as the criterion. We can consider this problem to illustrate the prediction of on-the-job or in-college performance from some score on a psychological test. The purpose of the exercise is selection, the selection of those persons with the highest predicted performance score Y. M_Y denotes the mean performance level of the population in question, and r denotes the correlation between the predictor x and the criterion Y.

We can consider prediction for persons who have been cross-classified on the basis of sex (S_1,S_2) and ethnicity (E_1,E_2), and who thus may be considered members of one of nine partially overlapping groups. Consider the following notation: the total (T); the four marginal groups (E_1,E_2,S_1,S_2); and the four joint or within-cell groups, E_1S_1, E_1S_2, E_2S_1, and E_2S_2. A person who is E_1S_1 could also be classified T_1E_1, or S_1. We shall assume that the slope of the regression is constant in the four marginal classifications (E_1,E_2,S_1,S_2) and nonconstant in the four joint classifications $(E_1S_1,E_1S_2,E_2S_1,E_2S_2)$.

The effect of labeling on the predicted value of Y can be seen by noting that the predicted value Y is obtained as a weighted average of the obtained predictor score x and the mean value of Y in the designated population. For example, for those designated E_1, disregarding sex, with a correlation $r = .5$, an x value of 480 converts to a predicted value of 470; for a person labeled E_2, that same x value converts to a predicted value of 510 (see Table 1). The computations are $Y = (.5)(480) + (.5)(460) = 470$, and $Y = (.5)(480) + (.5)(540) = 510$. Had all the applicants been treated as a single group, each of the two applicants under consideration would have had the same predicted Y score, which would be different from the two values we just computed. Clearly, from the point of view of the applicant, it is helpful to be identified with a successful population. That is, it is better to be labeled an S_1 rather than an E_1, because of the higher group mean. Similarly, a person classified E_1 would prefer to be classified E_1S_1, and an E_1S_2 would prefer to be classified as an E_1.

As a second example, consider a person with a 480 from S_1 and another with a 500 from S_2. These predicted Y scores are 500 and 490 (see Table 1). We see that test score and predicted score are inverted. As a third example, suppose prediction in E_2 is better than in E_1, so that we have a correlation of $r = .8$ in E_2. Now consider a person with a 520 from E_1 and a 480 from E_2; the corresponding predicted scores are then 490 and 492. In this case, the person from E_1 is penalized both because of the lower mean value and the lower correlation in E_1. Cole (1973) has argued eloquently that the unfairness arising from lower predictability in some groups as opposed to others is a legitimate matter of societal concern. This phenomenon can be seen in Table 1, equation (1), which shows that the weight given M_Y depends on r. In situations such as this, correlation in the subpopulations, $E_1 S_1$, $E_1 S_2$, $E_2 S_1$, $E_2 S_2$, will typically be higher than in the combined populations $E_1 E_2 S_1 S_2$, and the correlation in the total population will tend to be still lower. We need not detail the problems of unfairness that such an analysis causes. However, in such situations a legitimate business or public policy purpose may be served by using the smallest subpopulation for prediction rather than, say, the total population, even if such a practice means giving advantage to some persons and disadvantage to others.

Equation (1) and its analogues pervade statistical theory from simple least squares, as described here, to the most complex forms of Bayesian structural models. It, therefore, deserves our microscopic attention. Equation (1) is primarily a normatve prescription, developed from mathematical assumptions, that tells us how we ought to make estimates. It also, in a gross way, describes how people intuitively do make estimates when unaided by statistical help. Consider M_Y to be the knowledge that a person has about the group whose label he has placed on an applicant. That value reflects background information, and the value it takes will depend on the label placed on the applicant and our background knowledge about persons with that label. Consider x to be the direct information about this specific person (other than his group identification) and take r to reflect the amount, relevance, and strength of the direct information x. If the direct information x is small, of marginal relevance, or weak, then r will be small—possibly very near zero—and the predicted value will be M_Y. If the direct information x is substantial, relevant, and strong, then r will be close to one and the predicted value will be near x. Each of us examining our own decision processes would, I think, find that this description accurately reflects, generally, the way in which we process data. Equation (1) simply tells us how to do the job more precisely and coherently.

An apparent way to solve the problem of labeling is not to use labels and always use the largest group of persons available for prediction. There are many reasons why this is unacceptable. It can, for example, happen under pathological circumstances that a correlation of .8 can be found in populations $E_1 S_1$ and $E_1 S_2$, but when these two populations are combined into E_1 the correlation drops to near zero. Except in situations in which sample sizes are very small, much better prediction is generally made using smaller rather than larger units. This often creates a conflict. An applicant, the potential selectee, may be disadvantaged by being identified with a group having a lower mean. Public or business interests, in contrast, may be best served when prediction is greatest, that is, within smaller subpopulations.

In summary then, several points should be made. We must consider an individual in the context of our understanding of the world. No judgment or decision can be rendered without consideration of background information. Even the most ancient and most accepted methods of statistical analysis employ such background information. All modern Bayesian methods use both background and direct observational information, usually in the form of a weighted average. The process by which that background information is included involves labeling, which may be thought of as the identification of an individual with an appropriate group or subgroup of persons. The choice of a label may be critical in the computation of the predicted value for a given person, and that value may be critical for his or her future prospects. Also, our knowledge of the population with which that person is identified may be critical. If our knowledge is incomplete or incorrect, improper disadvantage or advantage may accrue to persons so classified. We also note a potential conflict between the public policy or business interests of the selector, who seeks optimum prediction, and the interests of selectees, who may be penalized by certain labelings.

Simpson's Paradox

Let us consider an example developed by Lindley and Novick (1981) that defines a fairly typical scenario for the use of statistical arguments in a sociolegal setting. This example will, we hope, show conclusively that we cannot just use the biggest group available and thus avoid all labeling, even if we agree to subordinate public policy and business necessity. We must, if sensible inference is demanded, directly confront the labeling problem, as difficult as it may be.

Let us consider an example of prison parolees. Suppose it is proposed that all parolees be required to participate in a weekly training program. In order to evaluate the potential usefulness of such a program, a brief study is done using some available parolees, some of whom have and some of whom have not had this training. The effectiveness of the training is measured by recidivism rates. At the conclusion of the study the report contains the following three statements: (1) Overall, training results in a higher rate of recidivism as compared to no training. Thus, in the total group, training is undesirable. (2) For men, training results in a lower rate of recidivism than no training. Thus, for men, training is desirable. (3) For women, training also results in a lower recidivism rate than no training. Thus, for women, training is desirable. The logical conclusion of this study then is that all male parolees should receive this training and all female parolees should also, but that if the sex of the parolee should inadvertently be omitted from the parole report, then the parolee should not be assigned to training. This paradoxical result and the conditions that may cause it deserve our careful study, because these conditions in moderate degree are typical in social science and legal research.

Most persons, including some of the statistically sophisticated, respond to the set of three statements with the comment that such results are not possible. To see that these three statements can be jointly and simultaneously true, the reader need only refer to Table 2. From Table 2a, men and women combined, we find that with training the recidivism rate is 50 percent and without training it is 40 percent. The "clear" indication is that training is ineffective and that we ought not to use this training program with any person from this combined group. However, on examining Table 2b, in which men and women are treated separately, we find that for men the recidivism rate for those who receive training is 60 percent, while the percentage is 70 percent for those who do not. For women the corresponding percentages are 20 percent and 30 percent.

We see, of course, that we have a true paradox, since when the data in Table 2b are combined they give the total values found in Table 2a. We have here an apparent violation of the "sure-thing principle," which says that if A is better than B given C, and A is better than B given $\bar{C}$ (where $\bar{C}$ is the complement of C), then A is better than B overall. A demonstration that the sure-thing principle is not necessarily violated by these data is given by Lindley and Novick (1981), the source of this example. I should also point out that the problem is not one of sampling error. If you like, increase the number of observations in each category a millionfold. The outcome is the same.

Let me emphasize that these kinds of data do arise in practice. Fallacies in the interpretation of data occur when analysts do not understand the phenomenon in question here. Two important examples of such errors are the Lankershire milk experiments, in which researchers concluded that milk retarded children's growth, and the Westinghouse Learning Corporation study of Head Start, in which researchers concluded that compensatory education retarded educational development.

The paradox I have referred to is known as Simpson's paradox (Simpson, 1951), although it was known to Cohen and Nagel (1934) much earlier. Its origins thus come from the Vienna school of logical positivism. The general ideas to be discussed here (but not the paradox itself) have been treated by a few authors (see particularly Zeisel, 1968). The resolution of Simpson's paradox—with a full discussion of its implications for social research, including points that go beyond previous treatment—is offered by Lindley and Novick (1981). The theory

Table 2. Simpson's Paradox

2a. Men and Women Combined   Conclusion

	R	$\bar{R}$	
T	20	20	40
$\bar{T}$	16	24	40
	36	44	80

Treatment undesirable

2b. Men and Women

	Men R	$\bar{R}$			Women R	$\bar{R}$	
T	18	12	30	T	2	8	10
$\bar{T}$	7	3	10	$\bar{T}$	9	21	30
	25	15	40		11	29	40

Treatment desirable

2c. Males Alone

	Rural R	$\bar{R}$			Urban R	$\bar{R}$	
T	9	1	10	T	9	11	20
$\bar{T}$	6	1	7	$\bar{T}$	1	2	3
	15	2	17		10	13	23

Treatment undesirable

that unravels the paradox is complex and depends on ideas that ought to be, but are not yet, part of the body of standard statistical discussion. In brief, the resolution involves the scrutiny of the labels one attaches to people, to ensure that one uses only those labels that best classify a new person as exchangeable with persons in the classification, and the consideration of how to logically relate an inference for this next person to past data.

In the example in question, one might be able to resolve the issue by studying the nature of the process, by specifying some assumptions that I shall not make explicit here, and then perhaps by concluding that the labeling in Table 2b is appropriate and, therefore, recommending training for all persons, male, female, or unspecified. However, if we take these numbers out of this context and supply new labels relevant to a new context, the opposite conclusion might hold with these same data. In the present notation the control $\bar{T}$ would be preferred to the treatment T, as has been demonstrated in an example given by Lord (1968) and discussed in detail by Lindley and Novick (1981).

A simpler approach to the problem, which many statisticians recommend but which others reject, is to examine a drawn sample with respect to variables that might affect the inference to ensure that the sample is representative. In the parolee example, it should be noted that while there are forty men and forty women in the study, thirty men have been assigned to treatment and only ten women. Such an observation leads some statisticians to discard the sample as unrepresentative and start again, or to block on this value ex post facto. Neither of these strategies is permissible in classical Neyman-Pearson theory, and the second is strictly forbidden.

Let us consider another approach to the parolee problem: Suppose the data for males are further categorized by rural and urban environments, as in Table 2c. We note that for males and for both the rural and urban environments, the control $\bar{T}$ is preferred to the treatment T. If one found the same result for women, then surely one could argue that since $\bar{T}$ is preferred to T in every smallest category (RM, UM, RF, UF,) it should be preferred overall. The correctness of this argument depends on the legitimacy of several assumptions and cannot be determined merely by scrutinizing the numbers.

Assume for the moment that after analyzing the data in Table 2b, we convinced ourselves that the conclusion that T should be preferred to $\bar{T}$ was appropriate. How confident could we then be that this result would sustain further analysis? Surprisingly, in most social science research the answer is "not too confident." Generally, we would have no assurance that a clever investigator would not be able to find another variable, in this case the rural-urban dichotomy, that challenges our conclusion. Call it the Horatio factor, for there are indeed, as Hamlet says to Horatio, "more things in heaven and earth . . . than are dreamt of in your philosophy." One might be inclined to take a shifting burden-of-proof approach in legal proceedings, and that might be appropriate in some cases, but I shall suggest later that this principle may need some modification. Some statisticians will insist that if we randomly assign persons to T and $\bar{T}$ and insist on large samples, this paradox will not occur. This contention may be true if the sample is large and the number of relevant variables is not. The paradox arises because of some relationship between the characteristics of a person and the labeling T and $\bar{T}$. But we must remember that in most social science and legal studies, and certainly in the evaluation of trial evidence, random assignment is rare indeed. Furthermore, in some studies any labeling refers to nontreatment variables directly associated with the person, so that no random assignment is possible. Children are not randomly assigned at birth to ethnicity, socioeconomic status, or parental educational level. Because these variables are correlated, any study of the relationship between heredity and such environmental variables may well be unapproachable by current types of analysis. We will shortly consider an example in which random assignment to T and $\bar{T}$ was clearly not possible.

Labeling and Evidence

The general technique of identifying persons with particular groups and then attributing to these individuals characteristics of the group is pervasive in legal proceedings. Attorneys generally attempt to identify their witnesses with groups whose members can be characterized as honorable, honest, wise, experienced, and responsible, with the implication that, because they are members of such groups, their testimony is credible. Cross-examination in the English and American legal systems is often characterized by an overt or covert attempt to identify the witness with some less favorable group, or to characterize the group in a less favorable way. Such labeling is not at all unlike the argument made in the earlier regression example concerning which of four possible categorical labels should be used in making a prediction for an examinee, or the question of considering evidence concerning the mean value in the chosen category.

Let us consider some hypothetical and theoretical examples, with only modest regard as to what an American court might now permit, what it ought to permit, or whether the offering of such evidence represents good legal strategy. Each of these issues needs to be addressed, and they are certainly part of the agenda for future research. Consider identification testimony given for the prosecution by a police officer, who presumably would be identified as such. The defense, wishing to rebut this testimony, might present the fact that on previous occasions this officer made ten positive identifications, nine of which later proved to be false. Most American courts would admit this evidence, primarily because it is related directly to the person whose credibility is in question, although such evidence might not be admissible in all circumstances or in all jurisdictions.

Now suppose, instead, that the defense attempted to introduce evidence that the record of accurate identifications of all police officers (or perhaps all officers in the relevant locality) was bad or even corrupt, and therefore, to some extent, we ought to suspect the testimony of this particular officer. Statistical logic would deem this evidence admissible, since it is relevant to the mean value in the population of officers (M_Y earlier) with which this particular officer is identified. American courts, however, now seem to be less likely to admit this testimony, though apparently admissibility is not necessarily ruled out. I am not arguing that this kind of evidence should necessarily be admissible, but questioning whether in some circumstances it should be. Difficulties arise both in admitting and failing to admit such evidence. We are being inconsistent if we admit regression analysis evidence that involves labeling and background information and do not admit background evidence in this situation. Incidentally, if such evidence were admissible, statistical theory would suggest that the prosecution in rebuttal should present more evidence about the particular officer, in effect increasing the value r in Table 1.

Consider now a lighthearted example, one which I hope will cause no offense. At trial the general moral character of the defendant sometimes becomes a central issue and the defense is able to introduce character evidence. Suppose one of the specifics of concern is the defendant's typical state of sobriety, and on this point, the defense establishes that the defendant is a regular churchgoer. Question: Might the prosecution then enter as evidence statistics that show conclusively that alcoholism is a much greater problem among churchgoers than nonchurchgoers? Probably not, but statistical theory would suggest that such evidence is relevant. Let me say that I am not unaware that this might be a foolish practical strategy for any prosecutor, but that is not the issue.

Actually, the statistic itself might evoke a variety of reactions. One former missionary, in response to this hypothetical example, was pleased by the statistic, saying that it indicated that the church was successful in reaching those persons who needed help. Other people might respond by arguing that persons ought not to be stigmatized because of their identification with some group. Of course, identification as a churchgoer has not generally been considered to be stigmatizing, but then perhaps identification as a nonchurchgoer also ought not to be, and perhaps it may be useful and appropriate in some situations to introduce some statistical evidence for this issue. The question is, ought it not be permissible to introduce evidence to correct what we know to be the erroneous prior beliefs of jurors, or should we be restricted only to the strategy of challenging such persons during jury selection? And indeed, can a juror be challenged for cause because his beliefs on important background issues are shown to be erroneous?

One major reason for not admitting background information is that it may, in some instances, tend to "inflame" a jury. That point is well taken. When we suspect that jurors will not accurately process information, it might, in some circumstances, be proper to disallow such evidence. The resolution to this problem is not simple, as this discussion bears out. One can only suggest tentatively that when such evidence seems important it may be necessary to use a "blue ribbon" panel that can process the information more accurately. This procedure, however, runs counter to Anglo-American tradition. An alternative is to have a court-appointed expert witness interpret data for the lay jury.

Quantitative Proof of Intentional Discrimination

Baldus and Cole (1977) offer a splendid and useful discussion of methodological and legal issues that arise from the use of quantitative methods to prove intentional discrimination against racial or ethnic minority groups. Almost as an afterthought, they describe a case involving an allegation of discrimination against blacks in apartment rentals.

> In *U.S.* vs. *Youritan Construction* (1973), fourteen pairs of black and white testers inquired about the availability of housing in defendants' apartments. The black and white testers were treated identically seven times (five yes and two no) and differently seven times (black favored once, 14 percent; white favored six times, 86 percent). The white tester therefore was preferred 36 percentage points (86 percent – 50 percent) more frequently than would be expected in an unbiased selection process. The weight of this evidence is very simply evaluated in probability terms. The chance of having the minority member accepted by a fair landlord in at least six out of seven differentially treated pairs is precisely the probability of obtaining "heads" at least six times out of seven tosses of a fair coin—namely, 8/128 or .0625. Such an occurrence is thus relatively rare (although it does not quite meet the commonly applied standard of less than once in 20 times or .05) [Baldus and Cole, 1977, p. 83].

Contrary to the statement in the middle of this paragraph, I would contend that the weight of evidence is *not* "very simply evaluated in probability terms," even when the background discussion preceding this paragraph is considered. It is, in fact, extremely difficult to draw any inference from the given data. Let me now alternate in the role of expert witness for Youritan Construction and for the United States and demonstrate how such data ought to be analyzed. I will not refer to the details of the case in question or, in the first instance, to the background discussion that preceded the cited material. My response is limited to the "case" as presented in the quoted paragraph, and I fictionalize as necessary to make my point.

First, in response to the material in the paragraph, one could argue that because there is a stable difference in acceptance rates, given the limited description of the "experiment" and the marginal character of the statistical results, no statistical analysis of this kind could prove anything other than adverse effect. We are not told precisely how the fourteen pairs of black and white testers were formed, only that they were carefully matched. Certainly if they were chosen randomly, then the only conclusion that could be made is that the black applicants seemed less desirable to the landlords than did the white applicants. Moreover, absolutely no evidence is presented here to suggest that the condition of blackness had anything to do with this judgment. No independent evidence of *intentionality* is provided. Granted, there are situations in which the statistics alone might lead to a tentative inference of intentionality; for example, if there have been no black jurors in twenty years in a county in which the population is 25 percent black. The general point is that there might be other variables associated with blackness that were the basis of the disparity. (In the real *Youritan* case the amount of evidence that blackness was the operative variable was enormous.)

Changing clients now, I report for the U.S. government that the paragraph tells us that the fourteen pairs were carefully matched on all important variables, except racial status, that might affect desirability as a tenant. These variables might have included educational level, income, numbers and ages of children, ownership of pets, and the like. The government's case immediately becomes much stronger, but it certainly should not be considered convincing in itself. Now again as consultant for Youritan, I would request an enumeration of these variables and the status of each applicant on each of these variables in order to verify that the matching was, in fact, adequate. Even small differences in favor of whites would be important, given the marginal character of the statistical analysis. But, for present purposes, let us stipulate that the matching was flawless on the indicated variables, and let us further stipulate that professional judgment would provide a consensus that these variables are legitimate indicants of desirability of tenancy and that a validation study would confirm this fact.

Given this much more strongly developed case by the plaintiff, however, Youritan Construction's statistical and legal position is by no means hopeless. To understand their next argument, consider the mathematically identical problem of determining whether or not there is a significant difference in the height of students at two universities, the University of Iowa (UI) and Iowa State University (ISU). The researchers draw a sample from each of fourteen matched departments in the two universities and a significant difference in favor of UI is found. On closer analysis, however, they observe that in the UI sample there are ten males and four females, while in the ISU sample there are four males and ten females. This is, of course, a most unlucky sample because actually there is a higher proportion of females at UI that at ISU. However, once the researchers discover the abnormality of this sample, they can compute a new test of significance after blocking on sex. When this is done, it is concluded that the average height of students at ISU is significantly greater than at UI. The important point here is that height and sex are correlated, but the initial analysis did not take this labeling into account. The researchers failed to recognize this Horatio factor and hence drew an incorrect conclusion.

Similarly, even if the United States presents evidence that the pairs were carefully matched on the basis of important variables, the consultant for Youritan can examine the sample to attempt to find a Horatio factor, a variable related to tenant desirability that has lower levels on average for blacks in the sample pairs. With only fourteen pairs, one is likely to find such a variable, though in fact the finding may be only a statistical aberration due to the screening of a large number of variables and selecting one that fits Youritan's needs. Make no mistake, the issue of intentionality raised in this case will not be settled with fourteen pairs of observations, nor indeed would the lesser allegation of adverse effect.

It has been suggested to me privately that the case for the United States can be strengthened even more if a statement can be entered into the record to the effect that the lessor selected the prospective tenants only with the aid of an application form and without the benefit of an interview and, further, if it is recorded that the racial status was entered randomly so that any correlation between ethnicity and the relevant selection variables arises from sampling variation. Indeed, at this point, the case for the United States would become exceptionally strong, and perhaps in conjunction with some independent testimony it might be overpowering. That experiment, of course, would be much more difficult to conduct.

However, even at this point there may be a further weakness in the analysis as presented by Baldus and Cole, and it is worth noting because it represents a very common but questionable strategy. The further weakness occurs because of the author's restriction in the statistical analysis to just those seven cases in which some differential treatment of blacks and whites occurred. But what of the seven cases in which identical treatment was found? The authors argue: "Pairs in which both applicants were accepted or both rejected could reflect a policy of equal treatment on the part of the landlord. On the other hand, they could indicate merely that the matched applicants in these pairs were so clearly attractive or unattractive that the landlord had essentially no other choice. Therefore, the only portion of the evidence that speaks unequivocally to the fairness of the landlord's policy is the group of pairs in which the candidates were treated differently" (Baldus and Cole, 1973, p. 83). I hope that most persons, on reflection, would find that argument unconvincing.

The counterargument is made by noting the large proportion of cases (50 percent) in which treatment was identical and the smallness of the sample. While the evidence in the seven cases of identical treatment may not be unequivocal, it does speak directly to the defendant's case and therefore cannot be ignored because a statistician is unable to easily produce an appropriate analysis. If there were 1,414 cases, instead of 14, and in 1,407 of these cases there was no difference in treatment, surely no attention would then be paid to the statistical analysis of just 7 cases. Detailed consultation with Youritan is necessary before one can provide any defensible analysis based on all fourteen cases to determine how much weight these other seven pairs should have. But one can speculate that any defensible analysis would reduce the force of evidence against Youritan. It is hard to say whether the strengthened case for Youritan that has been presented here fatally weakens the case for the United States. I suspect that the decision would depend largely on the prior beliefs that jurors brought to this trial. The value of r in this analysis is very small, and so the weight given to the value x from the seven (or fourteen) observations will be small. Thus the final judgment will depend heavily on the prior judgment that jurors bring to bear or, preferably, on other nonstatistical evidence offered by the plaintiff.

Let us now turn to a very similar case, described by Buss and Novick (1980), that might someday come to trial. A small firm, the National Testing Organization (NTO) screened several thousand answer sheets and looked for consistency of high-low difference of subscores on a six-part examination. Analysts identified twenty-six students, each having large differences in subtest scores, primarily between sections A and F. Using a computer, they compared the responses on each possible pair of these twenty-six examinees on each of the sections, a total of 1,650 comparisons. The pairwise statistical comparisons were made even though examinees took the test at a wide variety of locations. A significance test using a 1/10,000 pairwise significance level based on identical incorrect responses was used. Twenty-one significant differences were found among eleven examinees and the reports of scores of these examinees were withheld because these responses were not considered independent and, therefore, possibly not reflective of the true ability of the examinees.

There are many issues on which the NTO analysis can be criticized, three of which are central to our discussion. First, there is the clear multiple-comparison or selection problem, as Tribe (1971) calls it. If you flip a thousand coins ten times each, you can expect one to come up heads all ten times. In the NTO example, the pairwise significance level of .0001 bears no resemblance to the experimentwise value.

The multiple-comparison problem, which can be handled with some care, is not one of the more difficult problems in this case—except to the extent that NTO ignored it. A more difficult problem is the completeness of the evidence. NTO considered only jointly incorrect responses as evidence suggesting nonindependence of response. NTO, however, did not consider the number of items for which one examinee gave a correct response and the other an incorrect response. Surely a large number of such items would be evidence of independence and, in fairness, such evidence cannot be ignored. In fact, for at least two examinees, the number of such items was large.

There is a fundamental difference between standard applications of statistical methods and those involving persons in a legal context. If we are unfair in evaluating a fertilizer because we ignore some evidence, this neglect will be bad for us and our clients, but that is a risk we have chosen to take. But if we are unfair in a legal proceeding, another party, who has not chosen to accept such a risk, may be harmed. There is thus, I believe, an ethical imperative for a statisticican to be sure that all evidence is considered in such cases. In comparing heights in Iowa, the sex of the students was important evidence. If funding of the academic programs were dependent on the average height of students, it would be incorrect to argue that blocking on sex was unnecessary because in the long run everything would even itself out. In *Youritan* the number of like treatments was important evidence, and in the NTO case the number of items on which a pair of examinees obtained different scores was equally important. There is always the possibility that the addition of one more factor will overturn the entire analysis, and such factors should not be ignored.

Now I come to the final problem in the NTO case and the final problem to be discussed. As noted, some of the paired examinees actually took the examination at different sites, but this did not discourage NTO from making these comparisons of answer sheets. Presumably, the allegation of testing irregularity did not involve copying or other similar collusion. Actually, NTO did not carefully specify what might have happened, though there was some discussion that forms for one or two of the sections might have been compromised or that some tutoring firm had obtained unauthorized access to the examinations, and without knowledge of the examinees, used these forms in coaching.

If we take the possibility of coaching from illegally obtained exams as an alternative hypothesis, the statistical test would then be addressed to the null hypothesis of experimental independence of response of the examinees and, on rejection, the improper tutoring alternative might be accepted. But other secondary alternative hypotheses need to be ruled out before we can accept the hypothesis about tainted tutoring. For example, it would be necessary to demonstrate that the observed patterns of test scores did not occur because the students studied together, or they adopted a common test-taking strategy, or they jointly studied legitimately available items from previous tests in a common way. The possibility of ruling out all such alternative hypotheses is slim. Indeed, it is difficult to understand what evidence would distinguish between these hypotheses and that suggesting tainted tutoring. In the cited case, NTO simply stated that they considered and rejected all such hypotheses. The fundamental point is that in social research, as opposed to agricultural research, there are typically many competing alternative hypotheses to be considered once the null hypothesis is rejected. To accept just one of these without eliminating all others is unacceptable in science and, it is to be hoped, in law. It is for this reason that the case for the United States in *Youritan* is complex and not simple.

Now, as to the question of burden of proof in the NTO case. Perhaps, if the statistical analysis were otherwise flawless, one might suggest taking a shifting burden-of-proof approach. This stance might, however, be troublesome, considering the enormous financial burden that it would place on an examinee. Perhaps it is less of a problem in *Youritan*, but I wonder how much less.

Conclusion and Proposal

Despite the cataloguing of difficulties of statistical analysis in the law, one can be optimistic about such uses of statistics. But we must proceed carefully to preserve our credibility. There will surely be many situations in which we think that the evidence can be evaluated simply. But I doubt if evaluation will ever truly be a simple procedure. The difficulties outlined in this chapter apply in all but a few special cases. In cases such as *Youritan*, there is only a relatively artificial way of randomly assigning persons to race, and much in the way of realism is then lost. Still, this approach may be the only acceptable one in such situations. Thus, the question of introducing evidence through additional labelings will always be a crucial element, as will be the appropriateness of various possible labels.

Difficulties also arise in developing and presenting complex statistical analyses in adversarial proceedings before a lay jury. Perhaps when we recognize just how useful the careful probabilistic treatment of evidence can be, we will be prepared to provide the appropriate mechanism for its presentation. Perhaps, more to our central point, we must recognize that statistical analysis, in the context of evaluation, involves much more than textbook tests of hypotheses. The hypothetical debate in *Youritan* and the real debate in the NTO case represent more realistic scenarios.

We see that classical statistical methods are generally of little help in social science work. Random samples are not generally available. Substantial background information generally is available, and sample information is seldom overpowering. Furthermore, systems are complex rather than simple, so that the presence of Horatio factors can generally be anticipated. Thus post-hoc blocking seems to be a necessity, although it is not permissible in classical statistics. The inescapable conclusion must be that classical statistical methods must be abandoned. Fortunately, they can be replaced by a more helpful and coherent system, namely, Bayesian statistics.

The Bayesian system of statistical inference provides the only coherent system of inference. Background information can be incorporated in the analysis and blocking is always permissible, indeed, is often demanded. Finally, random sampling is not required. This last statement requires some elaboration. In Bayesian statistics the random sampling assumption can be replaced by a simpler assumption. But before we introduce this assumption, a brief review may be useful. In Bayesian inference all statements are normative and conditional. Given a stated model, a stated prior distribution, and sample data, a posterior distribution can be derived that tells what the investigator ought to believe about the unknown variables (parameters).

Part of the prior conditional statement must be a judgment about the sampled units with respect to the variable being measured. Specifically, it must be assumed that the investigators believe that the individual experimental units are exchangeable. They must have no reason for believing that one unit will yield a higher observed value than another. The important point is that this assumption is the only one analysts need make. They do not need to assume random sampling, and indeed random sampling is not an adequate assumption in the absence of exchangeability.

Consider the second part of that assertion. Formally, Bayes' theorem can be carried out a priori, under the assumption of random sampling. But if the data gathering yields differing values on related concommitant variables, then exchangeability will not be preserved and post-hoc blocking or covariation on these variables will be required by the conditional logic of Bayesian inference. In the Iowa case, the observed difference in the sex variable *cannot* be ignored. In classical analysis it must be ignored.

Now I return to the first part of my assertion, namely, that the investigator does not require an assumption of random sampling. In the context of typical applications of Bayesian inference, the assumption of exchangeability implies that in formal analysis the sample has the mathematical structure of a random sample and that the use of Bayes' theorem in its usual form is applicable. However, again, since exchangeability is the more primitive concept, it follows that it must be satisfied, as I have indicated.

We have now had more than half a century of formal statistical inference based on a system whose assumptions are necessarily and regularly violated in application. The adoption of the Bayesian approach relieves us of the discomfort associated with an incoherent and inapplicable system. A small price must be paid. We must learn to think carefully about all available information and not just the planned observations at hand. We must also learn to state our hypotheses and our conclusions more carefully. Significant results are possible, but the classical test of a point hypothesis against an unspecified alternative will never yield anything of significance. The social sciences have a right to expect more from the statistical profession.

References

Baldus, D.C, and Cole, J. W. L. "Quantitative Proof of Intentional Discrimination." *Evaluation Quarterly*, 1977, *1*, 53–85.

Buss, W. C., and Novick, M. R. "The Detection of Cheating on Standardized Tests: Statistical Analysis and Legal Rights." *Journal of Law and Education*, 1980, *9*, 1–64.

Cohen, M. R., and Nagel, E. *An Introduction to Logic and Scientific Method.* London: Routledge & Kegan Paul, 1934.

Cole, N. S. "Bias in Selection." *Journal of Educational Measurement*, 1973, *10*, 237–255.

de Finetti, F. *Theory of Probability.* London: Wiley, 1974.

Lindley, D. V., and Novick, M. R. "The Role of Exchangeability in Inference." *Annals of Statistics*, 1981, *9*, 45–58.

Lord, F. M. "An Analysis of the Verbal Scholastic Aptitude Test Using Birnbaum's Three-Parameter Logistic Model." *Educational and Psychological Measurement*, 1968, *28*, 989–1020.

Simpson, E. H. "The Interpretation of Interaction in Contingency Tables." *Journal of the Royal Statistical Society*, Series B, 1951, *13*, 238–241.

Tribe, L. H. "Trial by Mathematics: Precision and Ritual in the Legal Process." *Harvard Law Review*, 1971, *84*, 1329–1393.

U.S. v. Youritan Construction Company, 370 F.Supp. 643 (1973).

Zeisel, H. *Say It with Figures*. New York: Harper & Row, 1968.

10

David M. Rindskopf

Structural Equation Models in Analysis of Nonexperimental Data

In evaluation research, the randomized experiment provides the closest approximation to unbiased estimation of the effects of a program or treatment. Unfortunately, good randomized experiments, while they are often feasible (Boruch, 1975), are seldom attempted. Hence the evaluator usually must analyze data from groups of people who were not equivalent at the start of the experimental program. The problem is to find an analytic method that adequately adjusts for these preexist-

Note: Thanks go to Jay Magidson, Eva Rezmovic, Jerry Ross, Leroy Wolins, and Donald T. Campbell for providing comments on the first draft of this chapter. Preparation of this chapter was supported by grants from the National Institute of Education (NIE-C-74-0115) and from the National Institute of Mental Health (5T22MH00180).

ing differences, so that any remaining differences can be attributed to the program.

Some methods that have been advocated in the past, such as matching on pretest scores and analysis of covariance (ANCOVA), will often underadjust because they compensate only for the measured differences between people, not for true score (underlying) differences (Campbell and Boruch, 1975). Two of the most frequent reasons that these corrections are generally inadequate are (1) observed variables only measure some of the traits on which the groups differ (that is, specification error) and (2) observed variables are generally imperfect measures of the underlying traits (that is, measured error). For more detailed discussions of these errors, see Campbell and Boruch (1975), Campbell and Erlebacher (1970), Rubin (1974), and Wolins (1967). There are nonexperimental designs in which ANCOVA will provide unbiased estimates in spite of errors in the covariate; for example, when subjects are assigned to groups on the basis of the observed covariate—the regression discontinuity design. These conditions, however, seldom occur in field research.

We have noted that biases can occur in estimates of treatment effects because of omitted variables and errors of measurement. Under certain circumstances we can adjust for these problems by using techiques derived from the theory of structural equation models. This approach involves the following steps:

1. Construct one or more models of how underlying factors influence one another (structural model), and of how the observed variables are related to the underlying factors (measurement models). The entire analytic model is essentially a combination of path analysis (for the structural model) and factor analysis (for the measurement model).
2. Find out whether there are enough observed variables to solve all of the equations that those models generate (identification problem).
3. Solve the equations using a computer program such as LISREL.
4. Interpret the results. Does the overall model fit? What do each of the parameter estimates in the solution mean?
5. If none of the models tested fits the data adequately, construct different or more refined models or gather additional data, and then repeat the process.

Those familiar with factor analysis procedures will note that both exploratory and confirmatory procedures are involved in the use of structural equation models. The procedure is exploratory in that several different models are ordinarily tested and promising new ones refined until a reasonable fit is obtained. The procedure is confirmatory in that the researcher must have at least one explicit model showing how the variables are related to each other.

The following basic instructions in the use of structural equation models enable the reader to write a structural model, use that model to generate structural equations, and interpret the results of two different kinds of analyses using the methods of structural equation models to analyze nonexperimental data. For the sake of clarity, we use simplified models for our demonstrations. Readers unfamiliar with matrix representations of systems of equations and matrix multiplication may wish to consult Kerlinger and Pedhazur (1973) on path analysis, Long (1976), and Duncan (1975). The reader who is more statistically sophisticated may want to read some of the original work in the area by Bock and Bargman (1966), Bentler (1976), and Jöreskog and Sörbom (1979). Jöreskog's formulation of structural models and the notation he uses are followed in this chapter because Jöreskog and Sörbom (1976, 1978) have written several computer programs for the analyses described here. (These programs are available from International Educational Services, 1525 East 53rd Street, Suite 829, Chicago, Ill. 60615. Some of Jöreskog's earlier programs are available through the Educational Testing Service, Princeton, N.J. 08540.)

General Data Analytic Strategies Using Structural Models

The first step in a structural models approach is to generate all plausible models of how the variables could be structured; that is, which variables influence which other variables. When these are tested, either no model will fit the data, or exactly one model will fit, or more than one model will fit. If no model fits, then either the models or the assumptions for the analysis are incorrect. If one model fits, the next step is to examine individual parameter estimates in that model. But if more than one model fits the data, a search should be made for auxiliary data which would discriminate between them. It may be the case, for example, that two models will fit the data, the results from one indicating that the program had a positive effect, while the results from the other indicate a negative effect. One may need to collect additional data to resolve these inconsistencies.

Writing Structural Models. We start with a simple example that demonstrates the rules for writing the structural model—the model that relates the underlying variables to one another. Underlying variables fall into two classes: those assumed to have no other causes within the system of variables and those that are caused by other variables within the system. A variable that has no other causes within the system (and therefore must have all its causes outside the system) is called an *exogenous variable,* or an *independent variable.* Certain variables may be specified as exogenous because the factors influencing them have not been measured, and others may be specified as exogenous because their causal relations are irrelevant for determining the effects of interest in a particular study. A variable whose causes are other variables within the system is called an *endogenous variable,* or a *dependent variable.* Our primary interest in using structural equation models is to explain the variation in each endogenous factor in terms of variation in other factors. We use ξ to represent exogenous factors and η to represent the endogenous factors. If, as is usually the case, there is more than one independent or dependent factor, subscripts are used.

First, consider a case in which there are two independent and two dependent underlying factors, such as verbal and mathematical ability measured in 1975 and again in 1976 for the same group of people. Let ξ_1 represent mathematical ability in 1975, ξ_2 represent the number of hours of tutoring in mathematics received in 1975, η_1 represent mathematical ability in 1976, and η_2 represent the number of hours in tutoring in mathematics received in 1976. Figure 1 presents a diagram of a structural model for the four factors. In such diagrams, underlying (unobserved) factors are represented by circles, and observed variables by squares. If one factor is assumed to have a direct effect on another, this effect is represented by a straight line connecting them and an arrowhead to show the assumed direction of causation. Inde-

Figure 1. A Simple Structural Model

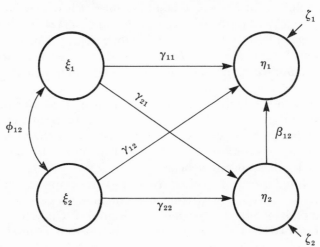

pendent factors that are correlated are represented by curved lines with a double arrowhead; this notation indicates that the direction of causation cannot be tested within the framework of this model. Note that independent factors are connected to each other only with curved lines and have no straight lines headed into them.

The arrows in Figure 1 show that tutoring in 1975 and achievement in mathematics in 1975 are assumed to be correlated (whether the correlation is positive or negative is not specified); that tutoring in 1976 is determined both by achievement in 1975 and tutoring in 1975; and that achievement in 1976 is determined by achievement in 1975, tutoring in 1975, and tutoring in 1976. These relationships are labeled as follows:

ϕ_{ij} denotes covariation between ξ_i and ξ_j and is represented by a curved arrow from one ξ to another.

γ_{ji} denotes a causal influence of an independent factor ξ_i on a dependent factor η_j.

β_{ji} denotes a causal influence of one dependent factor η_i on another, η_j.

The subscripts denote the termination point (effect) and origin (cause), in that order. For example, γ_{21} denotes the influence of ξ_1 on η_2. β_{12} denotes the influence of η_2 on η_1. Note that since ϕ denotes covariance, $\phi_{ij} = \phi_{ji}$; that is, the order of the subscripts on ϕ is irrelevant.

Finally, ζ represents the influence on the dependent factors of all factors other than the ones we have measured. Thus ζ represents what is commonly called the specification error, or error in equations, or omitted variables. The inclusion of these factors in the model, however, does not mean that we no longer have to worry about omitted factors: It means only that we can account for omitted factors that are uncorrelated with the independent factors. Omitted factors that are correlated with the independent factors still can present problems. The usual way to deal with such problems is to ignore them; a better, but still imperfect, way to proceed is to perform a sensitivity analysis (see Land and Felson, 1978; Rindskopf, 1978).

Rules for Writing Structural Equations. Once the model is diagrammed, the equations implicit in the model are easily obtained. There will be one equation for each dependent factor η_i. The righthand side of each equation consists of a term for each arrow going to the dependent factor. The term is computed by multiplying the source (either a ξ or an η) by the coefficient labeling the arrow. If the coefficient is not explicit, it is assigned the value 1. These terms are then summed, that is, the model is additive. From the structural model in Figure 1, we generate the following equations:

$$\eta_1 = \beta_{12}\, \eta_2 + \gamma_{11}\, \xi_1 + \gamma_{12}\, \xi_2 + \zeta_1$$

$$\eta_2 = \qquad\quad \gamma_{21}\, \xi_1 + \gamma_{22}\, \xi_2 + \zeta_2$$

These equations can be rearranged in order to expose the matrix formulation of the model. In order to do this, we subtract terms so that all parts involving dependent factors are on the left side, and all terms involving either independent factors or errors are on the right side. Note the implied zeros and ones as coefficients, which we use in the matrix representation.

$$1 \cdot \eta_1 - \beta_{12}\, \eta_2 = \gamma_{11}\, \xi_1 + \gamma_{12}\, \xi_2 + \zeta_1$$

$$0 \cdot \eta_1 + 1 \cdot \eta_2 = \gamma_{21}\, \xi_1 + \gamma_{22}\, \xi_2 + \zeta_2$$

The matrix formulation of this system of equations is as follows, with the name of each matrix written underneath:

$$\begin{bmatrix} 1 & -\beta_{12} \\ 0 & 1 \end{bmatrix} \begin{bmatrix} \eta_1 \\ \eta_2 \end{bmatrix} = \begin{bmatrix} \gamma_{11} & \gamma_{12} \\ \gamma_{21} & \gamma_{22} \end{bmatrix} \begin{bmatrix} \xi_1 \\ \xi_2 \end{bmatrix} + \begin{bmatrix} \zeta_1 \\ \zeta_2 \end{bmatrix}$$

$$\quad\ \ B \qquad\quad \eta \qquad\quad \Gamma \qquad\ \xi \qquad\ \zeta$$

The matrix equation representing the structural model is thus $B\eta = \Gamma\xi + \zeta$. To interpret these equations, remember that the ξ, η, and ζ are matrices of variables; that is, they represent measures on which each individual has a score. However, the B and Γ matrices contain parameters, or constants, that are the same for all people. The equations indicate the combination of scores on the dependent variables (factors) that are predicted for a person with a certain pattern of scores on the independent variables (factors); that is, the structural equations are simply regression equations.

Specifying the Measurement Models. Measurement models relate the observed variables to the underlying factors; one measurement model is for dependent variables, the other for independent variables. In diagrams of a measurement model, an arrow from a circle to a square indicates that the variable represented by the square measures to some extent the underlying variable represented by the circle. To represent the error of measurement in a variable, ϵ designates error in measurement in the dependent variable, and δ designates error of measurement in the independent variable. Readers familiar with multivariate analysis will recognize this as a factor analysis model.

To exemplify how a measurement model is used to generate equations, let us consider the model in Figure 2. We have two measures

Figure 2. A Simple Measurement Model

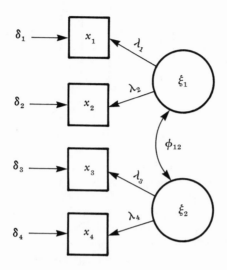

of each underlying independent variable: x_1 is the score on one mathematics test, x_2 is the score on another mathematics test, x_3 is the number of hours of mathematics tutoring as estimated by the teacher's memory, and x_4 is the number of hours of mathematics tutoring as estimated by the student's memory. In other words, we have two measures of mathematics ability, and two measures of the amount of tutoring in mathematics. We can use the measurement model to construct a set of measurement equations, just as we did with the structural model. There is one equation for each observed variable, which shows how that variable relates to the underlying variables. For our example, we have the following equations:

$$x_1 = \lambda_1 \, \xi_1 + 0 \cdot \xi_2 + \delta_1$$

$$x_2 = \lambda_2 \, \xi_1 + 0 \cdot \xi_2 + \delta_2$$

$$x_3 = 0 \cdot \xi_1 + \lambda_3 \xi_2 + \delta_3$$

$$x_4 = 0 \cdot \xi_1 + \lambda_4 \xi_2 + \delta_4$$

As before, the terms with zero coefficients are included so that the matrix formulation is clear. The matrix formulation is simply the factor analysis model:

$$
\begin{bmatrix} x_1 \\ x_2 \\ x_3 \\ x_4 \end{bmatrix} = \begin{bmatrix} \lambda_1 & 0 \\ \lambda_2 & 0 \\ 0 & \lambda_3 \\ 0 & \lambda_4 \end{bmatrix} \begin{bmatrix} \xi_1 \\ \xi_2 \end{bmatrix} + \begin{bmatrix} \delta_1 \\ \delta_2 \\ \delta_3 \\ \delta_4 \end{bmatrix}
$$

$$
x \quad = \quad \Lambda \qquad \xi \quad + \quad \delta
$$

This equation implies that each observed variable is a linear combination of unobserved variables, plus some error of measurement. The factor analysis model is just like the model for multivariate linear regression, except that the predictors' are unobserved variables. The elements of Λ are called *factor loadings*, or simply *loadings*.

The measurement model for the dependent variables is constructed in the same way, except that y's are used to denote observed dependent variables, and ϵ's are used for error terms. Also, in order to prevent confusion about the Λ's, they are subscripted: Λ_x refers to the independent variables, and Λ_y refers to the dependent variables. Thus, the two measurement models in matrix form are: $y = \Lambda_y \eta + \epsilon$, for dependent variables; and $x = \Lambda_x \xi + \delta$, for independent variables.

The Full Model and Its Representation. There are four matrices in the full model that have not yet been specified; these are the variance-covariance matrices of the errors in the observed dependent and independent variables, and the variance-covariance matrices of underlying independent variables and omitted variables. For most simple applications, the elements in ζ are considered to be either zero or uncorrelated; thus Ψ, their variance-covariance matrix, is either a null matrix (all zeros) or a diagonal matrix (all off-diagonal elements are zero). In general, Φ has variances of underlying independent variables (ξ's) in the diagonal and their covariances as off-diagonal elements. If the errors among the observed variables are assumed to be uncorrelated (as they usually are), then Θ_δ and Θ_ϵ, their error variance-covariance matrices, are diagonal. Table 1 summarizes the contents of each part of the structural and measurement models, listing each matrix, its size (in parentheses), and its description. There are n underlying independent variables, m underlying dependent variables, q observed independent variables, and p observed dependent variables.

Identification of the Model. Up to this point, we have assumed that there are sufficient data to test whatever model is developed. *Sufficient data* refers not to the sample size but to the number of observed variances, covariances, and (for some models) means. These factors determine whether the parameters in the model can be estimated. (We

Table 1. Components of the Structural Models

Matrix	Size	Description
ξ	$(n \times 1)$	Underlying independent variables
η	$(m \times 1)$	Underlying dependent variables
Γ	$(m \times n)$	Regression coefficients relating η to ξ
B	$(m \times m)$	Parameters for the structure of η
ζ	$(m \times 1)$	Other (unmeasured) factors influencing underlying dependent variables
Ψ	$(m \times m)$	Variance-covariance matrix of ζ
Φ	$(n \times n)$	Variance-covariance matrix of ξ
Λ_y	$(p \times m)$	Regression coefficients relating factors to observed dependent variables
Λ_x	$(q \times n)$	Regression coefficients relating factors to observed independent variables
Θ_δ	$(q \times q)$	Error variance-covariance matrix of observed independent variables
Θ_ϵ	$(p \times p)$	Error variance-covariance matrix of observed dependent variables

discuss more fully the importance of sample size later in this chapter.) Unfortunately, the complexity of models often exceeds the ability of experimenters to gather data. Researchers can adopt the following general stratgey: (1) Choose the models of interest, (2) determine the kind and amount of data necessary to test each model, (3) collect the appropriate data or simplify the models to fit the available data. Secondary analysts must usually adapt their models to the data, while researchers who are collecting data can often tailor their data collection to meet the specification of their models. An obvious corollary is that the original researcher must anticipate alternative analytic strategies so that appropriate data are collected for the investigation of the models of interest. In the field of structural equation models, the determination of the number of observed variables necessary to test a model is called the *identification problem*. This problem is analogous to the problem in elementary algebra of having a certain number of equations and a certain number of unknowns. If the number of unknowns is greater than the number of equations, then the system cannot be solved. Furthermore, certain equations may be redundant, so that even if there are more equations than unknowns, some unknowns may not be estimable from the data. Exactly the same situation holds with structural equation models: the unknowns (parameters) are elements of the matrices in the model, and the known values are the variances and covariances of the observed variables. A model usually consists of a complex system of equations with many unknowns, and it is often difficult to tell by inspecting these equations whether we can solve for each unknown.

The following examples show how the identification problem can be approached algebraically with simple models. The models used here for illustration are from factor analysis and, as such, represent only the measurement-model segment of the complete structural model.

Example 1: Two Observed Variables, One Trait. Suppose we have two observed variables; for example, scores on two different mathematics tests (x_1 and x_2). We want to test the proposition that these two tests actually measure one underlying ability (ξ), and we assume that each of the variables contains errors of measurement (δ_1 and δ_2). Figure 3 depicts the diagram and equations for this model. The

Figure 3. Two Variables, One Factor

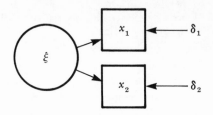

Structural equations:

$$x_1 = \lambda_1 \xi + \delta_1$$
$$x_2 = \lambda_2 \xi + \delta_2$$

Matrix formulation:

$$\begin{bmatrix} x_1 \\ x_2 \end{bmatrix} = \begin{bmatrix} \lambda_1 \\ \lambda_2 \end{bmatrix} \begin{bmatrix} \xi \end{bmatrix} + \begin{bmatrix} \delta_1 \\ \delta_2 \end{bmatrix}$$

$$\mathbf{X} = \Lambda\, \xi + \delta$$

Variance-covariance matrix:

$$\underset{(2\times2)}{\Sigma_x} = \underset{(2\times1)}{\Lambda} \quad \underset{(1\times1)}{\Phi} \quad \underset{(1\times2)}{\Lambda'} + \underset{(2\times2)}{\Theta_\delta}$$

equations are derived as described earlier in this chapter. Since we have two observed (dependent) variables, we derive two equations. From these, we derive the matrix formulation shown in Figure 3 and we posit the variance-covariance matrix of the observed variables. The derivation of the variance-covariance equation follows easily from the matrix formulation. In this equation, Σ_x is the variance-covariance matrix of the underlying factors. Since there is only one factor, we let $\Phi = [1]$, and Θ_δ is the variance-covariance matrix of the errors, which are uncorrelated. In our example, the following equations result from the model:

$$\Phi = [\ 1\ ]$$

$$\Theta_\delta = \begin{bmatrix} \theta_{\delta_1} & 0 \\ 0 & \theta_{\delta_2} \end{bmatrix}$$

$$\Sigma_x = \begin{bmatrix} \sigma_1^2 & \sigma_{12} \\ \sigma_{12} & \sigma_2^2 \end{bmatrix} = \Lambda \Phi \Lambda' + \Theta_\delta = \begin{bmatrix} \lambda_1^2 + \theta_{\delta_1} & \lambda_1\lambda_2 \\ \lambda_1\lambda_2 & \lambda_2^2 + \theta_{\delta_2} \end{bmatrix}$$

We have four unknowns (λ_1, λ_2, θ_{δ_1}, and θ_{δ_2}), but only the following three equations derived from the preceding matrix equation:

$$\sigma_1^2 = \lambda_1^2 + \theta_{\delta_1} \tag{1.0}$$

$$\sigma_{12} = \lambda_1\lambda_2 \tag{1.1}$$

$$\sigma_2^2 = \lambda_2^2 + \theta_{\delta_2} \tag{1.2}$$

Since we have more unknowns than equations, the system is not identified. We could get an identified model in several ways, but our theory has to be consistent with the assumptions of the modified model:

1. If either variable has no measurement errors, then either θ_{δ_1} or θ_{δ_2} is zero. Then we have one less unknown, and can solve the equations. For example, if $\theta_{\delta_1} = 0$, from equation (1.0) we obtain

$$\sigma_1^2 = \lambda_1^2 \text{ and } \lambda_1 = \sigma_1$$

From equation (1.1), we obtain

$$\lambda_2 = \sigma_{12}/\lambda_1 = \sigma_{12}/\sigma_1$$

and from equation (1.2),

$$\theta_{\delta_2} = \sigma_2^2 - \lambda_2^2 = \sigma_2^2 - (\sigma_{12}/\sigma_1)^2$$

2. If the measures have the same true-score variance, then $\lambda_1 = \lambda_2$. We can drop the subscript and just use λ. Then, from equation (1.1), we have

$$\sigma_{12} = \lambda^2$$

and from equation (1.0)

$$\theta_{\delta_1} = \sigma_1^2 - \lambda^2 = \sigma_1^2 - \sigma_{12}$$

and from equation (1.2)

$$\theta_{\delta_2} = \sigma_2^2 - \lambda^2 = \sigma_2^2 - \sigma_{12}$$

3. If the error variances are equal, $\theta_{\delta_1} = \theta_{\delta_2}$, which is unlikely to be the only assumption, then the system would be identified (proof omitted).

Note that in each case, making additional assumptions enables us to show that the system is identified by solving the equations for each unknown parameter in terms of the known variances and covariances of the observed variables.

Example 2: Three Variables, One Factor. Suppose that there are three observed variables which purportedly measure one underlying factor. We collect data on several hundred subjects and find that the correlation matrix of the observed variables is as follows:

$$\Sigma = \begin{bmatrix} 1.00 & .35 & .21 \\ .35 & 1.00 & .15 \\ .21 & .15 & 1.00 \end{bmatrix}$$

We have six known elements: three variances (all equal to one, since we have a correlation matrix), and three covariances (in this case, correlations). If we assume, as before, that the errors of measurement are uncorrelated, then we have six unknowns: the three elements of Λ and the three elements of Θ_δ (error variances). Our system of equations is then:

$$\begin{bmatrix} 1.00 & .35 & .21 \\ .35 & 1.00 & .15 \\ .21 & .15 & 1.00 \end{bmatrix} = \Sigma = \Lambda \, \Phi \, \Lambda' + \Theta_\delta = \begin{bmatrix} \lambda_1^2 + \theta_{\delta_1} & \lambda_1\lambda_2 & \lambda_1\lambda_3 \\ \lambda_1\lambda_2 & \lambda_2^2 + \theta_{\delta_2} & \lambda_2\lambda_3 \\ \lambda_1\lambda_3 & \lambda_2\lambda_3 & \lambda_3^2 + \theta_{\delta_3} \end{bmatrix}$$

$$\lambda_1^2 + \theta_{\delta_1} = 1.0 \qquad (2.1)$$

$$\lambda_2^2 + \theta_{\delta_2} = 1.0 \qquad (2.2)$$

$$\lambda_3^2 + \theta_{\delta_3} = 1.0 \qquad (2.3)$$

$$\lambda_1\lambda_2 = .35 \qquad (2.4)$$

$$\lambda_1\lambda_3 = .21 \qquad (2.5)$$

$$\lambda_2\lambda_3 = .15 \qquad (2.6)$$

To solve this set of equations, we start by concentrating on the last three equations, which contain just three unknowns. Dividing equation (2.4) by equation (2.5), we have $\lambda_2/\lambda_3 = .35/.21 = 5/3$. Multiplying this by equation (2.6) gives $\lambda_2^2 = (1.5)\ 5/3 = .25$. Thus, $\lambda_2 = .5$, and so $\lambda_3 = .15/.5 = .3$, and $\lambda_1 = .35/\lambda_2 = .35/.5 = .7$. The elements of Θ_δ are then found by subtraction in equations (2.1), (2.2), and (2.3).

We now return to the problem posed by complex systems. Although one can, in principle, solve them using these same techniques, in practice that approach is unwieldy, time consuming, and generally unproductive. Instead, it is better to try to analyze the data using, for example, Jöreskog's LISREL computer program, and choosing the option that gives standard errors. If no standard errors are produced, or if the standard errors produced are extremely large, then the model is probably not identified. Good generalizations about identification are few and far between, but this solution, while not perfect, is at least practical.

The identification problem is closely related to the problem of judging the model. When a system is exactly identified (as in our earlier example), any set of real data will fit the model. Thus, there are no checks we can make to see if the model is reasonable. In a few cases, we can judge the model as being unsatisfactory if the parameter estimates lie outside the admissible regions. If, in contrast, the model is overidentified, then there are more knowns than unknowns, and so there is some redundancy in the information; that is, there will be more than one estimate for some parameters. We could then check to see whether different estimates of parameters are consistent; if so, then the model becomes more reasonable. In actuality, though, the overall goodness-of-fit tests to be described later are more practical ways of deciding the usefulness of the model.

Two Approaches to Analyzing Nonexperimental Data

We now outline two approaches to the analysis of nonexperimental data using structural equation models. One approach separately models the behavior of each group (experimental and control), the other uses a so-called dummy variable to indicate group membership. In this latter approach, each subject is given a "score" of either 0 or 1, depending on whether he is in the control group or the experimental group. If the dummy variable is z, a person in the control group is scored $z = 1$. The designation of 0 or 1 to either group is arbitrary.

The most common method of analysis involves the use of a dummy variable in the model. For examples, see Magidson's (1977) reanalysis of Head Start data, and Linn and Werts (1977). The advantage of using a dummy variable is that the structural model can be used to test different theories of assignment to treatment. For example, if a theory assumes that assignment to treatment was determined by the score a child had on an IQ test, then this relationship can be tested by including it in the structural model. The disadvantages of using a dummy variable are that the use of a dichotomized variable violates the assumptions of the statistical model and that the structural relations may be different for the experimental group than the control group. As a practical matter, the effect of violating the assumptions will probably be small if there are about the same proportion of subjects in each group. If the structural relationships vary between groups, a model that uses a dummy variable will probably not fit the data.

The other method of analysis involves specifying separate models for each group and using estimated means on the underlying factors (instead of the observed variables) to compare the groups. Sörbom (1978) and Jöreskog and Sörbom (1976) provide examples of this type of analysis. This method allows one to easily test more than two groups (the dummy-variable approach would require multiple dummy variables); to test, within certain limitations, different models for different groups; and to satisfy the assumptions of the statistical model, since no dichotomous variable is used. This approach, however, does not provide for modeling assignment to treatment, which may be important in certain applications.

To exemplify the two approaches to structural models, we can analyze data from an evaluation of project Head Start. Our first example uses a dummy variable to indicate membership in the treatment group, and the second analyzes the Head Start and control groups separately. We used the computer program LISREL III to analyze the first example, and COFAMM for the second.

There are three sets of observed variables: background or socioeconomic status (SES) variables, scores from tests administered at the end of the evaluation, and the dummy variable for treatment assignment. The SES measures are mother's education, father's education, father's occupation, and family income. The outcome measures include two widely used standardized tests—the Illinois Test of Psycholinguistic Abilities (ITPA) and the Metropolitan Readiness Test (MRT). For this analysis, scores from subtests are combined to yield an overall score for each of the two test batteries. The data are presented in Table 2. An ordinary analysis of covariance (ANCOVA) of each dependent variable using all covariates indicated that students who participated in Head Start scored slightly lower (adjusted for initial differences) than students who did not, although the differences are not statistically significant.

Table 2. Overall Correlation Matrix for Head Start Data ($N = 303$)

	ITPA	MRT	MOTHERED	FATHERED	FATHOCC	INCOME
MRT	.652					
MOTHERED	.259	.275				
FATHERED	.246	.215	.516			
FATHOCC	.217	.255	.258	.285		
INCOME	.116	.190	.337	.209	.407	
TRTMENT	-.097	-.094	-.086	-.084	-.220	-.179

Note: ITPA   = Posttest: Illinois Test of Psycholinguistic Ability
     MRT   = Posttest: Metropolitan Readiness Test
     MOTHERED   = Mother's education
     FATHERED   = Father's education
     FATHOCC   = Father's occupation (scaled)
     INCOME   = Family income
     TRTMENT   = Treatment group (1 = Head Start; 0 = control)

Dummy-Variable Model. Figure 4 depicts a structural model that uses a dummy variable to indicate group membership. Since we assume that our covariates all measure socioeconomic status (SES), we make SES one of our underlying factors in the structural model and designate it as ξ_1. The other underlying independent variable, ξ_2, is the dummy variable for assignment to treatment. In this case, actual group assignment is the same as the underlying variable; thus, when we specify the measurement model we have one observed measure and no error of measurement for treatment assignment. We assume that our two posttests both measure the same trait, η_1 in the model. The parameter ϕ_{12} next to the curved arrow connecting ξ_1 and ξ_2 indicates that we

Figure 4. Structural Model for Head Start Analysis: Dummy-Variable Model

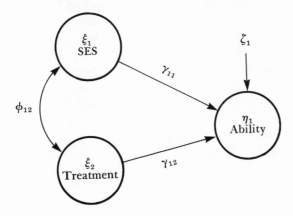

expect assignment to treatment to be correlated with SES; in fact, in a compensatory education experiment there should be a large negative correlation (high SES should indicate low probability of receiving the treatment). The other two arrows in the model indicate that both SES and treatment should affect ability. The equation implied by this measurement model is:

$$1 \cdot \eta_1 = \gamma_{11} \, \xi_1 + \gamma_{12} \, \xi_2 + \zeta_1$$

Thus,

$$B = [1], \, \eta = [\eta_1], \, \Gamma = [\gamma_{11}, \gamma_{12}], \, \xi = \begin{bmatrix} \xi_1 \\ \xi_2 \end{bmatrix}, \text{ and } \zeta = [\zeta_1].$$

In this model, ζ is specified as free, indicating that there may be other variables that are uncorrelated with ξ_1 and ξ_2 but do influence η_1. Since we are allowing ϕ_{12} to be free, the whole Φ matrix, which includes the variances of ξ_1 and ξ_2, as well as the covariances between them (in this case, there is just one covariance term), will be free. LISREL makes it possible to easily specify which variables will be free (in this case, the elements of Φ) and which will be fixed to some specified value (some of the elements of Λ will be specified as 0 or 1). If the need arises, it is also possible to constrain two or more elements to be equal; for example, if a model specifies that two variables are parallel measures, then the λ's and errors of measurement are equal for them.

The diagrams of the measurement models are presented in Figure 5. The model for the independent variables indicates that the SES variables are all measures of the underlying SES factor, but not of treatment assignment. Furthermore, all covariates are measured with error. Assignment to treatment, on the other hand, is measured without error, so $\delta_5 = 0$. Because there is no natural scale for the underlying variables, we arbitrarily set one of the λ's related to each factor, λ_1 and λ_5, equal to one. By fixing these parameters, we make the underlying factor have the same scale of measurement as the observed variable. This step also prevents the model from being unidentified. As the diagram for the dependent variables in Figure 5 shows, we consider both posttests to be measures of the same underlying factor, and both are imperfect measures of that underlying factor.

The following parameter matrices are associated with the measurement models; we use an asterisk (*) in Λ_x and Λ_y to indicate a fixed nonzero value:

$$\Lambda_x = \begin{bmatrix} 1.0^* & 0 \\ \lambda_2 & 0 \\ \lambda_3 & 0 \\ \lambda_4 & 0 \\ 0 & 1.0^* \end{bmatrix} \quad \Theta_\delta = \begin{bmatrix} \theta_{\delta_1} & \theta_{\delta_{12}} & 0 & 0 \\ \theta_{\delta_{12}} & \theta_{\delta_2} & & 0 & 0 \\ 0 & 0 & \theta_{\delta_3} & 0 & 0 \\ 0 & 0 & 0 & \theta_{\delta_4} & 0 \\ 0 & 0 & 0 & 0 & 0 \end{bmatrix}$$

$$\Lambda_y = \begin{bmatrix} 1.0^* \\ \lambda_7 \end{bmatrix} \quad \Theta_\epsilon = \begin{bmatrix} \theta_{\epsilon_1} & 0 \\ 0 & \theta_{\epsilon_2} \end{bmatrix}$$

In matrices of factor loadings (Λ_x and Λ_y), the first column corresponds to the coefficient for each variable on the first factor, the second column corresponds to the second factor. Thus, in Λ_x the first

Figure 5. Measurement Models for the Dummy-Variable Formulation

Independent Variables

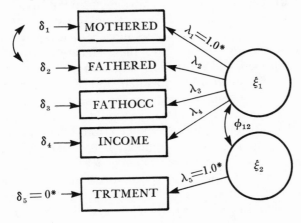

Dependent Variables

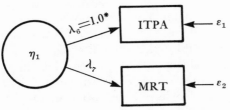

Note: An asterisk (*) denotes a fixed parameter.

column indicates that the first four variables measure SES, while the fifth, which is fixed at zero, does not. In the second column, the zeros in the first four rows indicate that the covariates do not measure the second factor, which is assignment to treatment condition. The variance-covariance matrices of the errors indicate that all variables except treatment are measured imperfectly and that the errors in mother's and father's education are correlated. (We allow for correlated errors here because people tend to choose marriage partners of similar educational level.)

Fit of the Model. First, we must check whether our model is consistent with the data. The simplest method is to examine the chi-square value associated with the goodness-of-fit test provided as part of the solution. The chi-square statistic is similar to any other null-hypothesis test in statistics: a small value of chi-square (which corresponds to a p value near 1.00) indicates that the model fits the data very well. A large value of chi-square (and a small value of p) indicates a poor fit. In our example, $\chi^2 = 21.0$ with 11 degrees of freedom ($p = .0334$). Thus, our model does not fit the data well. However, the fit is not exceptionally bad, so that minor adjustments in the model may enable us to find a good fit. (For pedagogical reasons, only a simple model was tested in this example. More complex models are necessary to provide a good fit to the data; such models for these data are discussed in Magidson, 1977 and 1978, and Bentler and Woodward, 1978.)

One problem with the chi-square test of goodness-of-fit is that the value of the statistic depends on the sample size. If a particular model tested with data from 100 subjects produces a chi-square value of 4.0, then the same model tested with data from 1000 subjects would be expected to yield a chi-square of about 40.0, or ten times as large as when fewer subjects were used. Thus, as with any statistical test, if enough subjects are used any hypothesized model could be rejected. Therefore, the chi-square statistic must be interpreted cautiously. One procedure is to estimate what the chi-square value would be if the sample size were "appropriate"; that is, if it were big enough to reject very poor models but not so big as to reject good models. To estimate the appropriate sample size, a reasonable rule is that it be five to twenty-five times the number of observed variables, since that is the usual number of subjects recommended for most multivariate analyses. With few variables—say, fewer than ten—a large number of subjects per variable might be reasonable. For our example, with six observed variables, we would probably want at least 150 (6 – 25) subjects. If we had 1500 subjects, we would divide the chi-square value by ten to estimate the value we would have obtained with 150 subjects. These rules are idiosyncratic—there is no consensus in the literature for interpreting the goodness-of-fit as reflected by chi-square values.

Another commonly used procedure for evaluating the fit of a model is to examine more directly how well the model predicts the obtained data. The estimates of the parameters in the solution can be used to predict the patterns of variances and covariances among the observed variables. If these predicted values are very close to the actual values in the data, then the model is acceptable. The difference between the predicted and actual value of each variance or covariance is defined as the *residual*. For our example, the residuals are listed in Table 3. A general rule is that if all of the residuals are less than .05 in absolute value, the model is acceptable, but of course the smaller they are the better. This method of assessing goodness-of-fit does not depend on sample size, since the predicted and observed values are independent of the number of subjects. (Note: Complete independence of the statistical test from sample size is not perfect either, since there should be more information in a larger sample, and thus the test can be more stringent. Perhaps some sort of intermediate statistic might be useful.)

Interpreting the Solution. Even though the fit of this model must be judged unacceptable, we will provide an interpretation for the parameter estimates as if the fit were acceptable. The solution for this model is shown in Figure 6. In the structural model, $\phi_{12} = -.143$, indicating a negative relationship between SES and assignment to treatment, as we had assumed would occur. This is a covariance; to get the correlation we must divide by the standard deviation (square root of the variance) of each of the underlying independent factors: $r_{12} = -.143/ \sqrt{(.242)(1.00)} = -.290$. There is a strong positive effect of SES on performance ($\gamma_{11} = .701$, with a standard error of .177, which is not shown in Figure 6), while there appears to be no effect of Head Start participation on performance ($\gamma_{12} = .016$, with a standard error of .049). Note that the sign of the effect has changed from negative (in the ANCOVA) to positive. Whether there really was a small effect, which because of the sample size was too small to detect statistically, is a matter of speculation (see Magidson, 1978).

A standardized solution, in which the original solution is rescaled so that all the underlying factors have a standard deviation of 1.00, is useful in that it provides a way to estimate the reliability of variables without much further calculation and it turns all of the elements of the Φ matrix into correlations instead of covariances. Figure 7 shows the standardized solution for the model we have been using. Note that $\phi_{12} = -.290$, as we calculated earlier.

In order to estimate the reliability of variables in our model, we make use of three facts: reliability is the ratio of true score variance to the sum of true score variance and error variance; the estimate of the true score variance for any variable in our model is the square of the factor loading (λ) in the standardized solution; and the estimate for the

Table 3. **Residuals for Dummy-Variable Analysis**

	MOTHERED	FATHERED	FATHOCC	INCOME	TRTMENT	ITPA	MRT
MOTHERED	.000						
FATHERED	-.057	.000					
FATHOCC	-.038	.000	.000				
INCOME	.032	.060	-.014	.000			
TRTMENT	.006	-.043	.041	-.020	.000		
ITPA	.013	-.096	-.103	.003	.087	.000	
MRT	-.006	-.077	-.046	.005	.051	.000	.000

Figure 6. Solution for the Dummy-Variable Model

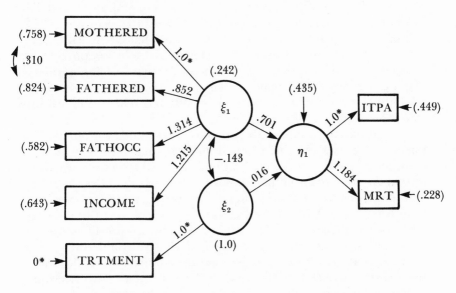

Note: An asterisk (*) denotes a fixed parameter. Numbers in parentheses are variances; those not in parentheses are regression coefficients.

Figure 7. Standardized Solution for the Dummy-Variable Model

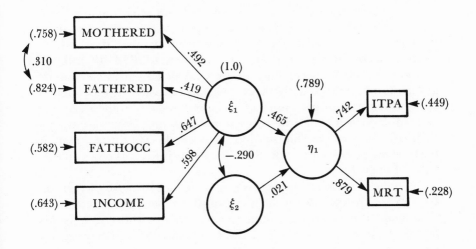

error variance for any variable in the model is the value in the diagonal of the Θ matrix corresponding to that variable. To compute the reliability of mother's education, we estimate the true score variance as $(.492)^2$, or .242, and the error variance as .758. Then the reliability is $.242/(.242 + .758)$, or .242. (In this example, the standardized solution provides an especially simple solution because the input is a correlation matrix instead of a covariance matrix.) For the achievement measures, the reliability of the ITPA is .551 ($= 1 - .449$) and that of the MRT is .772 ($= 1 - .228$).

How do the results of this analysis differ from the original analysis using ANCOVA? The original analysis concluded that the program may have been harmful, since the adjusted scores of the experimental group were lower than those of controls. Our analysis indicates that there is no negative effect due to treatment, and in fact there may have been a small positive effect. The difference arises because the ANCOVA underadjusted: The scores were adjusted for differences on the *observed* covariates, not on the *underlying* variable (SES). The LISREL analysis allowed us to estimate the relationship for the underlying variables, which in this case resulted in a more positive evaluation of the treatment than we would have made otherwise. In actual analyses, estimates of a program's effects might change from negative to either zero or positive, or from zero to positive, when a model is used that adequately corrects for initial differences on underlying variables instead of observed variables.

Separate-Groups Model. We now shift our attention to a model with a different analytic perspective. This model involves simultaneous factor analysis in two or more groups. While we used the computer program COFAMM for this analysis, the new LISREL IV program will give the same results. Each group is modeled separately, and the group means on the underlying variables are estimated by the program. The estimates of means and factor variances and covariances can then be used to write a true-score prediction equation for each group, and these equations can be compared to assess the effect of the treatment. If the lines are parallel, then the difference in the intercepts represents the effect of the treatment.

The first step in the process is to write the model for each group. In our case, the models for the two groups are identical, and the common model is presented in Figure 8. There are two underlying factors: ξ_1 is background status, and ξ_2 is posttreatment ability. There are four measures of background and two measures of ability. Because this is a factor-analysis model, there is no structural model (as there was with the previous model), just a measurement model. Thus, all underlying variables are independent variables, and all arrows connecting them are

Figure 8. Separate-Groups Model

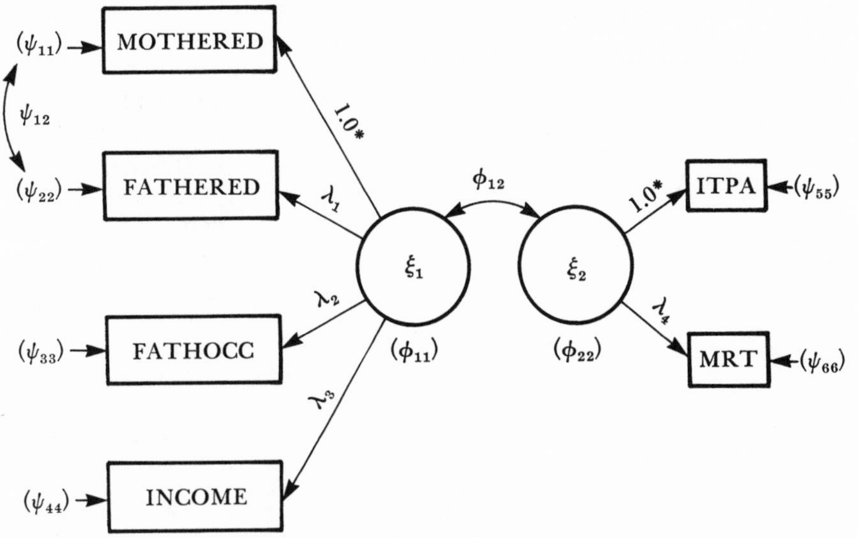

Note: An asterisk (*) denotes a fixed parameter; elements in parentheses are variances.

curved. The terms in parentheses in the model all indicate variances or covariances, while terms not in parentheses are regression coefficients (in this case, factor loadings). The distinction is made here to help remind the reader which terms must be squared when partitioning variance using the standardized solution.

Table 4 shows the parameter matrices of the model. Included in the table are labels for the rows and columns of each matrix, and asterisks to indicate which parameters are fixed. The factor loadings are in the Λ matrix. Note that by fixing certain elements at zero, we have specified that the covariates are measures only of the first factor, while the posttests are measures only of the second factor. As in the dummy-variable model, we have fixed one of the nonzero elements in each column at 1.0, in order to identify the model. In addition, we specify Λ for both groups to be equal, since the measurement process should be the same for both groups. The Φ matrix contains the variances and covariances of the two factors, and Ψ contains the variances and covariances of the errors of the observed variables. (The zeros are omitted from the Ψ matrix in Table 4.) Again, we allow the errors for mother's and father's education to be correlated. The two θ vectors contain the means of each group on each of the two factors. θ_1 contains the means for group 1, which are fixed at zero so that model will be

Table 4. Parameter Specifications in Separate-Groups Model

$$\xi_1(\text{SES}) \qquad \xi_2(\text{Ability})$$

$$
\Lambda \;=\; \begin{bmatrix}
1.0^* & 0 \\
\lambda_1 & 0 \\
\lambda_2 & 0 \\
\lambda_3 & 0 \\
0 & 1.0^* \\
0 & \lambda_4
\end{bmatrix}
\begin{matrix}
(\text{MOTHERED}) \\
(\text{FATHERED}) \\
(\text{FAHOCC}) \\
(\text{INCOME}) \\
(\text{ITPA}) \\
(\text{MRT})
\end{matrix}
$$

$$\xi_1 \qquad\qquad \xi_2$$

$$
\Phi \;=\; \begin{bmatrix}
\phi_{11} & \phi_{12} \\
\phi_{21} & \phi_{22}
\end{bmatrix}
$$ Note that $\phi_{21} = \phi_{12}$.

MOTHERED   FATHERED   FATHOCC   INCOME   ITPA   MRT

$$
\Psi \;=\; \begin{bmatrix}
\psi_{11} & \psi_{21} & & & & \\
\psi_{12} & \psi_{22} & & & & \\
 & & \psi_{33} & & & \\
 & & & \psi_{44} & & \\
 & & & & \psi_{55} & \\
 & & & & & \psi_{66}
\end{bmatrix}
$$

$$\xi_1 \quad\; \xi_2$$

$$
\Theta_1 \;=\; [\;\; 0^* \;\;,\;\; 0^* \;\;] \quad (\text{group 1 factor means})
$$
$$
\Theta_2 \;=\; [\;\; \theta_{21} \;\;,\;\; \theta_{22} \;\;] \quad (\text{group 2 factor means})
$$

Note: An asterisk (*) denotes a fixed parameter.

identified. We are interested only in the difference between the groups, and cannot determine where "the zero point" is on the factors. (See Jöreskog and Sörbom, 1979, for a discussion of identification in this type of model.)

The input to the COFAMM program consists of the means for each group on the observed variables, as well as the variance-covariance matrix of all variables for each group. Table 5 shows the means and the variance-covariance matrices for each group.

Table 5. Covariance Matrices and Means for Separate-Groups Analysis of Head Start

Control Group (N = 155)

Covariances	ITPA	MRT	MOTHERED	FATHERED	FATHOCC	INCOME
ITPA	15.218					
MRT	6.735	7.393				
MOTHERED	.953	.781	1.044			
FATHERED	1.002	.965	.686	1.428		
FATHOCC	.912	.759	.293	.488	1.423	
INCOME[a]	1.453	1.427	1.013	.832	1.495	10.491
Means	20.410	10.070	3.387	3.290	2.600	6.435

Head Start Group (N = 148)

Covariances	ITPA	MRT	MOTHERED	FATHERED	FATHOCC	INCOME
ITPA	14.175					
MRT	6.702	7.166				
MOTHERED	1.069	.707	1.065			
FATHERED	1.278	.418	.616	1.641		
FATHOCC	.842	.722	.281	.278	1.156	
INCOME	.837	1.404	.987	.617	1.073	7.012
Means	19.670	9.562	3.210	3.081	2.088	5.358

[a]Income is expressed in thousands of dollars per year.

The actual solution, which by itself is relatively uninformative, is in Table 6. Note, however, that the model does fit the data ($\chi^2 = 31.04$, $df = 22$, $p = .0952$). There is one set of estimates for each group. These estimates can be used to write regression equations for predicting a person's true score on posttreatment ability (ξ_1). In the regression

Table 6. Solution for Separate-Groups Model

	Control Group		Experimental Group	
Θ (Factor means)	(0* ,	0*)	(−.294 ,	−.631)

$$\Lambda \text{ (Factor loadings)} \quad \begin{bmatrix} 1.000^* & 0^* \\ 1.058 & 0^* \\ 1.479 & 0^* \\ 3.520 & 0^* \\ 0^* & 1.0^* \\ 0^* & .850 \end{bmatrix} \begin{bmatrix} 1.000^* & 0^* \\ 1.058 & 0^* \\ 1.479 & 0^* \\ 3.520 & 0^* \\ 0^* & 1.0^* \\ 0^* & .850 \end{bmatrix}$$

$$\Phi \quad \begin{bmatrix} .264 & .665 \\ .665 & 7.937 \end{bmatrix} \begin{bmatrix} .208 & .560 \\ .560 & 7.889 \end{bmatrix}$$

$$\Psi \quad \begin{bmatrix} .793 & .394 \\ .394 & 1.090 \\ & & .857 \\ & & & 7.255 \\ & & & & 7.334 \\ & & & & & 1.643 \end{bmatrix} \begin{bmatrix} .814 & .390 \\ .390 & 1.444 \\ & & .724 \\ & & & 4.447 \\ & & & & 6.310 \\ & & & & & 1.458 \end{bmatrix}$$

$$\chi^2 = 31.04, \ df = 22, \ p = .0952$$

Note: An asterisk (*) denotes a fixed parameter.

equations, we use the following notation: $\hat{\xi}_2$ is the estimated score of a person on factor 2 (ξ_2), θ_2 is the group mean on factor 2, ξ_1 is the actual score of a person on factor 1 (ξ_1), θ_1 is the group mean on factor 1. The general equation is

$$\hat{\xi}_2 - \theta_2 = \phi_{21}/\phi_{11} \, (\xi_1 - \theta_1)$$

For our example, the equation for the control group is

$$\hat{\xi}_2 = .665/.264 \, \xi_1 = 2.519 \, \xi_1$$

and for the experimental group

$$\hat{\xi}_2 + .631 = .560/.208\,(\xi_1 + .294)$$

Simplifying, we obtain

$$\hat{\xi}_2 = 2.692\,\xi_1 + .160$$

Comparing the equations for the two groups, we note that the lines are approximately parallel since the regression coefficients are almost identical. Furthermore, the equation for the experimental group lies slightly above that for the controls (for $\xi_1 = 0$, Head Start children are, on the average, .160 higher than the controls on ξ_2). This analysis is like an ANCOVA on estimated true scores, instead of on observed scores.

In addition to constructing the regression lines, we are interested in the distribution of individuals in each group around the regression lines. This distribution is even more important if the regression lines for the two groups are not parallel. If we assume that the distribution of true scores is bivariate normal for each group, we can construct confidence regions in the following manner: Let $\bar{X}$ be the vector $(\bar{X}_1, \bar{X}_2)$ of means of the independent and dependent underlying variable of either of the groups. Then let $X = (X_1, X_2)$ be a vector denoting a point on the edge of the confidence region which we want to construct, and let Σ be the covariance matrix of the two variables. Then the equation $(X-\bar{X})'\Sigma^{-1}(X-\bar{X}) = \chi^2_{\alpha=.90}$, $df = 2$ will yield the points on the 90-percent-confidence region when solved for X. (See Tatsuoka, 1971, for a more detailed description of this method of constructing regions of confidence.)

Figure 9 shows the 90-percent-confidence regions and the regression lines for both Head Start and control groups. The standardized solution was used to construct the plots. The MATRIX procedure, SAS User's Guide (1979), can be used to generate a set of data points that lie inside each confidence region and the results can then be plotted using the Statistical Analysis System (SAS) procedure PLOT or some other plotting package. As Figure 9 shows, the regression lines for the two groups are almost identical. Looking at the confidence regions, we clearly see that while Head Start children were lower on the initial underlying SES factor and on the posttest factor, there is no difference between Head Start and control children when initial differences are controlled. Another way to see this is to pick a point on the axis representing SES and compare the scores of Head Start with control children at that point. In each case, there is no difference between the groups on the posttest factor.

Figure 9. Head Start Data, 90-Percent-Confidence Regions

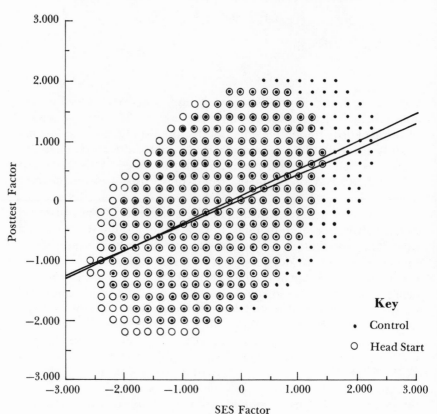

SES Factor

Pitfalls in the Use of Structural Models

Although structural models allow more realistic data analysis strategies than have ever been possible, several potential problems must be anticipated. The biggest temptation is to build the model after the data are collected, so that the model tested will be identified. For those who perform secondary analysis, this temptation is especially strong. The secondary analyst is using data that have already been collected, often with no plans having been made for such a sophisticated analysis.

The important first step, then, is to decide on the plausible models without reference to whether they can be tested with the data at hand. If the investigator is planning to collect data, then the study can be designed to facilitate choosing among the models. If the investigator is performing secondary analysis, the next step is to determine whether any of the plausible models can be tested. If not, then each model must be examined to see if certain assumptions can be relaxed or simplified to allow testing. Sensitivity analysis can often provide evidence as to whether proposed simplifications or relaxations of assumptions will seriously bias the results.

Another pitfall, implicit in the preceding discussion, is that some plausible model might be omitted from consideration. However, substantive knowledge of the content area, in addition to methodological sophistication, enables an investigator to construct a reasonably complete set of alternative models. Further, alternative models may be posited by other secondary analysts.

Analysts must also resist the temptation to accept a model that fits the data and thereby reject other plausible models that cannot be tested using the available data. These plausible models should not be slighted in favor of the model that can be tested.

Two problems are likely to arise in the interpretation of the statistical testing of models. First, as we discussed earlier, in evaluating goodness-of-fit tests, the chi-square statistic and its associated probability level should not be interpreted too strictly—consider the effect of sample size. Second, if two models each fit fairly well, be careful not to accept the best and reject the second-best if there is not really much difference in their fit. The design used in the study may make it impossible to decide between the models.

References

Bentler, P. M. "Multistructure Statistical Model Applied to Factor Analysis." *Multivariate Behavioral Research,* 1976, 11, 3–22.

Bentler, P. M., and Woodward, J. A. "A Head Start Reevaluation: Positive Effects Are Not Yet Demonstrable." *Evaluation Quarterly,* 1978, 2 (3), 493–510.

Bock, R. D., and Bargman, R. E. "Analysis of Covariance Structures." *Psychometrika,* 1966, 31, 507–534.

Boruch, R. F. "On Common Contentions About Randomized Field Experiments." In R. F. Boruch and H. W. Riecken (Eds.), *Experimental Testing of Public Policy.* Boulder, Colo.: Westview Press, 1975.

Campbell, D. T., and Boruch, R. F. "Making the Case for Randomized Assignment to Treatment by Considering the Alternatives: Six Ways in Which Quasi-Experimental Evaluations in Compensatory Education Tend to Underestimate Effects." In C. A. Bennett and A. A. Lumsdaine (Eds.), *Evaluation and Experiment: Some Critical Issues in Assessing Social Programs.* New York: Academic Press, 1975.

Campbell, D. T., and Erlebacher, A. "How Regression Artifacts in Quasi-Experimental Evaluations Can Mistakenly Make Compensatory Education Look Harmful." In J . Hellmuth (Ed.), *Compensatory Education: A National Debate.* Vol. 3: *Disadvantaged Child.* New York: Brunner/Mazel, 1970.

Duncan, O. D. *Introduction to Structural Equation Models.* New York: Academic Press, 1975.

Jöreskog, K. G., and Sörbom, D. *LISREL III: Estimation of Linear Structural Equation Systems by Maximum Likelihood Methods.* Chicago: National Educational Resources, 1976.

Jöreskog, K. G., and Sörbom, D. *LISREL IV: Analysis of Linear Structural Relationships by the Method of Maximum Likelihood.* Chicago: International Educational Services, 1978.

Jöreskog, K. G., and Sörbom, D. *Advances in Factor Analysis and Structural Equation Models.* Cambridge, Mass.: Abt Books, 1979.

Kerlinger, F. H., and Pedhazur, E. J. *Multiple Regression in Behavioral Research.* New York: Holt, Rinehart and Winston, 1973.

Land, K. C., and Felson, M. "Sensitivity Analysis of Arbitrarily Identified Simultaneous Equation Models." *Sociological Methods and Research,* 1978, *6*(3), 283–307.

Linn, R. L., and Werts, C. E. "Analysis Implications of the Choice of a Structural Model in the Nonequivalent Control Group Design." *Psychological Bulletin,* 1977, *47*, 121–150.

Long, J. S. "Estimation and Hypothesis Testing in Linear Models Containing Measurement Error: A Review of Jöreskog's Model for the Analysis of Covariance Structures." *Sociological Methods and Research,* 1976, *5*(2), 157–206.

Magidson, J. "Toward a Causal-Model Approach for Adjusting for Preexisting Differences in the Nonequivalent Control Group Situation: A General Alternative to ANCOVA." *Evaluation Quarterly,* 1977, *1*(3), 399–420.

Magidson, J. "Reply to Bentler and Woodward: The .05 Significance Level Is Not All-Powerful." *Evaluation Quarterly,* 1978, *2*(3), 511–520.

Rindskopf, D. M. "Secondary Analysis: Using Multiple Analysis Approaches with Head Start and Title I Data." In R. F. Boruch (Ed.), *New Directions for Program Evaluation: Secondary Analysis,* no. 4. San Francisco: Jossey-Bass, 1978.

Rubin, D. B. "Estimating Causal Effects of Treatments in Randomized and Nonrandomized Studies." *Journal of Educational Psychology,* 1974, *66*, 688–701.

Sörbom, D. "An Alternative to the Methodology for Analysis of Covariance." *Psychometrika,* 1978, *43*(3), 381–396.

Sörbom, D., and Jöreskog, K. G. *COFAMM: Confirmatory Factor Analysis with Model Modification.* Chicago: National Educational Resources, 1976.

Statistical Analysis System. *SAS User's Guide, 1979 Edition.* Raleigh, N.C.: Statistical Analysis System Institute, 1979.

Tatsuoka, M. M. *Multivariate Analysis: Techniques for Educational and Psychological Research.* New York: Wiley, 1971.

Wolins, L. "The Use of Multiple Regression Procedure When the Predictor Variables Are Psychological Tests." *Educational and Psychological Measurement,* 1967, 27, 821-827.

11

Leigh Burstein
M. David Miller

Regression-Based Analyses of Multilevel Educational Data

In this paper, we focus on three topics within the domain of regression-based analyses of multilevel data from quasi-experiments and field studies in educational research and evaluation. We first discuss the general questions of choosing a unit of analysis or choosing an analytical model. We then consider the use of within-group slopes as indices in between-group analyses and the estimation of within-group dependency and its role in analyses of multilevel data. These latter topics

Note: An earlier version of this paper was presented at the Institute for Research on Teaching, Michigan State University, East Lansing, December 10, 1977. This paper presents work partially supported by the National Institute of Education contract NIE G-78-0113 with the Center for the Study of Evaluation, University of California, Los Angeles, and by a grant from the Spencer Foundation to the Graduate School of Education, University of California, Los Angeles. The contents of the paper in no way reflect official opinions of those organizations and they are not responsible for the interpretations made herein.

reflect important substantive concerns in school-based nonexperimental investigation.

Overall, we believe that the major technical complication in the analysis of multilevel data from quasi-experiments and field studies is the inability of educational researchers to develop adequate theories about educational processes within groups (classrooms and schools) and to develop adequate methodology for analyzing the educational effects of such processes. The material presented here reflects an attempt to systematize the investigation of two important indices of within-group processes.

Choosing Units of Analysis and an Analytical Model

Efforts to identify the effects of education on pupil performance (for example, Coleman and others, 1966) have suffered from the complications caused by the multilevel character of educational data. Schools are aggregates of their teachers, classrooms, and pupils, and classrooms are aggregates of the persons and processes within them. The effects of education exist both between and within the units at each level of the educational system. Yet the majority of researchers of educational effects have restricted their attention to overall between-student, between-class, or between-school analyses.

Cronbach (1976) argues that the majority of studies of educational effects carried out thus far conceal more than they reveal, and that "the established methods have generated false conclusions in many studies" (p. 1). His concern is foreshadowed in the educational literature by the exchange among Wiley, Bloom, and Glaser as recorded by Wittrock and Wiley (1970), and by Haney's (1974) review of the units-of-analysis problems encountered in the evaluation of Project Follow Through.

Research on the differences between multiple regression models at different levels of aggregation and on the analyses of school effects at different levels indicates that there are substantial differences in the magnitudes of regression coefficients across levels for specific models; different variables enter the models at different levels; and aggregation generally inflates the estimated effects of pupil background and decreases the likelihood of identifying teacher and classroom characteristics that are effective. These results are reported by, among others, Burstein (1978), Burstein, Fischer, and Miller (1978), Hannan and Young (1976), and Keesling and Wiley (1974). These results are not very comforting for the researcher who wishes to draw conclusions about educational processes at one level but is constrained to analysis at a different level.

When faced with the analysis of multilevel data, most researchers try to choose among alternative units of analysis on the basis of theoretical or statistical considerations. Unfortunately, those who resort to theory either reject plausible alternative models (Bloom, 1970b; Brophy, 1975; Stebbins and others, 1977; Wiley, 1970) or find themselves unable to choose (Cline and others, 1974; Haney, 1974). Those who pick the appropriate unit on the basis of statistical considerations also face competing alternatives (Burstein and Smith, 1977; Glendening, 1976; Haney, 1974).

Haney (1974) elaborates the range of alternative considerations, citing four general types: the purpose of the evaluation (questions to be addressed), the evaluation design (nature of treatments, independence of units and treatment effects, appropriate size), statistical considerations (reliability of measures, degrees of freedom, analysis techniques), and practical considerations (missing data, policy research, multiple year comparisons, economy). Haney was unable to choose among units in his evaluation of Project Follow Through because the purpose of the evaluation dictated the child as the unit but the unit of treatment was the classroom; moreover, the multiyear character of Follow Through made classrooms impractical as units of analysis. Furthermore, since there was no random assignment at any level and the comparison children were not equivalent to treatment children, these considerations offered no relief.

To think of multilevel analyses simply as problems in the choice of a unit of analysis is inadequate. Phenomena of importance occur at all levels and need to be described and subjected to inferential analysis (Burstein and Linn, 1976; Cronbach, 1976). Once again, Haney's arguments are succinct and to the point: "Investigators ought to have a strong bias for studying various properties of the educational system at the level at which they occur; . . . variation in attributes of interest ought to be studied at those levels (or between those units) at which it does (or is expected to) occur. . . . If the hypotheses are explicitly stated in terms of mathematical models, the impact of shifting levels of analysis from one unit of analysis to another will be much more easily assessed than if they are not" (1974, pp. 96–97). Haney's arguments serve as justification for the research we describe in this chapter.

Decomposition into Between-Group and Within-Group Effects. A variety of competing points can be cited as traditional justification for the choice of either pupils or groups (classrooms or schools) as the appropriate unit of analysis in studies of educational effects. In general, the arguments cited are compelling and virtually irreconcilable if a choice must be made between pupil and group as the only unit. The multilevel character of educational data warrants analytical strategies tailored to the identification of educational effects at and within each level of the educational system. Moreover, the complexity of the choice depends on the type of study and the types of outcomes and processes under investigation.

Even in the simplest case, once a specific group membership is defined (for example, instruction from a specific teacher), any measure that varies over pupils can be decomposed into its between-group and within-group components. For example, consider the posttest or outcome performance Y_{ij} of pupil j in class i ($j = 1, \ldots, n$ persons per class; $i = 1, \ldots, k$ classes; for simplicity, we assume classes are equal in size) and the performance level X_{ij} of the pupil prior to entering the class (a pretest or some measure of entering ability). The relation of X_{ij} to Y_{ij} can be decomposed into between-class and within-class components (Burstein, Linn, and Capell, 1978; Cronbach, 1976):

$$
\begin{aligned}
Y_{ij} - \bar{Y}_{..} = &\ \beta_b(\bar{X}_{i.} - \bar{X}_{..}) && \text{Predicted between-class} \\
&+ \bar{Y}_{i.} - \beta_b(\bar{X}_{i.} - \bar{X}_{..}) && \text{Adjusted between-class} \\
&+ \beta_w(X_{ij} - \bar{X}_{i.}) && \text{Pooled within-class slope} \\
&+ (\beta_i - \beta_w)(X_{ij} - \bar{X}_{i.}) && \text{Specific within-class} \\
&+ \epsilon_{ij} && \text{Specific residual associated} \\
& && \text{with person } ij
\end{aligned}
$$

In this equation, β_b is the between-class slope from the regression of $\bar{Y}_{i.}$ on $\bar{X}_{i.}$, β_w is the pooled within-class slope from the regression of $(Y_{ij} - \bar{Y}_{i.})$ on $(X_{ij} - \bar{X}_{i.})$ across all classrooms, and the β_i are the specific within-class slopes from the regression of Y_{ij} on X_{ij} within the i classrooms.

The possible substantive interpretations of specific components and sets of components are important here. The main elements are the between-class slope, the adjusted between-class effect, the pooled within-class slope, and the specific within-class slopes. Often, this equation can be modified so that we have a global measure, T_i, of classes (for example, class membership, teacher quality, or treatment group) rather than the aggregation of individual scores represented by $\bar{X}_{i.}$. We hereafter refer to the effects associated with either $\bar{X}_{i.}$ or T_i as class effects without loss of generality.

One useful treatment of the multilevel analysis is provided by Cronbach (1976). Cronbach's justification for his proposed analysis is that the usual overall between-student analysis combines two kinds of relationships—those operating between collectives (reflected in β_b and adjusted class effects) and those operating among persons within collectives (reflected in β_w and β_i)—into a composite that is rarely of substantive interest. Cronbach reminds us that β_t, the overall between-student coefficient from the regression of Y_{ij} on X_{ij}, has been shown by Duncan, Cuzzort, and Duncan (1961, p. 66) to be a composite of β_b and β_w:

$$\beta_t = \eta_X^2 \beta_b + (1 - \eta_X^2)\beta_w$$

where η_X^2 is the intraclass correlation or correlation ratio of X. Cronbach recommends that between-group effects and individuals-within-group effects be examined separately. To determine between-group effects, Cronbach would examine

$$\bar{Y}_{i.} - \bar{Y}_{..} = \beta_{\bar{Y}T} T + \beta_b(\bar{X}_{i.} - \bar{X}_{..})$$

where the $\beta_{\bar{Y}T} T$ is the effect of teachers on mean outcomes after controlling for between-class differences in inputs. Individuals-within-group effects require us to examine

$$Y_{ij} - \bar{Y}_{i.} = \beta_w(X_{ij} - \bar{X}_{i.})$$

Thus, Cronbach's primary concerns are with the adjusted collective effects of instruction as reflected by the adjusted class mean outcomes and with the overall redistributive properties of classroom instruction as reflected by the pooled within-class regression, β_w.

Empirical Results from Multilevels Using International Educational Achievement Data. For the time being, we focus on the two estimators of most interest to Cronbach, between-group regression coefficients and the corresponding pooled within-group coefficients. Recent empirical analyses of data from the International Educational Achievement (IEA) Six Subject Survey (Burstein, Fischer, and Miller, 1978) dramatically demonstrate the distinct differences in interpretation that result from between-school and within-school analyses. This study investigated the factors influencing educational achievement in twenty-one countries, considering six subject areas (science, reading comprehension, literature, civics education, English as a foreign language, and French as a foreign language) at three age levels (basically, ten-year-olds, fourteen-year-olds, and students in their pretertiary year). Over 700 student, teacher, and school characteristics were measured.

Our investigation of educational effects models for fourteen-year-olds from the U.S. and Sweden in the IEA science achievement study shows that the effects of family background on science achievement were substantial, as usual, in the between-schools analysis of U.S. data but much smaller in Sweden (see Table 1). In fact, for fourteen-year-olds, the Total R^2 was larger than the Between-Schools R^2 in Sweden, which would be atypical for analysis of U.S. data.

In contrast, the effects of family background in the pooled-within-school analyses for the U.S. were substantially smaller and were essentially the same as the effects found in the pooled-within-school analysis for Sweden. One possible substantive explanation for these findings is that the two types of analyses reflect distinctions between

Table 1. Between-Student, Between-School and Pooled-Within-School Regression Analyses of Factors Affecting Science Achievement (RSCI) for Fourteen-Year-Olds from the IEA Study in the United States

| | Metric Regression Coefficients | | | | | |
| | Between-School | | Pooled Within-School | | Between-Student | |
Variable	United States	Sweden	United States	Sweden	United States	Sweden
Sex	-6.620 (3.90)	-3.362[a] (1.68)	-3.853[b] (11.30)	-5.281 (14.18)	-4.157 (11.87)	-5.165 (13.68)
Word knowledge	.876 (6.47)	.569[a] (3.24)	.812 (21.53)	.773 (18.36)	.861 (23.22)	.754 (18.02)
Father's occupation	.843 (2.87)	.194[a] (.67)	.307[b] (3.91)	.297 (3.64)	.487 (6.39)	.256 (3.26)
Number of books in home	3.577 (3.37)	1.217[a] (.92)	1.223[b] (5.36)	1.324 (5.04)	1.661 (7.20)	1.324 (4.99)
Grade	1.390 (1.69)	4.186[a] (2.49)	2.291[b] (5.25)	2.941[b] (7.25)	1.912 (5.24)	3.083 (7.65)
Science study	.110 (2.34)	-.149[a] (2.32)	.065[b] (3.90)	-.122[b] (5.70)	.066 (4.29)	-.125 (6.16)
Exploratory methods	.240 (1.50)	.382[a] (1.10)	.067[b] (1.25)	-.099[b] (1.31)	.130 (2.52)	-.064 (.85)
R^2	.72	.31	.31	.34	.39	.34

Note: The between-school analyses are run with each school weighted by the numbers of students. However, all t statistics were adjusted to reflect the number of schools rather than the number of students. The t statistics are reported in parentheses. For U.S. schools, $N = 107$; for Swedish schools, $N = 93$; for U.S. students, $N = 1,806$; for Swedish students, $N = 1,675$.
[a] Variable for which between-country differences were significant at $p < .05$.
[b] Within-country variables for which the between-school and within-school coefficients differ by at least two standard errors.

the countries in the political order governing the distribution of pupil backgrounds and school resources (specifically, the predominance of local control and community determination of school resources in the U.S. compared to national control and a policy of uniformity of resources in Sweden) and a similarity between the countries in their operation of the social order within schools (for example, interpersonal allocations of rewards within an institution).

Although this example illustrates other substantive issues, one methodological point is clear: Different types of analysis of multilevel data address different questions, and research on schooling typically asks questions at multiple levels.

Within-Group Slopes as Indices in Between-Group Analyses

Once researchers determine that the questions of interest or the statistical considerations warrant analyses of aggregated data, they must specify the types of between-group effects they expect to find. In particular, when one's purpose is to determine factors affecting pupil performance, it is possible that analyses of between-group means can hide important differences in the within-group distribution of pupil outcomes and educational inputs.

Several aspects of current schooling practices lead us to expect that within-school and within-class distributions of pupil performance vary. First, schools and classes do differ in the distribution of educational performance. Moreover, schools with the same mean outcome often exhibit different distributions of performance within school. An analysis of means alone could not be expected to account for such distributional differences.

Second, a variety of educational theories about the effects of specific schooling practices on within-group behavior argue for an examination of distributional properties other than group means. Obviously, at least the variability of performance is of interest in studies comparing individualized, competency-based, and open educational instructional programs with more traditional instructional practices. Also, research findings on the interaction between teaching style and learning style lead one to expect variable outcomes for pupils with similar entering characteristics and preferences taught by teachers with differing instructional styles.

Finally, the idea of using distributional characteristics in addition to the mean as criterion measures has been shown previously to merit consideration. Lohnes (1972) reports that standard deviations and skewness indices added to the explanatory power of means in his analyses of data from the Cooperative Reading Project. Klitgaard (1975) and Brown and Saks (1975) conclude that school and school-district standard deviations exhibit more significant relations with school characteristics than do school and school-district means.

Though they seek answers to different questions and use different methodologies, Lohnes, Brown and Saks, and Klitgaard apparently share our belief that educational outcomes are multifaceted and incompletely measured by simple group averages. There also seems to be a consensus that an educational theory can be developed which will link pupils' initial abilities and characteristics of the educative process to distributional properties of educational outcomes. We (Burstein and Linn, 1976; Burstein, Linn, and Capell, 1978) have elaborated a theory for the use of within-group slopes of outcomes on inputs as a criterion in educational effects studies. Wiley (1970) may have been the first to suggest this strategy. Our justification for considering within-group slopes as outcomes is derived from research on aptitude-treatment interactions (Snow, 1976). Putting our theory in its simplest form, we expect that different combinations of teachers and instructional practices result in varying distributions of educational outcomes for pupils with similar entering characteristics. For example, we hypothesize that among teachers who are equally effective in obtaining mean performance, the slopes of their students' performance will vary because some teachers use compensatory instructional practices that emphasize the improved performance of lower-ability students while others allow each child to learn at his or her own rate. (We would expect a flatter slope in the former case than in the latter.)

We (Burstein and Linn, 1976; Burstein, Linn, and Capell, 1978) have compared alternative analytical models for identifying educational effects for sets of hypothetical classrooms with heterogeneous slopes. Our principal findings are that, for the conditions studied, heterogeneous within-class slopes do make important differences in identified effects, differences that are not swamped by sampling variability in the estimation of slopes, and that certain analytical strategies exhibit good properties even in the presence of heterogeneity.

Although within-group slopes are conceptually appealing indices of educational effects, three points warrant further examination. First, it must be determined that slopes are sufficiently stable. Second, it must be demonstrated that slopes are potentially distinct from other group indices (for example, pre- and posttest means and standard deviations) in realistic situations. Finally, it must be shown that there exist realistic cases in which slopes are related to school and class characteristics after controlling for other background measures and other indices of group outcomes. We have already begun to investigate these points and now turn to them.

Stability of Slopes. The sampling variability of within-group slopes is substantially greater than that of the mean. For small samples, say, the size of a classroom, the sampling error of a slope is so large that it is questionable whether real differences in slopes may reasonably be distinguished from the noise; moreover, any outlier can dominate the slope. If the real differences in slopes are as large as those generated in Burstein and Linn (1976), then it is important to take them into account. Whether the differences in real classrooms are of similar magnitude is somewhat problematic at this stage, however.

Since students within a classroom are not a random sample, but are a fixed sample once the classroom is chosen, it is not clear how best to investigate the relative magnitude of signal and noise in the differences among within-classroom slopes. Linn and Burstein (1977) found little support for the notion that slopes vary systematically when they regressed a posttest in reading on a pretest in reading and only limited support for the notion based on a similar set of regressions for math using small samples of classrooms from the ETS Beginning Teacher Evaluation Study (BTES; McDonald and Elias, 1976). But these analyses are based on traditional confidence intervals that treat each class as if the students in it were a random sample from a population. As already noted, assumptions of random sampling are questionable in this situation.

While random sampling of students may not provide the best model, one does need to allow for disturbances in the observed slope due to idiosyncratic occurrences at the time of measurement. Just as an individual's observed score is distinguished from an underlying "true" score in classical test theory, one must distinguish between the observed measure for the group (in this case, the slope) and an underlying "true" slope.

Several approaches can be used to investigate the relative size of signal and noise in the within-group slope estimates. Confidence intervals can be computed for the within-group slopes for selected sets, as Linn and Burstein (1977) did for BTES data. The Jacknife procedure (Mosteller and Tukey, 1977) can also be used to estimate slopes and their stability.

Relations of Slopes to Other Group-Level Indices. If slopes are to provide a useful addition to the array of outcomes, they must be distinct from other indices. Linn and Burstein (1977) investigated this property of slopes for three separate data sets. They found that though pretest and posttest means correlated with one another in the range of .5 to .9, the correlations of within-group slope with either means or standard deviations (or, for that matter, with skewness and kurtosis indices and sample size) are much lower and, except for the pretest standard deviations (which are spuriously related to slopes), are rarely significant. These results suggest that slopes are sufficiently distinct from means and standard deviations to warrant further consideration.

Relation of Slopes to School and Class Characteristics. The final consideration in an investigation of the potential utility of within-group slopes is their relationships to measures of school and classroom processes. Preliminary results of an analysis of science achievement data on U.S. fourteen-year-olds in the IEA study (Burstein and Miller, 1978) provide tantalizing evidence of the possible value of this activity. Within-school slopes of science achievement on a verbal ability measure (assessed concurrently) were significantly and positively related to school mean responses of pupils on indices of exposure to science instruction and of the degree to which pupils reported instructional practices that emphasized exploration—discovery methods of instruction. These significant results occurred despite controls for pretest and posttest means and standard deviations, and pupil home background measures.

These results accord well with recent research on informal, open, individually guided, and unstructured instruction (see particularly Rosenshine, 1978, and Stebbins and others, 1977). Instruction that emphasizes student self-direction (selection) of learning goals and methods tends to exacerbate preexisting differences in pupils' skills. Higher-ability students tend to make more appropriate choices and achieve at a faster rate than lower-ability students. These steeper within-group slopes are consistent with expectations from other research and suggest the need for similar investigations with other data sets.

Estimating Within-Group Dependency in Multilevel Analysis

The problem of dependence among observations within groups is endemic to research on hierarchically nested school data, and can be especially critical when intact classrooms are investigated. Cronbach and Webb (Cronbach, 1976; Cronbach and Webb, 1975; Webb, 1977) have argued that when intact groups are assigned to instructional treatments, the students in those treatments cannot be considered independent units and therefore, the typical analyses based on all individuals pooled across groups can be justifiably criticized as inappropriate. The crucial problem in ignoring group membership is that educational treatments are not administered independently to individuals (Wiley, 1970). Individuals within the classroom have shared experiences. This nonindependence of individuals within the group can be expressed by an intraclass correlation structure. To ignore this intraclass structure, by treating individuals as independent by ignoring group membership, entails serious consequences (Walsh, 1947; Weibull, 1953).

Glendening (1976) provides a thorough discussion of the problem in the experimental-design frame of reference, summarizing the work of Glass and Stanley (1970) and Peckham, Glass, and Hopkins (1969). Glendening simulated the effects of violating the assumption of independence within the context of a balanced two-level hierarchically nested design, with subjects (S) nested within classrooms (C) and classrooms nested within treatments (T). She operationally defined independence as that condition wherein the expected mean square between classrooms, EMS$(C:T)$, equals that within classrooms, EMS$(S:CT)$. She found that a model in which the pupil is the unit or a conditional model in which a preliminary test of independence is followed by a choice of unit of analysis for testing treatment effects yielded spuriously small error terms and, therefore, too liberal tests of treatment effects. Glendening concludes that the researcher must make an a priori choice between the class (dependence) or the student (independence) as the unit, but acknowledges the complications of obtaining prior knowledge about independence of response.

While Glendening (1976) and Glendening and Porter (1976) focus on the implications of intraclass correlation for the analysis of experimental data, Webb (1977) is concerned with the antecedents of such intraclass relations in research on group process. Webb compares learning in interacting groups and learning singly, attempting to explain differences as a function of the characteristics of the individual, the group, and the group process. The group-process results provide a clue to understanding why some students learned best in groups, whereas others learned best singly. In general, group members who actively participated in discussions did better than those who did not actively participate, and did at least as well in groups as in individual learning. Active participation was related to pupils' ability ranking within the group and the range and level of ability in the group. Given the abilities of the students in a group, one could predict fairly well who interacted with whom and, consequently, who did best.

The results of this highly structured study suggest that knowledge of group processes in a particular class is crucial for understanding the degree to which students are working together—and therefore crucial for estimating degree of dependence in the class. Studying group process may be the only way to evaluate this dependence. Unless students in a class are receiving completely individualized instruction, rarely is it tenable to base analyses on the assumption of an intraclass correlation of zero. Unless all students are receiving exactly the same instruction and interact with fellow students in the same manner and for the same amounts of time, an intraclass correlation of one is unreasonable. Examination of lower-level processes will help locate the intraclass correlation on the continuum between zero and one. Webb suggests that these procedures may be generalized to real classrooms, considering interactions between teacher and students, interactions among students, and characteristics of students (abilities, personality variables) and teachers. Eventually, one may be able to predict student performance from a combination of these variables.

Clearly, research on most educational phenomena involves dependent observations. Dependence is not an all-or-nothing phenomenon—it exists in varying degrees. Dependence is a function of the factors one is measuring (the outcome) and the treatments or causes under study. It is also a function of the composition of the units and the nature of the grouping mechanism, as Webb (1977) demonstrates. Therefore tests for independence and adjustments for intraclass correlations are more appealing than automatic aggregation to the classroom level.

Analytical methods are needed that account for the degree of dependency and allow adjustments, when appropriate, to the estimated effects and associated estimates of precision. Moreover, estimators of dependency may be useful as indicators of classroom process. That is, it may be possible to relate these estimated relationships to characteristics of students, teachers, and instructional context.

Concluding Remarks

The topics discussed in this chapter are a subset of a broader range of issues and problems that require more attention over the next few years. Table 2 lists a variety of types of studies and types of outcomes for which multilevel analysis issues must be resolved. We cannot predict what form the final products of the investigation of the analysis of multilevel data will take, but some possibilities are apparent. We note a trend developing in educational evaluation for the conduct of what Glass (1976) has termed *meta-analysis* (see also Light and Smith, 1971). Persons conducting meta-analyses seek to accumulate knowledge about the effect and characteristics of a particular educational innovation by aggregating findings across numerous investigations of the phenomena.

There would seem to be a natural parallel to meta-analysis that is relevant to the examination of alternative methodological ap-

Table 2. Types of Studies and Outcomes for the Investigation
of Educational Effects

I. Type of Study

   A. Manipulation

      1. Experimental/True—"Units" assigned to alternative treatments or Treatment/nontreatments; some form of manipulation

         a. *Random Assignment of Pupils from Classrooms to Treatments—* Pupils randomly assigned to treatment conditions; treatment outside of normal class routine; treatment nongroup work

         b. *Random Assignment of Pupils from Classrooms to Groups—* Pupils randomly assigned to treatment groups; treatment outside normal class routine

         c. *Random Assignment of Pupils to Classes—*Pupils randomly assigned to classes; classes randomly assigned to treatments

         d. *Random Assignment of Partial Classes to Treatments—*Portions of class randomly assigned to different treatment conditions

         e. *Random Assignment of Intact Classes to Treatments—*Students assigned to classes on unknown nonrandom basis; intact classes assigned to treatments

      2. Experimental/Aptitude-Treatment Interaction—Conditions under 1 with additional question of interaction with entering characteristics

      3. Experimental/Longitudinal—Repeated measurement (master testing, sequential analysis of behavior and interaction patterns, persistence) in context of empirical studies

   B. Nonmanipulation

      1. Nonexperimental/Cross-sectional—Large-scale cross-sectional survey of pupils, teachers, classrooms, and schools for the purpose of establishing educational school/teacher effects model.

      2. Nonexperimental/Longitudinal—Large-scale longitudinal survey (For example, income maintenance, voucher study, Follow Through Evaluation)

      3. Nonexperimental/Outlier (residual) analysis—Develop indices of effects of system over and beyond what can be anticipated by entering characteristics

Table 2 (continued)

4. Nonexperimental/Contextual (compositional) effect—Examination of whether the composition, frog-pond, normative climate of institution has an effect

II. Type of Outcome

   A. Short-Term—Duration varying from a lesson to, say, a year

      1. *Specific Cognitive Objective*—Single content domain/objective in an instructional sequence

      2. *General Cognitive Objective*—Standardized achievement test or total score over multiple objectives of a Criterion Referenced Test

      3. *Affective Objective*—Attitude toward self and subject matter, efficacy

      4. *Group Behavior*—Peer socialization, group cohesiveness, group interaction

   B. Long-Term—Duration of multiple years, retrospective academic antecedents

      1. *General Cognitive Outcome*—Standardized test or cumulative grades (for example, SAT as outcome, prediction of future grades from earlier test scores)

      2. *Educational Attainment*—Level of education

      3. *Occupational Attainment*—Level of occupation (social stratification theory)

      4. *Career Plans and Career Satisfaction*

      5. *General Mental Health*

---

proaches for the analysis of multilevel data. There are two main obstacles to the development of appropriate methodologies in this context. First, the available methodological approaches vary greatly in the degree to which they are based on theory as opposed to being formulated ad hoc. Second, all currently available empirical data sets suffer from a variety of inadequacies which, taken singly, limit their usefulness in comparisons of alternative methodological approaches.

It is important to identify approaches that are practical as well as theoretically sound, that are usable with actual (and not only hypothetical) data. Therefore, we propose that in addition to the studies of the variation in analytical properties across approaches with hypothetical data, the alternative approaches be applied to a wide variety and sizable number of actual data sets, each with a potentially different set of inadequacies. In this way we hope to learn more about both the methods, their usefulness and behavior, and the influence of data limitations on the selection of methods.

References

Bloom, B. S. "Comments on D. E. Wiley, 'The Design and Analysis of Evaluation Studies.' " In M. D. Wittrock and D. E. Wiley (Eds.), *The Evaluation of Instruction: Issues and Problems.* New York: Holt, Rinehart and Winston, 1970a.

Brophy, J. E. *The Student as the Unit of Analysis.* Research report no. 75-12. Austin: University of Texas, 1975.

Brown, W., and Saks, D. H. "The Production and Distribution of Cognitive Skills Within Schools." *Journal of Political Economy,* 1975, *83,* 571-593.

Burstein, L. *Data Aggregation in Educational Research: Applications.* Technical report no. 1, Consortium on Methodology for Aggregating Data in Educational Research. Milwaukee, Wis.: Vasquez Associates, 1975.

Burstein, L. "Assessing Differences Between Grouped and Individual-Level Regression Coefficients: Alternative Approaches." *Sociological Methods and Research,* 1978, *7,* 5-28.

Burstein, L., Fischer, K., and Miller, M. D. "Social Policy and School Effects: A Cross-National Comparison." Paper presented at 9th World Congress of Sociology, Upsala, Sweden, August, 1978.

Burstein, L, and Linn, R. L. "Detecting the Effects of Education in the Analysis of Multilevel Data: The Problem of Heterogeneous Within-Class Regressions." Paper presented at Conference on Methodology for Aggregating Data in Educational Research, Stanford, Calif., October 1976.

Burstein, L., Linn, R. L., and Capell, F. "Analyzing Multilevel Data in the Presence of Heterogeneous Within-Class Regression" *Journal of Educational Statistics,* 1978, *3*(4), 347-383.

Burstein, L., and Miller, M. D. "Alternative Analytical Models for Identifying Educational Effects: Where Are We?" Paper presented at annual meeting of the American Educational Research Association, Toronto, Ontario,. Canada, March 1978.

Burstein, L., and Smith, I. D. "Choosing the Appropriate Unit for Investigating School Effects," *The Australian Journal of Education.*

1977, *21*, 65–79.

Cline, M. D., and others. *Education as Experimentation: Evaluation of the Follow Through Planned Variation Model.* Vols. 1A and 1B. Cambridge, Mass.: Abt Associates, 1974.

Coleman, J. S., and others. *Equality of Educational Opportunity.* Vols. 1 and 2. Washington, D.C.: U.S. Government Printing Office, 1966.

Comber, L. C., and Keeves, J. P. *Science Education in Nineteen Countries: International Studies in Evaluation.* Vol. 1. New York: Wiley, 1973.

Cronbach, L. J. *Research on Classrooms and Schools: Formulation of Questions, Design, and Analysis.* Occasional Paper, Stanford Evaluation Consortium. Stanford, Calif.: Stanford University, 1976.

Cronbach, L. J., and Webb, N. "Between-Class and Within-Class Effects in a Reported Aptitude × Treatment Interaction: Reanalysis of a Study by G. L. Anderson." *Journal of Educational Psychology,* 1975, *67*, 717–724.

Duncan, O. D., Cuzzort, R. P., and Duncan, B. D. *Statistical Geography: Problems in Analyzing Areal Data.* Glencoe, Ill.: Free Press, 1961.

Feige, E. L., and Watts, H. W. "An Investigation of the Consequences of Partial Aggregation of Microeconomic Data." *Econometrica,* 1972, *40*, 343–360.

Glass, G. V. "Primary, Secondary, and Meta-Analysis of Research." *Educational Researcher,* 1976, *5*, 3–8.

Glass, G. V., and Stanley, J. C. *Statistical Methods in Education and Psychology.* Englewood Cliffs, N.J.: Prentice Hall, 1970.

Glendening, L. "The Effects of Correlated Units of Analysis: Choosing the Appropriate Unit." Paper presented at annual meeting of the American Educational Research Association, San Francisco, April 1976.

Glendening, L., and Porter, A. C. *Interdependence and Selecting the Appropriate Unit of Analysis (or the Appropriate Analytical Model).* Technical Report No. 23, Consortium on Methodology for Aggregating Data in Educational Research. Milwaukee, Wis.: Vasquez Associates, 1976.

Haney, W. "Units of Analysis Issues in the Evaluation of Project Follow Through." Unpublished report, Huron Institute, Cambridge, Mass., 1974.

Hannan, M. T., and Burstein, L. "Estimation from Grouped Observations." *American Sociological Review,* 1974, *39*, 374–392.

Hannan, M. T., Freeman, J., and Meyer, J. W. "Specification of Models of Organizational Effectiveness." *American Sociological Review,*

1976 , *41,* 136–143.

Hannan, M. T., and Young, A. "Small-Sample Results on Estimation from Grouped Observations." Technical Report No. 24, Consortium on Methodology for Aggregating Data in Educational Research. Milwaukee, Wis.: Vasquez Associates, 1976.

Keesling, J. W., and Wiley, D. E. "Regression Models for Hierarchical Data." Paper presented at annual meeting of the Psychometric Society, Stanford University, Stanford, Calif., 1974.

Klitgaard, R. E. "Going Beyond the Mean in Educational Evaluation," *Public Policy,* 1975, *23,* 59–79.

Light, R. J., and Smith, P. V. "Accumulating Evidence: Procedures for Resolving Contradictions Among Different Research Studies." *Harvard Educational Review,* 1971, *41*(4), 429–471.

Linn, R. L., and Burstein, L. *Descriptors of Aggregates.* CSE Report Series, Los Angeles: Center for Study of Evaluation, 1977.

Lohnes, P. "Statistical Descriptors of School Classes." *American Educational Research Journal,* 1972, *9,* 547–556.

McDonald, F. J., and Elias, P. J. *The Effects of Teaching Performance on Pupil Learning.* BTES Phase II Final Report. Princeton, N.J.: Educational Testing Service, 1976.

Marco, G. L. "A Comparison of Selected Effectiveness Measures Based on Longitudinal Data." *Journal of Education and Measurement,* 1974, *11,* 225–234.

Mosteller, F., and Tukey, J. W. *Data Analysis and Regression: A Second Course in Statistics,* Reading, Mass: Addison-Wesley, 1977.

Peckham, P. D., Glass, G. V., and Hopkins, K. D. "The Experimental Unit in Statistical Analysis." *Journal of Special Education,* 1969, *3,* 337–349.

Rosenshine, B. V. "Formal and Informal Teaching Styles: A Review of S. N. Bennett and Others, 'Teaching Styles and Pupil Progress.'" *American Educational Research Journal,* 1978, *15*(1), 163.

Snow, R. E. "Learning and Individual Difference." In L. S. Shulman (Ed.), *Review of Research in Education.* Vol. 4. Itasca, Ill.: F. E. Peacock, 1976.

Stebbins, L. B., and others. *Education as Experimentation: A Planned Variation Model.* Vol. IV-A. Cambridge, Mass.: Abt Associates, 1977.

Walsh, J. E. "Concerning the Effect of Intraclass Correlation on Certain Significance Tests." *Annals of Mathematical Statistics,* 1947, *18,* 88–96.

Webb, N. "Learning in Individual and Small Group Settings." Unpublished doctoral dissertation, Stanford University, 1977.

Weibull, M. "The Distribution of t and F Statistics and of Correlations and Regression Coefficients in Stratified Samples from Normal Populations with Different Means." *Skandinavisk Aktuarietidskrift, [Scandinavian Actuarial]*, 1953, *36*, 407–416.

Wiley, D. E. "Design and Analysis of Evaluation Studies." In M. D. Wittrock and D. E. Wiley (Eds.), *The Evaluation of Instruction: Issues and Problems.* New York: Holt, Rinehart and Winston, 1970.

Wittrock, M. D., and Wiley, D. E. *The Evaluation of Instruction: Issues and Problems.* New York: Holt, Rinehart and Winston, 1970.

Lee Sechrest
William H. Yeaton

12

Empirical Bases for Estimating Effect Size

We have argued elsewhere (Sechrest and Yeaton, 1979) that statistical approaches to estimating the size of an effect obtained by an intervention have inherent limitations that make them hazardous to interpret. These limitations are conspicuous whether the studies are correlational, quasi-experimental, or experimental since they depend on the specific features of the design and implementation of the study. Consequently, the statistical estimate of the size of an intervention effect can neither be generalized to other studies nor be expected to have implications for extraexperimental decision making. This paper offers some alternative approaches that improve our ability to assess effects and reach conclusions about their real importance.

Any discussion of effect size must first consider the a priori strength of the treatment and the integrity with which it is carried out. (See Sechrest and Redner, in press, for a more detailed discussion of strength and integrity of treatment in criminal justice research.) We assert that *strength of treatment* refers to the a priori probability that a treatment could have the intended effect. For example, treatments designed to decrease the frequency of smoking range from a "treat-

Note: Preparation of this paper was supported by grant No. 1-R01-HS02702 from the National Center for Health Services Research.

ment" of one cigarette a day for five days to a very strong treatment bordering on punishment or cruelty. One must know something about the strength of a treatment in order to make recommendations about further implementation of the treatment, especially if the original test indicates that the treatment is ineffective.

Though the treatment protocol specifies a strong form, the actual treatment may not adhere to the specifications. We refer to the extent of such adherence as the integrity of treatment. For example, a rapid smoking treatment might require the client to take one puff of a cigarette every ten seconds during a fifteen-minute session over ten consecutive days. If the actual implementation of the treatment is less than ideal, this loss of integrity must inform one's expectation of the probable effect size. Therefore, all descriptions of treatments should include estimates of the strength of treatment and the methodology used to ensure integrity (Sechrest and others, 1979).

Stated simply, an experimental effect is the difference between the means for two independent groups or conditions. (See Sechrest and Yeaton, 1979, for further discussion of definitions of effect size in terms of contingency table, correlation, and regression analyses.) Examples of statements of effect size are "The body temperature of children in the experimental group was .9° lower than that of children in the control group" and "The rate of violent crime increased by 6 percent." These examples merely state the experimental (or quasi-experimental) findings; problems arise once one wishes to interpet such statements. Any meaningful interpretation is likely to require a judgment concerning the magnitude of effect produced. For example, one must judge whether a .9° difference in body temperature has any clinical significance. Is that difference sufficient to compel a physician to use the treatment that produced the difference? Similarly, one must judge whether a 6 percent increase in violent crimes is an alarming change or a relatively insignificant fluctuation. Such judgments require one to devise a measure of effect size.

Measures of effect size may be either relative or absolute, though relative measures are both more straightforward and more common. To illustrate, Cohen's d is an effect size measure found by taking the difference between two means and dividing by a standard deviation (Cohen, 1977). Hall (1978) uses this measure of effect size to assess the importance of sex differences in seventy-five studies of the ability to decode nonverbal cues. Hall aggregates effect size separately for auditory and visual cues (the mean effect sizes are .18σ and .32σ, respectively) and concludes that the contribution of visual cues to differences between sexes is the more important factor in the ability to decode nonverbal cues. Effect size measures can be used to compare results from different treatments within the same study or to compare the effect of similar treatments in different studies. Although it is possible to describe an effect size in absolute terms—for example, as .5σ—that description may lack force.

Evaluating Effect Size

Results of interventions in the social sciences are typically accompanied by a probability value indicative of the confidence that the findings could not have occurred by chance. Unfortunately, this significance level does not have any direct relation to the magnitude of the effect since the significance level depends on such factors as the number of cases studied and the care with which the study was conducted; it therefore has no necessary bearing on real-life decisions. We must decide whether a given difference between groups or a relationship between variables is large or small, important or unimportant. To assist in this decision, we offer two major categories of approaches: judgmental and normative.

Judgmental Approaches. Probably the most common method of evaluating the magnitude of an effect is based on an intuitive hunch. If a statistically significant finding *seems* large enough, researchers decide to follow up on the preliminary results. These intuititve judgments concerning effect size are not unreasonable. For example, Engelmann (1974), studying compensatory early education, reports a twenty-one point difference in IQ between experimental and control groups, a difference that we apprehend as large. Similarly we are likely to consider small the 6 percent difference in recidivism between two institutions for mentally defective delinquents that Bloom and Singer (1979) report.

We do not wish to disparage intuitive judgments of the magnitude of experimental effects. Intuition seems superior to the uncritical acceptance of all statistically significant effects as important or the assumption that results that are not statistically significant are unimportant. However, intuition alone does not provide a firm foundation for policy decisions.

To supplement intuitive judgments, one may seek the judgments of experts in a given field. Since experts have a realistic set of expectations about what constitutes significance, one may ask them to determine the degree of impressiveness of research results. This practice is traditional in behavioral psychology; data are "eyeballed" for their significance (for example, see Michael, 1974). However, a visual inspection of data may be impossible if a study is particularly complex or involves sophisticated statistical analyses. Sechrest (1976) maintains that there is a continuum of statistical analyses, varying from the transparent to the opaque, that determines a researcher's ability to make reasonable intuitive judgments. The *t* statistic represents a relatively transparent analysis; a canonical correlation is relatively opaque, as even experienced researchers find it most difficult to ascertain the social importance of a set of canonical correlations.

Many fields illustrate precedents for asking experts to assess the importance of change. Generals and admirals have always judged the degree to which changes in the military strength of enemy forces should elicit serious concern. Emlet and others (1973) sought the opinion of experts to determine the degrees of improvement in stroke victims that they judged to be clinically significant. Similarly, psychotherapy outcomes may be judged relative to the ability of treatment to improve depressive symptomatology.

A priori judgment of the potential effect of treatments that will be expressed in differential outcomes is also possible. We have submitted descriptions of smoking cessation treatments to experienced researchers, asking them to distinguish among treatments on a scale of probable effects. We then correlated their ratings with empirically obtained results and found an average correlation of .47. Some judges' correlations were better than .70. These results suggest that experts can make reasonably accurate predictions of the relative size of treatment effects.

Further credence to the value of expert judgments is revealed in an unpublished study (available from the authors) in which seventeen Fellows of the American Psychological Association were asked to estimate the strength of manipulations in five studies from the *Journal of Personality and Social Psychology*. The judges' estimates of manipulation strength were compared to the values reported in the study, and the correlations ranged from .55 to .95, with a mean correlation across the five studies of .76. A correlation of .84 was obtained when the average estimate for all judges was correlated with the actual manipulation-check value. With data such as these, we could examine two treatments judged to be equally strong that yield discrepant effect sizes and either question the integrity of the treatment or suspect that effects were mitigated by subject interaction.

Normative Approaches. Very often we assess the magnitude of an effect by comparing the effect to the same or similar effects occurring in like circumstances. For example, politicians describe an election as a "landslide victory," presumably because the margin between the winner's vote total and the nearest rival's is well (several standard deviations?) above the average difference achieved by other candidates in previous elections. They are implicitly employing a norm as the basis for describing a result as large.

More explicitly, one might judge the size of *experimental effects relative* to effects obtained by *very similar treatments*. If one finds that one smoking treatment is superior to 75 percent of previously tested smoking treatments and that its effectiveness lies above the 90th percentile for smoking treatments, one has a valuable finding for decision making. Cohen (1977) uses this perspective to justify his rule of thumb that effect sizes of at least .8σ should be considered large (since they occur so seldomly) while effect sizes of .2σ and below should be considered small (since they occur fairly frequently).

Using similar logic, Smith and Glass (1977) report an average effect size of .68σ difference between experimental and control groups, based on several hundred therapy outcome studies. They also report the standard deviation of effect size to be .67, enabling them to categorize specific treatments as small or large based on the extent of their departure from the mean effect size. Jeffrey, Wing, and Stunkard (1978) find that the mean weight loss of 11.0 pounds in their study compares favorably with a norm weight loss of 11.5 pounds calculated from twenty-one other studies of weight reduction. These illustrations demonstrate how empirically based norms allow quantitative comparison between treatments.

Researchers often present *separate norms* for experimental and control groups when their studies do not have control conditions or do not present data that enable a mean difference between experimental and control groups to be calculated. To illustrate one of the difficulties posed by such a practice, consider a smoking study that produces a 70 percent decrease in the experimental group, while another study, using exactly the same procedure, yields only a 50 percent decrease owing to a generally more recalcitrant sample. Although these treatments appear to be differentially effective, direct comparisons between studies tell us nothing about the treatment's relative efficacy as compared to its own group. Indeed, the control group may show equally impressive reductions.

Consider another hypothetical example, one involving a study reporting an effect size of .5σ where the normative mean effect size in the field is .7σ (posttest-pretest). Had the control group experienced a 15% greater attrition rate than the experimental group, the apparently reduced experimental effect might be attributable either to a weaker treatment or differential attrition. Should data from the normative sample average 1.0σ improvement for the experimental groups and .3σ improvement for the control groups, a finding of 1.0σ improvement in this particular experimental group and a .5σ improvement in this control group (1.0σ – .5σ = .5σ effect size) would tentatively indicate the reduced experimental effect to be a result of differential attrition.

Though norms for diverse sets of treatments, dependent variables, and subject samples might be established, more useful standards will probably involve homogeneous methods and results. For example, we examined thirty-two studies from volumes 30 and 31 of the *Journal of Personality and Social Psychology* that used rating scales to check the strength of manipulations or to measure changes in the dependent variable. We had supposed a fair degree of standardization and hoped to develop norms for expected effects from experimental manipulations. We were disappointed. No one scale was used in more than twelve studies, and we found sixteen different scales ranging from 4 to 201 points. Equally chaotic were the smoking modification studies. They differed in the length of the period studied after treatment and in their dependent variables, and not all data were reported at the same times for all groups in a given study. Such anarchy can no longer be tolerated if we are to develop meaningful norms.

In practice, it is often difficult to choose an appropriate normative standard. Classroom interventions are frequently evaluated by comparing the behavior of target subjects with peers in the same classroom who have not received treatment (for example, see Walker and Hops, 1976). For behavior problems, such local standards are reasonable. If an intervention's purpose is to improve reading ability, however, local norms are less justified since a case could as easily be made for state, regional, or national norms. No simple rule governs this choice. Researchers are likely to chose the norm that they judge to be most persuasive to the intended audience.

If we were afforded the luxury of data on the behavioral implications of commonly used measures, we could invoke what we call the *just-noticeable-difference approach,* modeled on the *jnd* unit in psychophysics. We can illustrate this normative approach by asking, "How much difference in intelligence makes a difference in behavior?" Cohen (1977) suggests that a small effect size of $.2\sigma$, or 3 IQ points, is not a noticeable difference in most instances, whereas a large effect size of $.8\sigma$, or 12 IQ points, is noticeable in most situations. Cohen's examples constitute the germ of a good idea, although systematic data sets are necessary to fully exploit this normative approach.

Commonly used measures in the social sciences are seldom accompanied by the *behavioral implications* of these measures. For example, how often does a person who rates his liking for a soft drink as "high" actually buy the drink? How poor an evaluation of a health clinic results in a potential client refusing to use it at all? These questions are best answered by deliberate empirical study, an orientation we think is sorely needed. One empirical paradigm that we have considered involves asking groups of judges to distinguish a "standard" person from comparison persons who possess varying degrees of, say, intelligence, anxiety, or ethnocentricity. By determining the point of difference that can be reliably discriminated, one determines an effect size of practical significance. Similar findings from diverse sets of studies might reveal that differences of some critical magnitude are detectable no matter what the measure.

In the field of applied behavior analysis, *social validation* methodology aims to establish relationships between behavior change and qualitative measures of this change (see, for example, Fawcett and Miller, 1975). Minkin and others (1976) provide an excellent example of this methodology in their study of conversational skills in predelinquent females. Subjective ratings of videotape conversations, pretraining and posttraining, were made by appropriate judges; significant, quantitative improvement was validated by substantial increases in the judges' ratings. The judges also rated the conversational ability of two norm comparison groups: university females and junior high females. We are persuaded that the differences obtained in this study can legitimately be termed large, since the posttreatment ratings were comparable to those attained by the normative group of junior high females. The fact that ratings did not fall within the range of the university females reemphasizes our previous point regarding the importance of the choice of an appropriate normative standard.

The goal of many interventions is to effect some normal state of functioning; compensatory educational programs and most medical interventions aim to alleviate some state of deficiency rather than to produce superior performance or health. We refer to this as *normalization*. For example, Ciarlo (1977) uses performance standards obtained from the community at large as a standard to judge the effectiveness of mental health interventions, and McKay and others (1978) use a comparison group of normal, middle-class children to measure the effects of their comprehensive educational and nutritional program on the IQ of barrio children in Colombia.

Because perfection is obviously an unrealistic criterion against which to evaluate research findings, researchers must attempt the difficult task of establishing a consensus on which realistic standards are, in principle, achievable. Williamson and others (1975) have suggested a measure of the percentage of achievable benefits achieved for evaluating health interventions. Devising such a standard is complicated because the implicit units on a scale of achievable benefits may not be of equal size. Still, the identification of a realistic standard may substantially improve the quality of our estimate of effect size.

We must, however, be cautious in our search for normal comparison groups. A normal comparison group of adults is a woefully poor standard against which to assess a pedestrian safety skills training program for young children (Yeaton and Bailey, 1978). Often, normal behavior is itself needful of improvement, as illustrated by the frequency with which drivers in New York City run stop lights (Freedman, 1975).

Cost-Benefit and Cost-Effectiveness Analyses

Cost-benefit and cost-effectiveness analysis represent two additional approaches to the problem of estimating effect size that may be appropriate in selected instances. The former seeks to establish that the benefits of a program outweigh the costs of producing it because even a small effect may be worthwhile if the costs of producing it are relatively trivial. The latter approach attempts to evoke absolute standards against which an intervention might be evaluated. Cost-benefit and cost-effectiveness analyses thus serve as judgmental aids in estimating the size of an experimental effect. Though considerations of cost are not nearly as critical to the social scientist as to the policy maker, effect size must often be weighted by the efforts required to produce them.

Dollars and cents calculations of cost are deceptively simple objective criteria on which to base a decision. Unfortunately, there are no universal rules for choosing among possible discount rates or adjustments for risk, to name but two subjective features that influence the analysis. Furthermore, these analyses are but one aspect of the decision process, and other considerations may be equally problematic. A particularly apt illustration is Cobb and Alvarez's (n.d.) study of Seattle's mobile cardiac care units. Their estimates suggest that it costs approximately $3500 to save a single life. In deciding whether this program is worthwhile, one needs to know the costs of saving a life by other means, the average life span of patients after treatment, the quality of their physical health after treatment, and the like.

Any social program that can document the saving of a single life can justify the efforts necessary to do so. A difficulty, of course, lies in determining whether the life was saved because of the intervention or simply by chance. Emergency medical squads in Seattle may claim a "save" upon submission of supporting evidence to a committee empowered to grant saves. This procedure allows analysts to compare different strategies for delivering emergency care and judge which is most productive.

Thus the task of quantifying social costs and benefits is often difficult if not impossible. Proxy measures, such as IQ test scores, may be used to compare the effectiveness of social programs if dollar estimates of benefit are not possible. Dollar estimates of cost may be equally formidable. What is the presumed psychological cost of a painful shot that may prevent illness or of a staff using techniques that submit them to significantly greater responsibility? Economic estimates of opportunity cost, distributional questions pertaining to actual recipients of benefits and costs, and alternative estimation techniques such as willingness to pay (Acton, 1976) further compound an already complicated set of procedures.

There appear to be few other absolute standards to judge the effectiveness of interventions. Virtually every example that we could muster, such as averting rapes, blindness, or child abuse, and the discovery and fostering of genius, must be judged in terms of the costs necessary to achieve them. Realistically, we are guarded in our optimism about supposing that outcomes have inherent values that cannot be questioned or weighted in some way.

Cost analyses are thus another of an imperfect set of techniques to assist the decision maker. However, ethical considerations and political acceptability cannot be neglected in the decision-making process. Failure to calculate the potential weight of these two factors may ruin an otherwise sophisticated estimation of effect size.

Treatments and Their Effects: An Integration

There need not be a relationship between a treatment and an effect; neither is there necessarily any relationship between an effect and a perceived effect. To explain the reasons for this conceptual independence, we need to define or redefine pertinent terms.

Treatments are relatively weak or strong: Cyanide is a strong treatment for the pains of living; a grain of aspirin is a weak treatment for migraine headaches. Treatments are also relatively appropriate or inappropriate. Strong treatments may have no effect if they are inappropriate to the problem at hand. For example, street patrols may affect the incidence of street crimes, but this strategy will not alter the rate of embezzlement, a problem clearly inappropriate to this treatment.

An effect, or an outcome, is a change in the phenomenon or related phenomena that the intervention was intended to alter. A perceived effect is the change believed to have occurred by either the providers or recipients of treatments. A program's effects may not be perceived by participants, or participants may assert imagined but unmeasured effects. Consider the following examples from various studies as illustrations of actual and perceived effect.

Milgram's (1963) studies of compliance with authority exemplify a treatment with large actual effects and large perceived effects. A large proportion of subjects responded to the experiment by expressing strong reactions to the experimental procedures. In other studies, the large effects may not be perceived or no effort may be made to assess changed perceptions. Engelmann (1974) reports a remarkable increase in measured IQ for children in the treatment group, though systematic reports of perceived change by parents and teachers are not included in the study.

A second type of treatment involves effects that are small as perceived and as measured. Most psychological research and many social interventions are characterized by statistically significant findings that are small in magnitude. Neither subjects nor experimenters are likely to be impressed by the changes. For example, Kelling and others (1974) report minimal changes in crime rates, citizen satisfaction, and the like associated with a relatively intensive police patrol intervention. Citizens did not perceive any changes from these efforts.

Some studies report large perceived changes despite small measured changes. Patients often express considerable enthusiasm for the effects of laetrile, although evidence of real physiological change is conspicuously absent. Conversely, large effects may be perceived as small. Fawcett and Miller (1975) studied the effects of a behavioral intervention designed to improve public-speaking skills. Though average behavior changes were dramatic, from 4 percent appropriate behavior during baseline to 90 percent subsequent to treatment, average rating-scale measures of perceived change were minimal, from 3.6 to 4.7 on a 7-point scale.

Treatments then may be characterized by their strength and the sizes of their perceived and real effects. A consideration of these three variables enhances our understanding of the relationship between various interventions and diverse outcomes. For example, consider weak treatments that result in large perceived effects and large measured effects. We should well be suspicious of treatments that meet this description. For instance, if a person experiences powerful effects after taking an apparently usual dose of medication, he may hypothesize that the medication was not of ordinary strength or guess that he had ingested a foreign substance. If the results of an intervention appear too large to be believable—say a 75 percent reduction in the recidivism rate of imprisoned felons associated with a group counseling program (see Lipton, Martinson, and Wilks, 1975)—they cast doubt on the outcome. One plausible explanation for such results is that the demand characteristics of the experiment produced a strong set to respond in a particular way (see Orne, 1962). In any case, such results are counterintuitive and seem to demand reinterpretation.

Strong treatments that yield a large effect and a large perceived effect are not problematic, except that they are rarely encountered.

Analogously, weak treatments that produce a small effect and a small perceived effect are problematic only in that they are so frequently encountered. As researchers become more sensitive to the strength, appropriateness, and integrity of their treatments, the preponderance of such examples should diminish.

Weak treatments that yield a small effect and a large perceived effect are exemplified by placebos. A placebo dose of alcohol is clearly a weak treatment that yields few measurable physiological effects, yet it may be experienced as potent by subjects (see Lang and others, 1975). Strong treatments that produce a small effect and a large perceived effect may be illustrated by certain psychoanalytic treatments. A long, intensive psychoanalysis can be a putatively strong treatment associated with small, actual changes, although patients may describe the changes in their life very favorably.

Weak treatments that produce large actual effects but small perceived effects are difficult to illustrate by cases; most instances of such data would demand reinterpretation. Strong treatments that produce large, measurable effects which may not be perceived are exemplified by the effects of alcohol on the skills of automobile drivers. Finally, strong treatments yielding small measured and perceived effects lead us to suspect that the treatment lacked integrity. For example, an investigation by *New York* magazine revealed that the alcoholic content of certain mixed drinks dispensed in a Manhattan bar was well below normal, thus the consumption of those drinks did not produce the expected effects. Another cause of such outcomes is that the treatment is simply inappropriate for the problem encountered; for example, penicillin does not affect viral infections.

To force a priori assessments of treatment strength and integrity that would be considered separate from their outcomes is, admittedly, unconventional. But this practice forces researchers to consider outcomes in the context of similar treatment application. And the result of such strong procedures should produce important effects perceived to be of real value by the reader.

References

Acton, J. P. "Economic Analysis and the Evaluation of Medical Programs." Paper presented at the Conference on Emergency Medical Services, Atlanta, 1976.

Bloom, H. S., and Singer, N. M. "Determining the Cost-Effectiveness of Correctional Programs: The Case of Patuxent Institution." Unpublished manuscript, Harvard University, 1979.

Ciarlo, J. A. "Monitoring and Analysis of Mental Health Program Outcome Data." *Evaluation*, 1977, *4*, 109–114.

Cobb, L. A., and Alvarez, H., III. "Medic I: The Seattle System for Management of Out-Of-Hospital Emergencies." Unpublished manuscript, University of Washington and Harborview Medical Center, n.d.

Cohen, J. *Statistical Power Analysis and the Behavioral Sciences.* (Rev. ed.). New York: Academic Press, 1977.

Emlet, H. E., and others. *Estimated Health Benefits and Costs of Post-Onset Care of Stroke.* Unpublished report, Johns Hopkins University, 1973.

Engelmann, S. "The Effectiveness of Direct Verbal Instruction on IQ Performance and Achievement in Reading and Arithmetic." In R. Ulrich, T. Stachnick, and J. Mabry (Eds.), *Control of Human Behavior.* Vol. 3. Glenview, Ill.: Scott, Foresman, 1974.

Fawcett, S. B., and Miller, L. K. "Training Public-Speaking Behavior: An Experimental Analysis and Social Validation." *Journal of Applied Behavior Analysis*, 1975, *8*, 125–135.

Freedman, J. "Running the Red." *New York*, November 17, 1975, pp. 117–118, 120.

Hall, J. A. "Gender Effects in Decoding Nonverbal Cues." *Psychological Bulletin*, 1978, *85*, 845–857.

Jeffrey, R. W., Wing, R. R., and Stunkard, A. J. "Behavioral Treatment of Obesity: The State of the Art, 1976." *Behavior Therapy*, 1978, *9*, 189–199.

Kelling, G. W., and others. *The Kansas City Preventive Patrol Experiment: A Technical Report.* Washington, D.C.: Police Foundation, 1974.

Lang, A. R., and others. "Effects of Alcohol on Aggression in Male Social Drinkers." *Journal of Abnormal Psychology*, 1975, *84*, 508–518.

Lipton, D., Martinson, R., and Wilks, J. *The Effectiveness of Correctional Treatment: A Survey of Treatment Evaluation Studies.* New York: Praeger, 1975.

McKay, H., and others. "Improving Cognitive Ability in Chronically Deprived Children." *Science*, 1978, *200*, 270–278.

Michael, J. "Statistical Inference for Individual Organism Research: Mixed Blessing or Curse?" *Journal of Applied Behavior Analysis*, 1974, *7*, 647–653.

Milgram, S. "Behavioral Study of Obedience." *Journal of Abnormal and Social Psychology*, 1963, *67*, 371–378.

Minkin, N., and others. "The Social Validation and Training of Conversational Skills." *Journal of Applied Behavior Analysis*, 1976, *9*, 127–139.

Orne, M. T. "On the Social Psychology of the Psychological Experiment: With Particular Reference to Demand Characteristics and Their Implications." *American Psychologist,* 1962, *17,* 776–783.

Sechrest, L. "Estimating Size of Effects in Health Research." Unpublished manuscript, Florida State University, 1976.

Sechrest, L., and Redner, R. "Strength and Integrity of Treatments in Evaluation Studies." *Criminal Justice Evaluation Reports,* in press.

Sechrest, L., and Yeaton, W. H. "Estimating Magnitudes of Experimental Effects." Unpublished manuscript, 1979.

Sechrest, L, and others. "Some Neglected Problems in Evaluation Research: Strength and Integrity of Treatments." In L. Sechrest and others (Eds.), *Evaluation Studies Review Annual.* Vol. 4. Beverly Hills, Calif.: Sage, 1979.

Smith, M. L., and Glass, G. V. "Meta-Analysis of Psychotherapy Outcome Studies." *American Psychologist,* 1977, *32,* 752–760.

Walker, H. M., and Hops, H. "Use of Normative Peer Data as a Standard for Evaluating Classroom Treatment Effects." *Journal of Applied Behavior Analysis,* 1976, *9,* 159–168.

Williamson, J. W., and others. "Health Accounting: An Outcome-Based System of Quality Assurance: Illustrative Application to Hypertension. Medical Care Outcomes: Assessment and Improvement." *Bulletin of the New York Academy of Medicine* (2nd series), 1975, *51,* 727–738.

Yeaton, W. H., and Bailey, J. S. "Teaching Pedestrian Safety Skills to Young Children: An Analysis and One-Year Followup." *Journal of Applied Behavior Analysis,* 1978, *11,* 315–329.

13

David B. Pillemer
Richard J. Light

Using the Results of Randomized Experiments to Construct Social Programs

Much of the debate about how experimentation should influence social policy centers on the adequacy of different research designs. A key question is whether or not controlled field trials are useful or necessary for conducting policy research. A strong case for the importance of randomization to assess program effects accurately has been made by such researchers as Campbell and Boruch (1975), Gilbert, Light and Mosteller (1975), and Riecken and others (1974). Randomly assigning

Note: This work was facilitated by grants from the National Institute of Education and the Spencer Foundation. We thank Terrence Tirnan for his helpful comments.

This chapter is adapted from L. Sechrest and others (Eds.), *Evaluation Studies Review Annual*, Vol. 4 (Beverly Hills, Calif.: Sage, 1979), pp. 717–726.

people to different treatment groups has the advantage that, for reasonably large samples, the groups are likely to have similar distributions on most background variables. Therefore, randomization allows the causal attribution of posttreatment group differences to the differential effects of the treatments.

Although randomization is desirable, it does not by itself ensure adequate social policy inferences. Equally important is the careful interpretation of research findings in order to improve our predictions of a program's probable effects in real-life settings. In this chapter, we focus on this inferential step, from experiment to implementation.

As part of a review of numerous social policy research topics, we have analyzed many research studies. For the major studies in each area, we have compared their reported findings and the quality of their research designs. These secondary analyses have helped to identify several methodological caveats that we believe are general and quite separate from the question of randomization. The caveats all pertain to situations in which a well-evaluated experimental treatment may perform unpredictably if implemented more widely.

We therefore present here three caveats that apply to a range of social policy research areas, including education, health, and criminal justice. Each caveat suggests a central role for secondary analyses of experimental studies in formulating social policy. Comparison of the major studies in an area serves two purposes: (1) to help identify situations in which the policy implications of experimental studies are unclear, and (2) to improve predictions of program success or failure in these situations.

Considering Relative Gain

Consider a new program developed to train paramedics. The program is to be evaluated, using the best research design possible. From a pool of forty applicants, twenty are randomly assigned to the training program and twenty to a control group. One year after the trainees have completed the program, a comparison is made. The results are clear; the twenty trainees are all employed, at good salaries, and their supervisors and patients are highly satisfied with their performance. The control group is not doing as well. The training program is apparently a success, as determined by a randomized field trial. The next step is to implement this program on a large scale and to give more people the same excellent training.

Next year the program is widely implemented. All 20,000 unemployed but trainable people in a city are given the paramedic training. What happens? The expanded program is a failure. A year later almost all of the trainees are unemployed. Why? Although there had been a demand for the 20 trained paramedics, there was not a demand for 20,000 trained paramedics. So the highly successful and well-evaluated experimental program broke down when expanded into a large-scale program.

This extreme example illustrates an important concept: In some social programs, the benefit that the program confers to any one recipient is a function of how many other people participate in the program. The program's value to the individual participant depends on the program's size. In this case, the more widely the training program is disseminated, the lower the expected benefit to any one trainee. Although the program may produce the same *absolute* increase in performance for all participants, the *relative benefit* that this increase confers to any individual decreases as the program size increases (that is, a relative gain constraint). We have rarely seen this simple point made in evaluations of job training programs, yet this is precisely the sort of caution that evaluators making policy recommendations cannot afford to forget.

A second example also illustrates that program value may depend on program size. Suppose a law school has 1,000 applicants for 100 places in its entering class. The school decides to accept the 100 people with the highest scores on an entrance exam. Professor Johnson alleges that she has developed a curriculum that can uniformly raise applicant's scores by 200 points on that exam. An evaluator is incredulous; he designs a randomized trial to assess the effects of Professor Johnson's curriculum. Forty applicants are randomly assigned to two groups of twenty; one group studies Professor Johnson's curriculum while the other receives no special training. After four months, the two groups are given the test and, shortly thereafter, the law school announces its selections. From the treatment group, all twenty applicants are accepted, while from the control group only two are accepted. Looking at the test scores, admission data, and excellent research design, the evaluator concludes that the new curriculum is indeed effective. Professor Johnson, encouraged by these exciting findings, sets up a chain of "prep schools" for the law school test. But next year, when the evaluator returns to see what happened to the graduates of Johnson's curriculum, he finds that the probability of being admitted for any applicant who takes the course has dropped from 100 percent to 10 percent, the value for the control group in the original evaluation.

What explains the program's large-scale ineffectiveness? All 1,000 applicants took the preparatory course, while the law school continued to accept only 100 students. As promised, the program may still have produced an average *absolute gain* of 200 points for its participants, but if all applicants took the course, no subgroup of applicants would experience a *relative gain* in test performance. As in the previous example, the benefit that this program confers to any one participant depends on how many other applicants also participated.

To assess accurately the relative gain afforded to program participants, it is necessary to consider the availability of *opportunities for success* as well as the ratio of the number of program participants to the total number of competing individuals. If there are many opportunities for success, an increase in the number of program participants may have little influence on the program's effectiveness. In the extreme case with as many opportunities available as there are competing individuals, the number of people who receive special program services is unimportant. Thus, in the law school admissions example, if there are 1,000 applicants and 1,000 acceptances, the number of applicants who participate in a special program to improve entry test scores is not related to program success as measured by the acceptance ratio.

As the number of opportunities for success decreases, increasing the number of program participants diminishes program effectiveness. For instance, with only 100 law school acceptances, increasing the number of people who attend the preparatory course severely limits the advantages provided to program participants. Clearly, relative gain depends on two factors—the number of opportunities for success and the ratio of program participants (n) to the total number of competing individuals (N). Both factors must be considered in a prediction of an experimental program's likelihood for success when implemented on a larger scale.

Secondary analysis makes possible a preliminary indication of whether a particular program has a relative gain constraint, if data on program effectiveness exist at several sites with different sampling fractions, n/N. If so, one can compare each site's sampling fraction with the program's demonstrated effectiveness. When those sites with larger fractions have smaller program effects, one should suspect that a relative gain constraint may be in operation.

The examples presented here underscore the importance of considering the *relative gain* experienced by any participant. But often *absolute gains* produced by large-scale program implementation are important in their own right. For example, if a program that produces uniform gains in children's reading skills is administered to all children, no participants will experience a relative gain. However, all of the children may benefit from the program, in terms of increased productivity, happiness, and so on. Programs that improve the general quality of life (such as those resulting in better health or increased life span) provide examples of situations in which absolute gain is of primary importance.

Unpredictable Interactions Between
Immediate and Follow-up Program Effects

Our second caveat concerns the potential hazards of judging the success of a program prior to observing the participants' performance later. For example, a treatment may result in considerable initial gains for its participants, yet these gains may dissipate when followed by incompatible programs. Or a program that initially appears to be a failure may combine productively with a follow-up program, resulting in an eventual "success."

As with the first caveat, the dangers of prematurely judging a program to be a success or a failure are not eliminated simply by conducting controlled, randomized field trials. In fact, evaluators may place high levels of confidence in the initial outcome of a well-prepared study, and deemphasize such "secondary" aspects of the study design as following participants longitudinally. When an initial program combines unpredictably with a follow-up program, the long-term outcomes may be poor.

The importance of following program participants longitudinally is widely noted in theory. A concrete illustration may be useful. From education, two evaluation studies provide an example of unpredictable interactions between preschool programs and elementary school. One study was conducted by Miller and Dyer (1971) and the other by Erickson and associates (1969). We have chosen these particular studies because they provide examples of the general methodological point that we wish to make; we are not trying to provide new substantive insights into preschool curriculums.

Both evaluations satisfied a number of experimental design criteria. In particular, assignment of subjects to treatments was at least partially randomized in both studies. Two types of programs were evaluated in each study: a regular, or traditional, Head Start program, and a highly structured Bereiter-Engelmann (B-E) curriculum. (Miller and Dyer use the label *traditional* to describe the regular program; Erickson refers to the regular preschool program as the *enrichment program* but emphasizes its traditional nature.) Erickson's preschoolers subsequently attended either B-E or regular kindergarten programs. Miller and Dyer's preschoolers moved on to either regular or highly academic Follow-Through kindergarten and first grade programs. We will focus on the long-term effects of the Bereiter-Engelmann (B-E) and regular preschool programs on one outcome measure—the Stanford-Binet Intelligence Test.

Erickson's results indicate that the B-E preschool program was superior to the regular program. Students in the B-E program demonstrated higher IQs than the traditional students following one year of preschool. In addition, B-E preschoolers remained above average intelligence one year after preschool regardless of the type of kindergarten (B-E or regular) they later attended. Traditional preschoolers were close to their age level in intelligence following either kindergarten experience, with those children attending B-E kindergarten scoring slightly higher than those in regular kindergarten.

Miller and Dyer's B-E preschoolers also demonstrated slightly higher IQs than traditional preschoolers immediately following preschool. However, while both the B-E and regular preschool groups experienced an overall decrease in IQ following preschool, B-E preschoolers decreased at a faster rate. This rapid decrease was due primarily to the poor test performance of B-E preschoolers in regular kindergarten and first grade. In contrast, the regular preschoolers' rate of IQ decreased more gradually in regular elementary school programs. As a result, the overall IQ performance of the regular preschoolers was higher than the B-E preschoolers by the end of first grade.

This example illustrates several methodological points. First, it demonstrates the critical importance of evaluating subjects' performances *longitudinally*. Had these studies reported only the immediate effects of preschool on students' IQ scores, the B-E program would have appeared superior in both studies. Since both studies were well designed, a large degree of confidence would have been placed in these convergent findings. However, we have seen that the effectiveness of the programs over time is not stable but depends strongly on what follows.

Second, the unpredictable interactions of preschool with follow-up programs were identified only by comparing the different preschool evaluations. Study of only one of the two reports would lead to different conclusions about the long-term effectiveness of the different preschool curriculums. Erickson's study indicates that the B-E curriculum is consistently superior, while Miller and Dyer suggest that the B-E preschool effectiveness dissipates rapidly when followed by regular schooling.

Once conflicting results are identified through secondary analysis, it is important to attempt to account for the discrepancy. A possible explanation for the example just cited is the use of imprecise treatment labels. The B-E and regular preschool programs may not have been identical in the two studies. And even if these two programs were similar, the follow-up programs certainly differed in some important aspects. The fact that Erickson's B-E preschoolers maintained a high

IQ performance in regular kindergarten while the performance of Miller and Dyer's B-E preschoolers dropped so sharply may be a result of substantive differences between similarly labeled programs. These conflicting results indicate that follow-up programs as well as the primary treatments need to be carefully defined and monitored.

Unpredictable Consequences of Implementing Experimental Treatments over Time

The long-term impact of a program depends to some extent on the experiences that follow it. Predicting the long-term impact of social programs becomes even more problematic when the effects may differ according to the tenure of the treatment. The long-term implementation of a particular treatment may exert a qualitatively different influence on participants than is indicated by the short-term experimental effect of the same treatment.

Studies investigating the effects on children from watching violence on television illustrate this point. There is some converging agreement among researchers that viewing violence on television causes children to act aggressively (Leifer, Gordon, and Graves, 1974). Several randomized experiments examining the immediate effects of exposing children to aggressive media content support this conclusion (see, for example, Hanratty and others, 1969; Drabman and Thomas, 1974).

Conclusions that can be drawn from the few longer-term experimental studies are less clear but suggest some conflict with short-term findings. For example, Feshbach and Singer (1971) manipulated the television watching of institutionalized boys over a six-week period. Half the subjects watched violent shows, while the other half viewed nonviolent shows. Surprisingly, certain subgroups of subjects who watched mostly nonviolent shows demonstrated more aggressive tendencies than subjects in the violent viewing group. Critics of this study (for example, Leifer, Gordon, and Graves, 1974) have stated that it contains serious methodological weaknesses and that Feshbach and Singer's unexpected finding of increased aggression in viewers of nonviolent shows may be artifactual. Wells (1973) replicated the study of Feshbach and Singer with some modifications. He found that while viewing of violent conditions increased physical aggression, a nonviolent television diet increased viewers' verbal aggression.

It is possible that limiting televised violence for different periods may qualitatively change the treatment. Short-term exposure to certain types of television shows does not alter children's normal viewing patterns. However, manipulation of children's television viewing over extended periods of time disrupts their normal viewing behaviors. For example, the control boys in Feshbach and Singer's study did not simply watch nonviolent shows; this "treatment" meant that they could not watch violent shows that they liked. It is possible that not allowing control subjects to watch their favorite shows resulted in their increased aggressiveness. Further, limiting children's exposure to violence on television for even longer time periods could result in another reversal of subject reactions. Over longer periods of time the control subjects' anger and aggressiveness might diminish.

We could continue to speculate about the possible effects of long-term changes in children's exposure to televised violence, but that is not the key issue here. The point is that qualitative differences may emerge in the effects of a treatment, depending on whether it is temporarily superimposed on naturally existing behaviors or whether it forces the reorganization of those behaviors. Short-term experiments—regardless of their quality—do not provide conclusive evidence about long-term implementations of similar treatments.

A second area of research on television—investigating the effects of advertising on children—also illustrates the difficulty of predicting the outcomes of long-term treatment implementation. As with violence on television, commercials have stimulated public and academic interest in recent years. A number of studies have measured the effects of television advertising on a variety of outcomes, such as children's purchase requests, attitudes, and consumer learning. Two principal findings emerge: (1) that the young child's understanding of commercials increases with age (Robertson and Rossiter, 1974; Rubin, 1972; Ward and Wackman, 1973), and (2) that short-term exposure to specific commercials may influence children's behaviors and attitudes (Atkin, 1975a, 1975b; Liefeld and others, 1974). The experimental studies by Atkin and Liefeld and others used randomization to some degree. The evidence suggests that although young children lack the sophistication to evaluate accurately the information presented in commercials, they are often influenced by television advertisements.

Citing this evidence, consumer advocate groups, such as Action for Children's Television, have called for the elimination of commercials directed toward children (Charren and Sarson, 1973). The Federal Trade Commission is currently studying whether formal regulations are appropriate. As with violence on television, however, it is difficult to predict the effects of severely limiting children's exposure to television commercials over long time periods. Although much of the present evidence may be interpreted as supporting consumer advocates' attempts to restrict television advertising, extreme limitations might result in unexpected outcomes.

One such outcome might be an impeded development of adult consumer skills. According to this position, it is necessary to watch commercials to learn to judge their merits more accurately. Thus, children may benefit more from the critical analysis of commercials, guided by parents or teachers, than from their prohibition. A counterargument is that television commercials directed toward children are not a necessary part of consumer socialization, especially since children are often exposed to advertisements directed to adults. Rather than advocate for one side or the other, we wish to illustrate how a long-term treatment implementation may have unpredictable consequences. Both viewpoints concerning long-term effects of eliminating commercials directed toward children are speculative. Existing studies do not provide conclusive evidence about the results of long-range changes.

Although it is often difficult to forecast the outcomes of long-term programs from the results of short-term experiments, existing research may still be useful in formulating social policy. Present policy should be based on the best available data. However, when the long-term impact of policy interventions is uncertain, policies should be frequently monitored for unintended long-term consequences. Secondary analysis is instrumental in comparing the results of experimental studies that differ in the length of the treatment. Conflicting results suggest that the tenure of a treatment is a critical determinant of program success.

A comparison of experimental studies' results with those of carefully done descriptive studies may also prove useful in identifying treatments that have unintended long-term consequences. Descriptive studies investigate subjects' naturally existing behaviors with observational techniques, interviews, or questionnaires. Their principal advantage is that they avoid the problem of artificially manipulating subjects' exposure to a treatment. These studies can provide valuable information about more stable influences on behavior. Unfortunately, the validity of cause and effect inferences based on descriptive data is difficult to assess. Despite this limitation, however, descriptive studies provide estimates of the effects of ongoing influences on human behavior. Thus, in application of the results of research studies for formulating policy, it may be useful to conduct analyses that compare the results of experimental and descriptive studies (Boruch, 1975). When the outcomes of descriptive studies conflict with experimental results, social programs based on the results of controlled experiments should be checked for unforeseen effects.

Conclusions

Conducting randomized experiments is not sufficient for determining if a program will be successful when implemented in nonexperimental settings. Our three caveats should be kept in mind before widely implementing an experimental program: the consideration of relative gain, the observation of participants' performance in follow-up programs, and the regulation of unanticipated consequences of long-term program implementations based on short-term experimental findings.

Secondary analyses may often identify policy areas where the results of different research studies conflict. However, these discrepancies are no cause for despair. Real treatment effects may often vary drastically, depending on such factors as the number of participants, the length of time the program is in operation, and the types of experiences that follow it. This information is invaluable for deciding how and where to implement similar programs.

Not everyone agrees that conflicting outcomes among studies may provide us with valuable information. Some researchers argue that if a large number of studies are available concerning the effectiveness of a program, we should be able to decide whether or not the program really "works." But this argument may oversimplify reality. Take the effects of busing on children's school achievement as an example. Some evaluation studies show substantial positive program effects, some show clear negative program effects, and the majority show no effect at all (Light and Smith, 1971). One way to consider all these studies is to search for convergence over time. This approach implies not only that a true average effect of busing exists but that it would be useful to know such an average and that as more studies are performed the true effect will be estimated more precisely. But what if this assumption is incorrect? Suppose that there are some settings in which busing is highly effective and other settings where busing has a disastrous effect on children's achievement. Then, as more studies and data accumulate, there is no reason to expect convergence of results. Secondary analysts should accept the variation of results not as confusion but as an accurate representation of reality. After acceptance of this idea, the next step is to identify setting-by-treatment interactions, so that policy makers can understand more fully under what precise circumstances a program will or will not work. For example, a researcher might want to see if busing works in small cities but not in large ones or with elementary school children but not with older students.

The three caveats we have discussed may serve the same purpose—to identify the particular settings in the real world where a well-evaluated experimental program is likely to succeed. Certain programs will be successful only when the number of participants is limited, if follow-up programs are compatible, or if a treatment is implemented for a certain length of time. The ultimate goal is to identify precisely those combinations of setting and program that lead to successful outcomes.

References

Atkin, C. *Effects of Television Advertising on Children: First Year Experimental Evidence (Research Report No. 1).* Washington, D.C.: Office of Child Development, June 1975a.

Atkin, C. *Effects of Television Advertising on Children: Second Year Experimental Evidence (Research Report No. 2).* Washington, D.C.: Office of Child Development, June 1975b.

Boruch, R. F. "Coupling Randomized Experiments and Approximations to Experiments in Social Program Evaluation." *Sociological Methods and Research,* 1975, *4*, 31–53.

Campbell, D. T., and Boruch, R. F. "Making the Case for Randomized Assignment to Treatments by Considering the Alternatives: Six Ways in Which Quasi-Experimental Evaluations in Compensatory Education Tend to Underestimate Effects." In C. A. Bennett and A. A. Lumsdaine (Eds.), *Evaluation and Experiment: Some Critical Issues in Assessing Social Programs.* New York: Academic Press, 1975.

Charren, P., and Sarson, E. "Children's T.V: Sugar Makes Cents." *News and Comment* (American Academy of Pediatrics), 1973, *24*,(6), 10–12.

Drabman, R. S., and Thomas, M. H. "Does Media Violence Increase Children's Toleration of Real-Life Aggression?" *Developmental Psychology,* 1974, *10*, 418–421.

Erickson, E., and others. *Experiments in Head Start and Early Education: Curriculum Structures and Teacher Attitudes (Final Report).* Washington, D.C.: Office of Child Development, November 1969.

Feshbach, S., and Singer, R. D. *Television and Aggression: An Experimental Field Study.* San Francisco: Jossey-Bass, 1971.

Gilbert, J. P., Light, R. J., and Mosteller, F. "Assessing Social Innovations: An Empirical Base for Policy." In C. A. Bennett and A. A. Lumsdaine (Eds.), *Evaluation and Experiment: Some Critical Issues in Assessing Social Programs.* New York: Academic Press, 1975.

Hanratty, M. A., and others. "Imitation of Film-Mediated Aggression Against Live and Inanimate Victims." In *Proceedings of the 77th Annual Convention of the American Psychological Association.* Washington, D.C.: American Psychological Association, 1969.

Leifer, A., Gordon, N., and Graves, S. "Children's Television: More Than Mere Entertainment." *Harvard Educational Review*, 1974, *44*, 213-245.

Liefeld, J. P., and others. "Television Advertising and Children: An Experimental Study." Unpublished manuscript, University of Guelph, Ontario, 1974.

Light, R. J., and Smith, P. V. "Accumulating Evidence: Procedures for Resolving Contradiction Among Different Research Studies." *Harvard Educational Review*, 1971, *41*(4), 429-471.

Miller, L. B., and Dyer, J. "Two Kinds of Kindergarten After Four Types of Head Start." Paper presented at the biennial meeting of the Society for Research in Child Development, Minneapolis, Minn., April 1-4, 1971.

Riecken, H. W., and others. *Social Experimentation: A Method for Planning and Evaluating Social Intervention*. New York: Academic Press, 1974.

Robertson, T. S., and Rossiter, J. R. "Children and Commercial Persuasion: An Attribution Theory Analysis." *Journal of Consumer Research*, 1974, *1*, 13-20.

Rubin, R. S. "An Exploratory Investigation of Children's Response to Commercial Content of Television Advertising in Relation to Their Stages of Cognitive Development." Unpublished doctoral dissertation, University of Massachusetts, 1972.

Ward, S., and Wackman, D. "Children's Information Processing of Television Advertising." In P. Clar (Ed.), *New Models for Mass Communication Research*. Beverly Hills: Sage, 1973.

Wells, W. D. "Television and Aggression: Replication of an Experimental Field Study." Unpublished manuscript, Graduate School of Business, University of Chicago, 1973.

14   *William J. Bowers*
Glenn L. Pierce

Capital Punishment as Deterrent:
Challenging
Isaac Ehrlich's Research

In this critique of Ehrlich's (1973, 1975a) research on capital punishment, we conclude that he has failed to provide any reliable evidence that the death penalty deters murder. His data are inadequate for the purposes of his analysis and he misapplies the highly sophisticated statistical techniques he employs. We begin with an evaluation of the data he uses to measure the critical variables in his theoretical formula-

Note: We wish to thank Andrea Carr, Elizabeth Chambers, Robert Kazarian, Phyllis Lakin, and Shari Wittenberg for their help in preparing this chapter. We also thank the staff of the Northeastern University Computation Center for providing frequent and extended access to the computer in connection with this work. This work was supported in part by Grant No. RR07143 from the U.S. Department of Health, Education, and Welfare.

Reprinted by permission of the Yale Law Journal Company and Fred B. Rothman & Company from *The Yale Law Journal*, 1975, *85*, 187–208, in which this material first appeared in slightly different form.

tion and then consider flaws in his analysis which would invalidate his conclusions even if his data were adequate. We conclude by explaining how Ehrlich's analysis produces results which seem consistent with the deterrence hypothesis when in fact they are not.*

Inadequacies in Ehrlich's Data

The credibility of Ehrlich's conclusions depends on the quality of the data he has used. For measures of the variables at the core of his theoretical analysis, he relies on the Uniform Crime Reporting System (UCRS) of the FBI (Ehrlich, 1975a, p. 406). The behavior he seeks to explain (the dependent variable) is the annual criminal homicide rate for the United States as reported by the UCRS, and his deterrence variables are the rates of arrest, conviction, and execution for homicide, which also come entirely or in part from the UCRS. Only if these data are sound throughout the full time period covered by Ehrlich's analysis do his findings deserve serious consideration.

The Dependent Variable. The FBI's national homicide statistics collected in the early years of the UCRS are unreliable. A staff report of the National Commission on the Causes and Prevention of Violence emphasizes this problem: "Many reporting agencies, especially in the nonurban areas, were slow in joining the UCR network; there were only 400 agencies reporting to the UCR in the 1930s, while today there are about 8,500. Thus trends of both violent and nonviolent crimes during the early years of the UCR are highly questionable as representative of national figures" (1969, p. 17). Furthermore, the President's Commission on Law Enforcement and the Administration of Justice warns that "figures prior to 1958, and particularly those prior to 1940, must be viewed as neither fully comparable with nor nearly so reliable as later figures" (1967 p. 20).

Ehrlich (1975a) indicates that he used "readjusted" estimates of the homicide rate supplied by the FBI. The FBI has periodically adjusted their estimates of offenses for earlier years on the basis of recent data on offences from jurisdictions that entered the reporting program after 1958. Yet to our knowledge there are no published indications of how the readjustments are performed. In any case, the adjustment of figures for as long ago as forty years on the basis of the current homicide levels of agencies recently added to the sample is of dubious value.

*The findings presented here are drawn from a more extensive and detailed critique of Ehrlich's work by the present authors (see Bowers and Pierce, 1975). That manuscript includes as appendices the full regression results for equations used to estimate coefficients in this chapter (appendix B, on file with *The Yale Law Journal*, 401A Yale Station, New Haven, Conn. 06520).

Less problematic are the willful homicide figures compiled by the Bureau of the Census. Unlike the voluntary reporting system of the FBI, census reports of willful homicide are mandated by law in each state. The annual collection of mortality statistics including willful homicide began in 1900, thirty years before the beginning of the FBI reporting system. By 1933, all states had met the 90 percent coverage requirement for admission to the national vital statistics program (U.S. Public Health Service, 1954). Thus, the census homicide statistics for the nation have been relatively complete since the early 1930s. (According to the U.S. Public Health Service, 1954, tests of the completeness of birth registrations made in 1940 and 1950 indicated that these statistics were, respectively, 92.5 and 97.9 percent complete. Although precise studies of the completeness of death registrations are not available for this period, the compilers of the vital statistics believe that they are even more complete than birth registrations.) Furthermore, the classification of "willful homicide" has remained essentially constant over time. The National Center for Health Statistics reports: "Since 1900, the causes of death have been classified according to seven different revisions of the International Classification of Diseases. Each revision has produced some breaks in the comparability of cause-of-death statistics. However, homicide is among the causes for which the classifications are essentially comparable for all revisions" (1967, p. 9). For these reasons, perhaps, the census homicide figures have gained a reputation for reliability, and have been used more widely than the FBI figures in previous studies of the deterrent effects of capital punishment (for example, Schuessler, 1952; Sellin, 1959).

If both FBI and census data provided accurate estimates of the homicide rate, the statistics would, of course, agree. Table 1 shows that the figures drawn from the two agencies are reasonably well correlated except during the 1930s, when the FBI's reporting system was in its inception. Notably, the FBI homicide estimates are 15 percent below the census figures for the 1930s, whereas the difference is only about 3 percent lower for the period after 1940. By all indications, these discrepancies are the result of inadequate sampling, reporting, and estimating in the early years of the UCRS.

The Deterrence Variables. The FBI data on arrest and conviction rates are even less reliable. The agencies reporting arrest and conviction statistics have remained a relatively small, self-selected subsample throughout most of the period during which these statistics have been compiled. Indeed, the arrest and conviction figures are based on such small and unrepresentative samples of law enforcement agencies that the FBI has made no effort to readjust earlier arrest and conviction figures on the basis of more recent returns.

Table 1. Correlations Between Homicide Rates Based on FBI
and Census Data by Decade

Effective Period	Annual Homicide Rates	Year-to-Year Changes in Homicide Rates
1933–1939	.24	–.69
1940–1949	.81	.86
1950–1959	.95	.76
1960–1969	.98	.79

Source: See Appendix, items 1 and 13.

The number of agencies reporting arrest data did not reach 2,000, or about one quarter of the total number of agencies, until the 1960s, and the number of agencies reporting convictions did not exceed 300 until the 1960s. The abrupt increase between 1960 and 1961 in agencies reporting convictions represents a major change in reporting practices for conviction statistics by the UCRS. Notably, in 1936, the first year in which conviction rates were reported, the figure Ehrlich used as a national estimate was based on only thirteen jurisdictions.

Further, the average size of jurisdictions reporting conviction data declined substantially in the late 1930s and also in the early 1960s. According to recent evidence, conviction rates are relatively low in the nation's largest jurisdictions. For example, in 1974, only 31.9 percent of those charged with homicide in jurisdictions with populations of 250,000 or more were convicted, as compared to approximately 50 percent in smaller jurisdictions (unpublished FBI data; on file with *The Yale Law Journal*). Hence the conviction data drawn from disproportionately large jurisdictions in 1936 and 1937 are apt to underestimate the national conviction levels for these years.

To show the importance of the effects of the values for 1936 and 1937 on the conviction estimates Ehrlich obtains for the missing years, we have estimated conviction rates for the years 1933–1937 on the basis of the data for the 1938–1969 period with the auxiliary equation used by Ehrlich to estimate the years 1933–1935 for the data from the 1936–1969 period.* As can be seen in Table 2, the reported conviction levels for these two years are far below those for other years—respectively –5.94 and –4.54 standard deviations below the mean conviction level for the period 1938–1969. Because the 1936 and 1937 conviction levels

---

*Ehrlich (1975b) (on file with *The Yale Law Journal*) supplies the auxiliary equations used to estimate the missing conviction values for 1933 through 1935.

Table 2. Comparison of Ehrlich's Conviction Rate Estimates with
an Alternative Estimation Procedure

	Ehrlich's Conviction Rates		Alternative Estimates	
	Annual Conviction Estimates	*Standard Deviations from the 1938–1969 Mean*	*Annual Conviction Estimates*	*Standard Deviations from the 1938–1969 Mean*
1937	30.3	−4.54	43.7	−.40
1936	25.8	−5.94	44.1	−.29
1935	28.3	−5.18	44.1	−.26
1934	26.9	−5.59	42.8	−.69
1933	30.2	−4.58	43.3	−.53

figure prominently in Ehrlich's estimation of missing conviction values for the years 1933–1935, the conviction rates for the entire period 1933–1937 are apt to be grossly biased in his analysis.

We have already noted that the reported conviction rates for 1936 and 1937 are far below the mean for the 1938–1969 period. The above comparison also makes clear that these reported rates are far below the values that would be estimated for these two years by applying Ehrlich's auxiliary equation to the data for the 1938–1969 period. Furthermore, Ehrlich's estimated conviction rates for 1933–1935 are also four to five standard deviations below the mean for 1938–1969; as the alternative estimates show, they would be far higher if they were estimated on the basis of the 1938–1969 time period rather than the 1936–1969 time period.

Finally, the measurement of execution risk—the key explanatory (or independent) variable in Ehrlich's work—is confounded by the inadequacies in the homicide, arrest, and conviction data, because execution risk, as defined by Ehrlich (1975a), incorporates all three of these variables. Thus, like his dependent variable, all of his measures of execution risk are in various ways and degrees biased negatively with respect to the criminal homicide rate. Random error in the number of homicides reported will tend to produce a negative correlation between the homicide rate and execution risk designated by PXQ_1 and PXQ_2, because the number of reported homicides in a given year, Q_t, is both the numerator of the homicide rate and a component in the denominator of these two execution measures (see Appendix, items 1 and 4). The remaining four measures of execution risk will tend to be negatively correlated with the homicide rate as a result of autocorrelated error in the reported number of homicides, because these measures all incorporate prior (lagged) homicide levels in one way or another. While we do not contend that all of Ehrlich's data are inaccurate, we have identified substantial problems with his core variables which cast doubt on his ability to perform a meaningful regression analysis.

Errors in Ehrlich's Regression Analysis

We have independently applied Ehrlich's regression technique to comparable data. On the basis of this replication, we find that his evidence of deterrence emerges only under restrictive assumptions about the form of relationships among the variables and only under a narrow selection of time period for analysis. The limitations required to obtain these results are not justified, since Ehrlich's regression model fits the data better without them. Thus, even if Ehrlich's data were free of errors, the analysis when properly conducted would not show that the death penalty has a deterrent effect.

Replication of Data and Regression Results. To ensure comparability in the replication of Ehrlich's regression analysis, we attempted to use exactly the same data as Ehrlich. Table 3 describes Ehrlich's and our variables and gives the means and standard deviations of their logarithms. In most cases, our means and standard deviations correspond quite closely to Ehrlich's. For eleven of the thirteen variables, they differ by no more than 3 percent, and generally by less than 1 percent. Differences of 2 or 3 percent may indicate that where alternates were available we chose a different data source than Ehrlich did. The two variables that show discrepancies of greater than 3 percent between the two data sets—the indexes of total per capita expenditures of governments ($XGOV$) and of per capita expenditures on police ($XPOL_{-1}$)—differ primarily in standard deviations.

Ehrlich's memorandum (1975b) describes the procedures that he used in obtaining his variables. For $XGOV$ and $XPOL_{-1}$, the two variables with significant differences between the two data sets, we believe that our measures more faithfully reflect Ehrlich's definitions of the variables. Although Ehrlich described $XGOV$ as per capita expenditures of local, state, and federal governments, his memorandum indicates that he actually used government purchases of goods and services and a price deflator for government purchases, instead of government expenditures and an appropriate price deflator. His memorandum also indicates that he failed to exclude defense purchases or expenditures. This is a serious oversight since defense expenditures and purchases represent resources not available for law enforcement activity. Our measure is based on government expenditures and excludes defense expenditures and purchases.

Table 3. Variables Used in the Regression Analysis: Annual Observations 1933–1969 (Means and Standard Deviations in Natural Logarithms)

Variable		Our Mean	Ehrlich's Mean	Our Standard Deviation	Ehrlich's Standard Deviation
Y_1	$(Q/N)°$ = Crime rate: offenses known per 1,000 civilian population	-2.853	-2.857	.156	.156
	$P°a$ = Probability of arrest: clearance rates.	4.497	4.997	.038	.038
	$P°c\|a$ = Conditional probability of conviction: fraction of those charged who were convicted of murder.	3.742	3.741	.172	.175
Y_1	$P°e\|c$ = Conditional probability of execution. PXQ_3 = the number of executions for murder in year $t+1$ as a percent of the total number of convictions in year t.	.172	.176	1.748	1.749
	L = Labor force participation rate of the civilian population.	-.544	-.546	.029	.030
	U = Unemployment rate of the civilian labor force.	1.743	1.743	.728	.728
X_1	A = Fraction of residential population in the age group fourteen to twenty-four.	-1.759	-1.740	.122	.118
	Y = Friedman's estimate of permanent income per capita.	6.889	6.868	.337	.338
	T = Chronological time (years).	2.685	2.685	.867	.867
	NW = Percent of nonwhite residential population.	-2.216	-2.212	.061	.063
	N = Civilian population in 1,000s.	11.944	11.944	.161	.161
	$XGOV$ = Per capita (real) expenditures on all governments in million dollars.	-7.753	-7.661	.256	.501
X_2	$XPOL_{-1}$ = Per capita (real) expenditures on police in dollars lagged one year.	2.200	2.114	.146	.306

Sources: See Appendix and Ehrlich, 1975a and 1975b. Ehrlich, 1975b, indicates that the mean of $P°a$ is incorrectly stated in his table, and that its true value is 4.497.

It was virtually impossible to replicate $XPOL_{-1}$ exactly because Ehrlich used an unspecified auxiliary regression equation to estimate unavailable police expenditure data for odd years prior to 1952. Furthermore, his memorandum indicates that he used a price deflator for government purchases rather than a price deflator for government expenditures, as we did.

We constructed two other variables differently than Ehrlich did. While A is described as the proportion of the residential population aged fourteen to twenty-four, Erhlich's memorandum (1975b) reveals that he used the number of fourteen- to twenty-four-year-olds in both the residential population and the armed forces overseas as a proportion of the total residential population. This is clearly inappropriate since youngsters in this age group overseas cannot contribute to the domestic homicide rate. The slightly greater standard deviation of our measure based exclusively on residential population figures undoubtedly reflects movements of this age group in and out of the country during the war years.

Secondly, NW is described as the proportion of nonwhites in the residential population, but Ehrlich (1975b) indicates that he took the number of nonwhites in the total population as a proportion of all those in the residential population. Moreover, he used annual estimates of the nonwhite population from the *Current Population Reports* for the 1960s (see Appendix) instead of readjusted estimates based on the 1970 decennial censuses. Again, our measure, based exclusively on residential population figures and readjusted annual estimates, is a more accurate representation of the variable as originally defined. In all cases where discrepancies exist, however, we have checked our data carefully, and we are satisfied that we have accurate measures of the variables.

With these data, we have reproduced Ehrlich's basic regression analysis. Table 4 contains the estimated effects of six different measures of execution risk on the criminal homicide rate. The effects are represented by partial regression coefficients (or elasticities), and their statistical significance is indicated by the ratio of these coefficients to their standard errors—the t values of the coefficients. (When the execution and homicide variables are in logarithmic form, the partial regression coefficients indicate the elasticity of the homicide rate with respect to execution risk—that is, the percentage change in the homicde rate that can be expected from a one percent change in execution risk. Thus, an elasticity of $-.068$ [associated with PXQ_2] means that a 1 percent increase in this measure of execution risk can be expected to yield a decrease of .068 percent in the homicide rate.)

Table 4. Estimated Effects of Execution Risk on the Criminal Homicide Rate

Six Alternative Measures of Execution Risk	Effective Period	Partial Regression Coefficients	t Values
PXQ_1	1935–1939	-.018	-0.69
PXQ_2	1935–1969	-.068	-3.15
PXQ_{1-1}	1936–1969	-.023	-1.12
TXQ_1	1938–1969	-.059	-2.76
PDL_1	1939–1969	-.065	-3.45
$P\hat{X}Q_1$	1935–1969	-.004	-0.11

Note: The definitions of these variables are contained in Ehrlich, 1975a, pp. 406–09.

The six measures of execution risk are alternative ways of representing the conditional probability of execution given conviction for murder. In five of the six measures, Ehrlich incorporates a delay between conviction and execution by dividing the number of executions in one year by the estimated number of convictions in the previous year. (PXQ_2 does not incorporate such a delay.) In two cases (TXQ_1 and PDL_1) he estimates execution risk at a given point in time in terms of the numbers of executions and convictions over a prior period of three or four years.

Note that two of Ehrlich's (1975a, p. 410) regression equations, PXQ_{1-1} and TXQ_1 in his Table 3, appear to be either misspecified or mislabeled in terms of the effective period of analysis. Given his data and analytic procedures, 1935 is the earliest possible beginning date for a regression analysis using any of the measures of execution risk. The first-stage regression estimates of arrest and conviction rates cannot be obtained prior to 1934 since values of many variables lagged one year are required by the reduced form equation. The modified first differences obtained in the second stage of the regression analysis by the Cochrane-Orcutt procedure cannot be obtained prior to 1935 since all exogenous and endogenous variables must be lagged one year. But with PXQ_{1-1} as the measure of execution risk (Ehrlich, 1975a, pp. 406–409), the earliest starting date is 1936. The reduced form first-stage equation requires that a lagged value of PXQ_{1-1} be used to estimate arrest and conviction rates, but the first legitimate value of PXQ_{1-1} is that for 1934, not for 1933, since the denominator of this measure incorporates values of homicides, arrests, and convictions lagged one year. This means that estimated arrest and conviction rates cannot be obtained before 1935 and that modified first differences cannot be estimated for periods beginning before 1936. Since Ehrlich gives 1935 as the beginning of the effective period, he may have used an erroneous (probably zero) value for PXQ_{1-1} in the first-stage estimation procedure.

With TXQ_1 as the measure of execution risk (Ehrlich, 1975a, pp. 406–409), the earliest beginning point for the effective period should be 1938. Since values of TXQ_1 depend on data from three prior years, the first values cannot be obtained before 1936; the first-stage estimation of arrest and conviction rates with lagged TXQ_1 cannot be made for years earlier than 1937, and hence modified first differences cannot be calculated for effective periods starting earlier than 1938. If, as Ehrlich indicates, 1937 is actually used as the beginning date of the effective period, lagged TXQ_1 in the first-stage equation will be an arbitrary (probably nonzero) value based on data from only two prior years (and a zero value for the third year).

PXQ_{1-1} and TXQ_1 are used more extensively than any of the other execution measures in Ehrlich's regression analyses, and in virtually all cases the effective period of analysis begins one year too soon. The following equations in both of his papers would appear to be misspecified, and therefore improperly estimated, in terms of the effective period of analysis: Equations 3 and 4 in Table 4 of Ehrlich (1973, p. 53), Table 3 of Ehrlich (1975a, p. 410), equations 2–5 in Table 5 of Ehrlich (1973, p. 54), equations 1–6 in Table 6 (Ehrlich, 1973, p. 55), Table 4 of Ehrlich (1975a, p. 410), and equations 3 and 4 in Table 7 of Ehrlich (1973, p. 57).

We believe these equations are not simply mislabeled but are, in fact, improperly specified with respect to the effective period of analysis. With the data generated from information in Ehrlich (1975b), we have estimated each of the above equations for its maximum proper effective period and for the apparently incorrect one indicated in Ehrlich's tabulations. In every case, we found that the results reported by Ehrlich correspond more closely with the estimates we have obtained for the incorrectly defined effective period. However, the resulting errors of estimation are probably small in magnitude since they enter the second-stage regression results through one of eighteen variables in the first-stage estimation of arrest and conviction rates.

Returning to the analysis presented in Table 4, we find that it shows a negative value for the regression coefficient associated with each of the six measures of execution risk. That is, the results of this initial regression analysis appear to indicate that, other things being equal, as the risk of execution among convicted offenders increases, the homicide rate decreases and, conversely, as execution risk declines, the homicide rate rises. For three of the six measures of execution risk, the estimated effect is at least twice its standard error, suggesting that the effect is not likely to have occurred by chance.

These results are similar to Ehrlich's (1975a, pp. 409–413). He finds negative coefficients, ranging from −.039 to −.068, for the six execution measures. In four cases, his negative coefficients are statistically significant. In addition, the relative strengths of the effects of arrest ($P^\circ a$), conviction ($P^\circ c|a$) and execution ($P^\circ e|c$) are the same as Ehrlich (1975a) reports. According to Ehrlich, "[t]he regression results regarding the effects of $P^\circ a$, $P^\circ c|a$, and $P^\circ e|c$ constitute perhaps the strongest findings of the empirical investigation. Not only do the signs of the elasticities associated with these variables conform to the general theoretical expectations, but their ranking, too, is consistent with the predictions" (1975a, p. 411). Thus, by reproducing the rank order of effects among arrest, conviction, and execution rates, we have replicated an especially important aspect of his regression results. Furthermore, our results are comparable to Ehrlich's in other respects (see Bowers and Pierce, appendix B, 1975, for the full regression results). The elasticities associated with alternative measures of execution risk are less in absolute magnitude than those associated with arrest and conviction rates, but relative to their standard errors, they tend to fall between those of the arrest and conviction measures. In addition, the signs of the elasticities associated with the remaining causal factors are the same as those obtained by Ehrlich.

Temporal Specification. If the results of a time-series regression analysis are a faithful representation of underlying causal processes, the values of the estimated coefficients will be independent of the specific time period chosen for the analysis. Thus, if the values of the coefficients associated with the various measures of execution risk change substantially when they are estimated for alternative time intervals, the negative values reported in Table 4 are not a reliable basis of inferring that capital punishment has a deterrent effect on murder.

Ehrlich addressed this issue by repeating the regression analysis for selected subperiods. He performed seven regressions in which varying numbers of years were removed from the beginning of the time series and two analyses in which three years were dropped from the end of the series. These alterations in the effective period of analysis do not appreciably change the elasticities associated with execution risk (see Ehrlich, 1973, 1975a). Ehrlich does, however, concede that the deterrent effects of arrest, conviction, and execution rates become weaker when as many as seven years are dropped from the recent end of the time series (Ehrlich, 1973, p. 70).

We find that all empirical support for the deterrent effect of capital punishment disappears when the five most recent years are removed from the time series that Ehrlich selected for analysis. Table 5 shows the estimated effects of execution risk on the criminal homicide rate for ten periods with successively earlier ending dates. For the period ending in 1964, there are no statistically significiant negative elasticities associated with the various measures of execution risk. For the period ending in 1963, the estimated elasticities have become positive in every case. Indeed, of the twenty-four coefficients reflecting the effects of execution risk for periods ending in 1963 and earlier, twenty are positive and only four are negative.

Furthermore, we find that the regression results are more adequate and consistent for the periods with earlier ending dates. The standard errors of the regressions are less, the F and R^2 statistics are consistently higher, and the Durbin-Watson statistics are generally more acceptable for the periods ending in 1960 and 1963 than for those ending in 1966 and 1969. (See equations 1.6–6.4 in Bowers and Pierce, appendix B, 1975. These statistical measures are tests for reliability of the regression results.) In addition, the estimated coefficients for the other variables in the regression equations for the two shorter periods are generally closer in value than in the equations for the longer periods.

Thus, not only does the evidence for deterrence disappear, but Ehrlich's more general theoretical formulation is weakened by our findings. When we examine the results for periods ending in 1964 or earlier, we find only three instances out of thirty possible results which conform to his rank-order predicitons of the relative strengths of the deterrence variables.

Hence for the periods in which the model gives evidence of being more adequately specified, the regression analysis consistently shows a slightly positive—though not statistically significant—effect of execution risk on the homicide rate.

Functional Form. Seldom does an initial theoretical formulation, such as Ehrlich's economic model of the determinants of murder, unambiguously dictate the mathematical function which describes the true relationships among the variables. When the functional form is open to question or when the analyst wishes to establish the generality of his findings, he will typically examine regression results obtained under different assumptions about the form of the model.

Ehrlich assumes that the factors which determine the murder rate have a multiplicative effect. Adopting a standard regression technique, he uses logarithmic values of the variables, in order to transform this multiplicative relationship into an equivalent linear form suitable

**Table 5. Estimated Effects of Execution Risk on the Criminal Homicide
Rate for Effective Periods with Successively Earlier Ending Dates**

Ending Date of Effective Period	Six Alternative Measures of Execution Risk					
	PXQ_1	PXQ_2	PXQ_{1-1}	TXQ_1	PDL_1	$P\hat{X}Q_1$
1969	-.018	-.068	-.023	-.059	-.065	-.004
	(-.69)	(-3.15)	(-1.12)	(-2.70)	(-3.45)	(-.11)
1968	-.026	-.069	-.030	-.059	-.069	-.049
	(-.99)	(-3.50)	(-1.41)	(-2.76)	(-4.09)	(-1.36)
1967	-.031	-.064	-.061	-.064	-.068	.060
	(-1.38)	(-3.65)	(-3.18)	(-3.64)	(-4.55)	(-1.98)
1966	-.020	-.055	-.053	-.050	-.056	-.043
	(-1.00)	(-3.79)	(-3.31)	(-2.88)	(-3.40)	(-1.59)
1965	-.016	-.041	.034	-.025	-.037	-.031
	(-.99)	(-1.51)	(-1.20)	(-.98)	(-1.53)	(-1.41)
1964	.028	-.021	-.017	-.009	-.013	.013
	(.91)	(-.70)	(-.58)	(-.34)	(-.40)	(.37)
1963	.057	.003	.003	.065	.048	.037
	(1.77)	(.08)	(.08)	(1.63)	(1.00)	(1.02)
1962	.052	-.030	-.021	.060	.021	.040
	(1.14)	(-.60)	(-.54)	(1.30)	(.35)	(.83)
1961	-.015	.041	.011	.086	.050	-.019
	(-.28)	(.67)	(.29)	(2.10)	(1.02)	(-.33)
1960	.013	.029	.009	.070	.067	.013
	(.24)	(.52)	(.25)	(1.72)	(1.36)	(.22)

Note: Variables are expressed as natural logarithms and *t* values are given in parentheses.

for regression analysis (See Johnston, 1972; Wonnacott and Wonnacott, 1970). Ehrlich (1975a, pp. 412–413) reports that his regression
results are not dependent on the specific assumptions he has made
about the form of the relationships among the variables—that there is
evidence of a deterrent effect even when he performs the regression
analysis with the natural values of his variables (which corresponds to
a linear rather than a multiplicative relationship among the variables).

Using the natural values of these variables, we have reestimated
the coefficients shown in Table 5 to obtain the results in Table 6.*

*When execution risk and homicide rates are expressed in natural values
rather than in logarithms, the regression coefficients indicate the change in the
homicide rate to be expected from a one unit change in execution risk. For

Table 6. Estimated Effects of Execution Risk on the Criminal Homicide Rate for Effective Periods with Successively Earlier Ending Dates

Ending Date of Effective Period	Six Alternative Measures of Execution Risk					
	PXQ_1	PXQ_2	PXQ_{1-1}	TXQ_1	PDL_1	$P\hat{X}Q_1$
1969	.00008	-.00061	.00132	.00135	.00085	.00054
	(.05)	(-.73)	(1.02)	(.64)	(.43)	(.33)
1968	.00038	-.00068	.00126	.00134	.00085	.00053
	(.25)	(-.79)	(.96)	(.61)	(.41)	(.34)
1967	.00021	-.00051	.00629	.00106	.00039	.00016
	(.16)	(-.63)	(.56)	(.47)	(.18)	(.11)
1966	-.00023	-.00040	-.00013	.00110	.00046	-.00046
	(-.20)	(-.52)	(-.17)	(.54)	(.22)	(-.38)
1965	-.00027	-.00027	-.00038	.00124	.00087	-.00053
	(-.29)	(-.40)	(-.60)	(.81)	(.52)	(-.55)
1964	.00009	-.00024	-.00034	.00104	.00123	-.00004
	(.11)	(-.37)	(-.57)	(.78)	(.78)	(-.04)
1963	.00026	-.00019	-.00023	.00123	.00189	.00022
	(.29)	(-.28)	(-.37)	(.87)	(1.10)	(.24)
1962	-.00030	-.00023	-.00032	.00058	.00120	-.00035
	(-.38)	(-.35)	(-.56)	(.53)	(.80)	(-.44)
1961	-.00032	.00027	-.00003	.00147	.00216	-.00044
	(-.50)	(.45)	(-.05)	(1.35)	(2.00)	(-.68)
1960	-.00004	.00041	.00005	.00139	.00235	-.00013
	(-.06)	(.69)	(.09)	(1.30)	(2.17)	(-.20)

Note: Variables are expressed in natural values whose coefficients are rounded to five decimal places, and *t* values are shown in parentheses.

There are, among the sixty estimates in Table 6, more positive than negative coefficients associated with the various measures of execution risk. Only two of them, both positive, are statistically significant. The direction and size of the estimated coefficients do not appear to be systematically affected by the choice of time period. In other words, the last few years of the time series, which are apparently responsible for

example, a coefficient of -.00061 (for PXQ_2 in the period 1935–1969) means that a reduction in the number of executions from ten to nine (per 100 convictions for murder) can be expected to increase the homicide rate from 5.00000 to 5.00061 (per 100,000 population), or to add twelve homicides for a population of 200 million.

the evidence of a deterrent effect when logarithmic values are used, yield no such evidence with the natural values of the variables.

Sources of Ehrlich's Deterrence Evidence

We have seen that Ehrlich obtains evidence of a deterrent effect only by imposing highly restrictive conditions on his analysis. One might assume that this evidence of deterrence reflects either a strong deterrent effect operating exclusively in recent years or a more pervasive effect obscured by data inadequacies in the early years. We show instead that Ehrlich's evidence is strictly a statistical artifact, not the reflection of a deterrent effect over the entire period of analysis or the most recent subperiod.

The Recent Years. What is it about the middle and late 1960s which causes the execution variables to show negative effects on the homicide rate when they are in logarithmic but not in natural form? The answer lies in the opposing trends in the two variables and in the nature of the logarithmic transformation. The national homicide rate, as reported by the FBI, rose precipitously in the middle and late 1960s to levels well above those of the 1940s and 1950s. Indeed, between 1962 and 1969 the homicide rate rose almost 60 percent to a level exceeded only by the rate for 1933. At the same time, executions literally came to an end. Hence execution risk—the number of executions among those convicted of murder—took on extremely low values, approaching zero, in the middle and late 1960s. In order to extend the effective period of analysis through 1969, Ehrlich had to generate nonzero execution rates for the years after 1967, since the logarithm of zero is not defined. He did this by supplying one nonexistent execution for 1968 and 1969 in the calculation of PXQ_2 (Ehrlich, 1975a, p. 409). A property of the logarithmic transformation is to emphasize variations at the lower range of a variable. For example, if execution risk is converted into logarithms, a difference between one and two executions per 1,000 convictions will be greater than a difference between 350 and 650 executions per 1,000 convictions. Consequently, the logarithmic transformation accentuates the decline in execution risk that occurred in the 1960s.

To show the effect of the logarithmic transformation on these low values of execution risk, we present in Table 7 the corresponding logarithmic and natural values of one of the six measures of execution risk for the years from 1960 through 1969. The natural values of execution risk have dropped from about 1 percent in the years 1960–1962 to less than .05 percent for the years 1966–1969. The values for the years after 1964 are all slightly more than one standard deviation below the

Table 7. Logarithmic and Natural Values of Execution Risk (PXQ_2)
for Each Year 1960-1969

	Logarithms		Natural Values	
	Absolute Value	Standard Deviations from the Mean	Absolute Value	Standard Deviations from the Mean
1969	-3.823	-2.524	.022	-1.123
1968	-3.873	-2.554	.021	-1.124
1967	-3.134	-2.103	.044	-1.114
1966	-3.774	-2.494	.023	-1.123
1965	-1.742	-1.252	.175	-1.059
1964	-1.456	-1.077	.233	-1.034
1963	-.642	-.580	.526	-.911
1962	.174	-.081	1.191	-.630
1961	-.042	-.214	.959	-.728
1960	.229	-.048	1.257	-.602

mean for the entire period from 1933 to 1969. Putting execution risk in logarithmic form greatly accentuates the decline. The difference between 1960 and 1969 in logarithmic values (from .229 to -3.823) is more than three times the corresponding difference in natural values (from 1.257 to .022). In fact, in the period from 1966 to 1969, the logarithmic values of execution risk are all more than two standard deviations below their mean. Thus, by using logarithmic values of execution risk, Ehrlich gives considerably more weight in his regression analysis to the extremely low values of this variable after 1964.

Ehrlich (1973, p. 70) has stated that the recent behavior of arrest and conviction rates as well as that of execution risk plays an important role in his regression results. To examine the effect of using the logarithmic values of execution risk and the possibility that the logarithmic transformation of arrest and conviction rates may also influence the regression results, we present, in Table 8, simple correlations of the arrest, conviction, and execution rates with the criminal homicide rate; these are shown for logarithmic and natural values of the variables and for time intervals with successively earlier ending dates from 1969 through 1960. The data for the recent years have an extraordinary effect on the correlation between the logarithms of execution and homicide rates; adding the last five years reduces the correlation from .836 to .123. In contrast, the recent data have much less effect on the correlation between the natural values of execution and homicide rates; adding the last five years reduces the correlation only from .729 to .553. These years have virtually no impact on the correlations, in either

Table 8. Correlations of Arrest, Conviction, and Execution Rates with the Homicide Rate for Effective Periods with Successively Earlier Ending Dates (for Logarithmic and Natural Values of the Variables)

Effective Periods	Arrest Rate ($P^a a$)		Conviction Rate ($P^c c\|a$)		Execution Rate (PQX_2)	
	Logarithms	Natural Values	Logarithms	Natural Values	Logarithms	Natural Values
1933–1969	-.809	-.832	-.504	-.516	.123	.553
1933–1968	-.801	-.818	-.488	-.496	.270	.644
1933–1967	-.793	-.809	-.492	-.497	.442	.720
1933–1966	-.791	-.808	-.496	-.499	.563	.758
1933–1965	-.792	-.809	-.496	-.499	.748	.773
1933–1964	-.795	-.813	-.494	-.497	.806	.772
1933–1963	-.806	-.824	-.488	-.491	.858	.763
1933–1962	-.820	-.837	-.495	-.500	.857	.750
1933–1961	-.819	-.835	-.505	-.511	.846	.741
1933–1960	-.814	-.831	-.518	-.526	.836	.729

Sources: See Appendix, items 2, 3, and 4.

logarithmic or natural form, of arrest and conviction rates with the criminal homicide rates. Thus, Erhlich's evidence of deterrence rests heavily on the relationship between the values of execution risk and homicide rates for the years after 1964.

This conclusion might suggest that the use of the death penalty at the very low levels of execution risk in the middle and late 1960s had a deterrent effect strong enough to produce a measurable effect over the entire period when these recent years are combined with earlier years. We examine this possibility in Table 9. It shows annual changes in the homicide rate relative to national changes in the homicide rate for the period 1962 to 1968 among states that increased or decreased the number of executions imposed for murder. The relative changes in homicide rate are expressed in homicides per 100,000 people, and are obtained by subtracting the changes in the national homicide rate from changes in the individual states.

If execution risk had a deterrent effect, states with declining numbers of executions would show a relative increase in homicide rate, and states with rising execution levels would show a relative decrease in homicide rate. But Table 9 demonstrates that there is no such pattern in the years since 1962. Among states which decreased executions, the homicide rate rose more than the national figure for two of the periods and less than the national figure for four. (However, one of these two periods, 1966–1967, involves only one state, representing 1 percent of the population.) Among states that increased executions, the change in homicide rate was below the national change in one comparison, very nearly the same in one case, and actually above in three of the five comparisons.

Table 9 also shows that the use of capital punishment during this period was restricted increasingly to a small minority of states. After 1964, no more than five states imposed executions in a single year, none of them imposed more than one execution per year, and none imposed executions two years in a row. In this situation, the national homicide rate cannot be expected to reflect possible deterrent effects presumed to occur primarily in the jurisdictions that actively use the death penalty. Thus, apart from problems of temporal specification and functional form, it would have been more appropriate, in view of the progressively restricted use of capital punishment in the nation, for Ehrlich to have shortened the effective period of analysis by removing the years after 1963, when no more than 10 percent of the states imposed executions, than to have extended the period of analysis two years beyond the end of exectuions in the United States.

Table 9. Annual Changes in Criminal Homicide Rate Among States Which Have Increased and Decreased Executions Relative to Annual Homicide Rate Changes in the Nation as a Whole for the Period 1962–1968

Annual Change	States Decreasing Executions			States Increasing Executions		
	Relative Homicide Rate Change	*Number of States*	*Population Proportion*	*Relative Homicide Rate Change*	*Number of States*	*Population Proportion*
1962–1963	-.10	14	.44	-.03	6	.17
1963–1964	.19	8	.33	-.33	3	.06
1964–1965	-.41	3	.13	.88	4	.05
1965–1966	-.93	4	.05	.50	1	.01
1966–1967	.62	1	.01	.09	2	.11
1967–1968	-.23	2	.11	—	—	—

Sources: States imposing executions for murder during this period are identified by Bowers (1974, pp. 400–401); criminal homicides annually by state were obtained from the Federal Bureau of Investigation, *Uniform Crime Reports* for the United States (Table 3, 1962–1964; Table 4, 1965–1968); annual population estimates by state taken from U.S. Bureau of the Census (1971). Changes in homicide rates for groups of states that increased and decreased executions are essentially the average of the annual changes in the states that comprise the group weighted by their respective population sizes. The data for these states are directly comparable with the national figures in the *Uniform Crime Reports.*

The Early Years. We have already described the unreliability of data for the 1930s. By reproducing his regression analysis for effective periods with later beginning dates, Ehrlich may have hoped to diminish the effects of measurement error in these early years. But he has thereby given greater weight to the years after 1964, which are responsible in the first place for his evidence of a deterrent effect.

To determine the effects of measurement error in the early years, we must first remove the idiosyncratic recent years, and then successively drop years from the beginning of the time series. Accordingly, we have performed regressions for periods with 1963 as the ending date and with successively later beginning dates from 1935 through 1940. The estimated coefficients for logarithmic and natural values of two measures of execution risk are shown in Table 10.

We know from Tables 5 and 6 that the elasticities associated with execution risk for effective periods ending in 1963 and earlier are more often positive than negative, though usually not statistically significant. In Table 10, the coefficients are again predominantly positive, and become even more so as years are successively dropped from the beginning of the time series. In fact, the effective periods beginning in 1938, 1939, and 1940 show positive effects for execution risk in all twelve cases. These positive coefficients are, of course, absurd from the viewpoint of the deterrence hypothesis, although they may not be altogether meaningless. (The possibility that, because of a brutalizing effect, capital punishment may encourage rather than deter murders is considered by Bowers and Pierce, 1975.) They do, however, indicate unambiguously that data inadequacies in the early years of the time series have not obscured deterrent effects of capital punishment. Indeed, by all indications there are no deterrent effects to obscure.

Conclusion

We have shown that Ehrlich's findings are not a reliable basis for inferring the effects of capital punishment on the criminal homicide rate. Flaws in Ehrlich's data cast doubt on the ability to perform meaningful regression analysis. The analysis itself yields evidence of a deterrent effect only by relying on the unusual nature of the years after 1964 and on the logarithmic transformation of the data. When the analysis is performed for more appropriate periods, the hypothesis that the death penalty deters murders finds no support.

Table 10. Estimated Effects of Execution Risk on the Criminal Homicide Rate for Effective Periods Ending in 1963 with Successively Later Beginning Dates

Beginning Date of Effective Period	Logarithmic Values (t Values in Parentheses)		Natural Values (t Values in Parentheses)	
	PXQ_{1-1}	$P\hat{X}Q_1$	PXQ_{1-1}	$P\hat{X}Q_1$
1935	–	.037	–	.000219
	–	(1.02)	–	(.24)
1936	.003	.034	–.000225	.000082
	(.08)	(.95)	(–.37)	(.08)
1937	.007	.038	–.000079	–.000004
	(.19)	(1.02)	(–.12)	(–.00)
1938	.038	.033	.001147	.000833
	(.91)	(.95)	(1.10)	(.64)
1939	.062	.061	.001858	.001772
	(1.39)	(1.73)	(1.35)	(1.20)
1940	.095	.056	.004581	.001848
	(1.95)	(1.56)	(3.03)	(1.19)

Note: PXQ_{1-1} is the measure of execution risk used most frequently by Ehrlich. $P\hat{X}Q_1$, of all the measures, is least biased by measurement error since the one year lagged homicide rate is only one of eighteen variables that figure in its estimation. Bowers and Pierce (Equations 13.1–16.3, appendix B, 1975) present detailed regression results for selected periods beginning in 1936, 1938, and 1940.

APPENDIX
Specific Data Sources Used in the Replication of Ehrlich's Regression Analysis

1. $(Q/N)°$ *Criminal Homicide Rate* = Number of criminal homicides per year/annual civilian population.
   (a) Q = Annual number of murders and nonnegligent manslaughters from 1933 to 1939. Revised figures, 1971, provided by the FBI.
   (b) N = Civilian population of the United States in 1,000s from 1933 to 1969 (U.S. Bureau of the Census, 1973).

2. $P°a$ *Clearance Rate for Criminal Homicide* = Fraction of murders and nonnegligent manslaughters cleared by arrest (Federal Bureau of Investigation, 1933–1969).

3. $P°c|a$ *Conviction Rate for Criminal Homicide* = Fraction of individuals found guilty as charged for murder and non-

negligent manslaughter (Federal Bureau of Investigation, 1936–1939). After 1962 separate estimates are reported in the FBI's *Uniform Crime Reports* annual bulletin. Estimates from the time series which is continuous over the 1936 to 1969 period were chosen. These estimates were generally based on larger population bases. The value for 1961 is the average of the 1960 and 1962 estimates. Values for 1933 to 1935 were obtained from Ehrlich (1973).

4. $P°e|c$ *Execution Risk for Criminal Homicide* (PXQ_1, PXQ_2, PXQ_{1-1}, TXQ_1, PDL_1, $P\hat{X}Q_1$). The measures of execution risk are all variations of the form E/C, where $C = Q·P°a·P°c|a$.

(a) E = The number of executions for murder (U.S. Bureau of Prisons, 1971).

(b) C = Number of convictions for murder.

(c) Q = The annual number of criminal homicides as defined in item 1(a).

(d) $P°a$, $P°c|a$ are as defined in items 2 and 3.

5. L *Labor Force Participation Rates.* For 1940–1969, $L = CL/(TN-TL+CL)$. For 1933–1939, $L = CL/(N - P13)$.

(a) CL, TL = The civilian and total labor force in 1,000s from 1933 to 1969 (U.S. Bureau of Labor Statistics, 1971).

(b) TN = Total noninstitutional population from 1940 to 1969 (U.S. Bureau of Labor Statistics, 1971).

(c) N = Annual civilian population as defined in item 1(b).

(c) $P13$ = Annual population thirteen years old and under from 1933 to 1939 (U.S. Bureau of the Census, 1965b).

6. U *Unemployment Rate of the Civilian Labor Force, 1933 to 1969.* Source: U.S. Bureau of Labor Statistics (1971).

7. A *Fraction of the Resident Population Fourteen to Twenty-Four Years of Age.* $A = (P1424)/(RP)$.

(a) $P1424$ = Number of persons fourteen to twenty-four years of age in the resident population. Sources, for 1933–1939, U.S. Bureau of the Census (1965b); for 1940–1949, U.S. Bureau of the Census (1954); for 1950–1959, U.S. Bureau of the Census (1965a); for 1960–1969, U.S. Bureau of the Census (1974).

(b) RP = Residential population in 1000s. References same as give in 7(a) for each of the respective time periods.

8. Y *Friedman's Estimate of Real Permanent Income per Capita.* The following equation was used to compute Y:

$$Y_t = (.330) \ Y_{t-1} + (.226) \ Y_{t-2} + (.154) \ Y_{t-3} + (.106) \ Y_{t-4} +$$
$$(.072) \ Y_{t-5} + (.049) \ Y_{t-6} + (.033) \ Y_{t-7} + (.023) \ Y_{t-8}$$

(a) The weights in the above equation were obtained from Karni, Table 33 (1971).

(b) Y_{t-1} through Y_{t-8} are logarithmic estimates of per capita real national income for the years 1925 to 1969. The national income figures were provided by Karni (1971). Population figures for per capita estimates for 1925–1929 were obtained from U.S. Bureau of the Census (1973); for 1930–1968, from U.S. Department of Commerce (1969).

(c) The per capita income was measured in terms of 1919 dollars using a price deflator obtained from Karni (1971).

9. *NW*   *Percent of Nonwhite Residential Population.* References same as given in item 7(a) for each of the respective time periods.

10. *N*   *Civilian Population in 1000s.* Reference same as given in item 1(b).

11. *XGOV*   *Per Capital Real Expenditures on All Governments in Millions of Dollars.* $XGOV = (FE + SLE - D)/RP*PD*10.$

(a) *FE, SLE* = Federal and state/local expenditure on all governments. Sources: for 1933–1938, U.S. Department of Commerce (1960); for 1939–1965, U.S. Department of Commerce (1966); for 1966–1969, U.S. Department of Commerce (1970).

(b) *D* = National defense expenditures. Sources: for 1933–1938, U.S. Department of Commerce (1960); for 1939–1952, purchases of goods and services, U.S. Department of Commerce (1966); for 1953–1969, purchases of goods and services, U.S. Department of Commerce (1970).

(c) *RP* = Residential population as defined in item 7(b).

(d) *PD* = Implicit price deflator for all governments. Sources: for 1932–1965, U.S. Department of Commerce (1966); for 1966–1969, U.S. Department of Commerce (1970).

12. *XPOL₋₁*   *Per Capita Real Expenditures on Police Lagged One Year in Dollars.* $XPOL = POLE*100,000/RP*PD.$

(a) *POLE* = Total police expenditure. Sources: for 1932–1966, U.S. Bureau of the Census (1969); for 1967–1969, U.S. Bureau of the Census (1971).

(b) *RP* = Residential population as defined in item 7(b).

(c) *PD* = Price deflator as defined in item 11(d).

13.   *Alternative Vital Statistics Estimates of Homicide.* Q = Annual number of willful homicides (minus the annual number of executions after 1948, when the two mortality categories were combined). Sources: for 1933–1936, U.S. Bureau of the Census (1933–1936); for 1937–1969, U.S. Bureau of the Census (1937–1945) and U.S. Public Health Service (1946–1969), all from annual reports.

References

Bowers, W. J. *Executions in America.* Lexington, Mass.: Lexington Books, 1974.

Bowers, W. J., and Pierce, G. L. "Deterrence, Brutalization, or Nonsense: A Critique of Isaac Ehrlich's Research on Capital Punishment." Unpublished manuscript, Center for Applied Social Research, Northeastern University, 1975.

Ehrlich, I. *The Deterrent Effect of Capital Punishment: A Question of Life and Death.* Working Paper No. 18, Center for Economic Analysis of Human Behavior and Social Institutions, Chicago: University of Chicago Press, 1973.

Ehrlich, I. "The Deterrent Effect of Capital Punishment: A Question of Life and Death." *American Economic Review,* 1975a, *65,* 397–417.

Ehrlich, I. "The Deterrent Effect of Capital Punishment: A Question of Life and Death—Sources of Data." Unpublished appendix, 1975b.

Federal Bureau of Investigation. *Uniform Crime Reports for the United States.* Washington, D.C.: Federal Bureau of Investigation, 1933–1969, (yearly).

Johnson, J. *Econometric Methods.* (2nd ed.). New York: McGraw-Hill, 1972.

Karni, E. "The Value of Time and the Demand for Money." Unpublished doctoral dissertation, University of Chicago, 1971.

National Center for Health Statistics. *Homicide in the United States 1950–1964.* Washington, D.C.: U.S. Department of Health, Education, and Welfare, 1967.

National Commission on the Causes and Prevention of Violence. *Crimes of Violence.* Staff report, National Commission on the Causes and Prevention of Violence, 1969.

President's Commission on Law Enforcement and the Administration of Justice (PCL). *Crime and Its Impact: An Assessment.* Washington, D.C.: Task Force Reports, 1967.

Schuessler, K. F. "The Deterrent Influence of the Death Penalty." *Annals,* 1952, *284,* 54–62.

Sellin, T. *The Death Penalty.* Philadelphia: American Law Institute, 1959.

U.S. Bureau of Labor Statistics. *Employment and Earnings*. Washington, D.C.: U.S. Department of Labor, 1971.

U.S. Bureau of Prisons, *National Prisoner Statistics Bulletin*. No. 46. Washington, D.C.: U.S. Department of Justice, 1971.

U.S. Bureau of the Census. *Mortality Statistics*. Washington, D.C.: U.S. Department of Commerce, 1933–1936, (yearly).

U.S. Bureau of the Census. *Vital Statistics of the United States*. Washington, D.C.: U.S. Department of Commerce, 1937–1945, (yearly).

U.S. Bureau of the Census. *Current Population Reports: Population Estimates and Projections*. Ser. P-25, No. 98. Washington, D.C.: U.S. Department of Commerce, 1954.

U.S. Bureau of the Census. *Current Population Reports: Population Estimates and Projections*. Ser. P-25, No. 311. Washington, D.C.: U.S. Department of Commerce, 1965a.

U.S. Bureau of the Census. *Current Population Reports: Population Estimates and Projections*. Ser. P-25, No. 310. Washington, D.C.: U.S. Department of Commerce, 1965b.

U.S. Bureau of the Census. *1967 Census of Governments*. Washington, D.C.: U.S. Department of Commerce, 1969.

U.S. Bureau of the Census. *Governmental Finances in 1969–1970*. Washington, D.C.: U.S. Department of Commerce, 1971.

U.S. Bureau of the Census. *Current Population Reports: Population Estimates and Projections*. (Ser. P-25, No. 499). Washington, D.C.: U.S. Department of Commerce, 1973.

U.S. Bureau of the Census. *Current Population Reports: Population Estimates and Projections*. (Ser. P-25, No. 519). Washington, D.C.: U.S. Department of Commerce, 1974.

U.S. Department of Commerce. *Historical Statistics of the U.S.: Colonial Times to 1957*. Washington, D.C.: U.S. Department of Commerce, 1960.

U.S. Department of Commerce. *The National Income and Product Accounts of the United States, 1929–1965 Statistical Tables*. Washington, D.C.: U.S. Department of Commerce, 1966.

U.S. Department of Commerce. *Survey of Current Business*. Washington, D.C.: U.S. Department of Commerce, 1969 and 1970.

U.S. Public Health Service. *Vital Statistics of the United States, 1950*. Washington, D.C.: U.S. Department of Health, Education, and Welfare, 1954.

U.S. Public Health Service. *Vital Statistics of the United States*. Washington, D.C.: U.S. Department of Health, Education, and Welfare, 1946–1969 (yearly).

Wonnacott, R., and Wonnacott, T. *Econometrics*. New York: Wiley, 1970.

15

Isaac Ehrlich

Capital Punishment as Deterrent:
Challenging the Reanalysis

Because of space limitations and the short time I have been given to prepare my response to the two critiques of my work published in this issue of the *Journal*, I shall confine myself principally to the critique by Bowers and Pierce (1975a). I do that not because the paper by Baldus and Cole (1975) does not warrant a detailed reply but because an elaborate response to the central issues they raise is contained in a study of mine now in progress which deals critically with published research by Sellin and others. (See, however, the sections on basic statistical errors, gaps between evidence and inference, and the measurement of the restraining effect of capital punishment—all are directly relevant to the Baldus and Cole *and* Bowers and Pierce works). I choose to focus on the Bowers and Pierce piece also because, as I hope to show, their work largely misinterprets and misapplies the framework I have developed for testing the deterrence hypothesis. Addressing their work critically

Note: Reprinted by permission of the Yale Law Journal Company and Fred B. Rothman & Company from *The Yale Law Journal*, 1975, 85, 209–227, in which this material first appeared in slightly different form.

This reply has been prepared in cooperation with Randall Mark.

provides the opportunity to elaborate upon some pertinent aspects of my research, hopefully for the benefit of interested scholars.

The conclusions of my time series study of murder basically are two: (1) that previous research never adequately tested a set of direct and specific implications suggested by a general theory of deterrence and (2) that my empirical findings, while tentative and inconclusive by the very nature of observational statistics, are not inconsistent with rather sharp implications emanating from this theory, including the hypothesized deterrent effect of the conditional risk of execution. Bowers and Pierce tacitly accept the first conclusion and seek to evade the second, evidently on faulty grounds. In their efforts to obscure the empirical findings, they have selectively deleted observations, utilized an inferior regression specification, considered irrelevant variables and correlations, and revealed in the process misunderstanding of elementary statistical concepts, as I discuss later in this chapter. They do not provide evidence based on systematic statistical analysis showing that capital punishment, or punishment in general, does not deter crime. Essentially, they make only the point that the observed deterrent effect of the risk of execution *can be* confounded when insufficient regard is shown for proper methods of hypothesis testing. Indeed, my principal response to Bowers and Pierce is that they concern themselves only with making a point (that is, confounding a result) rather than testing a hypothesis. There is a fundamental difference between a systematic and statistically coherent test of all the ramifications of a general hypothesis and an exercise in search of that set of circumstances which—for purely technical reasons—may weaken the effect of a single variable within a comprehensive model. Bowers and Pierce do not analyze the effects of variables other than the conditional probability of execution—variables such as estimates of apprehension and conviction risks and unemployment and labor force participation rates. Moreover, they do not address themselves at all to the question of the optimal form of testing for the deterrence hypothesis, given the technical limitations of observational statistics.

I shall respond in some detail only to the substantive issues raised by Bowers and Pierce and to a few of the arguments advanced by Baldus and Cole. Also, I shall point out only some of their more serious errors. For expositional convenience, the discussion below is ordered as seven general points.

Corroborating Evidence from Bowers and Pierce

First and foremost, the Bowers and Pierce work, however inadvertently, has lent considerable strength to the case for the deterrent effect of capital punishment, because their application of the theory and econometric methods outlined in my paper over the entire period considered in my analysis produces results quite similar to my own. This is noteworthy for several reasons.

First, their data set is not identical to the set of data that I utilized. Their comments indicate that at least four variables have been constructed differently in their work. Further, they allege that one of these differences, that concerning $XPOL_{-1}$, is due to my having an unspecific auxiliary analysis for estimating missing values of this variable. Their allegation is false: my memorandum on data sources (Ehrlich, 1975b) outlines in detail the auxiliary procedure utilized. (Bowers, among others, received a draft of this memorandum, which noted some errata in the published paper and which was completed in July 1975 by Randall Mark.) In addition, Bowers and Pierce utilize different values of $P°c|a$ than I did for the years 1933, 1934, and 1935, because they did not choose to apply the procedure I outlined for estimating these values. Their reference to "Ehrlich's conviction rates" for these years is misleading.

In addition, Bowers and Pierce do not accurately execute my regression analysis in which two measures of execution risk are used to test the hypotheses of the model. Their results in connection with these measures of execution risk are likely to be inferior to my own because they omit an observation; therefore their results are based on fewer degrees of freedom.

Bowers and Pierce suggest that all regressions of mine in which PXQ_{1-1} and TXQ_1 are used as measures of the conditional probability of execution are erroneous. They argue that I mistakenly utilized PXQ_{1-1} and TXQ_1 for the effective periods 1935–1969 and 1937–1969, respectively, whereas, they claim, the absence of data on PXQ_{1-1} in 1933 would require starting the effective period one year later in each case. They then speculate that an "erroneous (probably zero)" value of PXQ_{1-1} must have been inserted by the computer for 1933. Contrary to their speculation, however, PXQ_{1-1} in 1933 was estimated for use in all regressions with PXQ_{1-1} and TXQ_1 over the periods 1935–1969 and 1937–1969, respectively. The value of PXQ_{1-1} in 1933 is estimated as 7.16299 (percent). The estimate is based on published FBI data for the murder rate and for the murder-clearance ratio in 1932 and on an estimated conviction risk in that year.

Furthermore, Bowers and Pierce may have used computational procedures different from those I utilized. That their regression results and coefficients of serial correlation always differ from mine is consistent with this view. The calculations I reported were computed using the *Economic Software Package* (Cooper, 1973), into which R. C. Fair's three-round procedure is integrated. Bowers and Pierce (1975a) provide no documentation of their computational procedures.

Yet despite these differences, the regression results which Bowers and Pierce (1975a) report are "similar to Ehrlich's" (p. 196). More particularly, they confirm not only the apparent restraining effect of the conditional probability of execution on the murder rate but also my predicted ranking of estimates of elasticities of the murder rate with respect to the three deterrence variables—the probability of apprehension, the conditional probability of conviction, and the conditional probability of execution. This is at once a confirmation of the strength of my approach and a corroboration of the basic findings. The results stand out in contrast to previous allegations that no evidence exists suggesting that the death penalty may have a restraining effect on the frequency of murder in the population. How Bowers and Pierce attempt to obscure these results is the subject of the three following sections.

The Effects of Data Imperfections

Bowers and Pierce attempt to invalidate the results of my empirical investigation of the effects of deterrence variables (and these results alone) by posing, in effect, the extreme argument that data limitations prior to the 1960s preclude any empirical test of the deterrence hypothesis. (This direct implication of their remarks notwithstanding, Bowers and Pierce subsequently claim that their regression results are "more adequate and consistent" when they examine only subperiods ending early in the 1960s. Yet by their own analysis, data imperfections clearly are less important in the 1960s than in earlier periods). I do not agree with this general conclusion, and, in addition, I find their analysis concerning particular variables to be superficial and not constructive.

With respect to the dependent variable, the murder rate, the figures I have used are based on the Federal Bureau of Investigation's revised estimates of annual total murders and nonnegligent manslaughters. For the purposes of the empirical investigation, the FBI data are conceptually superior to the homicide series published in the *Vital Statistics of the United States* because the FBI category is defined to include only willful felonious homicides. Law enforcement officials, not health officials, bear the responsibility and undergo training for distinguishing willful felonious homicides from other homicides.

Although health officials are expected, when they can, to distinguish homicides from other violent "external" causes of death, namely accidents and suicides, they clearly experience much difficulty in drawing these distinctions. As late as 1970, for example, in which the *Vital Statistics* reports 16,848 homicides, a total of 5,384 violent deaths are classified as due to undetermined cause, that is, either accidental or purposeful (U.S. Public Health Service, 1970, p. 256). Indeed, by definition, the homicide data of the *Vital Statistics* explicitly include justifiable homicides and are likely to include some negligent manslaughters as well.

Homicides inflicted through legal intervention by police are included in the homicide count reported by the *Vital Statistics*. Only beginning in 1949 can such homicides be separated from the total. Moreover, the revised homicide data of the FBI reflect that agency's unique opportunity to incorporate into its estimates whatever homicide data have been collected by health officials. In constrast, the homicide figures tabulated for the *Vital Statistics* are never revised after the cutoff date for data collection for a given year. This failure to revise leads to an undercount of homicides pertaining to a given year because homicides occurring in that year that were not reported by the cutoff date are not added subsequently to that year's total.

In addition, information on death certificates, on which the *Vital Statistics* figures are based, sometimes may reflect classification of deaths only by medical cause rather than by external cause (such as accident or homicide), especially in those instances when death from homicidal assaults occurs later than the time of assault.

Because the *Vital Statistics* category includes some nonfelonious homicides, one would expect its homicide counts to exceed the FBI estimates. Yet, in every year from 1939 through 1961, the more narrowly defined FBI revised estimates are higher, by more than 900 in some years. Thus, Bowers and Pierce's (1975a, p. 189) statement that the FBI estimates differ from those of *Vital Statistics* by only about 3 percent for the period after 1939 is quite misleading in view of the magnitude of the year-to-year differences.

These comparisons suggest the importance of the technical considerations cited above that may lead to a significant underestimation of the relevant number of criminal homicides in the *Vital Statistics*. Tests which I have been conducting with independent bodies of data, and which I hope to report in the near future, indicate, nevertheless, that the effects of the deterrence variables—including the conditional probability of execution—on the homicide rate as reported by the *Vital Statistics* are qualitatively the same as those found in my time-series investigation.

With respect to the empirical measures of the apprehension and conviction risks, the critics raise the issue of whether the FBI data are "unrepresentative" in the earliest years of the sample period (Bowers and Pierce, 1975a, p. 190). Yet I have reported results demonstrating that the basic findings of my investigation are observed even without the presence of these early years in the observation set (see Erhlich, 1975a, equation 5 of Table 3 and equation 7 of Table 4). Moreover, their inference that the conviction data in 1936 and 1937 are biased because of a particular pattern observed in 1974 is purely conjectural and not founded upon any systematic analysis. Imperfections in data notwithstanding, my qualitative results in connection with the effects of apprehension and conviction risks over my entire sample period have been observed by others using the same FBI sources (see, for example, Vandaele, 1975).

More basically, though, the critics' attempt to discredit the empirical investigation on the basis of data quality is self-defeating to their own case. As is well known, *errors of measurement,* as they are termed in the econometrics literature, generally lead to underestimation of the true effects of an explanatory variable in a simple regression analysis when that variable is subject to random measurement imperfections (Johnston, 1972). If the true variables of interest were grossly misrepresented by their empirical counterparts, then the statistical implementation of the theory should have *failed* to demonstrate any of the effects theorized. In particular, only a remarkable coincidence could then explain the fact that, as predicted by my theory, the findings show that the probability of arrest (measured by the FBI's clearance ratios) had a proportionally larger impact on the murder rate than the conditional probability of conviction (derived from the FBI's statistics) and that the conditional probability of execution had the least effect. The FBI's reported figures on arrest and conviction in the 1930s surely were not tailored to my theoretical predictions thirty-odd years later.

The Effects of Deleting Observations

Curiously, Bowers and Pierce's remarks may convey the impression that I have artificially restricted the time span of my empirical investigation to test deterrence effects. The fact is that my empirical investigation was conducted for the longest time period for which necessary data were available at the time of my study. In contrast, Bowers and Pierce conduct the bulk of their analysis over arbitrarily restricted subperiods after deleting specific observations from the complete data set. Their assertion that "Ehrlich's regression model fits the data better without them" (Bowers and Pierce, 1975a, pp. 192–193) is based upon an erroneous method of inference, as I point out in a later section of this chapter. Here I shall address the consequences of discarding the information provided by the observations that they choose to omit.

Selective elimination of a sufficient number of observations from a regression analysis is a virtually foolproof method for reversing any single result derived from an original sample. Imagine, for example, a regression line verifying a negative association between the quantity demanded of corn and the price of corn. Since a majority of the data points typically will not lie on the regression line, the selective exclusion of data points can easily turn a significant negative relationship into an insignificant negative association or even a positive one. Such exclusions are particularly disturbing when the entire sample is relatively small. Indeed, the elimination of data points relating to murder in the 1960s—accounting for 17 percent or more of the full sample which I investigated—amounts to, in practice, the selective, nonrandom exclusion of observations crucial to an efficient estimation of the effects of key deterrent variables.

Omitting observations from the 1960s drastically reduces the variability in estimates of the conditional probability of execution and in the modified rates of change of these estimates, which are the actual regressors in the analysis. Whereas the rates of change in this variable had been quite stable for the preceding two decades, the objective (measured) risk of execution declined quite sharply starting about 1960. The sharp movement in the rates of change of the conditional risk of execution are, of course, not my invention—they accurately reflect the objective trend in the *true* risk of execution in the 1960s.

The fact that this trend concerns only twenty states that imposed execution in 1960 has no specific relevance in connection with the estimated deterrent effect of execution, contrary to the unsystematic discussion of Bowers and Pierce (1975a, p. 201). Only a subset, and typically a minority, of states enforced the death penalty in any given year. Many fewer than twenty applied the death penalty in every year from 1933 to 1967. Moreover, aggregating over states which had executions and states which did not implies that the estimated elasticity of the murder rate with respect to execution risk is likely to be biased downward relative to the true elasticity (see Ehrlich, 1975a, p. 408).

The inferences drawn by Bowers and Pierce, concerning murder rate and execution changes in particular states during the 1960s, are based on a faulty methodology. Their analysis of yearly changes in murder rates and executions in specific states over the six-year period 1962–1967 fails to control for the different trends in apprehension and conviction risks or in any other relevant determinants of murder across these states. It considers the absolute number of executions rather than the theoretically relevant conditional risk of execution in each state. It is based on comparisons which are not capable of identifying the relevant causal relationships in specific cases. Furthermore, the overwhelming trend in all the states compared over this subperiod was toward a complete cessation of executions. The occasional deviations from that trend in each state in a single year cannot serve as a statistically meaningful basis for the classification of states into those with increasing or decreasing executions. These fundamental shortcomings in Bowers and Pierce's independent analysis pertaining to the 1960s further underscores the importance of applying the *full* econometric framework utilized in my study over as long a period as the data permit in order to isolate the deterrent effect of the death penalty. In addition, murder-clearance ratios, used as objective estimates of the probability of arrest for murder, also exhibit little variability over a specific subperiod ending in the early 1960s. Thus, variability in arrest and execution risks is particularly small between the late 1930s and the early 1960s.

It is a well-known principle that a minimum amount of variability is necessary to perform a regression analysis. Indeed, an *efficient* sample designed for the purpose of estimating via a regression format the partial effects of specific explanatory variables on a dependent variable is one which maximizes the range of a variability in the regressors. Imagine, again, the attempt to confirm the negative association between prices and quantities demanded of corn. The attempt would fail if the subperiod selected by a researcher for his regression analysis is one in which corn prices or their rates of change, whichever are relevant, are relatively stable. The appropriate inference, however, is not that the theory of demand fails to explain movements in corn purchases but rather that the selected subperiod cannot be utilized to estimate the partial effect of corn prices on quantities demanded. The importance of such considerations is apparent in my time-series analysis not only in connection with deterrence variables but also in relation to the effect of the unemployment rate on the frequency of murder. While the association between the latter two variables is found to be positive over the entire sample period, this association weakens substantially when the subperiod relating to the 1930s is excluded from the observation set. The significance of the 1930s in connection with movements in the unemployment rate is well known.

A related consideration is that the estimates of the objective risk of execution show a strong time trend over the subperiod ending in the early 1960s. Specifically, the graph plotting the logarithms of these estimates over the time period from the late 1930s to the early 1960s appears to be nearly a negatively sloped straight line. Over the same subperiod the murder rate in the United States also exhibits a continual, systematic negative trend. Because of the significant negative trend in estimates of both the frequency of murder and the conditional risk of execution, the estimated effect of the latter on the former over this specific subperiod may simply reflect the effect of pure time trend.

The differences between regression results based on the full sample and those based on subperiods ending in the early 1960s, including those reported by Bowers and Pierce (1975b, pp. 24–26), are consistent with the arguments developed above. Not only does the effect of execution risk appear to become quite weak as data points are deleted, but the effect of apprehension risk also becomes weak due to lack of variability. As indicated above, the effect of unemployment is also sensitive to the deletion of specific subperiods. More importantly, the negative partial effect of the time trend on the murder rate, which was verified over the entire period considered in my study, becomes "insignificant" in Bowers and Pierce's regression results for subperiods ending in the early 1960s, although over those specific subperiods the murder rate continually declined. (The term *significance* here is used heuristically only to indicate relatively low standard errors. Standard tests of significance do not apply in connection with simultaneous equation estimation procedures.) Hence the effect of pure trend should have been found to be even more pronounced over these periods. The fact that the effects of both the risk of execution and time trend weaken suggests a high degree of competition or multicollinearity (see Johnston, 1972, 159–167) between the two variables over subperiods ending in the early 1960s.

The absence of variability and the presence of multicollinearity are hardly unique to my study but occur frequently in time-series regression analyses. The conventional remedy to such problems is to *extend* the sample size so that variability may be enhanced and the separate effects of highly related explanatory variables may be extricated and identified. I have pursued this procedure from the outset in my efforts to extend the sample size into the early 1930s and up to the late 1960s. Bowers and Pierce pursue just the reverse course. Following my own report of weak results obtained from subperiods ending in 1963, they go on to perform most of their independent estimations over subperiods in which little meaningful analysis can be conducted.

As for the unfounded claim that somehow "significant" deterrent effects of execution risk and other punishment variables are "present" only in a short span of time relating to the 1960s and are not to be found in earlier (or later) periods, I plan to demonstrate in the near future, through evidence based on statewide data in earlier years, that the deterrent effects of certainty and severity of punishment—including punishment by execution—are not uniquely associated with a specific set of data points. Further independent evidence on this point is provided by Yunker (1975). Yunker's analysis, conducted over a sample period extending through 1974, yields results indicating that the murder rate declines as the risk of execution rises. The statistical methodology he uses, however, is different from my own.

The Merits of the Logarithmic Format

In the empirical implementation of my general theory of participation in illegitimate activities (see Ehrlich, 1974, 1975a), I consistently have emphasized a logarithmic-linear specification of the relevant equations. However, as my following comments will show, while the logarithimic-linear specification appears to be preferable on analytical and experiential grounds, the qualitative results from my time-series study do not depend exclusively on this functional form.

The logarithmic-linear form can be justified on practical grounds if the elasticities of a dependent variable with respect to a set of explanatory variables are assumed to be constant to the first order of approximation. A logarithmic-linear specification is a superior regression format when the magnitude of the errors in the data are thought to be proportional to the level of the variables that the data purport to measure. It would be rather implausible, for example, to assume that the magnitude of underreported and misreported crime is independent of the level of reported crime. This assumption is implicitly invoked by use of the linear specification in the natural values of the variables, the functional form stressed by Bowers and Pierce (1975a, p. 199). More plausibly, one may assume that the magnitude of reporting errors is proportional to the level of the relevant statistics (see Ehrlich, 1974). Furthermore, in the case of murder investigation, the dependent variable of interest is the rate of capital murder rather than the rate of criminal homicide, the actual measure utilized. Previous researchers (for example, Sellin, 1959) have assumed that the capital murder rate and the total homicide rate are proportionally related. It would be convenient at least, then, to use a logarithmic-linear specification which enables a direct estimation of elasticities. Moreover, similar considerations also apply to the observed probabilities of apprehension, conviction, and execution, each of which is based upon data relating to reported willful felonious homicides rather than the true level of capital murders. All these considerations suggest that the efficient functional form underlying the murder supply function is likely to be one that utilizes the logarithms of the dependent variable and the key independent variables. And indeed, "prior information" accumulated through my past work on crime has led me to emphasize the logarithmic-linear regression because of its observed relative efficiency.

Bowers and Pierce could have tested statistically for the optimal functional specification of the estimated supply-of-offenses function. In particular, they could have examined the efficiency of the logarithmic-linear specification relative to a specification that is linear in the natural values of all variables. In research now in progress, I have conducted statistical tests of optimal transformations based on a likelihood ratio method. As I plan to demonstrate, the conclusion emerging from these tests is that the logarithmic-linear format not only is decisively superior to the format using the natural values of the variables but that the former generally cannot be rejected as the optimal form within the class of single-parameter power transformations. Bowers and Pierce's demonstration that their regression results tend to deteriorate when running the regressions with natural numbers shows only that they evade the question of which of the two transformations is more appropriate. Hence they not only prefer testing the deterrence hypothesis for subperiods of sharply limited usefulness, but they also prefer an inferior regression format.

As I noted in my paper, the basic results from that study were found to be unaffected qualitatively by the choice of functional form. The regression equation given here was performed with the antilogarithms (that is, the natural numbers) of the same set of variables used to derive the results reported in my published paper, and indicates that the qualitative deterrent effects of apprehension, conviction, and execution are not exclusively dependent on a specific functional form. This estimated equation pertains to the effective period 1935–1969. The murder rate is represented by $q°$; the risks of apprehension, conviction, and execution are represented by $P°a$, $P°c|a$, and PXQ_1, respectively; other symbols can be interpreted from Table 2 of my published paper, Ehrlich (1975a, p. 409), and the numbers in parentheses denote ratios of estimated regression coefficients to their standard errors. The estimate for $\hat{\rho}$ is -.119. Not only is the direction of the effect of every variable the same as is found with the logarithmic-linear specification, but the predicted ranking of the elasticities of the measures of the three deterrence variables also is observed.

$$q° = \quad .245 \quad - .000891\Delta*P°c|a \quad - .000830\Delta*P°a \quad - .00385\Delta*PXQ_1$$
$$(3.806)\ (-3.771) \qquad\qquad (-1.573) \qquad\qquad (-3.024)$$

$$- .238\Delta*L + .147\Delta*A + .000115\Delta*Y_p + .000269\Delta*U$$
$$(-2.476) \qquad (2.428) \qquad (5.504) \qquad\qquad (1.462)$$

$$- .00372\Delta*T$$
$$(-6.857)$$

Although the specification in natural numbers appears to be clearly inefficient in view of prior information and other tests, time-series regression estimates derived via that format in this equation nevertheless indicate the existence of the expected deterrent effects. (Yunker, 1975, performed regressions with natural numbers only. His regression analysis also indicates the existence of a deterrent effect associated with the risk of execution in the United States.)

Basic Statistical Errors in My Critics' Work

Bowers and Pierce's critique refers to errors in my analysis. The fact is that I have learned of no single error in either my theoretical analysis or the statistical methodology used to implement the theory. In contrast, the work by Bowers and Pierce is riddled with errors and demonstrations of misunderstanding of basic statistical principles. A few examples will illustrate.

The R^2 statistic is essentially irrelevant in connection with a two-stage least squares regression analysis or the related three-round procedure used in my study. Yet, with no qualification whatever, Bowers and Pierce cite this statistic in conjunction with every estimated equation which they report (1975b). More seriously, they use the R^2 statistic as a basis for inference.

The R^2 statistics, as well as standard errors of the regressions, computed for subsamples having different ending dates, are relied on by Bowers and Pierce to draw the startling inference that regression results are "more adequate and consistent for the periods with earlier ending dates" (1975a, p. 198). Their lack of regard for, indeed their apparent lack of awareness of, the diminishing degrees of freedom associated with smaller and smaller subsamples is astonishing. Even if the regression analysis were based on the ordinary, or classical, least square procedure, comparison of R^2 statistics and standard errors of the regressions across subsamples with successively smaller degrees of freedom would be improper: As Bowers and Pierce surely know, when the number of degrees of freedom is zero, the R^2 statistic necessarily is unity. It should be noted that the deletion of observations from the full set of observations led Bowers and Pierce to estimate regression equations in which the number of observations is as low as twenty-two while the number of parameters estimated in the reduced-form regression analysis is nineteen. They apparently fail to recognize that estimated regression coefficients based on successively smaller degrees of freedom become increasingly imprecise. In particular, estimates based upon so few degrees of freedom as those Bowers and Pierce stress are unlikely to be adequate for rejecting the hypothesis of no deterrent effects.

Unfortunately, on this point, as others, Baldus and Cole (1975, p. 180) uncritically accept the inferences drawn by Bowers and Pierce and other critics and, thus, implicity commit the same errors. Without providing any valid grounds for their assertions, Baldus and Cole even more emphatically assert their judgment that the subperiod analysis provides estimates somehow superior to those obtained from the full sample.

At the end of their article, Bowers and Pierce (1975a) report results from regressions in which they replace the conditional probability of execution—the theoretically relevant variable—with the absolute number of executions. A finding of a positive association between homicide rates and the number of executions is cited as evidence of the "brutalizing" effects of capital punishment. Bowers and Pierce do not recognize, however, that the positive association may be expected on purely technical grounds. Where there are no homicides there can be no convictions or executions. In contrast, when murder rates rise, with arrest, conviction, and execution risks constant or rising, the number of convictions and executions also would rise. A positive (or zero) associaton between criminal homicides and the number of executions thus is hardly surprising. Indeed, more than twenty years ago this relationship was noted by Schuessler (1952), who recognized that this correlation does not constitute a test of the deterrence hypothesis.

Schuessler's work is cited by Bowers and Pierce (1975b, p. 2), as well as by Baldus and Cole (1975, p. 183), who also fail to recognize the technical association between homicide and execution rates. It might be noted that Schuessler (1952, pp. 59–60) went on to attempt a test of the deterrence hypothesis by measuring the simple correlation coefficient between homicide rates and a measure of the risk of execution in forty-one executing states over the period 1937–1949. Although he found the correlation coefficient to be −.26, indicating that the murder rate falls as execution risk rises, and although this negative association turns out to be significant statistically at the 5 percent level for a one-tail test, neither Bowers and Pierce nor Baldus and Cole mention this result.

Although I have focused in this discussion on errors contained in the Bowers and Pierce paper, I should point out that the Baldus and Cole paper also is seriously flawed. For example, Baldus and Cole criticize my study because "the second-stage regression does not hold fixed" (1975, p. 182) the cluster of variables denoted as X_2 in Table 2 of my published work. However, these variables serve in the role of "omitted exogenous variables" in the murder supply equation. The remark shows that Baldus and Cole do not understand the simultaneous equation framework underlying my study. Exogenous variables such as those summarized under X_2 *must* not be held constant in estimating the structural murder supply function. If they were, the two-stage least squares procedure would become meaningless. Their effects, however, are integrated appropriately in the estimation procedure through their incorporation in the reduced form regression analysis. This error by Baldus and Cole betrays quite a fundamental misunderstanding of the methodology which they have undertaken to evaluate. Indeed, in their comparisons of my research with that of previous researchers, they do not note the prime benefit of utilizing the simultaneous equation framework—that it attempts to identify the direction of the causal relationship between the frequency of murder and the deterrence variables. The direction of that relationship is not self-evident. For example, in times of high murder rates, states may be more inclined to convict and execute offenders, or even reinstate the death penalty, than in times of low murder rates. The simple association between these variables thus may give the appearance that, for example, an increase in the risk of execution "leads" to an increase in the murder rate, even though the opposite is true. A simultaneous equation estimation framework is designed to identify causal relations and thus avoid potentially biased results.

The Gap Between Evidence and Inference in Previous Research

Bowers and Pierce (1975b) and, in greater detail, Baldus and Cole (1975), rely heavily on previous research, especially that of Sellin, as evidence against the deterrence hypothesis. In this section, I shall briefly comment on the research by Sellin and others concerning the deterrence hypothesis.

The principal shortcoming of Sellin's research and related work is that the approach taken and the methods applied do not permit a systematic test of the main implications of the general theory of deterrence, a theory which posits that potential offenders respond to incentives. The shortcoming is basic because the implications following from the *general* deterrence hypothesis are what Sellin was attempting to challenge empirically (see, for example, Sellin, 1961). Yet his work neither develops nor tests the full range of implications following from the theory that he attempts to reject; nor is a competing theory developed and tested. In addition to implying that punishments in general, and executions in particular, may deter crime, the general deterrence hypothesis provides the testable expectation that punishments imposed only with relative infrequency will have less impact than those imposed with a high degree of certainty. The theory of deterrence predicts not only the direction of effects of, for example, equal percentage changes in the relevant apprehension, conviction, and execution risks, but also the relative order of magnitude of these effects. Although the basic premise of these and other testable implications is that, on balance, potential offenders respond to incentives, Sellin never devised an analytical framework for rejecting this general hypothesis. More significantly, to my knowledge Sellin never reported any parametric or nonparametric statistical tests that could justify his rather strong conclusions. In all, there exists a considerable gap between the limitedly useful evidence provided by Sellin and others following his methodology and the rather emphatic inferences drawn.

Two examples may illustrate this conclusion. Sellin has compared homicide rates in "abolitionist" and "retentionist" states, as defined by the legal status of the death penalty. But Sellin never accounts for the extent of the actual enforcement of the penalty in retentionist states. Yet by his own analysis, the suggested relevant variable is the risk of execution, not merely its legal status, for "were [the death penalty] present in the law alone it would be completely robbed of its threat" (Sellin, 1959, p. 20). The point is far from being subtle. In a number of "retentionist" states whose homicide rates are compared to neighboring abolitionist states, the execution risk was negligible throughout the entire period investigated by Sellin. For example, in Vermont, New Hampshire, South Dakota, and Nebraska, the death penalty was imposed only rarely after 1920; Massachusetts had no executions after 1947. Not surprisingly, with no allowance for actual execution risks, Sellin's simple graphical comparisons of homicide rates across different states do not *appear* to uncover considerable differences. (As indicated above, Sellin's observations are not supported by statistical inference tests.) But could such observations justify Sellin's (1967) conclusion that the presence of the death penalty—in law or practice—does not influence homicide death rates?

This deficiency is even more glaring in tests attempted by Bowers (1974) in another work to determine the effect of the moratorium on executions in the United States. (Baldus and Cole, 1975, cite this work by Bowers as corroboration of Sellin's findings.) Following Sellin's methodology, Bowers compares the levels of murder rates in nine arbitrarily chosen mixes of neighboring states in the four years preceding and subsequent to the judicial moratorium. He reports similar patterns in most groups. However, the plain fact is that *none* of the states in eight of the nine groups had a single execution throughout the period. And in the ninth group, Bowers creates a dubious distinction between New York, classified as abolitionist, and New Jersey and Pennsylvania, classified as retentionist, although New York ceased all executions in 1963—the same year as New Jersey and one year after Pennsylvania.

That such comparisons are used as a basis for inference about the deterrent effect of capital punishment taxes one's imagination.

A second general shortcoming characterizing previous research on this issue by Sellin and others is the absence of any sytematic standardization of data so that the effect of execution risk can be isolated from the effects of other factors that not only may influence the murder rate but also are expected to be systematically related to the risk of execution. Clearly aware of the general problem, Sellin (1959) has emphasized the need to compare states that are "as alike as possible" (p. 21). However, his assumption that neighboring states satisfy this prerequisite is unacceptable. Pairs of neighboring abolitionist and retentionist states, such as Illinois and Wisconsin, Michigan and Indiana, or Massachusetts and Rhode Island, differ in their economic and demographic characteristics, in their crime rates and law enforcement activity, and presumably also in their medical services available to victims of aggravated assaults. The perfunctory analysis of Baldus and Cole (1975, p. 177) on this point shows little appreciation of the issues involved. At Table 3 their list of data purportedly for one year is a mix of data drawn from two different years (1960 and 1966). Yet the issue on which they are leveling evidence is the extent to which Sellin "controlled for other factors" in each and every year of the forty-odd years considered in his studies. There still exists substantial variation in the variables Baldus and Cole compare within the five groupings of states they consider. They have not presented data for the sixth grouping considered by Sellin. The data sources they cite for the construction of their permanent income measures for the states are not capable of generating such statewide measures. Their inferences about the impact of specific variables on the murder rate in each state are not based on any systematic analysis. In three of their five cases, a retentionist state has the lowest homicide rate within a particular grouping—a fact they choose not to mention. By Baldus and Cole's analysis this fact might be viewed as evidence for deterrence. I am not suggesting, however, that such inference can be justified given the fragmentary nature of the analysis. More generally, I question the logical basis for preferring a statistical method that provides only indirect and incomplete control for specific variables expected to have an impact on the crime rate over a regression analysis attempting to control these variables directly.

In addition, as my analysis has shown (Ehrlich, 1975a, p. 406), variation in the legal status of the death penalty occasionally may be a result, rather than a cause, of changes in murder rates and thus may give rise to an apparent positive association between the two variables. For these reasons, the true effect of the death penalty on the murder rate

cannot readily be inferred from simple comparisons of the sort performed by Sellin and others.

The Proper Measurement of the Restraining
Effect of Capital Punishment

My critics (Bowers and Pierce, 1975a, p. 6; Baldus and Cole, 1975,
pp. 177-183) allude to my having inappropriately or incompletely
estimated the deterrent effect of capital punishment because I neglected
the interdependencies among apprehension, conviction, and execution
risks. The fact is that I have stressed and integrated these interpeden-
dencies both in my theoretical analysis and in the empirical investigation. Both pairs of authors suggest that the only proper means of
estimating the deterrent effect of the death penalty is by allowing
apprehension and conviction risks to "vary" with execution risk rather
than by holding them "constant," thereby estimating the "total" effect
of the penalty. In fact, I have treated empirically both the "partial"
effect of execution risk—by controlling for the apprehension and conviction risks—and the observed "total" effect—by estimating the effect
of execution risk through a reduced form regression analysis controlling only for exogenous and predetermined variables. The former
procedure is without question the only proper way of verifying the
hypothesized deterrent effect of execution risk, for the theory predicts
that an increase in the conditional risk of execution at *given* levels of
apprehension and conviction risks would have a deterrent effect on the
incentive to commit murder. For the quite distinct purpose of evaluating the overall desirability of capital punishment as an instrument of
policy, both estimation procedures, in principle, can provide useful
guidance. Indeed, both are reported in my study. Although the "total"
effects associated with a few measures of execution risk appear somewhat smaller than their estimated "partial" effects, the quantitative
differences are generally small.

It should be pointed out, in this connection, that my critics
misconstrue the theoretical predictions relating to the "total" deterrent
impact of the risk of execution. While unwarranted movements in
execution risk are expected to induce opposite movements in apprehension and conviction risks, the magnitudes of the resulting effects
will not necessarily offset the effect of the initial change in execution
risk. Moreover, the theory implies that no such compensatory movements are expected when the initial shift in execution is viewed as

*warranted.** For example, if there were universal agreement that reinstatement of capital punishment under specific conditions were socially optimal, then there is no compelling reason to expect that juries would be less inclined to convict offenders charged with capital crimes. Levels of apprehension and conviction risks could also be maintained through an appropriate allocation of resources to specific law enforcement activities. Thus estimates of "partial" effects of execution risk, as well as of apprehension and conviction risks, provide useful information from a policy viewpoint.

Concluding Remarks

The basic issue underlying my theoretical and empirical investigation of murder has not been merely the deterrent efficacy of the death penalty but the more general issue of offenders' responsiveness to incentives. My time-series analysis of the trend of murder in the United States should not be evaluated as an isolated experiment but rather as part of the more general research into offenders' behavior. Viewed in this more general context, the new research by myself and other social scientists in recent years has lent considerable support to the proposition that, in the aggregate, potential offenders respond to both negative and positive incentives. The growing body of new research by economists and sociologists has indicated the existence of deterrent effects of severity and certainty of punishment as well as other systematic regularities attributable to the effects of incentives. (See, for example, Carr-Hill and Stern, 1973; Ehrlich, 1974; Fleisher, 1966; Gibbs, 1968; Phillips, Votey, and Maxwell, 1972; Rottenberg, 1973; Smigel-Leibowitz, 1965; Title, 1972; Vandaele, 1975; Yunker, 1975.) These conclusions have been demonstrated in studies using data from different times and different places. My research on the deterrence effect of capital punishment has produced results compatible with this new evidence.

*In reference to these possible compensatory changes in apprehension and conviction risks, both Bowers and Pierce (1975b, p. 6) and Baldus and Cole (1975, p. 182) cite an exercise in an unpublished paper by Passell and Taylor (1975, on file with *The Yale Law Journal*), as evidence that the "total" effect of execution risk on the murder rate is likely to be positive. Ironically, neither pair of authors apparently understands the exercise by Passell and Taylor, which has nothing to do with the "compensatory" changes under discussion. In fact, I believe that the exercise by Passell and Taylor is internally inconsistent and irrelevant, but since their paper has not been published yet, I will not address their exercise here.

The bulk of my critics' analyses challenges neither the theoretical formulation of the deterrence hypothesis nor the statistical techniques used in the theory's empirical implementation. Neither Bowers and Pierce nor Baldus and Cole present valid tests that reject the deterrence hypothesis. Furthermore, Baldus and Cole do not present evidence of their own. They rely mainly upon Sellin's work as evidence, which I have discussed briefly here. Their discussion merely repeats other authors' inferences and judgments concerning the deterrence hypothesis which may prove to be unjustified or premature. It is beyond the scope of this discussion to deal with these other works. I hope that their work does not baffle the lawyer pondering the merits of using an economic approach to law or of using statistical techniques to study legal questions. The statistical methodology is quite useful and relevant when appropriately applied. Contrary to the inferences of Bowers and Pierce, their study does not present statistically meaningful evidence that the risk of execution has no deterrent effect, let alone that it has a "brutalizing" effect, on the frequency of murder in the population.

In this reply, I have elaborated upon some aspects of my research which, because of space limitations, have not been fully discussed in my published paper on the death penalty. Needless to say, my discussion here is not a substitute for the published paper. The paper discusses the analytical framework underlying the general deterrence hypothesis, which is the main issue of concern in my research. It also elaborates upon the methodology needed for meaningful tests of that hypothesis. The paper also stresses the limitations of the empirical investigation and the tentative nature of the findings. Indeed, as I stated, conclusions based on studies of historical data necessarily are qualified in view of the difficulties of measuring efficient empirical counterparts of relevant theoretical constructs and in view of intrinsic limitations of statistical inference. However, data imperfections are likely to work *against,* not in favor of, the theorized deterrent effect of punishment and the effects of incentives in general. It is thus remarkable that the evidence of my time-series analysis and additional research repeatedly has proven not inconsistent with rather sharp predictions emanating from the deterrence hypothesis. I have not claimed, however, that my research settles the issue of the deterrent effect of capital punishment. Nor have I advocated the use of capital punishment. As I stressed in my paper, the issue of deterrence is but one of a myriad of issues related to the efficiency and desirability of capital punishment as a social instrument for combating crime. The study of the deterrent effect of capital punishment is of considerable independent importance in connection with the hypothesis that potential offenders on the whole respond to incentives. Research on this issue undoubtedly will benefit in the long run from legitimate attempts to use more efficient data and statistical techniques than those heretofore employed in studies of capital punishment.

References

Baldus, D. C., and Cole, J. W. L. "A Comparison of the Work of Thorsten Sellin and Isaac Ehrlich on the Deterrent Effect of Capital Punishment."*Yale Law Journal*, 1975, *85*, 170–186.

Bowers, W. *Executions in America*. Lexington, Mass: Lexington Books, 1974.

Bowers, W., and Pierce, G. "The Illusion of Deterrence in Isaac Ehrlich's Research on Capital Punishment." *Yale Law Journal*, 1975a, *85*, 187–208.

Bowers, W., and Pierce, G. "Deterrence, Brutalization, or Nonsense: A Critique of Isaac Ehrlich's Research on Capital Punishment." Unpublished manuscript, Center for Applied Social Research, Northeastern University, 1975b.

Carr-Hill, R. A., and Stern, N. H. "An Econometric Model of the Supply and Control of Recorded Offenses in England and Wales." *Journal of Public Economics*, 1973, *2*, 289–318.

Cooper, J. *Econometric Software Package*. Chicago: University of Chicago Press, 1973.

Ehrlich, I. "Participation in Illegitimate Activites: An Economic Analysis." In G. Becker and W. Landes (Eds.), *Economics of Crime and Punishment*, 1974.

Ehrlich, I. "The Deterrent Effect of Capital Punishment: A Question of Life and Death." *American Economic Review*, 1975a, *65*, 397–417.

Ehrlich, I. "The Deterrent Effect of Capital Punishment: A Question of Life or Death—Sources of Data." Unpublished appendix, 1975b. (Available from *The Yale Law Journal*.)

Fleisher, B. *The Economics of Delinquency*. Chicago: Quadrangle Books, 1966.

Gibbs, G. "Crime, Punishment, and Deterrence." *Study of Social Science Quarterly*, 1968, *48*, 515–530.

Johnston, J. *Econometric Methods*. (2nd ed.). New York: McGraw-Hill, 1972.

Passell, P., and Taylor, J. "The Deterrent Effect of Capital Punishment: Another View." Discussion Paper No. 74-7509, Department of Economics, Columbia University, February 1975.

Phillips, L, Votey, H. L., Jr., and Maxwell, D., "Crime, Youth, and the Labor Market." *Journal of Political Economics*, 1972, *80*, 491–504.

Rottenberg, S. (Ed.). *The Economics of Crime and Punishment.* Washington, D.C.: American Enterprise Institute for Public Policy Research, 1973.

Schuessler, K. F. "The Deterrent Influence of the Death Penalty." *Annals,* 1952, *284,* 54–62.

Sellin, T. *The Death Penalty.* Philadelphia: American Law Institute, 1959.

Sellin, T. "Capital Punishment." *Federal Probation,* 1961, *3*(4), 25.

Sellin, T. "Executions in the United States." In T. Sellin (Ed.,), *Capital Punishment.* New York: Harper & Row, 1967.

Smigel-Leibowitz, A. "Does Crime Pay? An Economic Analysis." Unpublished master's thesis, Columbia University, 1965.

Title, C. R. "Crime Rates and Legal Sanctions." *Social Problems,* 1972, *16,* 409–423.

U.S. Public Health Service. *Vital Statistics of the United States.* Vol 2. Washington, D.C.: Department of Health, Education, and Welfare, 1970.

Vandaele, W. "The Economics of Crime: An Econometric Investigation of Auto Theft in the United States." Unpublished doctoral dissertation, University of Chicago, 1975.

Yunker, J. "The Deterrent Effect of Capital Punishment: Comment." Unpublished manuscript, on file with the *Yale Law Journal,* 1975.

16   *Hernando Gomez*

Reevaluating
Educational Effects
in the Cali Experiment

Educational and psychological literature has been long concerned with
the problem of measurement and analysis in longitudinal research
programs. The need for coherent methodology has its origin in a con-
ception of the individual as a performer whose behavior changes with
time, rather than as a static respondent, and in social scientists' interests in understanding developmental trends rather than the individual's state at a given time. Furthermore, modern psychometric theory
has generated techniques that are at least partly adequate in dealing
with the individual himself, rather than groups of individuals, when
longitudinal data are available. This achievement has some implications for research-based policy in that developed societies are likely to

Note: Support for this research was provided by NIE-C-74-0115 and
NIE-G-79-0128. The data on which this reanalysis is based was supported primarily by the Ford Foundation. The author wishes to thank Benjamin Wright
for his assistance. This material was presented at a meeting of the International
Statistical Institute in New Delhi, India.

inquire more frequently about individual development rather than group performance. Bock (1976), for example, points out that industrial nations are reaching the barrier of zero-growth population but that the same is not true for economic development. In the near future, there will be fewer children in grammar schools, and the resources available to education will continue to grow. What will educational researchers and educational psychologists do? One humane response is to shift our attention to quality rather than quantity in education.

Latent trait theory will play a notable role in such an accomplishment. This technique, when combined with longitudinal designs in field experimentation, provides almost all the elements necessary for individual assessment, judging from the work of Rasch (1960) and Bock (1976). These contributions notwithstanding, several problems in analyzing longitudinal data for groups must be solved before we begin to implement an individualistic approach. To be specific, the researcher must confront the problem of analyzing a data matrix in which treatment groups and different occasions of measurement are summarized in a multivariate, time-structured vector of observations. If the instruments that render the observed values remain the same along the time continuum, a multivariate approach to the repeated measures design, as suggested by Bock (1963), is powerful in understanding group trends and group differences. This approach assumes that the factorial composition of the observations is the same on all occasions. If the instruments differ from one measure to the next, as often they do, a model such as the one suggested by Jöreskog and Sörbom (1976) facilitates understanding the factorial composition of the different multivariate vectors of observations as well as the linkages among them. However, factor analytic techniques are not always appropriate for providing evidence of group differences in such a situation. Both factor analysis and multivariate analysis of variance, for example, demand that the measures have the same units along the time continuum. Although taken for granted, there often is no evidential reason to assume that ordinary tests of intelligence, achievement, attitude, and so forth are on an interval scale, as the parametric techniques require.

The objective of this paper is to elaborate on the commensurability and continuity of the observed variables. First, we discuss measurement theory, especially the properties of achievement tests and of the estimates of children's ability that they generate. Then we describe the application and test of the theory, using data from field experiments on enrichment programs for improverished Colombian children. Our secondary analysis of existing data was conducted in the interest of exploring measurement theory.

Commensurability

A scale may be defined as *commensurable* if it has units along a continuum. Interval scales that are unique up to a linear transformation constitute an adequate metric for parametric techniques such as analysis of variance and factor analysis. Thus, in order to perform an adequate evaluation of a set of longitudinal data, we must assure that the variables are measured on an interval scale. To obtain that assurance in testing situations, we may think of the reponse to a test item as the result of an interaction between two parameters: the item's difficulty and subject's ability. However, the interaction generates a qualitative observation in that we classify a subject according to whether a variable defining a response process exceeds or does not exceed the item threshold. The model suggested by Rasch (1961) formally replaces this qualitative observation by measurable quantities, relating the response process to response probabilities. So, for example, the probability of success for a given child on a test item j is defined by $\exp(\theta_s - \delta_j)/1 + \exp(\theta_s - \delta_j)$, where θ_s = ability parameter for child s, and δ_j = difficulty of item j.

The objective then is to estimate the parameters that determine the probability of success on a given item so one can make comparisons among stimuli or individuals. At best, one would like to have a comparison base for individuals that is independent of the particular stimuli or items to which the respondent has been exposed. Similarly, a comparison base for test items that is independent of the particular sample of individuals providing responses allows for more interpretable comparisons. These two properties in abilities and difficulties are what Rasch has termed *objectivity*. They are better understood if we assert that abilities are item-free and difficulties are person-free (Wright, 1967).

Later developments in the field of latent trait theory suggest that evidence for the contention that an interval scale has been achieved can be generated by establishing a relationship between differences in the scale to item response probabilities (Bock, 1976). Other authors, such as Samejima (1969), are of the opinion that the metric properties of ability and difficulty estimates generated under the model are only ordinal. Perline (1977) suggests that several models have been proposed that do yield interval scales. By relating parameters estimated using the Rasch model to the additive conjoint measurement model, he concludes that the Rasch approach could be applied in many situations where conjoint measurement is being attempted. This conclusion holds only if the model properly fits the data. The theoretical arguments must be verified, however, with empirical work. Samejima (1969) suggests relating the estimates obtained with latent trait models to an external criterion that is known to be measured on an interval scale. In this chapter, we apply Samejima's approach to verify that the estimates are in fact suitable for parametric analysis.

Continuity in Measurement

A major problem in longitudinal research is that tests generally top out when the time span is relatively large. Therefore, researchers are often confronted with the need to change the test instruments half-way through a study or even at each occasion of measurement. If completely different tests are used for different occasions, a satisfactory analytic strategy is not available. More often, researchers keep a set of items in common between measures of ability on two consecutive occasions. This practice is probably not an unreasonable one, since the intervals of measurement in longitudinal studies are relatively short in comparison to the subject's rate of development. Assuming that this is the case, it is relatively easy to develop a method that allows us to evaluate longitudinal data. For the sake of simplicity, we explain the principal axioms of the method by appealing to an example, rather than to complex theoretical discussions.

In the simplest case, the data we confront involve only three testing periods. Suppose the researcher has used test A to evaluate the outcome of an education program on the first occasion of measurement. Since a test will often be useful for only two occasions, good practice would indicate that a new test, B, should be used in conjunction with test A to evaluate outcome on the second occasion. The same principle underlies the use of tests B and C in the third testing period. Notice that this is an extreme situation, since one sometimes has the opportunity to use the same test on more than two occasions. If the factor composition for all the tests is identical throughout occasions, a psychometric model such as the one proposed by Rasch is suitable for the estimation of abilities on a common scale in all the testing points.

Abilities estimated with test A are in the same scale, and scores represent developmental change between the first and second occasions of measurement. The same holds for abilities estimated with test B on occasions two and three. However, abilities estimated with test B on these occasions are in scales with different origin to those estimated with A on occasions one and two. The problem is then to understand how to establish a link between the two sets of abilities.

Let $C_{i,j}$ represent the test items in common between occasions i and j with $j < i$, and let $C_{i,k}$ represent items in common between occasions i and k with $k > i$. Further, let $\hat{\theta}_{i,j}$ and $\hat{\theta}_{i,k}$ be the abilities estimated with tests of length $C_{i,j}$ and $C_{i,k}$, respectively. The principle of objective comparison implies that estimates obtained with tests $C_{i,j}$ and $C_{i,k}$ are equal, but they have scales with different origin. Under the principle, the following relationship must hold:

$$\hat{\theta}_{i,j} = \beta_0 + \beta\hat{\theta}_{i,k} \tag{1}$$

β_0 can be defined as a shift operator that translates the origin of the scale of the $\hat{\theta}_{i,k}$ abilities to equate with $\hat{\theta}_{i,j}$, since β by the objective comparison principle must be equal to one. If we sum over all the sample of examinees, ℓ, a proper estimate of the shift operator is:

$$\beta_0 = \frac{1}{n} \sum_{\ell=1}^{n} (\hat{\theta}_{i,j} - \hat{\theta}_{i,k})_{\hat{\ell}} \tag{2}$$

where n is the number of subjects in the sample. Given that abilities and item difficulties are in the same metric (Rasch, 1961), an estimate of β_0 can also be obtained by using item difficulties in two consecutive occasions where the same test was administered (Wright and Mead, 1975).

The theory outlined here is subject, of course, to empirical verification. The same approach was employed by Wright (1967) in calibrating a test with both extremes of the same population. Wright found that original test scores produce different test characteristic curves when groups of "smart" and "dumb" persons (Wright's terminology) were used as target populations. When raw test scores were replaced by abilities estimated using the Rasch procedure, the test characteristic curve was the same for both groups. A similar approach can be found in Goulet, Linn, and Tatsuoka (1975); however, these authors suggest that their analyses do not support the dual claim of item-free person measurement and person-free test calibration indicated by Wright. In the present example, we could talk about vertically equated tests only if the correlation between abilities estimated with tests A and B on occasion two, or tests B and C on occasion three is exactly one except for sampling or calibration errors. A plot of these two sets of abilities should fall on a straight line with a slope of one and an intercept β_0.

A Numerical Example

Data for the present application comes from a randomized longitudinal study on nutrition and mental development. Briefly, the study involved a randomized experiment undertaken in the field to estimate the relative effects of nutrition and education programs on children from Colombian barrios. It is one of the few large-scale, formal experiments to assay the effect of programs on preschool children, and one of a still smaller number of tests to assay effects over a reasonable time span. Detailed information about the study and a summary of the evaluation is presented in McKay and others (1978); only technical details about the procedure are included here. (See also Chapter Seventeen.)

The data matrix is a 5×5 array where columns correspond to occasions and rows to treatment groups. Different tests of cognitive performance were used during the five-year longitudinal study. At the beginning of the study, a standard test battery was adapted for local use and served as the criterion. However, the researchers expected that the tests would reach a ceiling after the third testing period. That is, the test would no longer contain items which were sufficiently difficult to serve as a basis for accurate characterization of children's ability. For this reason, the Wechsler scale for children (WPPSI) was introduced on the third testing occasion and the WISC-R on the fifth. The number of tests employed on each of the five occasions of testing were respectively: eleven, eleven, fifteen, fourteen, and eleven. The number of tests used on consecutive occasions varied: eleven tests were common to first and second test occasions: ten were common to second and third; nine were common in the third and fourth; eleven were given on both fourth and fifth occasions. The total number of test items available after test calibration for estimating ability of each child were, on consecutive occasions: 126, 131, 105, 82, and 79.

Factor Composition. In a longitudinal evaluation of an education program of the kind under examination, it is necessary to assure that the same trait or traits underlie the covariance structure for the tests along the entire time span. This assurance helps to guarantee that inferences about a developmental trend are meaningful and provides a basis for the calibration of tests, since local independence must be assumed. Difficulties in making this assurance arose in performing factor analyses in this study, since the number of items is too high for available computer software. To circumvent the problem, Cronbach's α was computed within tests as an index of interval consistency. The smallest α obtained was of the order of .78, and it was then assumed that each of the tests was essentially unifactorial. A more adequate procedure that can be recommended for future studies is to factor analyze within-test tetrachoric correlation matrices, although difficulties might arise when some of them are not positive definite.

Taking into account the internal consistency coefficients, we obtained total scores for each of the tests, and we performed factor analyses within occasions for this reduced number of variables. Cattell's scree test indicated that a single-factor model would be adequate in reproducing the covariance matrices for occasions one through four (Gomez, 1973). For occasion five, Rezmovic (1976) found that a two-factor model was adequate to fit the data; however, these two factors correlated .86.

Parameter Estimation. A computer program developed by Wright and Mead (1975) was used to calibrate the tests for each measurement occasion. Criteria such as item discrimination, item-test correlation, and a chi-square statistic suggested by Wright and Panchapakesan (1969) provided adequate information about the goodness of fit of the model. Those items that did not meet requirements were dropped, since they contribute to poor fit for the overall model. The most common cause of poor fit, after unidimensionality was established, were differences in item discrimination; under the Rasch model, all discrimination indexes should be close to unity. Models developed by Birnbaum (1968), Bock (1972), Lord (1952), and Samejima (1969) do not require equality in discrimination power of the test items, and so these are preferable if the researcher has special reasons to believe that items with different discriminating power must be retained.

The data matrix for the present application provided for eight different calibrations along the five occasions of measurement: two calibrations for each of occasions two, three, and four, and one calibration each for occasions one and five. Although the correlation coefficients were not exactly one as hypothesized in the model given in Equation 1, they are large enough as to suggest that vertical equation has been achieved. For example, correlations between two sets of ability estimates in testing periods two and four were .96 and .92, respectively. Further, data plots reveal that abilities fall on a 45° straight line.

Once the estimates for the shift parameter were obtained by Equation 2, longitudinal scores were computed by using the following relationship:

$$\hat{\theta}_t = \hat{\theta}_{t-1} + \sum_{k=1}^{t} (\beta_0)_k \qquad (3)$$

Figure 1 displays developmental trends for the five treatment groups along the occasions of measurement as obtained by this procedure. It is important to notice that Figure 1 is a parsimonious solution for the present longitudinal study since it very well summarizes the information contained in approximately 40,000 cards. Briefly, the results imply that the children involved in the educational enrichment program perform notably better than an otherwise equivalent control group, the effects of the treatment are larger to the extent that duration of involvement is greater, and the rate of growth in cognitive achievement can be affected dramatically by the program in the age ranges considered in the experiment. For a detailed explanation of the educational implications of results and the limits on generalizability of the findings, see McKay and others (1978).

Commensurability. The argument for equal intervals in the present data is considerably strengthened by the fact that the increase in

**Figure 1. Estimates of Ability of Children in Each of Five Groups,
Using the Rasch Model as a Basis for Estimation**

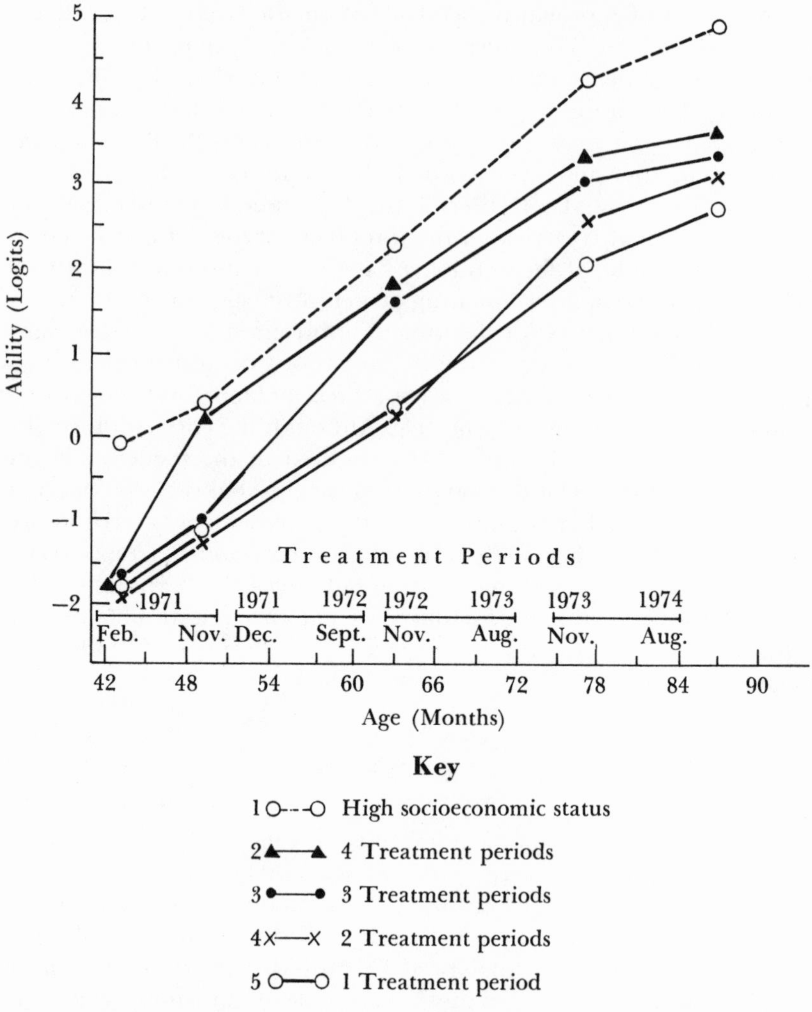

Key

1 O---O High socioeconomic status

2 ▲——▲ 4 Treatment periods

3 ●——● 3 Treatment periods

4 X——X 2 Treatment periods

5 O——O 1 Treatment period

group means in the nontreated group (group five in Figure 1 and
before occasion five) is essentially linear. Since physical growth in this
range also appears to be linear, from the data produced in the same
experiment, it is very likely that an equal interval measure of general
cognitive functioning has been achieved. This assertion receives
further confirmation if we consider the relationship between physical
growth and ability for group 5, prior to receiving treatment. This
analysis reveals that, for the ranges of 12 to 17 kilograms and –2.0 to
+2.0 logit units of ability, the relationship between an index of physical
growth and ability is linear.

Table 1. Abilities of Children in the Experimental Groups, as Estimated by Tests on Occasion Five

Group	Stanford-Binet (IQ)	Rasch Scores (Logits)	Differences Between Group 1 and Other Groups	
			Binet Units	Rasch Scores Scaled to Binet Units
1	109.2	4.9		
2	92.4	3.7	16.8	17.1
3	88.2	3.4	21.0	21.4
4	86.6	3.2	22.6	24.2
5	82.0	2.7	27.2	30.0
Within-groups standard deviation	13.5	.97		

External Validity of the Procedure. Six months after the experiment was discontinued, the Stanford-Binet (form L-M) was applied to all the children who participated in the longitudinal study. This provided a unique opportunity to check the validity of the ability estimates provided by the Rasch analysis. Table 1 shows the means for the ability score at testing occasion five and the Stanford-Binet results six months later. Since it is difficult to establish an origin which makes both estimates comparable, the best we can do is to take differences among the groups and, by using the within-groups standard deviation for each scale, transform differences in ability scores to the same units of the Stanford-Binet. Table 1 also shows differences of each of the groups with respect to group 1.

Summary and Conclusions

To the extent that social scientists' inquiry moves towards a better understanding of individual's change over time, longitudinal research and the demand for methods of analysis in this field will continue to grow. This paper provides additional evidence that latent trait theory is a suitable methodology for analyzing time structured data. In particular, there is ample justification for the idea that applying this theory, the estimates of the abilities of children have a metric with equal units along the scale. Beyond this, the theory allows adequate vertical equation of general tests of intelligence, achievement, and so forth. As shown on the numerical example here, it is not necessary to maintain the same tests along the time span of longitudinal studies.

The fact that a fairly complex longitudinal set of data, such as the one analyzed here, was reduced to a parsimonious description that does not demand a sophisticated knowledge of statistics, suggests that latent trait theory can facilitate communication between methodologists and decision makers, at least with respect to final results and graphical descriptions of them.

References

Birnbaum, A. "Some Latent Trait Models and Their Use in Inferring an Examinee's Ability." In F. M. Lord and M. R. Novick (Eds.), *Statistical Theories of Mental Test Scores*. Reading, Mass.: Addison-Wesley, 1968.

Bock, R. D. "Multivariate Analysis of Variance of Repeated Measurements." In C. W. Harris (Ed.), *Problems of Measuring Change*. Madison: University of Wisconsin Press, 1963.

Bock, R. D. "Estimating Item Parameters and Latent Ability When Responses Are Scored in Two or More Nominal Categories." *Psychometrika*, 1972, *37*, 29–51.

Bock, R. D. "Basic Issues in the Measurement of Change." In D. N. M. De Gruitter and L. J. T. van der Kamp (Eds.), *Advances in Psychological and Educational Measurement*. London: Wiley, 1976.

Bock, R. D. "Univariate and Multivariate Analysis of Time-Structured Data." In J. R. Nesselroade and P. B. Baltes (Eds.), *Longitudinal Research in Human Development: Design and Analysis:* New York: Academic Press, 1979.

Gomez, H. *The Cali Nutrition, Health, and Education Project: Technical Report*. Cali, Columbia: Human Ecology Research Station, 1973.

Goulet, R. L., Linn, R. L, and Tatsuoka, M. M. *Investigation of Methodological Problems in Educational Research: Longitudinal Methodology*. Urbana: University of Illinois, 1975.

Jöreskog, K. G., and Sörbom, D. *Statistical Models and Methods for Analysis of of Longitudinal Data*. Research Report 76–1. Uppsala, Sweden: Department of Statistics, University of Uppsala, 1976.

Lord, F. M. *A Theory of Test Scores*. New York: Psychometric Society, 1952.

McKay, H., and others. "Cognitive Growth in Malnourished Colombian Children." *Science*, 1978, *200*, 270–278.

Perline, R. "The Rasch Model as Conjoint Measurement." Unpublished mansucript, Committee on Methodology of Behavioral Research, University of Chicago, 1977.

Rasch, G. *Probabilistic Models for Some Intelligence and Attainment Tests*. Cophenhagen, Denmark: Danish Institute of Educational Research, 1960.

Rasch, G. "On General Laws and the Meaning of Measurement in Psychology." *Proceedings of the Fourth Berkeley Symposium on Mathematical Statistics and Probability Theory,* 1961, *5,* 321–333.

Rezmovic, V. "Factorial Invariance of the WISC-R in Groups Differing in Experimental Treatments." Paper presented at the meeting of the American Psychological Association, Washington, D.C., September 1976.

Samejima, F. "Estimating Latent Ability Using a Pattern of Graded Scores." *Psychometrika Monogrpah,* Supplement No. 17, 1969.

Wright, B. D. "Sample-Free Test Calibration and Person Measurement." In *Proceedings of the 1967 Invitational Conference on Testing Problems.* Princeton, N.J.: Educational Testing Services, 1967.

Wright, B. D., and Mead, R. J. *CALFIT: Sample-Free Calibration with a Rasch Measurement Model.* (Research Memorandum No. 18). Chicago: Department of Education, Statistical Laboratory, University of Chicago, 1975.

Wright, B. D., and Panchapakesan, N. "A Procedure for Sample-Free Item Analysis." *Educational and Psychological Measurement,* 1969, *29,* 23–24.

Isaac I. Bejar
Victor Rezmovic

17

Assessing Educational and Nutritional Findings in the Cali Experiment

Malnutrition is believed to adversely affect cognitive development (Kaplan, 1972). As many as 40 percent of the world's children under the age of six suffer some form of protein-calorie deficiency. Consequently, it is important to determine what can be done to avoid irreparable damage to such children. One implication for policy is that a high priority should be the elimination of malnutrition, not just because of its potential effect on cognitive development (which some believe to be not established, for example, Warren, 1973), on economic productivity, and on well-being, but as a matter of human rights as well. It is in this context that the importance of the experiment to be reanalyzed here, the Cali Project, can be appreciated.

Briefly, the Cali Project was designed to improve the cognitive development of malnourished Colombian preschoolers. The compen-

Note: Funding for this reanalysis was provided by the National Institute of Education Contract NIE-C-74-0115 and Grant NIE-G-79-0128.

satory treatment consisted primarily of educational and nutritional components. Unlike most social innovations, the Cali project was a randomized experiment, not a quasi-experiment, and for this reason can provide more definitive information about the effects of ameliorative programs on children.

The original investigators found that the comprehensive treatment, consisting of a nutritional and an educational component, was effective in enhancing the cognitive development of participating children, and that the nutritional treatment was effective in improving the physical development of participating children (McKay and others, 1978). (See also Chapter Sixteen.) The purpose of the reanalysis reported here is to verify these results and to assess the independent contribution of the educational treatment relative to that of the nutritional treatment on cognitive development. In this chapter, we review the Cali Project and its findings, and then turn to the results of our reanalysis concerning the effectiveness of the treatment components.

Review of the Cali Project and Findings

The Cali Project was sponsored by the Human Ecology Research Station (HERS), an institution created in 1968 by Leonardo Sinisterra with the assistance of the Council for Intersocietal Studies at Northwestern University, and with major financial support from the Ford Foundation. HERS was initially part of the Universidad del Valle, but became an independent organization in 1972. This review is based on the second progress report (McKay, McKay, and Sinisterra, 1973) of the Cali research, a more recent published paper (McKay and others, 1978), and on conversations with Hernando Gomez.

The study was undertaken in Cali, Colombia, a rapidly gowing city of nearly one million inhabitants. The target population of the experiment consisted of families living in a poor district known as Union de Vivenda Popular (UVP). The socioeconomic characteristics of the district are low, with a monthly per capita income of less that $10 in 1970. Most employed parents are engaged in unskilled construction work, factory work, street vending, and the like.

In August 1970, a house-to-house canvas of 7,500 homes of UVP was conducted to identify families with children having birthdays between June and November 1967. Subsequent screening was based on the families' willingness to participate and their children's qualification for the study. Children with an inappropriate birthdate or serious neurological dysfunction, and those who had moved from the UVP were disqualified. Upon completion of these screenings, the 333 most nutritionally deprived children were included in the study.

The children were divided into seven groups. Groups 1, 2, 3, and 4 received the comprehensive treatment—a combination of nutritional and educational treatment—for four, three, two, and one years, respectively. Groups designated 61, 62, and 63 received only the nutritional treatment for four, three, and two years, respectively, and the educational treatment only during the fourth year.

The children were assigned to the treatment groups in the following manner. The geographical area of the UVP was divided into twenty sectors. For each sector, a score based on the mean height, weight, and per capita family income was computed. Based on this score, the twenty sectors were ranked. Each of the first five sectors was assigned randomly to either groups 1, 2, 3, 4, or 61, 62, and 63. Each sector had between thirteen and nineteen children. The process was repeated for the next three sets of five sectors. A test for initial group equivalence was performed and indicated that blocking and randomization had resulted in construction of very similar groups. It is also important to note that the families of the children were not told to which groups they had been assigned.

The regimen for groups 1, 2, 3, and 4 consisted of an educational and a nutritional program. The curriculum of the educational program was focused on the development of cognitive processes, language, social abilities, and psychomotor skills (McKay, McKay, and Sinisterra, 1973). The children participated in the program for about four hours a day. The nutritional treatment was designed to satisfy 75 percent of the recommended calorie and protein intake. Groups 1 through 4 received the nutritional treatment while they were at the school set up for the experiment. The children in groups 61, 62, and 63 received the nutritional treatment at home, but periodic visits were made to ensure that the food was consumed and not being sold. In addition to the cognitive and nutritional treatment groups 1 through 4 received educational instruction on personal hygiene.

Three kinds of outcome variables were measured: cognitive, nutritional status, and socioeconomic. Our interest here is limited to the nutritional and cognitive measures. Nutritional status indicators, such as height and weight, were collected before the treatment began and again at the end of each treatment year; an additional measure was taken midway through the third treatment year. Thus, seven systematic observations were made of each child. A variety of cognitive measures were also collected throughout the study. Among these were specially adapted Spanish versions of several well-known tests such as the WISC. Test data were collected at the very beginning of the study and at the end of each year of treatment. All participating children were tested at each of the five test periods.

Results of the Original Evaluation

In the original analysis (McKay and others, 1978), estimates of ability for each child at each measurement period used a one-parameter Rasch model (Gomez, 1978; Rasch, 1960; Wright, 1977). Then the data were restructured according to a revised group classification (groups 1, 2, and 3 remained the same; 4 was combined with 61, 62, and 63) and analyzed as a one-way multivariate analysis of variance. The analysis indicated significant differences among the groups in their growth profile. Inspection of the means suggested a very definite pattern. The profiles of untreated groups were parallel, but the groups under treatment showed a sharp increase in ability, and these increases were statistically significant. The nature of the gains was such that the later the children entered the program, the smaller the gain. However, a comparison of treated groups with a group of children of high socioeconomic status who did not participate in the experiment indicated that the latter excelled on the Stanford-Binet by about three months.

The original results strongly suggest that a combination of nutritional and educational intervention can be effective in accelerating the cognitive development of disadvantaged children. Moreover, gains appeared to have endured one year after the intervention was terminated (McKay and others, 1978), in contrast to the usual finding in compensatory educational research that effects of the intervention dissipate over time.

Nevertheless, scientific method and social policy urge that several aspects of the data receive further analysis. First, cognitive development as measured by the Rasch model may be too broad a variable to determine exactly what specific gains the program achieved. More specific analyses can determine what types of cognitive abilities were influenced most. Little was reported on the effect of the nutritional intervention on physical growth. Because of the randomized design, the Cali Project may well be the only study that can shed some light on this effect. Finally, it is not clear from the results presented how much of the effect on cognitive development is due to the nutritional treatment and how much is due to the educational treatment. The project's data are pertinent to this question, which is important enough to merit further analysis.

Reanalysis of the Cognitive Data

In our attempt to corroborate some of the original findings with respect to cognitive development we limited our attention to the results based on the WISC-R during the last year of treatment. Our choice was motivated by the knowledge that the WISC-R is a well-known instrument whose results can be readily interpreted by others. Second, by restricting our attention to the last year of treatment, we considerably simplified the analysis while maintaining the longitudinal nature of the data; that is, although our reanalysis was based on a single point in time, we were able to tell whether the number of years of treatment differentially affected cognitive development.

Table 1 presents estimates of the raw-scale group means on the seven WISC-R scores at the end of the experiment. The means for a group of middle-class Colombian children has been included for comparative purposes. In general, this latter group has the highest mean on all subscores followed in order by groups 1, 2, 3, and the combination of groups 4, 61, 62, and 63. A univariate analysis of variance on each subscore (excluding the middle-class group) showed that the differences were statistically significant for all but the Similarities and Vocabulary subtests.

In analyzing these findings in perspective, we examined earlier research which suggests that performance on the various subtests of the WISC-R is explained by two psychological factors in samples of normal children. In particular, we hypothesized that a two-factor structure would also be adequate to explain the correlations among WISC subtests within each treatment group. We also hypothesized the structure to be invariant across treatment groups; that is, that the factor loadings and unique variances of each subset would be the same in each group. This is a strict requirement, but one that is necessary to make interpretable comparisons (Bejar, 1980).

The hypothesis that two factors were adequate for each group was tested by means of conventional maximum likelihood factor analysis (see Chapter Ten). The goodness-of-fit test yielded a chi-square of 39.4, with 32 degrees of freedom and $.10 > p > .05$. In contrast, the corresponding test statistic for a single-factor hypothesis yielded a chi-square of 111, with 60 degrees of freedom and $p < .001$, suggesting the need for two factors. The Tucker-Lewis index of fit for the two-factor solution was .985, adding further, related support for a two-factor solution.

Having established the plausibility of a two-factor model, we hypothesized the following pattern matrix to hold in each group. In the matrix, X depicts a loading that is free to take any value and 0 indicates the loading is restricted to be zero. We expected the first factor, verbal IQ, to be determined exclusively by terms of the first four subtests: the second factor, performance IQ, by the last three subtests. No other restrictions were imposed on the solution. This analysis yielded a chi-square statistic of 53, with 35 degrees of freedom and $p =$

Table 1. Scores on WISC-R Subtest for Four Experimental Groups and a Middle-Class Comparison Group

	Middle Class N = 54	Group 1 N = 49	Group 2 N = 51	Group 3 N = 51	Group 4[a] N = 96	Grand Mean[b]	F[b]	p
Information	7.4	4.8	4.4	4.1	3.8	4.20	3.18	.014
Arithmetic	7.1	5.5	5.2	4.9	4.0	4.75	6.50	.001
Vocabulary	18.1	12.6	12.6	12.1	11.4	12.03	1.80	.120
Similarities	9.6	6.3	5.6	6.7	5.7	6.02	.82	.510
Block design	11.6	7.3	6.5	4.9	3.8	5.31	7.50	.001
Mazes	15.3	10.7	9.4	8.5	6.8	8.47	4.80	.001
Picture arrangement	12.3	5.8	3.7	3.2	2.1	3.41	9.90	.001

[a] Includes children in groups 61, 62, and 63.
[b] Excludes the middle-class group.

	Verbal IQ (Factor 1)	Performance IQ (Factor 2)
Information	X	0
Arithmetic	X	0
Vocabulary	X	0
Similarities	X	0
Block design	0	X
Mazes	0	X
Picture arrangement	0	X

.03. Although the lack of fit is of borderline significance, the equality of the factor patterns across treatment groups was accepted as a reasonable approximation.

Finally, the model was restricted further by imposing the constraint that unique variances must be equal across groups. In this analysis, the factor means were estimated as well. The resulting chi-square of 257, with 103 degrees of freedom and $p < .0001$, suggests that the unique variances across treatment groups were not of the same magnitude. However, since no trend indicated that the magnitude of the unique variances was a function of the treatment group, we believe that this lack of invariance does not introduce a systematic bias in the comparison of factor means across groups. The parameter estimates for the model and the factor means are shown in Table 2. The means on both factors are monotonic functions of the number of years of treatment, with the lowest mean obtained by the group that received only one year of educational treatment.

Our secondary analyses then confirm the general conclusions reached by the Cali group, with only a few differences with respect to details. First, our reanalysis shows a pattern of general development and a pattern of the effect of educational enrichment programs that does not differ appreciably from that described in McKay and others (1978). Increases are remarkable; they are clearly linked to the intervention program and the point of its introduction. This conclusion confirms that of the Cali group, even though our assumptions about the underlying structure of cognitive abilities differ somewhat from the assumptions made in the original analyses. In particular, we believe that the assumption of a two-factor model for cognitive abilities is somewhat more plausible than a one-factor model for these children, based on sequential fitting of the factor models to the available data. Our finding is a clarification of earlier Cali results and a confirmation of earlier independent work on the structure of cognitive development.

Table 2. Two-Factor Solution for WISC-R Data

Variable	Loadings		Unique Variance
	Factor 1	Factor 2	
Information	.706	0	.809
Arithmetic	.559	0	.495
Vocabulary	.661	0	.826
Similarities	.585	0	.655
Block design	0	.406	.322
Mazes	0	.389	.674
Picture arrangement	0	.840	.702

Group	Factor Means					
1	1.374	1.131	$\Phi_1 = \begin{matrix} 1.591 \\ 1.487 \end{matrix}$ 3.351		$\Phi_2 = \begin{matrix} .779 \\ .640 \end{matrix}$ .558	
2	.819	.873				
3	.760	.365	$\Phi_3 = \begin{matrix} .969 \\ .526 \end{matrix}$ .727		$\Phi_4 = \begin{matrix} .829 \\ .427 \end{matrix}$ .162	
4[a]	0	0				

[a] Group 4 includes children from Groups 61, 62, and 63.

Effect of Nutritional Treatment on Weight and Height

A second objective of our reanalysis was to examine the effect of nutritional intervention on physical growth.* Such assessment is important in its own right and also serves as evidence of the implementation of the comprehensive treatment. Thus, if we find that physical growth is not a function of years of treatment, it would be reasonable to question how well either nutritional or educational treatments were implemented and indeed whether the ordering of the factor means just presented can be attributed fairly to the treatments.

The Cali investigators obtained a large number of physical measures. Our reanalysis of their data is limited to height and weight since these are the most commonly used measures of health status. For this analysis, we combined the experimental groups that received the nutritional treatment for the same length of time; that is, we combined groups 1 and 61, and similarly 2 and 62, and 3 and 63.

The plots of the mean weight and height as a function of mean age at the time of measurement for combined groups reveal no dramatic differences, but they do not appear to be superimposed on each other either. The development curves for height, for example, differ for

*A more-detailed reanalysis of the physical variables can be found in Bejar (in press a).

each group; if the curves were indistinguishable from one another, then one would suspect, in the absence of any more sophisticated analyses, that the nutritional treatments were ineffective. As a matter of fact, the departures from coincidence, especially toward the end of the experiment, appear to be a function of the duration of the treatments. Tables 3 and 4 contain the means, standard deviations, the pooled within-group correlation matrix, and standard deviations for these data. The tables are presented here to permit the reader to independently analyze the pooled data.

There are two major options for the analysis of such growth data: the mixed-model approach and the multivariate approach. Bock (1975) discusses both; their application to these data are discussed in detail by Gomez (1978). The mixed-model approach is based on a univariate analysis of variance formulation for a three-way factorial design: children, groups, and occasions. Groups are crossed with occasions; children, the random factor, are nested within groups. The multivariate approach is based on a one-way classification with repeated measures (occasions) as the dependent variables.

Contemporary practice suggests that the choice between these two approaches should be based on the structure of the pooled within-group covariance matrix of the repeated measures. If the matrix exhibits compound symmetry (Winer, 1971), then the correlations across occasions are roughly constant, and the mixed model is appropriate. If the matrix does not exhibit compound symmetry, the mixed model approach will not yield a valid probability value for the null hypothesis. Although some corrective measures can be taken, it is not clear that such corrections can encompass all covariance matrices that deviate from compound symmetry. The multivariate approach, in contrast, always yields a valid probability value, regardless of the covariance matrix of the repeated measures. However, the multivariate approach is less powerful, since in effect it must estimate the covariance matrix, and a subtantial number of degrees of freedom are lost. We have capitalized on the multivariate approach on heuristic grounds: The univariate model can always be derived from the multivariate output, and existing multivariate programs are quite flexible with respect to the kinds of designs that can be analyzed.

The Cali data show high positive correlations between contemporaneous gains in weight and height. For example, the correlation between general elevation for height and weight is .75, and the correlation in gains from the beginning of the study to the first testing period is .33. Under these conditions, the appropriate test of overall group differences is obtained from a multivariate analysis of variance (MANOVA) with gains in height and weight as dependent variables.

Table 3. Means, Standard Deviations, and Correlations for Untransformed Weight Data

	N	0	1	2	3	4	5	6
				Time				
					Means			
Group 1	65	11.75	12.65	13.74	15.36	16.43	18.07	18.85
Group 2	63	11.85	12.49	13.32	14.82	16.05	17.61	18.45
Group 3	64	11.90	12.49	13.35	14.50	15.70	17.70	18.57
Group 4	48	11.51	12.11	13.04	14.17	15.12	16.75	17.78
					Standard Deviations			
Group 1	65	1.09	1.12	1.11	1.48	1.55	1.96	2.07
Group 2	63	1.00	1.09	1.27	1.32	1.45	1.58	1.67
Group 3	64	1.24	1.33	1.46	1.62	1.57	1.64	1.83
Group 4	48	1.33	1.40	1.53	1.63	1.75	2.00	2.03
				Pooled Within-Group Correlations ($df = 236$)				
		1.000						
		.905	1.000					
		.864	.908	1.000				
		.790	.832	.896	1.000			
		.740	.784	.843	.916	1.000		
		.680	.739	.789	.872	.943	1.000	
		.623	.677	.730	.814	.899	.947	1.000
				Pooled Within-Group Standard Deviations				
		1.16	1.23	1.34	1.51	1.57	1.79	1.90

Note: Weight expressed in kilograms.

Table 4. Means, Standard Deviations, and Correlations for Untransformed Height Data

	N	\-	\-	Time	\-	\-	\-	\-
		0	1	2	3	4	5	6
Means								
Group 1	65	.880	.909	.948	1.001	1.051	1.103	1.137
Group 2	63	.877	.900	.939	.989	1.039	1.092	1.130
Group 3	64	.874	.897	.933	.980	1.026	1.088	1.128
Group 4	48	.874	.903	.938	.989	1.028	1.081	1.124
Standard Deviations								
Group 1	65	.047	.047	.044	.042	.043	.044	.046
Group 2	63	.042	.044	.042	.045	.045	.047	.049
Group 3	64	.042	.044	.045	.045	.042	.039	.040
Group 4	48	.049	.051	.053	.057	.056	.060	.055
Pooled Within-Group Correlations ($df = 236$)								
		1.000						
		.957	1.000					
		.940	.959	1.000				
		.880	.914	.948	1.000			
		.848	.879	.918	.969	1.000		
		.790	.826	.871	.936	.967	1.000	
		.745	.781	.821	.887	.934	.959	1.000
Pooled Within-Group Standard Deviations								
		.045	.046	.046	.047	.046	.047	.047

Note: Height expressed in meters.

The resulting statistic $F(42,662) = 4.13$, $p < .0001$ indicates that the group differences are appreciably different. This result was to be expected; to see if the treatment functioned as intended, we must examine the results a little more closely.

The left-hand portion of Table 5 reports the univariate F statistics for successive gains in weight and height. Group differences in gains are evident for both measures. Further, the contrasts presented in Table 5 show that the gains in weight and height are a function of the treatment. These comparisons between groups 1 through 3 and group 4 are adjusted for the correlation among them due to unequal cell sizes. The pattern of gains indicates that the largest gains, compared to group 4, occur initially in group 1, then 2, and then 3 (in that order). Finally, group 4 gains most rapidly during the last measurement period. The pattern is fairly clear for the weight measure but less so for height.

Strictly speaking, the significance level for the univariate F statistics are not valid due to the correlation between corresponding gains in weight and height. This situation requires the use of step-down procedures in order to arrive at proper significance levels. The step-

Table 5. Univariate F's and Orthogonalized Estimates of Effects
for Weight and Height

Time Interval Variable	Univariate		Contrasted Pairs			Step-Down
	F	p	1 and 4	2 and 4	3 and 4	p
			Weight			
1–0	4.67	.003	.29	.04	-.02	.01
2–1	2.63	.05	.16	-.10	-.06	.04
3–2	8.17	<.001	.49	.37	.02	<.001
4–3	2.23	.08	.13	.28	.25	.14
5–4	6.59	<.001	.01	-.06	.37	.10
6–5	1.70	.17	-.26	-.19	.16	.67
			Height			
1–0	3.37	.02	.00	-.05	-.06	
2–1	1.74	.16	.05	.04	.01	
3–2	1.76	.16	.02	-.02	.04	
4–3	9.79	<.001	.10	.11	.06	
5–4	9.83	<.001	-.01	.00	.09	
6–5	3.39	.02	-.08	-.05	-.03	

Note: We use 0 to represent baseline scores at the beginning of the experiment, 1 to represent scores at the first posttreatment testing period, and so on.

down F's were computed by means of an analysis of covariance with weight gains as the dependent measure and corresponding height gains as covariates; the resulting significance levels appear in Table 5. As we see, the significance of all but one of the gains is unchanged; that exception is the gain from the fourth testing occasion to the fifth. Overall, the analysis suggests that the observed differences in gains are due to the treatment rather than to any within-group relationships such as the natural association between weight and height.

Implications

The two preceding analyses show that there was an improvement in both cognitive and physical development. It seems obvious to attribute the gains in physical development to the nutritional component of the treatment, but it is not equally obvious that the gains in cognitive development are due to the educational component of the treatment since it was always given in conjunction with the nutritional treatment. Given the putative relationship between nutrition and intelligence (Kaplan, 1972), is an analyst justified in concluding that the Cali experiment demonstrates that a nutritional program is sufficient to improve physical and cognitive development of underprivileged children?

A full answer to this question requires a more extensive examination of the Cali data base than we undertook here, and indeed members of the original Cali staff are initiating more thorough analyses (see also Bejar, in press b). We limited our reanalysis to the regression of performance of WISC subtests on three indices of physical development at the last measurement period. More specifically, our data consisted of the correlation matrix for the following variables: height, weight, head circumference, and the Information, Vocabulary, and Similarities subscores of the WISC. The correlation matrix, shown in Table 6, was computed by pooling the 244 children for whom complete data were available from all experimental groups. The correlation matrix thus reflects both within- and between-group variation.

The multiple R associated with each regression is not significant, which implies that at the end of the treatment period cognitive status, as measured by the three WISC subtests, did not depend on nutritional status, as measured by height, weight, and head circumference. This result suggests that both the nutritional and educational treatment are needed to improve cognitive growth. Our reanalysis of the cognitive data shows that variation in WISC performance at the end of the experiment could be attributed to the comprehensive treatment. Our reanalysis also shows between-group variability attributable

Table 6. Intercorrelations Among Height, Weight, Head Circumference, and Information, Vocabulary and Similarities WISC Subscores ($N = 244$)

	A Height	B Weight	C Head Cir- cumference	D Information	E Vocabulary	F Similarities
A	1.000					
B	.717	1.000				
C	.318	.145	1.000			
D	.122	.075	.146	1.000		
E	.098	.109	.088	.440	1.000	
F	.055	.085	.001	.367	.377	1.000

to the nutritional treatment at the end of the experiment, although we did not directly address this relationship. The causal agents of these two sources of variability must therefore be the two different treatments. The nutritional treatment enhances physical development while the educational treatment enhances cognitive development. Such development, of course, is only the immediate benefit of treatment. Over time, both treatments may interact to help the development of individuals.

References

Bejar, I. I. "Biased Assessment of Program Impact Due To Psychometric Artifacts." *Psychological Bulletin*, 1980, *87*(3), 513–524.

Bejar, I. I. "Does Nutrition Cause Intelligence? A Reanalysis of the Cali Project." *Intelligence*, in press a.

Bejar, I. I. "The Effect of Nutritional Intervention on the Height and Weight of Malnourished Colombian Preschoolers." *Evaluation in the Health Profession*, in press b.

Bock, R. D. *Multivariate Statistical Methods in Behavioral Research*. New York: McGraw-Hill, 1975.

Gomez, H. "The Analysis of Growth." Unpublished doctoral dissertation, Department of Psychology, Northwestern University, Evanston, Ill., 1978.

Kaplan, B. J. "Malnutrition and Mental Deficiency." *Psychological Bulletin*, 1972, *78*, 321–334.

McKay, H., McKay, A., and Sinisterra, L. *Stimulation of Intellectual and Social Competence in Colombian Preschool Age Children Affected by the Multiple Deprivations of Depressed Urban Environ-*

ments: Second Progress Report. Cali, Colombia: Human Ecology Research Station, 1973.

McKay, H., and others. "Cognitive Growth in Colombian Malnourished Children." *Science,* 1978, *200,* 270–278.

Rasch, G. *Probabilistic Models for Some Intelligence and Attainment Tests.* Copenhagen: Denmark Pedagogical Institute, 1960.

Warren, N. "Malnutrition and Mental Development." *Psychological Bulletin,* 1973, *80*(4), 324–328.

Winer, B. J. *Statistical Principles in Experimental Design.* (2nd ed.). New York: McGraw-Hill, 1971.

Wright, B. D. "Solving Measurement Problems with the Rasch Model." *Journal of Educational Measurement,* 1977, *14,* 2.

18

Leroy Wolins

Reanalyzing Studies of Race Differences in Intelligence:
Scale Dependent Mistakes

Although it may seem evident to some philosophically oriented individuals that researchers' mistakes fit into classes, the specification of those classes may not be immediately useful to the researchers. Mistakes that are noted in published research are often directed at audiences with interests in substantive issues rather than those interested in research strategy and methodology. However, if a classification of commonly made mistakes avoids substantive issues, it may not be meaningful to researchers. In this chapter, I discuss a class of mistakes that is frequent in published reports. I present spurious findings in research on race differences in IQ, delineate the concept that holds these spurious findings together, and illustrate essential procedures for making certain inferences about differences among races through data analysis.

Note: This chapter was supported by National Institute of Education contracts NIE-C-74-0115 and grant NIE-G-79-0128.

The class of mistakes discussed herein is labeled *scale dependent mistakes*. These are not statistical mistakes, although statistical mistakes may be involved. They are more often mistakes in inference based on proper statistics. That is, scale dependent mistakes are psychological, educational, or sociological mistakes in that factual, well-known information about our measuring instruments make untenable the inferences drawn from some of the research articles discussed here.

Race Differences in Variability of IQ

It is commonly found that we measure people with low IQs more precisely than people with high IQs. That is, if individuals are given several forms of an IQ test, individuals with high IQs display more variability in performance than individuals with low IQs. Thorndike and Hagen (1961) discuss this problem relative to an old edition of the Stanford-Binet. Table 1 reproduces their data.

Thorndike and Hagen (1961) report, "For this test, the variation that may be expected from one testing to another is very much higher for children with average and above average IQs than for retarded children" (p. 187). This same idea is developed relative to binomial error models by Lord and Novick (1968, chap. 23) and noted by Willerman (1979, p. 42) in connection with the standard error of a predicted score. The finding, when ignored, leads to inappropriate inferences from data.

For example, Brody and Brody (1976, p. 194) cite several older studies indicating that blacks vary less than whites on IQ tests and they offer several reasons for this. In particular, they discuss mean and variance differences between race independently, as if mean and variance were independent of one another in such data. They do not recognize the empirical property of the scale, that standard error is dependent on

Table 1. Standard Error of IQ as a Function of IQ Level

IQ Level	Standard Error of IQ
130 and over	5.2
110–129	4.9
90–109	4.5
70–89	3.8
Below 70	2.2

Source: Thorndike and Hagen, 1961; Terman and Merrill, 1937.

IQ level. When one peruses the literature, it is clear that the variability of blacks on a particular IQ test is not noticeably different from that of whites at the lower IQ levels. For example, Brody and Brody report that Kennedy, Van De Riet, and White (1963), in their large normative study of the Stanford-Binet in the southeastern United States, found that the black variance was 57 percent the size of the white variance. Given the well-known differences in average IQ in these two groups and the information in Table 1, no substantive explanation may be necessary. That is, the observed differences between blacks and whites may result, at least in part, from the scale and thus may not require a psychological or genetic explanation.

This scale dependent mistake may seem obvious in retrospect, but it occurs frequently and less obviously in other contexts. Willerman (1979, p. 131) infers that racial differences in IQ increase with socioeconomic status, presenting data from the research of Broman, Nichols, and Kennedy (1975). Willerman (1979, p. 440) also presents data based on research by Heber, Dever, and Conry (1968) that indicates the difference in the incidence of low IQ in blacks and whites increases as socioeconomic level decreases. These results are expected, at least in part, from the data given in Table 1.

According to Broman, Nichols, and Kennedy (1975), children of high socioeconomic level score higher on IQ tests than children of lower socioeconomic level. This result is similar for blacks and whites but seems more marked for whites, whose mean IQ is 95.6 in the lowest quarter of the socioeconomic scale and 110.9 in the upper quarter. Four-year-old black children show a mean IQ of 88 in the lowest level and 98.1 in the upper 25 percentile. However, as Table 1 indicates, higher-scoring groups display more variability than lower-scoring groups. Given that the mean and variance (or standard deviation) are positively correlated and that whites score higher than blacks, one expects this difference to increase with increasing socioeconomic level. In fact, if one isolated a subgroup of whites with a lower mean IQ than the main group, separated these into low, medium, and high socioeconomic levels, one would find the same pattern of increasing difference with increasing socioeconomic status.

Analogous phenomena are prevalent in the biological sciences. Men are taller than women and also more variable in height. Whites are taller than Orientals and more variable in height. In inches, the differences between the sexes are larger for whites, and thus racial differences in height are larger for men. Of course, racial differences in IQ relative to socioeconomic level do not necessarily behave like sexual differences in height relative to race. But the increase in racial differences that accompanies an increase in socioeconomic level can be removed by a transformation that also tends to homogenize the variance, a fact that certainly casts doubt on the substantive interpretation of the results.

The complexity of the problem increases when one attempts to compare profiles of test scores between races. However, the problem of comparing groups at different levels of one scale cannot be viewed as an entirely different problem from comparing relative performance of groups on different scales. Knowing the procedure used to score and administer the Stanford-Binet, one may assert that the lower-socioeconomic blacks responded, with few exceptions, to *different* questions than did the upper-socioeconomic whites, and it is only when different groups take the same test that scores are comparable. As a result, one may be confident that individuals have comparable scores to the extent that their mean scores are alike.

The problem can also occur with conventional multiple-choice tests in which every individual responds to each item. Test results may not be comparable because difficult items have little influence on low scores and easy items have little influence on high scores. Thus, the problem of comparing races at different levels of a single scale is not separate from the problem of comparing racial differences on different scales. The latter seems to be more important, however, because noting racial differences on a single scale is less heuristic: One may speculate why differences between races are relatively large on one measure but small on another, and such speculation may guide further research.

Comparing races on different scales in a meaningful way is difficult, but possible, judging from the work of Lesser, Fifer, and Clark (1965). They compared profiles of children in four ethnic groups on four types of tests: Verbal, Reasoning, Number, and Space. The profile for each of the ethnic groups was ascertained for a group of middle-class children and for a group of lower-class children. One observes from inspecting these results, depicted in Figure 1, that the shape of the middle-class and lower-class profiles within each ethnic group are similar. But the differences among ethnic groups suggest that the ethnic groups perform qualitatively differently from each other. This result cannot reflect a scale dependent mistake because socioeconomic differences result in large differences in average performance but do not result in profile differences within ethnic groups.

In contrast to the findings of Broman, Nichols, and Kennedy (1975), these results indicate that socioeconomic differences are largest for blacks. However, one notes that the tests used by Lesser, Fifer, and Clark (1965) are binomially scored. Thus the relatively small socioeconomic differences displayed by Jews and Puerto Ricans could be due to "ceiling" and "floor" effects, respectively. The small socioeconomic

Figure 1. Comparison of Test Performances of Middle- and Lower-Class Children from Four Cultural Groups

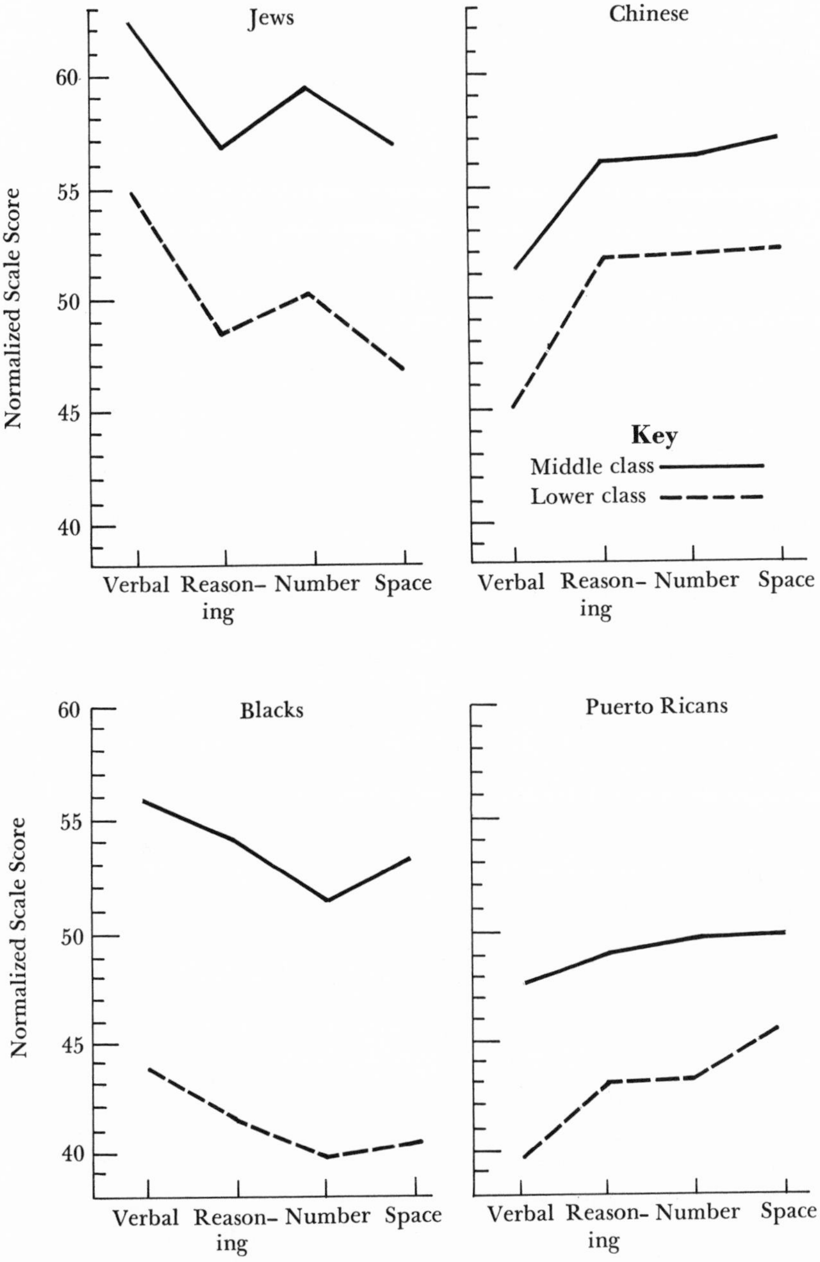

Source: Lesser, Fifer, and Clark (1965).

differences for Chinese, as compared to blacks, seem to require a psychological explanation since differences for these two groups occur in the same part of the scale. The important point for the present context is that the apparent conflict between these two results is resolved by taking cognizance of the measurement scale.

Racial and Ethnic Differences
in Forward and Backward Digit-Span Tests

Unlike Lesser, Fifer, and Clark (1965), Wolins (1978a) asserts that Jensen and Figueroa's (1975) comparison of blacks and whites on backward and forward digit-span tests is meaningless because the average performance differences between the groups were so large, particularly on the backward measure, that unequal-sized scale intervals offered at least as good an explanation of the observed differences as the racial explanation.

Let us first consider data of the kind that Jensen and Figueroa use to provide partial support for their views. Reschly's (1978) data were used to compare the factor structure of the Wechsler for four racial-ethnic groups: whites, blacks, Mexican-Americans (Chicanos) and Native-American Papagos. For each of these groups forty or more children were tested at each of five elementary and junior high school levels: grades 1, 3, 5, 7, and 9. Although racial-ethnic differences on the digit-span measures was the focus of the research, grade in school, socioeconomic level, and IQ measures were used to search for groups comparable in level of performance so that profile differences in the digit-span measures could be properly evaluated. This sample is described by Reschly and Jipson (1976).

Jensen and Figueroa (1975) base their inference that blacks and whites differ qualitatively in intelligence on two lines of evidence. First, blacks perform much lower than whites on the backward digit-span measure but only slightly lower than whites on the forward measure. Second, the backward measure correlates more highly with other measures of IQ than the forward measure, particularly for blacks. Thus, the data analyses I present here are divided in two major parts: one concerning mean differences, the other, correlational differences. Socioeconomic differences are briefly discussed.

Mean Differences in Digit-Span Measures for Four Racial Groups. In order to identify groups of people differing in race who perform at comparable levels on the digit-span measures, I used several strategies. First, races were compared on the two digit-span measures at the five grade-in-school levels to ascertain whether or not the rank ordering of the race differences in performance on the digit-span measures depended on grade-in-school. Second, all subjects, regardless of race or grade-in-school, were placed on fifteen ordered categories on the basis of the full-scale raw score on the Wechsler to see if the rank ordering of the racial differences on the basis of difference in performance on the digit-span measures depended on intelligence level. Each of these ordered categories contained fifty-six or fifty-seven individuals. Third, racial differences for the individual items on the forward and backward digit-span measures were ascertained to determine if the rank ordering of these racial differences depended on the difficulty of the items. Fourth, the races were further subdivided according to sex and to place of residence (rural or urban) to determine if these racial differences were consistent for these subgroups.

The results from the first analysis are presented in Figure 2. They are consistent with those of Jensen and Figueroa in that forward-backward digit-span differences are somewhat larger for blacks and these differences do not seem to depend on grade-in-school or location on the scale. However, the difference between blacks and whites is small compared to that between Chicanos and Native-American Papagos (see Appendix). The forward-backward differences for Chicanos are much smaller than for either whites or blacks, while the forward-backward difference for Native-American Papagos is much larger than for either whites or blacks.

The results presented in Figure 2 are consistent regardless of place of residence for the white and Chicano groups. That is, forward-backward differences do not seem to depend on place of residence. Additional analyses, which are not displayed here, show that these forward-backward racial differences are consistent for both sexes, although forward-backward differences tend to be smaller for white females than white males. In addition, these forward-backward racial differences hold up for individual items. There are seven items in each digit-span measure, and they vary in difficulty according to the number of digits the child is asked to repeat (or repeat backwards) to the examiner. The first item in the forward measure has three digits and the seventh item has nine digits. For the backward measures the number of digits varies from two to eight. This analysis reveals that forward-backward racial differences for items containing each of these numbers of digits tend to rank the four racial-ethnic groups the same way. Not all item pairs are equally discriminating for all racial groups, but for items 2, 3, and 4, racial-ethnic differences appear consistent.

The division of the sample into fifteen categories on the basis of full-scale Wechsler scores results in very small sample sizes and an erratic picture. The use of broader classes produces results similar to those presented in Figure 2.

Figure 2. Mean Raw Score for the Forward and Backward Digit-span Measures by Race, Grade-in-School, and Place of Residence

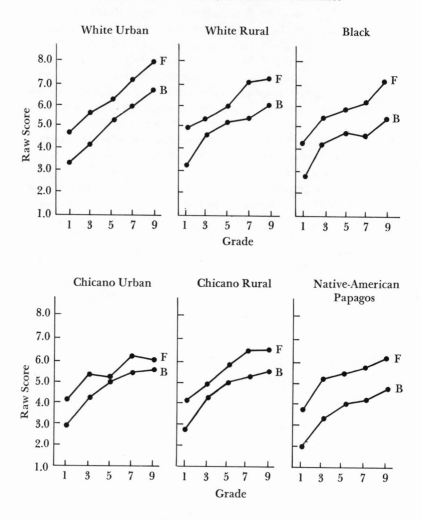

Correlational Differences for the Four Racial-Ethnic Groups. Reschly (1978) found that the factor structure was similar for all racial-ethnic groups, but he did not include the digit-span measures. Table 2 presents the correlations between these latter two measures and the correlation of the digit-span measures with the subscales. All these correlations are based on raw-score data including all subjects in each racial-ethnic group. That is, no correction for age or grade was made because such corrections would obscure any relationship between the size of these correlations and the location of a group on the scale.

The results presented in Table 2 are not consistent with those reported by Jensen and Figueroa: here the backward measure is a better measure of the Wechsler subscales for all racial groups but blacks, whereas Jensen and Figueroa report the backward measure as the better one particularly for blacks. Table 2 suggests the forward measure is generally better for blacks, particularly for three of the subscales: Comprehension, Picture Arrangement, and Mazes. The superiority of the backward measure as a measure of intelligence is most marked for the Native-American Papagos. The Chicanos and whites are most similar in this regard.

One explanation of this superiority of the backward measure for Native-American Papagos might be that items in the backward mea-

Table 2. Correlations Between Raw Scores for Digit-Span Measures and Their Correlations with Raw Scores on the Wechsler Scales ($N \sim 230$)

	Whites		Blacks		Chicanos		Native-American Papagos	
	F	B	F	B	F	B	F	B
Forward digit span (F)	—	60	—	48	—	58	—	49
Backward digit span (B)	60	—	48	—	58	—	49	—
Information	52	58	56	52	46	55	44	54
Picture completion	45	49	40	40	44	45	44	52
Similarities	49	58	50	46	44	51	37	49
Picture arrangement	36	38	53	41	37	40	32	51
Arithmetic	50	60	52	56	46	53	43	58
Block design	44	49	42	43	41	44	38	54
Vocabulary	47	54	52	54	51	55	42	46
Object assembly	33	48	41	45	38	37	37	49
Comprehension	52	59	58	49	47	48	35	43
Mazes	38	43	49	42	43	42	30	47

Note: Decimals have been omitted.

sure are more discriminating at lower intelligence levels. In the low-intelligence range, the slope of the function relating item difficulty to intelligence level is quite steep for two of the seven items and moderate for a third. In contrast, only one of the seven forward items displays a steep slope at these lower levels and two display moderate slopes. Since Native-American Papagos score particularly low on the backward measure, it is a superior measure of intelligence for them. However, this explanation should also apply for blacks since they also score relatively low on the backward measure—but, of course, it does not.

No control for socioeconomic level was possible in this study because practically all the variability in this measure occurred between groups rather than within groups. The correlations of the forward and backward scores by group and grade are mostly near zero and negative almost as often as positive. Although one can find support for the use of socioeconomic variables as covariates of this sort even in the current literature (Wildt and Ahtola, 1978), recent criticism of such use (Woodward and Goldstein, 1977; Wolins, 1978b) should discourage future publication of such results.

Discussion and Conclusions

The mean qualitative differences in cognitive behavior between blacks and whites found by Jensen and Figueroa (1975) are only partially supported by this study. Differences between blacks and whites are greater on the backward digit-span measure than on the forward digit-span measure. However, the largest differences in this regard occurred between Native-American Papagos and Chicanos. If one considers the Chicanos as a racial mixture of Native-American Papagos and whites (Kephart, 1960), then it becomes difficult to attribute the observed differences to race.

The correlational differnces between races observed here contradict those found by Jensen and Figueroa. The forward measure appears to be the better measure of intelligence for blacks, and the backward measure is better for the other three racial groups, especially the Native-American Papagos. The backward measure is better for the Native-American Papagos, the group showing the largest correlational differences for the digit-span measures, because their performance on the measure is very low and the measure is more discriminating at lower levels of intelligence. The remaining correlational differences between the digit-span measures are erratic, and no explanation is evident. However, one observes that within a race the size of the difference in the correlation of the two digit-span measures depends on the subscale. For example, the second largest discrepancy occurs for whites on the Object Assembly subtest: for the forward measure $r = .33$, and for the backward measure $r = .48$. Thus these correlational differences might be explained by how effectively the items in the subscales discriminate at various levels. That is, subscales containing more items that discriminate well at lower levels of intelligence should correlate better with the backward measure. This result would, of course, be most marked for groups that score relatively low on intelligence scales since the two digit-span measures appear to differ most in how well they discriminate at these lower levels.

Part of the difference between these results and those of Jensen and Figueroa could result from methodology. They used scores adjusted for age, while I did not. However, since age-adjusted scores cannot be related to any particular part of a scale, one cannot determine whether the observed racial differences stem from a scale artifact. Further, if these qualitative racial differences occur within age groups, they should be evident in comparisons of raw scores. Raising or lowering a pair of scores, depending on the age of the respondent, should not alter the relative difference between them. Consequently, I can see no compelling reason to look at age-adjusted scores.

Although the correlational differences among these races for the digit-span measures might be explained by the scale, one cannot explain away the racial differences in the relative performance on these digit-span measures. The most cogent question arising from these analyses is: What are the motivational or cultural differences that produce the large difference between Chicanos and Native-American Papagos?

Appendix

Although inferential statistics are only tangentially relevant to the content of this article, after perusal of the data I feel comfortable with the following:

| | $\bar{X}$ | | S | | | | | |
	F	B	F	B	r_{FB}	N	$\bar{D} = \bar{X}_F - \bar{X}_B$	S_D^2
Whites	6.21	4.94	2.06	1.87	.60	252	1.277	3.12
Blacks	5.68	4.21	1.99	1.94	.48	237	1.477	4.01
Chicanos	5.34	4.47	1.78	1.72	.58	223	.870	2.56
Native-American Papagos	5.05	3.46	1.80	1.82	.49	237	1.586	3.31

$$\text{Critical ratios: } Z = \frac{\bar{D}_i - \bar{D}_j}{\sqrt{\dfrac{S_{D_i}^2}{N_i} + \dfrac{S_{D_j}^2}{N_j}}}$$

Critical Ratios Comparing Forward-Backward Differences Between Races

	W	B	C	N
Whites (W)		-1.17	2.63	-1.90
Blacks (B)			3.60	- .62
Chicanos (C)				-4.49
Native-American Papagos (N)				

These critical ratios exceed conventional significance levels only when the Chicanos are compared to the other three groups.

References

Brody, B. D., and Brody, N. *Intelligence: Nature, Determinants, and Consequences.* New York: Academic Press, 1976.

Broman, S. H., Nichols, P. L., and Kennedy, W. A. *Preschool IQ: Prenatal and Early Developmental Correlates.* Hillsdale, N.J.: Erlbaum, 1975.

Heber, R., Dever, R., and Conry, J. "The Influence of Environmental and Genetic Variables on Intellectual Development." In H. J. Prehm, L. A. Hamerlynch, and J. E. Crosson (Eds.), *Behavioral Research in Mental Retardation.* Eugene: University of Oregon Press, 1968.

Jensen, A. R., and Figueroa, R. A. "Forward and Backward Digit Span Interaction with IQ: Predictions from Jensen's Theory." *Journal of Educational Psychology,* 1975, *67*, 882–893.

Kennedy, W. A., Van De Riet, V., and White, J. C., Jr. "A Normative Sample of Intelligence and Achievement of Negro Elementary School Children in the Southeastern United States." *Monographs of the Society for Research in Child Development,* 1963, *28* (90, entire issue).

Kephart, C. *Races of Mankind, Their Origin and Migration.* New York: Philosophical Library, 1960.

Lesser, C. S., Fifer, G., and Clark, D. H. "Mental Abilities of Children from Different Social-Class and Cultural Groups." *Monographs of the Society for Research in Child Development,* 1965, *30,* (4, entire issue).

Lord, F. M., and Novick, M. R. *Statistical Theories of Mental Test Scores.* Reading, Mass.: Addison-Wesley, 1968.

Reschly, J. " WISC-R Factor Structures Among Anglos, Blacks, Chicanos, and Native-American Papagos." *Journal of Consulting Psychology,* 1978, *46,*(3), 417–422.

Reschly, D. J., and Jipson, F. J. "Ethnicity, Geographic Locale, Age, Sex, and Urban-Rural Residence as Variables in the Prevalence of Mild Retardation." *American Journal of Mental Deficiency,* 1976, *81*(2), 154–161.

Terman, L. M., and Merrill, M. A. *Measuring Intelligence.* Boston: Houghton-Mifflin, 1937.

Thorndike, R. L., and Hagen, E. *Measurement and Evaluation in Psychology and Education.* New York: Wiley, 1961.

Wildt, A. R., and Ahtola, O. T. *Analysis of Covariance.* Beverly Hills, Calif.: Sage, 1978.

Willerman, L. *The Psychology of Individual and Group Differences.* San Francisco: W. H. Freeman, 1979.

Wolins, L. "Interval Measurement: Physics, Psychophysics, and Metaphysics." *Educational and Psychological Measurement,* 1978a, *38,* 1–9.

Wolins, L. "Secondary Analysis in Published Research in Behavioral Sciences." In R. F. Boruch (Ed.), *New Directions for Program Evaluation: Secondary Analysis,* no. 4. San Francisco: Jossey-Bass, 1978b.

Woodward, J. A., and Goldstein, M. J. "Communication Deviance in Families of Schizophrenics: A Comment on the Misuse of Analysis of Covariance." *Science,* 1977, *197,* 1096–1097.

19

Joel M. Moskowitz
Paul M. Wortman

Reassessing the Impact
of School Desegregation

Although more than a quarter of a century has passed since the *Brown* decision (U.S. Supreme Court, 1954), it remains not only a landmark civil liberties case but also an outstanding example of applied social research. The testimony and brief presented by social scientists contained an implicit theory of how desegregation should lead to beneficial social outcomes (see Linsenmeier and Wortman, 1978; Stephan, 1978). The theory consisted of a sequence of causal processes that would follow from desegregation. Briefly, it was assumed that desegregation would decrease racial prejudice; that this, in turn, would lead to an increase in the self-esteem of minority children; and that this would be reflected in higher academic achievement by them. This theory was eloquently summarized in the text of the opinion. In noting the harmful effect of segregation on minority children, Chief Justice Warren stated, "To separate them from others of similar age and qualification solely because of their race generates a feeling of inferiority as to their

Note: The work on this chapter was supported in part by Contract No. C-74-0115 from the National Institute of Education. The authors thank Hernando Gomez and Charles Reichardt for their helpful suggestions.

status in the community that may affect their hearts and minds in a way unlikely ever to be undone" (U.S. Supreme Court, 1954).

Gerard and Miller's (1975) study of desegregation in Riverside, California, focused on testing this theory and related theories of personality and achievement. However, after an exhaustive examination, they concluded (Miller, 1975, pp. 284–285): "There were few substantial changes reflected in the personality measures, particularly those anticipated to be most strongly related to achievement: the measures of achievement motivation, anxiety, and self-worth. . . . The pesonality variables assumed to be most directly related to achievement were even more disappointing. . . . Here the personality model failed completely." The researchers did find a somewhat more positive picture for personality factors that might mediate the child's adjustment to the desegregation experience. The investigators collected pre- and post-desegregation data on the following five fifteen-item, paper-and-pencil measures—taken from a variety of existing personality instruments—general anxiety, school anxiety, others' attitudes, self-attitudes, and need for school achievement (Green, Miller, and Gerard, 1975). They report statistically significant changes in all these personality traits over time. In particular, general anxiety decreased after the first year of desegregation and remained low after three years; school anxiety dropped after the first year, but then increased; and the favorableness of others' attitudes increased, while self-attitudes dropped slightly then returned to their predesegregation level (except for Mexican-Americans, who stayed the same over time). Only on the measure of achievement need (administered to grades 4 through 6) was there a consistent decrease over time. However, there were no differential changes among the ethnic groups studied over time. Moreover, the investigators dismissed these results by noting that the modest correlations between these variables and achievement (the absolute value of r ranged from .12 to .24) did not account for much of the total variance.

Given the inconsistencies in these results, the present reanalysis seeks to verify the validity of the negative conclusions concerning this theory of desegregation. Our general approach is to occupy the methodological "high ground" by reanalyzing that portion of the data set permitting the highest quality design and, hence, presenting the fewest threats to internal validity. As we shall see, there is some disagreement over the quality of the research design (specifically, whether or not random assignment was used). After examining this issue, we applied recently developed analytic approaches appropriate to a "worst-case" quasi-experimental design situation. Whereas the original investigators examined only academic achievement for this particular subpopulation, we include the full set of personality variables noted earlier. By employing more appropriate analytic methods and examining the entire theory for the strongest portion of the data set, we intended to obtain a clearer test of the findings and a more consistent pattern of results. This subset of the sample is composed exclusively of Mexican-American students and thus also provides a test of the generalizability or external validity of the theory derived primarily from research on black children. In fact, as far as we know, the Riverside School Study (RSS) is the only major investigation of the effects of desegregation that involves Hispanic students.

The Riverside School Study Analyses

Data for the Riverside School Study (RSS), collected from 1965 through 1971, assessed the intellectual and personality development of 1,731 public school students. The students, who were in grades kindergarten through sixth in 1965–66, were composed of three ethnic groups: Anglo-American (41 percent), Mexican-American (36 percent), and black (23 percent).

In the fall of 1966, planned school desegregation was begun in Riverside through the busing of minority children to predominantly Ango-American schools. As a segregated control group was unavailable, the original investigators primarily examined differences between ethnic groups before and after school desegregation. Such a preexperimental design in which nonequivalent groups simultaneously receive the treatment is subject to numerous threats to internal validity (see Campbell and Stanley, 1966; Cook and Campbell, 1979). Furthermore, the design cannot directly assess the effects of desegregation on each group.

Fortunately, within the overall sample existed a subsample of Mexican-American students who were desegregated in two waves one year apart. All these students attended the same elementary school, Casa Blanca, prior to desegregation. The original investigators were not entirely certain how these students had been assigned to the waves: "As far as we can tell from questioning the school officials involved, the assignment of children to each of the waves was made on a random basis" (Singer, Gerard, and Redfearn, 1975, pp. 76–77); "pupil selection at Casa Blanca for the two waves of desegregation was not explicitly random" (Redfearn and Gerard, 1975, p. 59). It seems unlikely that the school officials implemented a scientific random assignment plan; in calling the plan "random," they were probably referring to the absence of a systematic assignment procedure. Thus it is unlikely that random assignment did occur, an issue we will address later.

The original analysis of the effect of school desegregation on the Casa Blanca subsample examined the two waves of children for pre-desegregation differences in 1965–66 on measures of reading achievement, intelligence, classroom grades, sociometric popularity, and socio-economic background. The *only* difference between the two groups was in predesegregation reading achievement: Students in the 1966 desegregation wave scored significantly lower than those in the 1967 wave (Redfearn and Gerard, 1975). For these reasons the original researchers (Singer, Gerard, and Redfearn, 1975, p. 78) assumed that the groups were "approximately comparable, randomly selected samples from the same population" and employed an experimental pretest-posttest control group design.

They chose to conduct analyses only of the reading achievement data. The raw test scores were first standardized to the same mean and standard deviation within each grade and then averaged together. Analysis of variance was performed on these scores, with the year deseg-regated, or wave, (1966 and 1967) and time of testing (1965–66, 1966–67, 1967–68, 1968–69) as the two factors. The investigators found a significant overall difference between the groups, which reflected the initial difference, but they found no group-by-year interaction. In addi-tion, a repeated measures analysis of variance and a covariance analysis performed on these scores yielded no reliable differences. The researchers concluded that the additional year of desegregation expe-rienced by the 1966 wave had no effect on reading achievement (Singer, Gerard, and Redfearn, 1975).

This analysis strategy can be expanded and strengthened in a number of ways through secondary analysis. First, the Casa Blanca analysis should not be confined solely to examining effects of school desegregation on reading achievement. Other measures of theoretical importance were systematically collected before and after desegregation and were comparable for both waves of students. Since theory predicted that these measures would be affected by desegregation, they should also be analyzed for this subsample. Such analysis would take full advantage of the strong comparisons provided by the Casa Blanca stu-dents. Thus, the present analysis complements the earlier analysis of the Casa Blanca sample by examining the effect of an additional year of school desegregation on other variables, including general anxiety, school anxiety, perceived others' attitudes, self-attitudes, and achieve-ment need. We could not examine math achievement scores because they were not systematically collected.

Secondly, analyses of achievement should, when possible, be performed within grades and not across grades. St. John (1975), review-ing school desegregation effects, found that younger children generally benefit more than older children from school desegregation on measures of academic achievement, indicating the importance of age or grade level. Stephan (1978) reports a similar finding for self-esteem. The importance of age is also acknowledged in other parts of the RSS in which age-related effects were investigated (see Gerard, 1975, p. 17). In addition, we note that in the RSS reading tests were administered at different times of the year for different grade levels. Hence, the period of time between testings was not identical for all grades, and the original investigators' aggregation of data across grades may be misleading. In the present study, separate analyses were performed for each grade level on the reading achievement measures.

Finally, recent developments in the analysis of quasi- or non-experimental design (see Bock, 1975) facilitate the analysis of data even if, at worst, random assignment was not used. The statistical analyses chosen by the original investigators were probably the best available at that time, but even if one accepts their assumption of random assignment, in each analysis they ignored an important assumption of the statistical model selected. Performing an analysis of variance on data taken from the same subjects over time violates the assumption that observations within each level of a factor (time) are independent from observations in each other level (Winer, 1971). The repeated measures analysis of variance is also flawed, as this approach assumes the homogeneity of covariances (Winer, 1971). Roughly speaking, such homogeneity means that if variances are similar, the observed correlations between all pairs of repeatedly assessed standardized measures must be equal within sampling error. Such a requirement is probably too restrictive for these data, as it is for most longitudinal data (McCall and Appelbaum, 1973). Since the analysis of covariance was performed in conjunction with one of these two procedures (which one was not specified), it too is open to criticism. Our reanalysis avoids most of these problems by applying newer methods that do not require these assumptions.

Secondary Analyses

We first examined the pupil assignment or selection process by considering predesegregation parental attitudes. We used a nonequivalent control group design, with appropriate statistical methods, to estimate the effect of desegregation. This design can provide an unbiased estimate of the treatment effect if the statistical model accounts for the selection differences. A popular strategy that may control for these differences is the analysis of covariance in which a single posttest score is adjusted for differences on the pretest score(s). However, measurement error in the pretest(s) yields biased estimates of treatment effect with this model (Cochran, 1968).

To correct for pretest unreliability, one regresses the pretest scores toward their group means using an estimate of the within-group pretest reliability (Porter and Chibucos, 1974). These estimated true scores are used as the covariate(s) instead of the observed pretest scores. Some methodologists (Campbell and Boruch, 1975; Kenny, 1975) suggest that under certain circumstances the pretest-posttest correlation constitutes the most appropriate correction factor (see Reichardt, 1979, for a more detailed discussion). When one does not have extensive knowledge of the selection process, as in the present case, a reasonable strategy is to employ a range of values to correct for unreliability in an attempt to bracket the unbiased estimate of the treatment effect (see Wortman, Reichardt, and St. Pierre, 1978). This strategy has been employed by a number of investigators and yields somewhat different results than the uncorrected covariance analysis.

When there is only one pretest and posttest, the analysis of covariance (ANCOVA) is employed, but where there are multiple posttests, as in longitudinal studies like RSS, a multivariate analysis of repeated measures, or multivariate trend analysis should be applied (Bock, 1975; Finn, 1969; Poor, 1973). This statistical model requires that the measures be multivariate normal and be commensurable or have the same scale of measurement, and that the covariance structures of the two waves be homogeneous. In this approach, orthogonal polynomial contrasts are generated for the repeated measures. A univariate analysis of variance is performed on the individual's mean scores to determine group differences, a test for the main effect of the group or treatment factor. A multivariate analysis is performed on the mean vector of polynomial contrasts over all individuals to test for the main effect of the repeated factor, and is peformed on this vector among the levels of the group factor to test for an interaction between the group and repeated factors. The predesegregation score can be employed as a covariate to adjust for predesegregation group differences in the test for the main effect of the group factor (see Winer, 1971, pp. 796–803).

In sum, the present study estimates the effect of an additional year of school desegregation on the intellectual and personality development of a group of Mexican-American elementary school students. We used a nonequivalent pretest-posttest control group design in which the controls were students from the same school who were desegregated a year later. We analyzed each grade level separately to detect treatment differences in reading achievement. Univariate and multivariate analyses of covariance were applied, using a range of values to correct for pretest unreliabilities. In the multivariate case, correcting for measurement error in the covariate should be considered an exploratory procedure as no one has yet devised an algebraic proof that this technique yields unbiased treatment estimates. Personality measures are separately analyzed for grades K through 3 and 4 through 5 using ANCOVA and corrections for unreliability in the predesegregation measures.

Design. The subjects were 291 Mexican-American children in grades kindergarten through 5 attending the Casa Blanca public elementary school in Riverside, California, in 1965–66. The treatment group, or 1966 wave, consisted of 142 children who entered desegregated receiving schools in the fall of 1966. The remaining 149 children composed the control group, or 1967 wave. The latter children entered desegregated receiving schools in the fall of 1967.

The six cohorts correspond to the students at each grade level in 1965–1968. Reading achievement data were collected for cohort K each spring from 1966 through 1969; for cohort 1 each spring from 1966 through 1968; for cohort 2 in the spring of 1966 and 1967 and the fall of 1968 and 1969; for cohort 3 in the spring of 1966 and the fall of 1967 and 1968; for cohort 4 in the fall of 1965 and 1967; and for cohort 5 in the fall of 1965 and 1968 (for further details, see Singer, Gerard, and Redfearn, 1975, p. 75). The personality measures consisted of the instruments described earlier, including general anxiety, school anxiety, perceived others' attitudes, and self-attitudes. They were administered to the entire sample. In addition, grades 4 and 5 received a need-for-school-achievement measure. The analysis employed two administrations of the personality test battery: the first in the spring of 1966, and the second one year later.

The design of this secondary analysis is a modification of the basic nonequivalent control group design (Campbell and Stanley, 1966, pp. 47–50). The design, in its general form, includes multiple posttest measures. In addition, the control group (1967 wave) received the treatment, school desegregation, one year after the treatment group (1966) received it. Hence, only the first posttest (given in 1966–67) clearly assesses the effect of school desegregation on the treatment group relative to the control group. Subsequent posttests reflect the effect of the additional year of school desegregation on the treatment group.

Analyses. To clarify the selection process, our first analysis examined predesegregation differences among the attitudes of the parents toward desegregation for the two waves of students. Our second analysis investigated the potential biases of selection and attrition upon the reading achievement measures. Finally, we analyzed the reading achievement measures for each grade (as of 1965–66). We analyzed the personality measures separately for grades K through 3 and 4 through 5 (as of 1965–66) to correspond with the original analyses and thus simplify the comparison of results.

For cases in which we have only one posttest (reading achievement and personality for grades 4 and 5), we performed a univariate analysis of covariance using the corresponding predesegregation measure as a covariate (see Appendix, item 1). Adjustments for the unreliability of the pretest have been carried out over a range of values (see Wortman, Reichardt, and St. Pierre, 1978) and results are reported for a pretest reliability value of .50 (see Appendix, item 2). We selected this reliability value to represent a general lower-bound estimate of the pretest-posttest correlation. The value may actually be too low for the achievement tests but is likely a good estimate for the personality tests. Use of this relatively low value provides covariance analyses that reflect maximal adjustments for unreliability in the covariate, as advocated by Campbell and Boruch (1975).

For cases in which we have multiple posttests (reading achievement for K through 3), we standardized the scores for each testing occasion, using the pooled within-group standard deviation to create a common measurement scale. We then performed a multivariate trend analysis of repeated measures (Bock, 1975, pp. 458–461; see Appendix, item 3). The standardization procedure does not allow one to delineate overall trends over time (that is, to test for a main effect for occasions) as the group mean scores at each testing occasion are forced to sum to zero. The analysis can determine overall group differences—main effect for treatment—and differences between the groups over occasions—interaction between treatment and occasions (see Appendix, item 4). The latter analysis allows one to determine whether the slopes representing the two groups' scores over time are parallel, a determination that influences the interpretation of the main effect. The analysis corresponding to the main effect for treatment uses the corresponding predesegregation measure as a covariate and also uses this measure regressed to its group mean with a reliability estimate (r_{xx}) of .50.

Parental Attitudes Toward Desegregation. Parental attitudes toward desegregation were measured in the summer of 1966, prior to the desegregation of both waves of children. Mothers and fathers of children in the 1966 wave were more favorable toward desegregation than parents of children in the 1967 wave $(F(1,252) = 6.60, p = .01; F(1,184) = 4.90, p = .03$, respectively). These results suggest that the selection process for the 1966 wave may have depended upon the parents' volunteering their children to be desegregated, although selection may have occurred by some other nonvoluntary means. If parental attitudes were assessed after the initial selection was made public, cognitive dissonance (Brehm and Cohen, 1962) or self-perception theory (Bem, 1967) could account for this observed attitudinal difference. That is, parents who know their children are soon to be desegregated may be expected to be more favorable toward desegregation. From an analysis of available data it is impossible to reconstruct with any degree of certainty the selection process.

Cohort and Attrition Effects. Predesegregation scores from 1965–66 were analyzed using a two-factor analysis of variance (ANOVA) to examine cohort and attrition effects. One factor was the desegregation wave, either 1966 or 1967, and the other an indicator that categorized the data as either from the analyzed sample or from the attrited sample. The finding of a main effect for wave would indicate a cohort effect, while a main effect for sample would imply a systematic attrition effect. An interaction between the factors would indicate differential attrition, that is, that one wave lost either higher or lower scorers on the predesgregation measure relative to the other.

The analysis was performed separately for each of the six cohorts on the reading achievement measures. A cohort effect was found for grade 1 on reading achievement, $F(1,43) = 3.95$, $p = .05$. First-grade students in the 1966 wave scored lower on predesegregation reading achievement than those in the 1967 wave. No other significant effects were found.

The analysis was also performed on each of the personality measures for grades K through 3 and for grades 4 and 5. The only significant result was an overall attrition effect on the perceived others' attitudes measure for grades 4 and 5, $F(1,56) = 10.44$, $p = .002$. Interestingly, both waves lost students who perceived that others had less favorable attitudes toward them in 1966.

Effects of Desegregation on Reading Achievement. The means and standard deviations of the unstandardized reading achievement tests are presented in Table 1. The differences between the waves on the predesegregation measures are generally small, with the exception of the grade 1 cohort reading achievement. The standardized differences range from +.19 for cohort K to –.57 for cohort 1 in reading achievement. The size of the estimated effects of desegregation on reading achievement is presented in Table 2. The unadjusted effects of desegregation by testing occasion are generally small and range from .004 to –.063. The covariance adjusted effects are also generally small in magnitude. Tests of the significance of these effects also appear in Table 2. The covariance analysis of the mean effect of desegregation on reading yields a negative effect for cohort 1 that approaches significance ($p = .06$), but this effect is attenuated when the covariate is adjusted for unreliability.

Table 1. Means and Standard Deviations of Reading Achievement Measures

Cohort (Grade in 1965–66)	Wave	N	Pretest		Posttest 1		Posttest 2		Posttest 3	
			Mean	S.D.	Mean	S.D.	Mean	S.D.	Mean	S.D.
K	1966	11	41.93	9.75	18.71	13.27	27.64	10.84	39.93	16.13
K	1967	24	39.69	12.36	22.65	9.25	25.19	9.09	42.27	14.62
1	1966	19	27.45	12.20	24.55	11.74	36.20	17.94		
1	1967	19	35.63	16.66	38.32	15.97	52.21	21.46		
2	1966	12	35.00	11.99	47.75	14.85	242.83	7.85	46.92	9.80
2	1967	21	37.91	10.50	47.91	16.11	242.95	9.21	47.86	13.71
3	1966	12	51.08	12.59	33.42	14.02	36.27	16.66		
3	1967	20	54.65	13.93	41.90	12.13	42.45	16.67		
4	1966	11	235.27	5.60	33.91	8.67				
4	1967	15	238.60	9.03	36.07	11.82				
5	1966	13	246.15	9.87	262.69	10.07				
5	1967	12	247.25	11.52	264.50	14.07				

Note: For grades K through 3 and 6, the Stanford Achievement Test (SAT) was used. For grades 4 and 5, the Sequential Test of Educational Progress (STEP) was used.

Table 2. Multivariate Analyses of Reading Achievement by Cohort

Cohort (Grade in 1965–1966)	Desegregation × Occasion					Covariance Adjusted Desegregation Effect							
						$r_{xx} = 1.00$				$r_{xx} = .50$			
	Linear Effect	Quadratic Effect	F	(df)	p	Mean Effect	F	(df)	p	Mean Effect	F	(df)	p
K	-.080	.170	0.78	(2,32)	NS	.013	0.01	(1,32)	NS	-.028	0.06	(1,32)	NS
1	.004	—	0.00	(1,36)	NS	-.208	3.67	(1,35)	.06	.071	0.30	(1,35)	NS
2	-.063	.071	0.65	(2,30)	NS	.038	0.08	(1,30)	NS	.094	0.46	(1,30)	NS
3	-.044	—	0.23	(1,30)	NS	.254	2.42	(1,29)	NS	-.198	1.39	(1,29)	NS
4	—	—	—			.560[a]	0.14	(1,24)	NS	2.198[a]	1.91	(1,24)	NS
5	—	—	—			.444[a]	0.07	(1,23)	NS	.005[a]	0.00	(1,23)	NS

[a] These measures have not been standardized.

Effects of Desegregation on Personality Adjustment. The means and standard deviations of the personality measures are presented in Table 3. The standardized differences in the predesegregation measures between waves are small, from -.08 to +.36. The covariance adjusted effects appear in Table 4 along with the corresponding tests of significance. One year of desegregation had no detectable effect on the general anxiety, school anxiety, or perceived attitudes of others for students in cohorts K-3 who had been desegregated (1966 wave) relative to those who had not yet been desegregated (1967 wave). The desegregated students did reflect a significant decrement in self-attitudes relative to other students, $F(1,162) = 4.93$, $p < .05$. For cohorts 4 and 5, one year of desegregtion had no detectable effect on general anxiety, school anxiety, self-attitudes, or achievement motivation. Desegregated fourth and fifth graders in the 1966 wave did perceive that others had significantly more favorable attitudes toward them than did those not yet desegregated (1967 wave).

Univariate or multivariate covariance analyses were performed on each of the above postdesegregation measures with the corresponding predesegregation (1965–66) score employed as a covariate. In addition, each analysis was performed with the predesegregation score regressed halfway to its group means ($r_{xx} = .50$) to correct for unreliability in the covariate. The analysis strategy attempted to bracket the true estimate of the desegregation effect with the results from these two analyses. Inspection of Tables 2 and 4 reveals little difference in the outcomes of these two analyses on each of the measures, suggesting that any nonequivalence of the two Casa Blanca waves due to the selection process was not serious.

Conclusions. The secondary analysis partially confirms the principal investigator's assessment of the effects of school desegregation on Mexican-American children's intellectual and personality development in Riverside, California. We found no effect of school desegregation on reading achievement, confirming the original study's conclusions. We employed the same pretest-multiple-posttest control group design as the original study, but used multivariate covariance procedures and corrections for unreliability in the covariate. Also, our analysis was performed within cohorts, unlike the earlier study. The absence of desegregation effects, even with a rather large correction for measurement error in the covariate, provides somewhat greater credence for the original conclusion.

That the results of the reanalyses of reading achievement and personality adjustment were not affected by the covariate being corrected for unreliability may indicate that the initial differences between the waves created by the selection process were largely insubstantial.

Table 3. Means and Standard Deviation of Personality Measures

Cohort (Grade in 1965–66)	Type of Measure	Wave	N	1966 Measure		1967 Measure	
				Mean	S.D.	Mean	S.D.
K-3	General anxiety	1966	66	108.33	4.04	108.27	4.23
K-3	General anxiety	1967	108	108.01	3.88	107.20	4.01
K-3	School anxiety	1966	65	105.14	2.95	104.71	2.77
K-3	School anxiety	1967	113	104.89	2.63	104.29	2.29
K-3	Self-attitudes	1966	61	109.31	2.18	107.92	2.72
K-3	Self-attitudes	1967	104	108.89	2.19	108.66	2.56
K-3	Others' attitudes	1966	64	110.53	2.02	110.66	2.06
K-3	Others' attitudes	1967	103	110.19	2.29	110.53	2.42
4-5	General anxiety	1966	28	108.00	4.00	107.50	4.30
4-5	General anxiety	1967	31	108.00	3.93	108.19	3.76
4-5	School anxiety	1966	28	106.79	3.22	107.43	10.85
4-5	School anxiety	1967	32	106.91	3.65	107.56	16.06
4-5	Self-attitudes	1966	24	108.67	2.88	108.33	2.96
4-5	Self-attitudes	1967	25	107.60	2.99	107.48	2.82
4-5	Others' attitudes	1966	25	110.44	2.31	111.88	1.79
4-5	Others' attitudes	1967	18	110.50	2.55	110.06	3.10
4-5	Achievement need	1966	26	105.96	2.36	105.81	5.20
4-5	Achievement need	1967	30	105.67	1.83	106.00	3.38

Table 4. Univariate Analyses of Personality Measures

| Cohort (Grade in 1965-66) | Type of Measure | Covariance Adjusted Desegregation Effect | | | | | | | |
| | | $r_{xx} = 1.00$ | | | | $r_{xx} = .50$ | | | |
		Mean Effect	F	(df)	p	Mean Effect	F	(df)	p
K-3	General anxiety	.461	2.53	(1,172)	NS	.386	1.76	(1,172)	NS
K-3	School anxiety	.167	1.22	(1,176)	NS	.126	0.79	(1,176)	NS
K-3	Self-attitudes	-.450	4.93	(1,162)	.05	-.526	6.63	(1,162)	.05
K-3	Others' attitudes	-.014	0.01	(1,164)	NS	-.089	0.28	(1,164)	NS
4-5	General anxiety	-.347	0.70	(1,56)	NS	-.347	0.70	(1,56)	NS
4-5	School anxiety	-.028	0.01	(1,57)	NS	.012	0.01	(1,57)	NS
4-5	Self-attitudes	.055	0.08	(1,46)	NS	-.316	1.04	(1,46)	NS
4-5	Others' attitudes	.930	9.63	(1,40)	.01	.948	10.00	(1,40)	.01
4-5	Achievement need	-.156	0.38	(1,53)	NS	-.215	0.76	(1,53)	NS

Although the results appear robust under the newer covariance models, it is possible that these models may be biased in the same direction as the original ones. Our uncertainty about the selection process precludes us from drawing firm conclusions from the nonequivalent control group design. Researchers may wish to explore the efficacy of more flexible structural equation models in controlling for selection differences in this design (Magidson, 1977).

With regard to the effects on personality development, results of the present study support the original finding on only two of the five measures examined. The research designs we employed to reanalyze the effects of school desegregation on personality development also provide a more direct test than did the original of the effect on Mexican-American children's personalities. Because our analysis was limited to pre- and one-year postdesegregation, we limit our comparison with the original analysis to the one-year effects of desegregation. The original study found decreases in measures of general anxiety, school anxiety, self-attitudes, and need for school achievement, and an increase in perceived favorableness of others' attitudes, between 1965 and 1967 for all ethnic groups (Green, Miller, and Gerard, 1975). Such changes in these measures, however, may reflect historical and maturational effects. Our analysis of the Mexican-American students ruled out many of these sources of invalidity, thus enabling us to draw stronger inferences. We find a positive effect for one year of school desegregation on the perceived favorableness of others' attitudes of the older children, a negative effect on self-attitudes of the younger children, and no effects on the other three measures. Thus, the results of the primary and secondary analysis generally correspond on only two of the five measures, others' attitudes and self-attitudes. Our results indicate that one year of school desegregation generally had little effect upon the personality development of the Mexican-American children.

Two Problems for Future Research

Our secondary analyses suggest that the early years of school desegregation had little effect on the intellectual and personality growth of Mexican-American elementary school children in Riverside, California. We had difficulty interpreting the effects we did find as they did not form any systematic patterns. The absence of systematic effects is frequent in school desegregation research (St. John, 1975) and points to two related problems for evaluation research in this area.

The first problem is that school desegregation is not a well-specified treatment, as has been implicitly assumed. In general, school desegregation entails a complex set of organizational changes within the schools and within the larger community. As far as we know, no one has yet compiled a complete list of these changes. Riverside's desegregation program was somewhat atypical; school desegregation occurred only after one school was destroyed by arson, and the Mexican-American community was strongly opposed to desegregation, preferring to keep their local community school (Hendrick, 1975, p. 42). Only one-way busing was used, and average class size increased significantly in the years following desegregation—a factor recently shown to lower achievement (Glass and Smith, 1979). Furthermore, the percentage of minority students in the average classroom increased each year after desegregation; in 1970–71 minority students constituted 22 percent of the sample classes, a ratio that approximated the distribution of minority students in the district as a whole. Finally, desegregation was not a uniform experience in all classrooms. Some schools had special workshops for teachers and special programs for students, others did not; and evidence suggests systematic differences in teachers' attitudes and behaviors with regard to minority students (Johnson, Gerard, and Miller, 1975; but also see Chapter Seven). However, the original RSS design precluded using classes as the unit of analysis since data were not collected on all students. While data were obtained on all minority children, only a random sample of white children, matched for grade and school, were selected. In sum, school desegregation is a highly complex package of social change processes, and by no means is it a well-specified intervention.

Second, as we have noted, no one theoretical framework describes or predicts the effects of school desegregation or even identifies all the important parameters. Instead, the desegreation researcher must be eclectic, applying pieces of theories drawn from virtually all the social sciences. This method often forces one to ignore many important aspects of the social change processes and often leads one to draw overly simplistic assumptions that force one later to engage in speculative retrospective interpretations. A coherent theory of desegregation is essential to evaluative research of desegregation and, ultimately, to the development of programs to implement desegregation.

Our secondary analysis supports the original investigators' contention that the personality-based theory of desegregation is untenable. If anything, our study indicates a more uniform pattern of no effects. However, one of the underlying assumptions of the theory is that desegregation promotes interracial contact. As Gerard (1975, p. 18) notes int describing the hypotheses examined in the RSS investigation: "This assumption implies that there is a fluid social structure in the classroom: that the racial subgroups will not segregate themselves into work and friendship cliques." And yet, after an extensive examination of this assumption, Gerard, Jackson, and Conolley (1975, p. 237) conclude, "The unprecedented amount of data we have examined points unmistakably to the conclusion that, with the exception of playground interaction, little or no real integration occurred during the relatively long-term contact situation represented by Riverside's desegregation program. If anything we found some evidence that ethnic cleavage became somewhat more pronounced over time." Furthermore, Johnson, Gerard, and Miller's (1975) discussion of teacher effects lends some support to the potential benefits of social contact. Teachers low in discrimination were found to facilitate interracial contact through the use of small groups, while those high in discrimination did not. Students of the former teachers received higher grades and test scores. Moreover, Slavin and Madden (1979) present evidence that interracial contact resulting from cooperative work groups in school classrooms significantly improves race relations.

In light of this discussion it seems premature to conclude that the personality model failed completely. But many scholars and social commentators have interpreted the findings in just this way (see Coleman, 1978; Stephan, 1978). Unfortunately, the failure of the theory has often been confused with busing itself. Miller (1975, p. 303) takes a more positive view, concluding, "Beyond desegregation, additional procedures must be developed to foster integration of the minority child into the classroom social structure and academic program." Thus we must realize that the issue is not the appropriateness of school desegregation, but the development of educational programs to obtain the benefits of integration.

APPENDIX

1. The model for measures with one posttest:

$$(a) \quad Y_{ij} = \mu + \alpha_i + \beta(X_{ij} - \bar{X}..) + e_{ij}$$

where Y_{ij} = postdesegregation score for student m in wave i
  μ = overall mean
  α_i = desegregation effect
  X_{ij} = predesegregation score for student j in wave i
  $\bar{X}..$ = overall mean of predesegregation measure
  β = coefficient of within-group linear regression of Y on X
  e_{ij} = error component for student j in wave i
 and (b) $\epsilon_{ij} \sim \text{NID } (0.\sigma_e^2)$
  (c) X is random variable distributed independently of e.
  (d) The within-class regression coefficients are homogeneous.

2. The model for adjustments for pretest unreliability:

$$X_{ij}^* = \bar{X}_{i.} + r_{xx}(X_{ij} - \bar{X}_{i.})$$

where X_{ij}^* = predesegregation measure of student j in wave i adjusted
            for unreliability
      $\bar{X}_{i.}$ = mean of predesegregation measure for wave i
      r_{xx} = reliability estimate
      X_{ij} = predesegregation score for student j in wave i

3. The model for measures with multiple posttests:

(a) $Y_{ijk} = \mu + \alpha_i + w_{ij} + \gamma_k + (\alpha\gamma)_{ik} + \beta(X_{ij} - \bar{X}_{..}) + e_{ijk}$

where Y_{ijk} = postdesegregation score for student j in wave i at time k
      μ = overall mean
      α_i = overall effect of desegregation
      w_{ij} = individual-difference component for student j in wave i
      γ_k = overall effect of time k
  $(\alpha\gamma)_{ik}$ = interactive effect of wave i and time k
      β = coefficient of within-group linear regression of Y on X
      X_{ij} = predesegregation score for student j in wave i
      $\bar{X}_{..}$ = overall mean of predesegregation measure
      e_{ijk} = error component for student j in wave i at time k
and (b) $w_{ij} \sim$ NID $(0,\sigma_w^2)$, $\epsilon_{ijk} \sim$ NID $(0,\sigma^2)$
    (c) The random components are assumed similar and inde-
         pendently distributed in both waves.
    (d) The within-class regression coefficients are homogeneous.

4. The parameter estimates for the case of three posttests:

(a) linear: $.707/2[(y_{1.1} - y_{1.3}) - (y_{2.1} - y_{2.3})]$
(b) quadratic: $.408/2[(y_{1.1} - y_{2.1}) - 2(y_{1.2} - y_{2.2}) - (y_{1.3} - y_{2.3})]$
(c) mean: $1/6[(y_{1.1} + y_{1.2} + y_{1.3}) - (y_{2.1} + (y_{2.2} + y_{2.3})]$

where $y_{i.k}$ = postdesegregation score for wave i (1 = 1966 wave,
                2 = 1967 wave) at time k averaged over students.

References

Bem, D. J. "Self-Perception: An Alternative to Dissonance." *Psychological Review*, 1967, *74*, 183–200.
Bock, R. D. *Multivariate Statistical Methods in Behavioral Research.* New York: McGraw-Hill, 1975.
Brehm, J. W., and Cohen, A. R. *Explorations in Cognitive Dissonance.* New York: Wiley, 1962.

Campbell, D. T., and Boruch, R. F. "Making the Case for Randomized Assignment to Treatments by Considering the Alternatives: Six Ways in Which Quasi-Experimental Evaluations in Compensatory Education Tend to Underestimate Effects." In C. A. Bennett and A. A. Lumsdaine (Eds.), *Evaluation and Experiment: Some Critical Issues in Assessing Social Programs.* New York: Academic Press, 1975.

Campbell, D. T., and Stanley, J. C. *Experimental and Quasi-Experimental Designs for Research.* Chicago: Rand McNally, 1966.

Cochran, W. G. "Errors of Measurement in Statistics." *Technometrics,* 1968, *10,* 637–666.

Coleman, J. S. "Can We Integrate Our Public Schools Without Busing?" *Chicago Tribune,* September 17, 1978, Section C, 1.

Cook, T. D., and Campbell, D. T. *Quasi-Experimentation: Design and Analysis Issues for Field Settings.* Chicago: Rand McNally, 1979.

Finn, J. D. "Multivariate Analysis of Repeated Measures Data." *Multivariate Behavioral Research,* 1969, *4,* 391–413.

Gerard, H. B. "The Study." In H. B. Gerard and N. Miller (Eds.), *School Desegregation.* New York: Plenum Press, 1975.

Gerard, H. B., Jackson, T. D., and Conolley, E. S. "Social Contact in the Desgregated Classroom." In H. B. Gerard and N. Miller (Eds.), *School Desegregation.* New York: Plenum Press, 1975.

Gerard, H. B., and Miller, N. *School Desegregation.* New York: Plenum Press, 1975.

Glass, G. V., and Smith, M. L. "Meta-Analysis of Research on Class Size and Achievement." *Educational Evaluation and Policy Analysis,* 1979, *1,* 2–16.

Green, D., Miller, N., and Gerard, D. S. "Personality Traits and Adjustment." In H. B. Gerard and N. Miller (Eds.), *School Desegregation.* New York: Plenum Press, 1975.

Hendrick, I. G. "The Historical Setting." In H. B. Gerard and N. Miller (Eds.), *School Desegregation.* New York: Plenum Press, 1975.

Johnson, E. B., Gerard, H. B., and Miller, N. "Teacher Influences in the Desegregated Classroom." In H. B. Gerard and N. Miller (Eds.), *School Desegregation.* New York: Plenum Press, 1975.

Kenny, D. A. "A Quasi-Experimental Approach to Assessing Treatment Effects in the Nonequivalent Control Group Design." *Psychological Bulletin,* 1975, *82,* 345–362.

Linsenmeier, J. A. W., and Wortman, P. M. "The Riverside School Study of Desegregation: A Reexamination." *Research Review of Equal Education,* 1978, *2*(2), 1–40.

McCall, R. B., and Appelbaum, M. I. "Bias in the Analysis of Repeated Measures Designs: Some Alternative Approaches." *Child Develop-*

ment, 1973, *44,* 401–405.

Magidson, J. "Toward a Causal Model Approach for Adjusting for Preexisting Differences in the Nonequivalent Control Group Situation: A General Alternative to ANCOVA." *Evaluation Quarterly,* 1977, *1,* 399–420.

Miller, N. "Summary and Conclusions." In H. B. Gerard and N. Miller (Eds.), *School Desegregation.* New York: Plenum Press, 1975.

Poor, D. D. "Analysis of Variance for Repeated Measures Designs: Two Approaches." *Psychological Bulletin,* 1973, *80,* 204–209.

Porter, A. C., and Chibucos, T. R. "Selecting Analysis Strategies." In G. D. Borich (Ed.), *Evaluating Educational Programs and Products.* Englewood Cliffs, N.J.: Educational Technology Publications, 1974.

Redfearn, D., and Gerard, H. B. "The Overall Research Design and Some Methodological Considerations." In H. B. Gerard and N. Miller (Eds.), *School Desegregation.* New York: Plenum Press, 1975.

Reichardt, C. S. "The Statistical Analysis of Data from Nonequivalent Group Designs." In T. D. Cook and D. T. Campbell (Eds.), *Quasi-Experimentation: Design and Analysis Issues for Field Settings.* Chicago: Rand McNally, 1979.

Rindskopf, D. M. "Secondary Analysis: Using Multiple Analysis Approaches with Head Start and Title I Data." In R. F. Boruch (Ed.), *New Directions for Program Evaluation: Secondary Analysis,* no. 4. San Francisco: Jossey-Bass, 1978.

St. John, N. H. *School Desegregation: Outcomes for Children.* New York: Wiley, 1975.

Singer, H., Gerard, H. B., and Redfearn, D. "Achievement." In H. B. Gerard and N. Miller (Eds.), *School Desegregation.* New York: Plenum Press, 1975.

Slavin, R. E., and Madden, N. A. "School Practices that Improve Race Relations." *American Educational Research Journal,* 1979, *16,* 169–180.

Stephan, W. G. "School Desegregation: An Evaluation of Predictions Made in *Brown* v. *Board of Education.*" *Psychological Bulletin,* 1978, *85,* 217–238.

U. S. Supreme Court. *Brown* v. *Board of Education of Topeka,* 1954, 347 U.S. 483.

Winer, B. J. *Statistical Principles in Experimental Design.* New York: McGraw-Hill, 1971.

Wortman, P. M., Reichardt, C. S., and St. Pierre, R. G. "The First Year of the Education Voucher Demonstration: A Secondary Analysis of Student Achievement Test Scores." *Evaluation Quarterly,* 1978, *2,* 193–214.

20 *Margaret E. Boeckmann*

Rethinking the Results of a Negative Income Tax Experiment

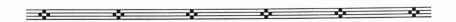

Attrition, the loss of sample subjects, and the consequent loss of data are of continuing concern to researchers involved in longitudinal studies (Wortman, 1978). The question is whether individuals who refuse to continue their participation in the study are systematically different from those who continue to participate. If they are, the attrition is nonrandom, and research results based on the reduced sample will not be generalizable to the population of which the sample was originally

Note: An earlier version of this chapter was presented at the annual meeting of the Southern Sociological Society, April 1978. Analysis of this material began when the author was a summer Fellow in Evaluation Research at Northwestern University; continuing research was supported by a grant from the University Committee on Research of the George Washington University. The contributions of the following persons are gratefully acknowledged: Donald T. Campbell, Thomas Cook, and the editors, for helpful comments and analytical advice, and Bruce Foster for programming assistance.

representative. This loss of representativeness places external validity, or the ability to generalize, in question (Campbell and Stanley, 1966).

In experimental research, a second, potentially more serious, consequence of nonrandom attrition is the degeneration of the original, randomly constituted, experimental and control groups into nonequivalent comparison groups. This type of attrition, called differential attrition, threatens internal validity by making it difficult to determine whether the experimental treatment had any effect. In the presence of differential attrition, posttreatment differences are no longer strictly attributable to the experimental treatment. In fact, a possible consequence of differential attrition is the production of pseudoeffects that are attributed to the experimental treatment although the treatment has actually had no effect, or even a different, but undetected, effect. Differential sample loss can also produce a false finding of no difference between groups.

If attrition is random both within and between treatment groups and is uncorrelated with subject characteristics related to the experimental treatment, there is no cause for concern. However, researchers submit that attrition is rarely random, that those remaining in the sample differ in various characteristics from the original sample (Riecken and others, 1974). At this stage in the development of social science field experimentation, some sample loss seems inevitable. Thus, it is incumbent upon the researcher not only to report the extent of the loss, but also to evaluate critically the potential for bias resulting from it. To accomplish this task, it is necessary, at a minimum, to collect pretest data that might be related to attrition (Jurs and Glass, 1971). If analysis of the data for missing subjects appears to be random, these missing data can be estimated using standard regression techniques without biasing the results. If attrition is found to be nonrandom and external validity is threatened, the population to which results can be generalized must be redefined. If the experiment has lost internal validity, the attrition analysis can suggest the direction of bias and contribute to circumspect interpretations of results.

In this chapter, we analyze the consequences of nonrandom attrition in a randomized field experiment, the New Jersey Negative Income Tax Experiment (NJE). The extent of the attrition is described; hypotheses are generated concerning the direction of the potential bias resulting from attrition; approaches to analyzing attrition are explored; and results of some preliminary analyses are presented. The data for this analysis were obtained from the Institute for Research on Poverty at the University of Wisconsin.

The New Jersey Experiment (NJE)

The NJE was the first in the current series of large-scale social science field experiments designed to provide information that would contribute to policy discussions (see Watts and Rees, 1977). The experiment addresses an issue of both theoretical and political importance—the work response of eligible families to a negative income tax, that is, a basic income guarantee with a tax on earned income (Green, 1967). The issue has theoretical importance because classical economic theory predicts a reduction in work effort in response to a negative income tax but not the magnitude of the response to various combinations of guarantees and tax rates. This lack of specificity precludes an accurate estimate of the reduction in work effort and the resulting cost of a negative income tax program. The NJE was designed to estimate the extent of the reduction in work effort in response to various guarantee and tax rate combinations.

The experimental sample consisted of 1,357 male-headed families with income at or below 150 percent of the official poverty line. Families were chosen by random sampling of poverty tracts in Trenton, Paterson-Passaic, and Jersey City in New Jersey, and Scranton in Pennsylvania. Families were randomly assigned to one of eight experimental treatments or a control group by Conlisk and Watts' (1969) optimum-allocation model. Families assigned to the treatment groups received cash payments according to a particular guarantee and tax rate combination. The amount of the cash payment, or transfer, depended on the amount of the basic income guarantee and the portion of the earned income that was taxed, according to the stipulations of the experimental condition. For example, if the income guarantee were $3,000 and the tax rate 50 percent, a person (or family) earning $4,000 would be "taxed" $2,000 (at the 50 percent rate) and would receive a transfer of $1,000, instead of the zero-income transfer of $3,000, producing a total income of $5,000.

The most generous experimental treatment provided an income guarantee equal to 125 percent of the official poverty line and a tax rate of 50 percent on earned income. The least generous treatment was a guarantee of 50 percent of the poverty line with a tax rate of 30 percent on earned income. An experimental family continued to receive transfer payments until its earned income equaled the "breakeven" income, or the amount of the income guarantee divided by the tax rate. For example, the breakeven income for a guarantee of $3,000 and a tax rate of 50 percent is $6,000.

The experimental goal was to determine which tax rate and income guarantee combination produced the smallest reduction in work effort or labor supply. In each site, both experimental and control families responded to quarterly interviews for three years, providing information on a number of variables, including how much they worked. These data were analyzed to determine the effect of a negative income tax on work effort and a series of other behaviors.

The analyses of family earnings and hours worked presented in the final report were quite complex, and the results rather ambiguous (Watts and Rees, 1977). In the aggregate, there were no statistically significant differences between the experimental and control families on measures of work effort. However, when the sample was disaggregated by ethnicity, several important, and unanticipated, results emerged. The hours and earnings of white and Spanish-speaking experimental families were lower than those of their respective control families, although the experimental-control differences for the Spanish-speaking families were generally smaller than those for whites. For blacks, the experimental families had higher earnings than their controls and a small difference in the number of hours worked. Since the results for black families counter the expectations of orthodox economic theory, they have been the focus of a great deal of attention, speculation, and concern.

The ethnic variations in work response are the subject of the secondary analysis presented in this chapter. The alternative hypothesis under consideration is that the reported results are an artifact of differential attrition between the experimental and control groups, rather than a response to the experimental treatment.

Sample Loss. In the final report, *attrition* is defined as a family leaving the sample entirely. By this definition, NJE suffered differential attrition. The greatest subject loss occurred in the control group (0 percent guarantee, 0 percent tax rate), as shown in Table 1. Attrition was so high among the controls that 141 families were added to that group a year after the experiment began. These families are referred to as "new controls" in the code book and their data were added to the data collected on the other families, although they were excluded from the final labor supply analysis.

There was also differential attrition in the experimental groups. The rate of the income guarantee and the tax rate affected attrition: attrition was negatively related to the income guarantee ($r = -.89$) and positively related to the tax rate ($r = .98$). A relationship between participation in the experiment and financial gain characterized the experiment from the beginning. During enrollment, the most noticeable difference between families who chose to enroll in the experiment and those who refused was the size of the enrollment check: the higher the check, the greater the probability of a family's enrolling.

Table 1. Sample Allocation and Attrition by Experimental Treatment

Income Guarantee[b]	Tax Rate[a]				Total
	0	30	50	70	
0	$n = 632$[c] $x = 160$ $a = 25.3$				$n = 632$ $x = 160$ $a = 25.3$
50		$n = 48$ $x = 7$ $a = 14.6$	$n = 73$ $x = 20$ $a = 27.2$		$n = 121$ $x = 27$ $a = 22.3$
75		$n = 101$ $x = 9$ $a = 8.9$	$n = 117$ $x = 19$ $a = 16.2$	$n = 85$ $x = 22$ $a = 25.9$	$n = 303$ $x = 50$ $a = 16.5$
100			$n = 77$ $x = 12$ $a = 15.6$	$n = 86$ $x = 15$ $a = 17.4$	$n = 163$ $x = 27$ $a = 16.6$
125			$n = 138$ $x = 9$ $a = 6.5$		$n = 138$ $x = 9$ $a = 6.5$
Total	$n = 632$ $x = 160$ $a = 25.3$	$n = 146$ $x = 16$ $a = 10.9$	$n = 408$ $x = 60$ $a = 14.7$	$n = 171$ $x = 37$ $a = 21.6$	$N = 1,357$ $X = 237$ $A = 20.1$

Note: n = size of original sample; x = number attrited; a = percentage rate of attrition.
[a] The tax rate is the percentage of the family's income that is deducted from the income guarantee to determine the transfer payment.
[b] The income guarantee is expressed as a percentage of the official poverty line.
[c] Includes the 141 families added to the control group during the second year.

Attrition rates over the experiment's three years ranged from 25 percent in the control group to 6 percent in the group having the highest income guarantee. Total attrition was approximately 20 percent. Many more families were excluded from the final labor supply analysis, which included only those families that remained intact and responded to questionnaires throughout the experiment. Consequently, the final analysis was conducted on 693 families, or 51 percent of the original sample. Although there are some data on all attrited families, the researchers decided that, for their purposes, the "continuous," or unattrited, sample was the most appropriate for the final analysis.

An important observation, which will be elaborated later, is that similar analyses performed on different subsamples of the NJE data yield different results. Hence, in evaluating results from NJE, one must specify which operational definition of attrition is being employed and which data are being used. Since the results in the final report are based on the continuous sample, the focus of the present reanalysis is the continuous sample and the operational definition of attrition used to generate that sample.

   Prior Analyses of NJE Attrition. Riecken and others (1974) suggested that attrition be analyzed as an outcome variable. Such an analysis appears in a draft of the final NJE report. Peck (1974) regressed attrition on a number of family characteristics in order to determine which of these characteristics was a significant determinant of attrition. He used the entire experimental sample, excluding the 141 new controls and families formed from the original families' breaking up and forming new families, for a sample of 1,213, almost twice the sample size used for most of the final labor supply analyses.

   Peck defined attrition as the loss of a quarterly interview and determined that 27 percent of all families present at preenrollment missed at least one interview. His analysis includes the following family characteristics as predictor variables: experimental site, family type (nuclear or nonnuclear), ethnicity, presence of second spouse, age of family head, education, experimental treatment, preenrollment income, current income, labor force participation, quarters on welfare, and preenrollment housing status. Peck reports that attrition rates differ considerably by site, with Trenton and Paterson-Passaic experiencing the highest attrition and Scranton the lowest. As expected, experimental status was related to attrition—groups with high guarantees and low tax rates had lower attrition. None of the income or labor force participation variables were significant; however, nuclear families, families in public housing, nonwelfare families, and white, non-Spanish-speaking families had significantly lower attrition rates. Peck notes that significant factors related to attrition, other than experimental status, could be "considered determinants of family stability, basic competence to cope with society, and mobility" (1974, p. Cl-12); the more stable families were the ones most likely to remain in the sample.

   Peck suggests that attrition could lead to biased coefficient estimates. If the experimental-control comparisons on certain predictor variables were significant, analysis would yield incorrect conclusions, and such pseudoeffects threaten internal validity. Since the experimental-control differences in work effort were generally nonsignificant (with the exception of the unexpected ethnic differences), Peck hypothesizes that an intact sample might have produced more consistent results, with significant differences in the observed overall work effort. This hypothesis was based on the notion that, in addition to their tendency to drop out of the sample, the more unstable individuals would work less, and thus contribute to a negative labor supply response had they remained in the sample.

Rethinking and Reanalyzing the Results of the NJE

Perhaps families do not alter their behavior when participating in a temporary program, either because they lack the options to alter their work effort or because they recognize the temporary nature of the experiment and are unwilling to risk a change in work effort for a short-term program. Then a plausible hypothesis is that an intact sample would have produced no experimental-control differences in work effort. This hypothesis requires a new explanation of the observed experimental results, especially the ethnic variation. One possible explanation is that differences attributed to the experimental treatment reflect only differential attrition and not a true experimentally induced behavioral response.

In the final report, the preenrollment status of the continuous sample is compared with the total sample. A 5 percent difference between the continuous sample and the total sample on family size, income, and earnings is reported (Watts and others, 1977, p. 11). However, when the continuous husband-wife sample is extracted from the total sample, and means calculated for the unanalyzed portion of the sample (hereafter referred to as the attrited sample), the differences between the continuous and attrited samples at preenrollment on measures of the dependent variables are nontrivial.

Table 2 shows the total family earnings and average total family hours worked per week at preenrollment for the continuous and attrited families. The difference in average total family earnings at preenrollment between the continuous and attrited families is well over 10 percent. When the sample is disaggregated by ethnicity, there are several marked discrepancies between the continuous and attrited samples. Similar results appear for average total family hours worked per week. Although the extent of the disparity between the samples is not great, the direction is consistent; the attrited sample scores substantially lower (for all but two comparisons) than the continuous sample on both measures of work effort.

This systematic loss of families initially lower on measures of work effort (with the exception of control black and experimental Spanish-speaking families) could be described as differential attrition within treatment groups, and therefore, a threat to external validity, but not necessarily to internal validity (Jurs and Glass, 1971). Internal validity is compromised only if there is differential attrition between treatments.

Table 2. Family Earnings and Hours Worked for the Continuous and Attrited Samples

	Average Weekly Total Family Earnings at Preenrollment			Average Total Family Hours Worked per Week at Preenrollment		
	Continuous Sample	Attrited Sample	Difference[a]	Continuous Sample	Attrited Sample	Difference[a]
Total sample (N = 1,357)	94.8 (693)[b]	82.2 (664)	13.3%	40.6 (693)	37.8 (664)	6.9%
Experimental	95.0 (425)	79.8 (300)	16.0%	40.6 (425)	37.1 (300)	8.6%
Control	94.5 (268)	84.1 (364)	11.0%	40.7 (268)	38.3 (364)	5.9%
Whites						
Experimental	100.2 (181)	81.7 (51)	18.5%	42.3 (181)	38.5 (51)	8.9%
Control	98.0 (129)	78.9 (79)	19.5%	42.2 (129)	36.3 (79)	13.9%
Blacks						
Experimental	94.4 (151)	77.1 (131)	18.3%	40.3 (151)	34.7 (131)	13.9%
Control	89.7 (83)	88.1 (137)	1.7%	36.2 (83)	38.6 (137)	-6.3%
Spanish-speaking						
Experimental	85.9 (93)	81.8 (118)	4.8%	37.8 (93)	39.2 (118)	-3.7%
Control	93.6 (56)	83.2 (148)	11.1%	43.9 (56)	39.2 (148)	10.7%

[a] Differences expressed as a percentage of continuous sample.
[b] The numbers of families are shown in parentheses.

Jurs and Glass (1971) suggest a method for testing whether attrition is nonrandom on measured variables. This method employs an analysis of variance (ANOVA) to assess attrition. Within this framework, the treatment factor (T) refers to experimental or control group status in the experiment and the group factor (G) refers to continuous or attrited sample status. If the sample allocation model has resulted in random assignment to experimental and control groups on measured variables, there should be no significant differences between the treatment groups (T) on these variables. Similarly, there should be no difference between the continuous and attrited samples on measured variables if attrition has been random within treatment groups. If the differences between continuous and attrited samples (G) are significant, external validity is threatened. If the treatment by group interaction $(T \times G)$ is not significant, attrition is unrelated to the treatments, that is, the loss between experimental and control groups is random. If the $T \times G$ interaction is significant, there is differential attrition between experimental and treatments, and internal validity is threatened.

In the current analysis, we look at two separate measures of the dependent variable: total family hours worked and family earnings. To determine whether differential attrition is a plausible rival explanation for the ethnic differences reported in the original analysis, we must specify two criteria—the probability level to be used in assessing the statistical significance of the observed differences and the consistency of the pattern of results.

First, we must consider whether the conventional statistical standard, $\alpha = .05$, is adequate in this case. Here, the null hypothesis is that groups do not differ with respect to measured preenrollment status, that is, that the influence of attrition can be considered random. The present case requires us to select a criterion level that is not so stringent as to falsely reject the random attrition hypothesis nor so weak as to fail to detect the phenomenon of interest, nonrandomness. The selection of a reasonable criterion depends on the desired power of the particular analysis.

In a similar statistical situation, Kirk (1968) suggests that a numerically large level of significance, $\alpha = .10$ or $\alpha = .25$, be used in order to detect nonrandomness. Since we seek to establish the existence of differences other than those resulting from the experimental treatment, the large criterion $\alpha = .2$ is appropriate in our analysis of the null hypothesis.

To specify the consistency of the pattern of results, which serves as a check on the pervasiveness of the influence of attrition, is not as easy a task. Here, the direction of preenrollment differences must be examined in relation to the postintervention results. The extent to which these findings are consistent across each of the three subgroups lends additional credibility to the conclusion that the original findings could be attributed to the influence of differential attrition.

Results of the Reanalysis of the NJE

The influence of differential attrition on the previously reported ethnic differences was assessed using the Jurs-Glass procedure for family earnings and number of hours worked, separately. The results of this analysis are summarized in Tables 3 and 4 (for family earnings and number of hours worked, respectively) for the entire sample, including the new controls.

As shown in Tables 3 and 4, none of the differences between experimental and control groups are statistically significant. However, differences between continuous and attrited samples (G) are consistently present (across each ethnic sample) for family earnings and present for the white subgroup on number of hours worked. These comparisons suggest that attrition may have compromised external validity. With respect to internal validity, the analyses reveal significant interaction terms for the black subsample on total family earnings and family hours worked and for the latter variable only for the Spanish-speaking subsample. Thus, some pseudoeffects may be present since there is some indication of differential attrition.

To determine whether the continuous experimental and control families differed before any experimental intervention, we compared their hours worked at preenrollment (see Table 5). One of the comparisons is significant according to the statistical criterion established earlier: The comparison between Spanish-speaking subsamples shows the control families working more hours than the experimentals at preenrollment. This pretreatment difference is important since a reported result of the final labor supply analysis was that Spanish-speaking families demonstrated a negative labor supply response, that is, that experiments worked less than controls. The attrition analysis (see Table 4) shows a significant interaction term for Spanish-speaking families. This term indicates nonrandom attrition between groups on family hours worked, suggesting that attrition may be responsible for observed postintervention differences. We must consider the important possibility that preenrollment differences, whatever their cause, may be reflected in the final labor supply results.

The difference in total family hours worked between control and experimental black families in the continuous sample is marginally within the criterion (see Table 5), which suggests a preintervention difference. This difference between experimental and control black

Table 3. Total Family Earnings at Preenrollment

	Entire Sample			Whites			Blacks			Spanish-Speaking		
	df	F	p	df	F	p	df	F	p	df	F	p
Between treatments (T) (Experimental compared with control)	1	.52	—	1	.23	—	1	.74	—	1	.81	—
Between Groups (G) (Continuous compared with attrited)	1	23.75	.001	1	11.51	.001	1	5.25	.02	1	2.74	.09
Treatments by groups interaction ($T \times G$)	1	.82	—	1	.003	—	1	2.77	.09	1	.57	—
Within TG	1,353			436			498			411		

Table 4. Average Total Family Hours Worked per Week at Preenrollment

	Entire Sample			Whites			Blacks			Spanish-Speaking		
	df	F	p	df	F	p	df	F	p	df	F	p
Between treatments (T) (Experimental compared with control)	1	.31	—	1	.125	—	1	.02	—	1	1.09	.29
Between Groups (G) (Continuous compared with attrited)	1	6.64	.02	1	5.02	.02	1	1.29	.26	1	.36	—
Treatments by groups interaction ($T \times G$)	1	.24	—	1	.22	—	1	4.17	.04	1	2.06	.15
Within TG	1,353			436			498			411		

**Table 5. Average Total Family Hours Worked per Week for the
Continuous Sample at Preenrollment**

	Experimental		Control		Z Value	Percentage Difference
Total sample	40.6	(425)	40.7	(268)	− .061	0.2
Whites	42.3	(181)	42.2	(129)	.043	0.2
Blacks	40.3	(151)	36.2	(83)	1.250	10.2
Spanish-speaking	37.8	(93)	43.9	(56)	−2.020	13.9

families is in the opposite direction from that observed for the Spanish-speaking families, and both differences are in the same direction as those reported in the final report. Consequently, in the absence of any behavioral response to the experimental treatment, the experimental and control portions of the continuous black sample would be different on measures of the dependent variable.

Although none of the differences in family earnings (see Table 6) between continuous experimental and control families at preenrollment are within the established range of statistical significance, the differences between the Spanish-speaking experimental families and their control families, and the black experimental families and their control families are in the same direction as the reported original results. The continuous Spanish-speaking experimental families and the continuous black control families earned less than the black experimental families. Consequently, even if there were no true change in labor supply response due to the NJE, at the end of the experiment black experimental families would appear to have a positive labor supply response and Spanish-speaking experimental families a negative one. Once again, the attrition analysis (see Table 3) indicates that differential sample loss could be responsible for this observed difference in total family earnings for blacks ($p = .09$), although there appears to be no between-treatment difference due to attrition for the Spanish-speaking families, on this measure.

The principal investigators offered the following explanation for the black differences: Black control families had a relatively difficult time in the labor market and therefore showed a decreased work effort, making the experimental families only look as if they were responding positively to the experimental treatment. This historical explanation threatens the internal validity of the experiment, introducing "specific events occurring between the first and the second measurement in addition to the experimental variable" (Campbell and

Table 6. Average Family Earnings for the Continuous Sample at Preenrollment

	Experimental		Control		Z Value	Percentage Difference
Total sample	95.18	(425)	95.54	(268)	.155	0.7
Whites	100.24	(181)	98.02	(129)	.367	2.2
Blacks	94.40	(151)	89.73	(83)	.534	4.9
Spanish-speaking	86.60	(93)	93.64	(56)	−1.10	7.5

Stanley, 1966, p.5). However, the attrition analysis provided in Table 4 indicates that attrition-related differences in family hours worked, across treatment groups, is signifcant for blacks ($p < .04$). This non-random attrition between treatment groups is a threat to the internal validity of the experiment and suggests an alternative explanation for the observed differences between the black experimental and control groups.

Discussion. The principal investigators, aware of preenrollment differences between groups, introduced a seventeen-variable control function into all their analyses to adjust for these differences. A basic assumption of such a correction is that all covariates are reliably measured. In reality, this assumption is rarely met, resulting in an underadjustment (Campbell and Boruch, 1975). Consequently, it is possible that the experimental treatment had no effect on work effort, with the reported results merely reflecting pretreatment differences between the comparison groups.

The differences among ethnic groups were the surprise of the experiment and the center of much discussion. However, these differences emerged only after a series of refined analyses. When simple analyses showed no differences between experimental and control groups, the investigators undertook the more refined analyses that yielded the ambiguous ethnic differences. These unanticipated differences were difficult to interpret theoretically; and further exploration was limited by the sample size, reduced substantially by attrition. Thus one must exercise caution in interpreting these results. Analyses of a new series of income maintenance experiments (the Rural Experiment, the Gary Experiment, and the Seattle-Denver Experiment) may either confirm or contradict the NJE findings. If ethnic variation in work response is found in all the experiments, that result will have heightened credibility. However, the results of this reanalysis for the NJE indicate that internal validity was most likely compromised for the black and probably the Spanish-speaking subsample. Thus, little, if any, confidence should be placed in these results without further substantiating evidence.

The results of the attrition analysis in Tables 3 and 4 also indicate that external validity was compromised. In six of the eight comparisons, the between-group differences were found to be significant. Although external validity was already limited by restricting participants to urban, male-headed families, the between-group differences are still a matter of some concern. Individuals who choose not to participate in a three-year experiment may elect to participate in a national program once it becomes established policy. Since the treatment level was negatively related to attrition, with the greatest loss from the control group, attrition may be considered a behavioral response to the treatment. Consequently, if everyone were subject to uniform treatment, as would be the case in a national program, the families who participate may be very different from those who continued to participate in the experiment. Thus, estimates based on a sample reduced by attrition will not be generalizable even to that population. Experimental results that are not generalizable to a larger population expected to be covered in a national program are only minimally relevant to policy-making decisions.

Conclusions. There are two kinds of conclusions one can draw from this analysis. One is specific to the case at hand. The other generalizes to other cases. Specifically, this analysis suggests that differential attrition has compromised both the internal and external validity of the results of the NJE. Furthermore, it suggests that the direction of the bias has been to underestimate a negative labor supply response for the black subsample, and to overestimate it in the case of the Spanish-speaking subsample. It also suggests that the compromised external validity may limit severely the usefulness of results for policy makers.

The general lesson concerns the limitations of analyses applied to flawed data. In the case of a true experimental design, the advantage of the technique stems from the ability to make valid comparisons between treatment and control groups. However, if the groups lose comparability, all the cautions of quasi-experimental research must be invoked. Sophisticated analyses cannot substitute for the loss of comparability. Adjustment procedures are only approximate, and when they are used the possibility of incomplete adjustment must be considered. Consequently, it is imperative to document, and even model, the sample loss so that results will be interpretable.

References

Campbell, D. T., and Boruch, R. F. "Making the Case for Randomized Assignment to Treatments by Considering the Alternatives: Six Ways in Which Quasi-Experimental Evaluations in Compensatory Education Tend to Underestimate Effect." In C. A. Bennett and A. A. Lumsdaine (Eds.), *Evaluation and Experiment*. New York: Academic Press, 1975.

Campbell, D. T., and Stanley, J. *Experimental and Quasi-Experimental Designs for Research*. Chicago: Rand McNally, 1966.

Conlisk, J., and Watts, H. "A Model for Optimizing Experimental Designs for Estimating Response Surfaces." In *Proceedings of the Social Statistics Section, American Statistical Association*. Washington, D.C.: American Statistical Association, 1969.

Green, C. *Negative Taxes and the Poverty Problem*. Washington, D.C.: Brookings Institution, 1967.

Jurs, S. G., and Glass, G. V. "The Effect of Experimental Mortality on the Internal and External Validity of the Randomized Comparative Experiment." *Journal of Experimental Education*, 1971, *40*, 62–66.

Kirk, R. F. *Experimental Design: Procedures for the Behavioral Sciences*. Belmont, Calif.: Brooks/Cole, 1968.

Peck, J. "The Problem of Attrition." In H. Watts and A. Rees (Eds.), *Studies Relating to the Validity and Generalizability of the Results: Part C of the Final Report of the New Jersey Graduated Work Incentive Experiment*. Madison, Wis.: Institute for Research on Poverty, 1974.

Rees, A. "The Labor-Supply Results of the Experiment: A Summary." In H. Watts and A. Rees (Eds.), *The New Jersey Income Maintenance Experiment*. New York: Academic Press, 1977.

Riecken, H. W., and others. *Social Experimentation: A Method for Planning and Evaluating Social Intervention*. New York: Academic Press, 1974.

Watts, H. W., Poirier, D., and Mallar, C. "Samples, Variables, and Concepts Used in the Analysis." In H. Watts and A. Rees (Eds.), *The New Jersey Income Maintenance Experiment*. Vol. 2. New York: Academic Press, 1977.

Watts, H., and Rees, A. *The New Jersey Income Maintenance Experiment*. Vol. 2. New York: Academic Press, 1977.

Wortman, P. M. "Differential Attrition: Another Hazard of Follow-up Research." *American Psychologist*, 1978, *33*, 1145–1146.

21

Steven M. Director

Examining Potential
Bias in Manpower
Training Evaluations

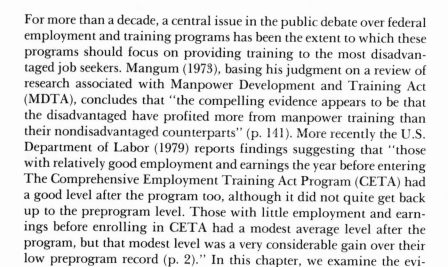

For more than a decade, a central issue in the public debate over federal
employment and training programs has been the extent to which these
programs should focus on providing training to the most disadvantaged job seekers. Mangum (1973), basing his judgment on a review of
research associated with Manpower Development and Training Act
(MDTA), concludes that "the compelling evidence appears to be that
the disadvantaged have profited more from manpower training than
their nondisadvantaged counterparts" (p. 141). More recently the U.S.
Department of Labor (1979) reports findings suggesting that "those
with relatively good employment and earnings the year before entering
The Comprehensive Employment Training Act Program (CETA) had
a good level after the program too, although it did not quite get back
up to the preprogram level. Those with little employment and earnings before enrolling in CETA had a modest average level after the
program, but that modest level was a very considerable gain over their
low preprogram record (p. 2)." In this chapter, we examine the evi-

356

dence cited by Mangum and the Department of Labor and find that the reported pattern of earning gains could have occurred as an artifact of the analyses employed, even in the absence of any true differential effect of participation in the training programs.

Both of the studies analyze pre- and postprogram data on large samples of trainees. A control group, composed of nontrainees, was not available for either study. When comparisons between a trainee and control group are not possible, it is not surprising (or inappropriate) that researchers devote their efforts to making comparisons between subsets of the trainees. However, such designs cannot determine what proportion, if any, of the postprogram earnings gain was due to the training. If one assumes, however, that in the absence of training all trainees would have experienced the same earnings gain, it may be possible to determine which individuals benefited the most from training. Unfortunately, while both studies make this assumption, they employ analytical strategies that are inappropriate to it. Both studies compare a group chosen on the basis of low preprogram earnings with a group chosen on the basis of high preprogram earnings. It has been well documented that these types of comparisons can produce a regression artifact that results in differential postprogram earning changes even in the absence of any differential program effects (see Campbell and Boruch, 1975).

Analysis of Mangum's Evidence

Mangum (1973) relies on data from a nationwide MDTA outcome study conducted by a research group named Decision Making Information (DMI). In this study, DMI interviewed 5,169 persons who were a randomly selected sample of both institutional and on-the-job training (OJT) enrollees who left MDTA training, either because they dropped out or completed the training, during 1969. The DMI study classified as "disadvantaged" those individual heads-of-households with pretraining annual earnings below the Social Security poverty minimum for families of their size. In addition to meeting this income criterion, disadvantaged individuals belonged to one of the following groups: (1) those aged under twenty-two or over seventy-seven, (2) those having less than a high school education, (3) those belonging to a minority group, or (4) those physically or mentally handicapped. Based on this definition of disadvantaged, DMI calculated pretraining and posttraining annual income for MDTA enrollees (see Table 1). Within both the institutional and OJT groups, the disadvantaged enrollees attained posttraining income gains that were almost twice that of their nondisadvantaged counterparts.

Table 1. Pre- and Posttraining Income of MDTA Enrollees

	Pretraining Annual Income	Posttraining Annual Income	Income Gain	Expected Artifactual Gain $(r = .6)$	Adjusted Gain $(r = .6)$
Institutional enrollees					
Disadvantaged	$2,036	$3,363	$1,327	$248	$1,079
Nondisadvantaged	4,032	4,732	700	−551	1,250
OJT enrollees					
Disadvantaged	2,212	3,862	1,650	351	1,299
Nondisadvantaged	4,209	5,078	869	−447	1,316

Source: Pre- and posttraining annual income data taken from Mangum, 1973.

We can determine whether differences of such magnitude could plausibly have resulted from regression artifacts. Essentially, this analysis simply requires an examination of the plausible influences on observed income. That is, an individual's earnings at a point in time can be viewed as the sum of permanent and transitory components. More formally, this relation may be written as follows:

$$Y_1 = Y^* + u$$

and

$$Y_2 = Y^* + G + T + v$$

where Y_1 = observed preprogram earnings
  Y^* = the permanent component of Y_1
  u = the transitory component of Y_1
  Y_2 = observed postprogram earnings
  G = the change in permanent earnings due to factors other than the training
  T = the effect of training on permanent earnings
  v = the transitory component of postprogram earnings
It is assumed that u and $v \sim N(\phi,\sigma^2)$ and that the covariances $C(u, Y^*)$, $C(v,Y^*)$, and $C(u,v)$ are zero. The expected prepost change is therefore:

$$(Y_2 - Y_1) \ T + G + u$$

Even if T and G were equal across all trainees, differences in u would produce differences ·in $(Y_2 - Y_1)$. By estimating the expected regression toward the mean, u, and subtracting this from the observed pre- to postprogram change, a comparison of $T + G$ between the disadvantaged groups can be made. The results of this analysis are reported in Table 1. Estimates of the expected regression artifact were obtained from:

$$u = (Y_{1i} - Y_1)(1 - r)$$

where Y_{1i} = mean preprogram earnings for the ith group (disadvantaged or nondisadvantaged)

Y_1 = mean preprogram earnings of the combined groups (disadvantaged and nondisadvantaged)

r = $V(Y^*)/[V(Y^*) + V(u)]$, variance of the permanent component of earnings divided by the sum of the variances of the permanent and error components

Campbell and Boruch (1975) suggest using the pretest-posttest correlation as an estimate of r for taking into account imperfect reliability of the pretest measure. While this correlation is not reported in the DMI study, Cooley, McGuire, and Prescott (1976) report autocorrelations of annual earnings of MDTA trainees of .69 over one year, and .50 over two years. Since the time elapsed between pre-and postprogram measure was about eighteen months, a value of .6 was used as a reasonable estimate of r (the autocorrelation) for the adjusted gains presented in Table 1.

The adjusted gains for the disadvantaged and nondisadvantaged institutional trainees differ by $171. The adjusted gains for the disadvantaged and nondisadvantaged OJT groups differ by only $17. In both cases the adjusted gains are surprisingly close, suggesting that there was no significant between-group difference in $(G + T)$. If one is willing to assume (as Mangum does implicitly) that G is equal in both groups, it follows that there were no group differences in the impact of training (T). The greater observed gain for the disadvantaged enrollees was probably due to the fact that this group, which consisted of the lower tail of the preprogram earnings distribution, regressed upward toward the distribution mean, while the nondisadvantaged regressed downward toward the distribution mean.

Analysis of the Department of Labor's Evidence

The Department of Labor's findings were reported as highlights of a major study of 320,000 individuals who entered CETA between January and June 1975, and later left the program either as dropouts or upon completion of the program. One aspect of the analysis, performed for the Department of Labor by Westat, Inc., was the sorting of individuals based on their preprogram labor force status and a comparison of their pre- and postprogram earnings. The results of this analysis are reported in Table 2. Similar to the DMI data, postprogram gains were inversely related to preprogram earnings. Since this comparison, too, is between groups chosen because of their position on the preprogram earnings distribution, it is again possible that the observed pattern of gains is the result of regression artifacts. In fairness to Westat, Inc., it should be noted that they did not interpret the obtained differences as effects of CETA participation, rather these were attributed to the passage of time.

The same procedure used to adjust the DMI data was applied to the Continuous Longitudinal Manpower Survey (CLMS) data, and the results are shown in Table 2. A value of $r = .6$ reduces the range in income gains from \$3,400 to \$1,384. This analysis could be interpreted as evidence that, while their magnitudes are much smaller than originally suggested, group difference in postprogram gains do exist. A second possibility is that a lower estimate of the autocorrelation (r) should have been used in the adjustment process. This possibility is made more credible by the fact that quarterly, not annual, earnings are used in the CLMS analysis. Since transitory components affect quarterly averages more than annual averages, we would expect lower autocorrelation for these data. If the adjustments are recalculated using $r = .4$, the difference between the largest and smallest gain is less than \$500 (see Table 2). This difference, considerably smaller than the \$3,400 reported in the original calculations, is probably not sufficient to be of much significance for policy makers.

We can further test the possibility that the pattern of results reported by the Department of Labor is the result of a regression artifact by comparing the gains using a variable correlated more highly with permanent earnings than observed earnings. A proxy variable that probably satisfies this criterion is educational attainment. According to the U.S. Department of Labor (1978), for the CLMS sample, the average earnings gain (the difference between fourth-quarter earnings after training and fourth-quarter earnings prior to training) of those persons with fewer than twelve years of education was \$200 or 6 percent, and for those with twelve or more years of education was \$1,280 or 38 percent. These results suggest a quite different conclusion than that offered by the Department of Labor (1979), namely that the disadvantaged (as defined by educational attainment) benefited least from CETA training. While the use of proxy variables may decrease the threat of regression bias, due to a higher correlation of the covariate and better specification of permanent income, it does not remove the ambiguity always associated with simple pretreatment-posttreatment designs. For example, this analysis still leaves unanswered the question

Table 2. Pretraining Earnings, Observed Change, and Adjusted Change for CETA Participants

Employment Experience in Year Before Entry into CETA Program	Earnings in Fourth Quarter Before Entry	Raw Gain from Fourth Quarter Before Entry to Fourth After Entry	Expected Artifactual Gain ($r = .6$)	Adjusted Gain ($r = .6$)	Expected Artifactual Gain ($r = .4$)	Adjusted Gain ($r = .4$)
Predominantly not in labor force ($N = 76,600$)	$ 890	$2,300	$ 980	$1,320	$1,470	$ 830
Predominantly unemployed ($N = 81,000$)	1,900	1,610	576	1,034	684	926
Other ($N = 114,900$)	5,050	–290	–684	394	–1,026	736
Predominantly employed ($N = 48,400$)	5,930	–1,100	–1,036	–64	–1,554	454

Source: Data on participants' earnings and raw gain in earnings are taken from U.S. Department of Labor (1978).

of whether the gains of the high school graduates represent larger benefits from CETA or just the benefits of a high school education.

Conclusion

Attempts, such as those contained in this chapter, to adjust for expected artifacts can be of only limited value. The adequacy of the results obtained through these adjustment procedures is dependent upon a number of assumptions. The two most critical are that the group means are, in fact, drawn from a normal distribution around the grand mean, and that an appropriate value of r is employed in the adjustment process. Given these caveats, the primary purpose of this chapter is not to provide adjusted estimates of the differences in program effects but to demonstrate that under a variety of plausible alternative assumptions, differences as large as those reported in the studies considered could be merely the result of a methodological artifact, regresson toward the mean. Other researchers using similar methods have also reached the same conclusions (see Wortman, Reichardt, and St. Pierre, 1978). As a consequence, policy makers should not rely upon adjusted estimates, but should encourage investigators to obtain other evidence less subject to these artifacts.

Unfortunately, such evidence is not readily available. I am aware of only one recent study (Borus, 1978) that explicitly tested for an interaction between program effects and disadvantaged status using a comparison group design. Though the comparison group in this study was not constituted using randomization, it is, nonetheless, superior to pretreatment-posttreatment analyses. Borus (1978) reports that the benefits from training were positively related to average wage in the year before training and inversely related to receipt of public assistance in the year before training. This finding and the present analysis of the CLMS data suggest that we should reject the conclusion that the disadvantaged benefit most from governmental training programs.

References

Borus, M. E. "Indicators of CETA Performance." *Industrial and Labor Relations Review,* 1978, *32,* 3–14.

Campbell, D. T., and Boruch, R. F. "Making the Case for Random Assignments to Treatments by Considering the Alternatives: Six Ways in Which Quasi-Experimental Evaluations in Compensatory Education Tend To Underestimate Effects." In C. A. Bennett and A. A. Lumsdaine (Eds.), *Evaluation and Experiment: Critical Issues in Assessing Social Programs.* New York: Academic Press, 1975.

Cooley, T. F., McGuire, T. W., and Prescott, E. C. *The Effects of MDTA Manpower Training Programs.* Carnegie-Mellon University Working Paper No. 85-75-76. Pittsburgh, Pa.: Carnegie-Mellon University, 1976.

Mangum, G. L. *A Decade of Manpower Development and Training.* Salt Lake City, Utah; Olympus, 1973.

U.S. Department of Labor. *Continuous Longitudinal Manpower Survey, Followup Report No. 1.* Washington, D.C.: U.S. Department of Labor, 1978.

U.S. Department of Labor. *Summary of Highlights of Continuous Longitudinal Manpower Followup Report No. 1.* Washington, D.C.: U.S. Department of Labor, 1979.

Wortman, P. M., Reichardt, C. S., and St. Pierre, R. G. "The First Year of the Education Voucher Demonstration: A Secondary Analysis of Student Achievement Test Scores." *Evaluation Quarterly*, 1978, 2(2), 193-214.

22

Clifford B. Hawley
William T. Bielby

Research Uses
of Longitudinal
Survey Data
on Women

In this chapter, we summarize the substantive findings from a long series of secondary analyses of the mature women cohort of the National Longitudinal Survey (NLS) of Labor Market Experience. In this sense, we follow Hyman's (1971) tradition of secondary analysis, which addresses social science issues through the reanalysis of archived sample surveys. Our report has three purposes. We begin our report with an evaluative survey of two major substantive areas of labor market research: labor supply and demand. We then present a summary of an important methodological innovation developed by users of the NLS data on mature women. We conclude with a description of topics that have been neglected in the research on the data and recommendations for future research.

Let us begin with an overview of the scope and history of the NLS data. Since 1966, the Center for Human Resource Research (CHRR) of Ohio State University and the U.S. Bureau of the Census, under separate contracts from the Manpower Administration of the U.S. Department of Labor, have collaborated in conducting the NLS of Labor Market Experience. Based on a national probability sample, the complete NLS data set is comprised of four cohorts: men who, at the inception of the study, were forty-five to fifty-nine years of age; young women and young men between the ages of fourteen and twenty-four; and women thirty to forty-four years of age. These four groups were selected to be periodically interviewed because each is confronted with particular labor market problems (unemployment for the young cohorts, labor market reentry problems for mature women). This report focuses on the mature women cohort (for details of the NLS data, see Center for Human Resource Research, 1976).

The NLS data set has figured prominently in evaluations of the effects of social programs. For example, Director (1979) used the NLS data on younger cohorts in his assessment of the extent to which bias existed in previous outcome analyses of Manpower Training Programs. His procedure, a double pretest, requires the use of archival data (see Wortman, Reichardt, and St. Pierre, 1978). Thus, not only have the NLS data been useful for assessing hypotheses about labor experience, but also they have been used in the evaluation of social programs. We hope, through this discussion, to facilitate further use of these data.

In July 1977, we began collecting published articles identified in the NLS *Handbook* and *Newsletter*. We also solicited published and unpublished papers, sending letters to all users of the NLS data as identified from the *Handbook, Newsletter,* and the Department of Labor's list of projects funded by the Office of Manpower Research and Development. In addition, Herbert S. Parnes provided us with published and unpublished papers by the staff of CHRR. The present report on the uses of the data on mature women is revised and expanded from our review of research on all four NLS cohorts (Bielby, Hawley, and Bills, 1979). We focus on research published or forthcoming in professional journals and books rather than on the in-house research of the CHRR staff. Much of the latter appears in the widely distributed *Dual Careers Monograph Series* (see Jusenius and Shortlidge, 1975; Parnes and others, 1975; Shea, Kim, and Roderick, 1973; Shea, Spitz, and Zeller, 1970). Also, some of the major findings have been summarized by Sexton (1977) and Andrisani and others (1977). (Readers may obtain a complete list of the extensive research based on the NLS data file by writing the authors.)

Labor Supply of Women

In the 1960s the determinants of female labor supply were thought to be well understood. Women's increasing participation in the labor force in the face of a rising standard of living was at first viewed as an anomaly to economic theory, which suggested that rising incomes would bring increasing demands for leisure. This apparent anomaly was resolved by Mincer (1962), who placed female labor supply in a family context and focused both on female wages and other family income as determinants of women's decision to work. Mincer showed that declines in the labor force participation of married women due to husbands' rising income (an income effect) were more than offset by the positive labor supply effects of rising wages for women (a substitution effect).

Mincer's research prompted a sharper focus on the alternatives to wives' working—both leisure and housework. Researchers explored the relationship between the home productivity of married women and family composition—the number and ages of children in the household. Cain (1976) and Bowen and Finegan (1969) confirm that the rise in female wages is the driving force behind the great increases in female participation in the labor force, and, equally important, they confirm that for married women, family composition plays an extremely important role in the decision to work. The presence of children, especially young children, was repeatedly found to have a large negative effect on the labor supply of married women. This finding stimulated new research on fertility and its determinants (Schultz, 1974). The well-established inverse relationship between number of children present and female labor supply suggests that the decision to have children and the decision to work are interdependent.

The 1970s witnessed extensive research in the area of labor supply. Continuing policy debates over income maintenance programs motivated much of the research, and the family model of labor supply allowed more rigorous testing of hypotheses. Difficulties in interpreting the results of the New Jersey and other income maintenance experiments attested to the inadequacy of traditional estimates of the labor supply function and highlighted some of the deficiencies of a family labor supply model that suppresses dynamic considerations (Greenberg, 1972). The principal topics of recent research on the female labor supply are: (1) the endogeneity of certain "independent" variables, such as assets, work experience, and family composition; (2) the importance of jointness in wage-hours choices; (3) the process of human capital accumulation within the household and home investments in children; (4) the efficient and unbiased estimation of the labor supply function.

The research studies we will discuss all use the NLS data on mature women, and thus have two advantages over earlier research. First, the individual or the family is the unit of analysis, whereas larger aggregates, such as a census tract, characterized much of the research in the 1960s. Second, the longitudinal nature of the NLS data allows investigators to examine labor supply over the span of the life cycle. Researchers usually measure labor supply by annual hours or weeks worked; the NLS data permit measures over longer intervals of time.

Household Decision Making and Female Labor Supply. Interest in women's participation in the labor force over the span of their adult lives has led to careful comparisons of their work during the interval between leaving school and parturition and their work after the birth of their first child. Sandell (1977) estimated the separate labor supply functions for these two periods for a sample of mothers and confirms that rising female wages have a positive effect on married women's labor force participation. Like Mincer, he shows that female labor force participation is greater, other factors being equal, when a husband's current income is temporarily below his permanent income. For mothers, he finds that the substitution effect of wages on labor supply declines substantially when certain attitudinal variables and prior (prepartum) job experience are included as independent variables. Prior job experience, a favorable attitude toward working mothers, and a perceived favorable attitude of the husband toward the respondent's working all have positive effects on female labor supply (see also Kim, 1972). Interpretation of such attitudinal variables requires some care. Presumably they represent an orientation toward the labor market. Thus either these variables capture differences in women's attitudes toward being homemakers or reflect rewards for working that cannot be captured by an own-wage variable alone.

Rosenberg (1972) investigates the relationship between fertility, family composition, and labor force participation. His research indicates that increases in female labor force participation in the past have largely been due to changes in household composition, with the independent effects of wages on participation playing a smaller role.

Fleisher (1977) matches the NLS surveys of mature women and young men to create a mother-son sample. He investigates the relationship between the mother's time at home and her education and her son's educational attainment, intelligence, and early labor market experience. While he finds little relationship between a mother's time at home and her son's schooling, he offers evidence that a mother's education interacts with her time at home to affect her son's educational attainment and wages in the labor market.

Much of the recent research on the labor supply of married women and its relationship to fertility behavior uses the Chicago model of family labor supply, or as it is called by its practitioners, "the new home economics" (Schultz, 1974). The model depicts an interrelationship between the demand for children and the demand for market goods. The commodity "children" is taken to have two dimensions, quality and quantity, and household purchases occur up to both margins (Becker and Lewis, 1973; DeTray, 1973; Willis, 1973).

Of the papers using the NLS data, the one most faithful to the Chicago model is Fleisher and Rhodes' (1979). Their model relates wife's wages, work experience, and number and quality of children to her education, age, race, and her husband's education and wages at age forty. Many of their results are similar to findings yielded by simpler approaches: Blacks earn lower wages; schooling positively affects wages; and women earning higher wages have fewer children. One curious result is that husband's wage is strongly and directly related to wife's wage. The authors posit a job-search theoretical explanation for this, but alternatives include shared human capital, marriage selection, or a within-family, "old boy" network. Their most surprising result is a positive influence of number of children on the labor force participation of married women. While we question the robustness of this result, their paper represents the first foray into simultaneous structural estimates of fertility and female labor force participation, using NLS data. Related efforts to estimate wages, labor supply, and fertility based on simultaneous equations are presented by Cain and Dooley (1976), using 1970 census data.

Kniesner (1976b) explores a single parameter of the family labor supply model: the cross-substitution effect between one's hours of work and spouse's wage rate. Most previous estimates of the income effect on married women's hours of work were based on an estimate of other family income (mostly the husband's). These estimates presume that husband's earnings are given, that his wage has no effect on the supply of her labor, nor does her wage have any effect on the allocation of his time between the household and the market. Using data from the first interview of the older men and mature women, Kniesner finds evidence that one's hours of work and spouse's wage rate are positively related. For this sample, hours of work of each spouse are also positively related, a relationship unlikely to be uniform over the life cycle.

One limitation of the Chicago model of family labor supply is its static nature. As such, the wage rates of each spouse are formally taken to be exogenous. In practice, to overcome the suppression of dynamic considerations, a wage rate equation for each spouse is commonly estimated on the basis of his or her education and work history. But the causation between work histories and wages for women is a difficult one to understand. Do women withdraw from the labor market because of low expected wages or is their low participation the cause of their low expected wages?

The relationship between women's participation in the labor market and their wages is also examined by Mincer and Polacheck (1974) and Sandell and Shapiro (1976), and we review their work later in this chapter, in our discussion of sex discrimination.

Child Care and Welfare. Shortlidge and Brito (1977) analyze how working women with children under fourteen handle childcare responsibilities, using the 1971 NLS data on mature women and young women. Their analysis relates the use of various forms of daycare (family, nonfamily, at home, outside the home) to age of children, mother's wages and hours worked, mother's education, and other variables. Using multiple classification analysis, they relate the use of family or nonfamily daycare to household composition, characteristics of the mother's job, personal characteristics, and geographical location. Their most interesting result is that both women's earnings and education are positively related to use of nonfamily daycare after controlling for other factors such as household composition and availability of relatives in the community of residence. They also provide estimates of the cost of childcare for each hour worked by the mother. Costs averaged $.37 per hour worked for children under three, and $.27 an hour for children aged three to five, or between 15 and 20 percent of working women's wages. For school-age children, the cost was much smaller. This study provides valuable information on the consumption patterns working women choose, but it is unable to overcome the simultaneity of supply and demand in order to disentangle the determinants of that choice. The restriction of the sample to working women gives us no estimates of how the presence of children forms barriers to labor market entry for nonworking women. (But Heckman, 1974a, 1974b, and 1976, provides a discussion of factors that influence labor market participation.)

In a related study, Shortlidge, Waite, and Suter (1975) compare the 1971 NLS mature women survey of childcare arrangements with the 1965 Current Population Survey (Low and Spindler, 1968). They document the still small, but increasing, reliance of working women on group daycare centers for their children, as within-home substitutes become increasingly unavailable or prohibitively expensive. The greatest increase in use of group centers is among nonwhite women with preschool children, an increase most likely due to federal programs aimed at that population. The authors also discuss increased suburbanization, increased female labor force participation, and changes in the female occupational structure as factors responsible for the secular change in childcare arrangements.

While Shortlidge and his coauthors document the kinds of child care used by employed women, Heckman (1974a) examines the labor supply effects of programs that lower the cost of formal childcare arrangements. He seeks to determine whether the availability of affordable daycare would cause nonworking mothers to work, or working mothers to work more hours, or not affect most mothers, particularly those who rely on relatives to provide childcare. Heckman, using the 1967 mature women data, restricts his analysis to those families with spouse present and at least one child under ten. For both blacks and whites, he finds that child care costs are inversely related to the presence of a relative or older sibling in the home and length of residence in the area, and positively related to husband's hours of work and residence location within the area. Heckman estimates the women's asking wage, and for both blacks and whites, asking wage is positively related to years of education and labor market experience. (For the statistical procedure to determine asking wage, see Heckman, 1974b.)

A summary of Heckman's results is beyond the scope of this paper. In fact, the results seem subordinate to the innovative approach to the direct measurement of the marginal rate of substitution along an indifference curve and the statistical procedure employed. Heckman does find cases in which childcare subsidies would prompt nonworking mothers to work and would thus reduce net government welfare costs.

Meyer (1975) and Shea (1973) use the 1967 mature women survey to examine the relationship between welfare benefits and the willingness to work. Meyer estimates labor supply functions for black and white women. For both groups he finds that net wages (the difference between earned wages and forgone welfare benefits) have no significant effect on hours worked, as income and substitution effects seem to balance out. Instead, respondent's education and job experience, self-reported health status, and the presence or absence of preschool children are the major determinants of annual hours worked.

Shea (1973) selected a sample of nonworking women who said they would accept a job in their area. Women who had the most work experience were most willing to return to work if a job were available. He also reports that current white welfare recipients were slightly less willing to return to work; white and black welfare recipients named an asking wage less than $.25 an hour higher than nonrecipients.

Finally, Rosen (1976a, 1976b) used the 1967 mature women survey data to test a model that estimates the tax perception for white wives. Since married females are likely to be secondary earners, their first dollar earned is taxed at the same marginal rate as their spouse's last dollar. Consistent with his derivations from economic theory, his results indicate that labor supply is responsive to net wages rather than gross wages.

Marital Instability. A utility-maximizing approach to understanding the social behavior of the individual over his or her life cycle seems to be the ultimate goal of the new home economics. Becker (1973, 1974) uses this principle to develop a theory of marriage in terms of the expected costs and benefits to each party of such a union. The new home economics takes the union as given to predict the demand for children and the allocation of time to household and outside work on the basis of nonlabor income and each spouse's household and market productivities. No one has yet proposed a complete well-integrated theory of family formation and the allocation of time to investment, home, and market activities. Nevertheless, economists have begun to examine the subject of divorce and separation.

Using the 1967 NLS data on mature women, Cherlin (1976a, 1976b, 1977) and Kniesner (1976a) studied a sample of white, nonfarm, married women between the ages of thirty and forty-four. To investigate the determinants of marital instability, he relates divorce or separation between 1967 and 1971 to a set of independent variables, such as length of marriage, actual or expected wage of the wife relative to that of the husband, and number of children under eighteen. Cherlin concludes that the wife's relative wage, the number of children, and large age differences between spouses are positively related to divorce or separation, while the presence of young children is negatively related to marital instability. In a similar analysis, Kniesner (1976a) reports that, other factors being equal, families with many children and low levels of assets are more likely to experience divorce or separation. He found no independent effect of race on marital dissolution.

Such research suggests that the relationship between marital instability and children is a complex one. The presence of young children does seem to delay and perhaps inhibit divorce or separation. Becker, Landes, and Michael (1977) report similar findings, and show that the relationships of the number, presence, and ages of children to marital dissolution change with the length of marriage. Thus the analyses of marital instability by Cherlin and Kniesner should be interpreted with caution since these analyses are confined to the older female cohort, women in their thirties and forties.

Bahr (n.d.a) examined some determinants of marital instability for all four NLS cohorts and finds that net assets have a significantly positive effect on marital stability. In another paper (n.d.b) using the data from the young women sample, he finds that the importance of assets differs according to the age at which the couple married. Net assets did not have a positive influence on marital stability for those who married in their teens. Unlike Kniesner, Bahr finds significant racial differences in the probability of marriage dissolution; however, Bahr fails to consider other variables that may be causally related to marital instability, in particular, family composition and female wages. (For related studies of marital instability, based on the University of Michigan's Panel Study of Income Dynamics, see Ross and Sawhill, chap. 3, 1975.)

Recent quantitative research on marital instability explicitly measures net benefits from dissolution. While some microeconomic variables, such as wife's wage, have shown consistent (and in this case, positive) effects on marital instability, the amount of variation explained by commonly used attribute variables is very small, especially when the population analyzed is fairly homogeneous with respect to age.

As this summary shows, research on the relationship between women's household and market activities has benefited from the NLS data on mature women. We note that far more attention has been devoted to the labor allocation of married women than to the social forces that operate on single women. We are unaware of any research based on the NLS data that studies the relationship between single women's participation in the labor force and their decision to marry and choice of partner. Furthermore, we feel that the postsecondary educational attainment of women is an aspect of behavior that is still only vaguely understood. Research that delineates the multiple motivations behind such educational acquisition should be part of the social science agenda of the 1980s.

Labor Demand

Survey data on the socioeconomic attributes of individuals seem ideally suited for research on labor supply, labor force participation, and human capital models of individual status attainment. Moreover, the NLS data on mature women have provided the basis for considerable normal-science research in those areas. In recent years, however, social scientists have debated the appropriate representation of demand or structural determinants of social processes. A number of labor market theories have been offered to explain socioeconomic inequality (Doeringer and Piore, 1971; Edwards, Reich, and Gordon, 1975; Thurow, 1975). Radical and Marxist theories of socioeconomic inequality study phenomena such as conflicts between interest groups, class domination, and exploitation (Bonacich, 1976; Bowles and Gintis, 1975; Gordon, 1972; Wright and Perrone, 1977). These approaches often stress the importance of the attributes of jobs and their arrangement in an occupational hierarchy.

For example, according to dual labor market theory, women and minority groups are often confined to the secondary job sector, in which workers obtain lower wages, have less opportunity for career advancement, and receive lower returns for their productive capabilities. Discrimination against specific groups is typically assessed by decomposing group differences in socioeconomic success into three components: a portion attributed to differential individual human-capital endowments and other predetermined personal characteristics, a portion attributed to discrimination from differential returns to those characteristics, and a residual differential attributed to direct discrimination. A direct stratification of a sample of individuals into labor market sectors on the basis of occupation or industry can provide a somewhat more direct test of dual hypotheses, but biases may be introduced if the sample is stratified on an endogenous variable (Cain, 1976). Both techniques have been used with the NLS data.

Sex Discrimination in the Labor Market. The hypothesis that discrimination channels women into occupations that offer lower wages, fewer opportunities for advancement, and lower return to workers' human-capital investments, has been presented as an alternative to neoclassical human-capital explanations for sexual differences in labor market experience. The NLS data on mature women have been used as evidence to support both views. Polachek (1976, 1977) and Mincer and Polachek (1974), using the detailed labor force experience measures in the 1967 NLS mature women data, contend that sex differences in the labor market are largely due to the intermittent character of female participation in the labor force and the lower postschooling human-capital investments of women. Polachek further argues that occupational segregation by sex is a consequence of a rational choice by women who expect their participation in the labor force to be discontinuous. These women choose occupations characterized by less atrophy, that is, occupations in which the depreciation of human capital that occurs during interruptions is small.

Sandell and Shapiro (1976) point out an apparent misspecification by Mincer and Polachek (1974) and find that the human-capital depreciation incurred during time spent at home was substantially overstated. According to Sandell and Shapiro, sex discrimination plays a much larger role in the earnings gap, with perhaps a fourth of the gap attributable to the differential labor market experience of males and females.

Jusenius (1976) directly approaches the human-capital explanations of Polachek and others, specifying a wage model for NLS mature women (1972 data) stratified into three occupational segments according to skill. She reports that the higher the level of skill, the higher the returns to education and to recent and long-term experience, and the lower the disadvantage to a woman in a female sex-typed occupation. Women in the lowest strata are disadvantaged both in human-capital endowments and returns to those endowments. These results are presented to show that labor market segmentation, as defined by both skill level and occupational segregation by sex, produces an economic disadvantage to women over and above that due to discontinuous labor force participation.

Suter and Miller's (1973) study, one of the first studies using NLS data to examine sex discrimination, examines the following data: (1) NLS women aged thirty to forty-four in 1967; (2) NLS "career women" (women who worked at least six months in three fourths of the years since leaving school); (3) all men aged thirty to forty-four in the March 1967 Current Population Survey; (4) black men aged thirty to forty-four in the March 1967 Current Population Survey. They find that education, occupational status, and work experience explain more variation in income for women than for men. More specifically, there is less variation in income among women of the same education, occupational status, and experience than there is among men who are equivalent on the same attributes. Women receive lower returns to education and occupational status; 38 percent of the overall gap between mean income for men and women remains after controlling education, experience, and occupational status. Their analysis is largely descriptive and does not directly address the competing explanations of labor market outcomes for women.

In a replication and extension of the study by Suter and Miller (1973), Treiman and Terrell (1975) compare status attainment models of education and occupational prestige for working women (NLS mature women data) to similar models for men of the same age (data from the 1962 Occupational Changes in a Generation Survey, Blau and Duncan, 1967). They find the distribution of occupational prestige and years of schooling to be nearly identical for men and women, and the processes of attaining these outcomes quite similar. However, their research neither speaks to the different career choices, expectations, and aspirations young men and women make while in school, nor addresses occupational segregation by sex as manifest in intrafirm authority structures and internal labor markets.

Treiman and Terrell (1975) compare earnings functions for working NLS women and their husbands. Working white wives earn 42 percent as much as their husbands, working black wives, 54 percent. White working women obtain a return from years of schooling only one fourth as large as their husbands, and returns from occupational status about three fourths as large as their husbands. If the mean attributes of white husbands are applied to the equation for wives, the overall earnings gap is reduced by less than one half. However, they note that much of the differential return and residual gap could be attributable to family contingencies and decisions made within the household.

When the earnings functions of black working wives and their husbands are compared, the differences are not nearly as large as those detected for whites. Working black wives receive nearly the same return from education and hours usually worked as do their husbands, and actually receive a slightly higher return from occupational status. Differential endowments account for only about one third of the overall wage gap between working black wives and their husbands. Treiman and Terrell note that, overall, the earnings functions of both black wives and husbands fall about midway between those of white wives and the earnings functions of their husbands. They suggest that white wives appear to exercise the most discretion over whether to become committed to labor market or family activities.

Treiman and Terrell thus show that black and white mature women have qualitatively different labor market experiences. Hudis (1977) and Mincer and Polachek (1974), also using the 1967 data, replicate the finding that black women receive greater returns from education. However, working black women acquire less education, are in lower-status jobs, and earn less on average than white women. Consequently, "only those few black women who have managed to surmount their problems of background and discrimination and acquire an occupation equal to that of the average woman attain comparable income" (Treiman and Terrell, 1975, p. 192). Hudis (1977) presents evidence that suggests that the greater returns from education and occupational status occur primarily among black women with more labor market experience. Of course, the greater return from education and occupation among black women could be interpreted in the opposite direction—a black woman with one less year of education or one less unit of occupational status is marginally disadvantaged more than a comparable white woman. Black women applying for better-paying jobs may be more closely screened with respect to education and occupation than are white women.

Intergenerational Mobility of Women. The influence of social origins on the socioeconomic success of women has received little attention in the past decade. One reason for the scarcity of research on the intergenerational mobility of women is that there exist few data sets appropriate for such research. Perhaps more importantly, sociologists have been reluctant to address the conceptual problems of incorporating family decision-making processes and the structure of job opportunities for women into models of mobility.

Among the few studies that examine the occupational mobility of women are two, primarily descriptive, that use the NLS data on mature women. Tyree and Treas (1974) use 1967 data to replicate their findings, obtained from other data, on marital mobility. They find that the marital mobility patterns of women (from parental head of household's occupation to husband's occupation) are more similar to the intergenerational occupational mobility patterns of men than they are to the mobility patterns of women. Men and women differ more in their respective occupational destinations than in their destinations in marriage, and "about twice as many working women would have to change jobs as wives would have to change husbands for the two sexes to have the same mobility matrices" (p. 300). Rosenfeld (1978) uses the same data to show that mother's occupation, as well as father's occupation, influences the mobility patterns of women. While both studies suggest role modeling and occupational segregation as underlying mechanisms, these concepts are not incorporated into the analyses.

Labor Demand and Structural Factors. Several demand or structural perspectives have not been applied to research based upon the NLS data. Very little research focuses explicitly on job competition, queuing mechanisms for rationing jobs, screening, and signalling processes. The few exceptions include descriptive papers on job rationing by Furstenberg and Thrall (1975) and by Thrall and Furstenberg (1975). While screening hypotheses are admittedly difficult to test (Cain, 1976; Lazear, 1977), some explicit conceptual models have been proposed (Spence, 1973; Starrett, 1976), and Thurow (1975) suggests how queuing processes and statistical discrimination result in labor market disadvantages for women. Since the NLS data contain considerable information on the process whereby individuals search for and acquire jobs, they provide an opportunity for a major empirical contribution to research in this area.

Issues of labor supply and labor demand intersect in the areas of unemployment, job separation, and job search. The two recessions of the 1970s and the high rates of unemployment experienced in times of high aggregate demand have stimulated considerable empirical research about the nature of unemployment and its relation to levels of unemployment benefits. But little of this research has focused upon the unemployment experience of women. Indeed, the research has yet to contribute significantly to our understanding of unemployment among men, and the conceptual and methodological complications introduced by the more frequent entrance and exit from the labor force among women makes the successful modeling of female unemployment seem intractable at present. Nevertheless, Sandell (1977) and Furstenberg and Thrall (1975) use NLS data on mature women in two exploratory attempts to approach this issue.

The detailed information on unionization in the NLS data on mature women has yet to be studied. Many widely used surveys, such as the census and Current Population Surveys, provide no information on unionization, while others simply provide an indicator of labor union membership. But since 1971, the NLS data on mature women indicate whether earnings are set by a collective bargaining agreement, whether the respondent is a member of the union, and the type of union that negotiates the agreement. However, effective analysis of the unionization data for mature women may be difficult. In assessments of the effects of unionization from microsurvey data, there often exists an implicit assumption of historical equilibrium. This assumption is particularly problematic for the kinds of jobs typically held by women. For example, white-collar jobs in the public sector may have recently become unionized because of low wages, and the resulting effect of such unionization on the market may not yet be fully established. In contrast, many private-sector industrial unions may be far past that stage. In the blue-collar private sector, observed wage differentials are more likely to reflect the activities of unions. While earnings functions incorporating this dynamic dimension of unionization might be considerably more complex, they would also be more convincing. Studies based on a dynamic mode could use the longitudinal NLS data to examine the long-term effects of unionization on wages and other job-related rewards.

Finally, we know very little about the processes by which women are recruited into or excluded from positions of authority. Access to authority hierarchies should have a central place in a comprehensive structural explanation of sex discrimination, but the NLS does not collect information on respondents' position in an authority hierarchy. We hope that future editions of the surveys include measures of this characteristic.

Methodological Research on Subsample Selectivity Bias

NLS data on mature women have been used in the exposition of recently developed techniques for assessing the effects of subsample selectivity bias in estimating models of labor market processes. A problem encountered in the estimation of labor supply and wage equations for women is that no wage is observed for nonworking women. Heckman (1974b, 1976; see also 1974a) developed a procedure for estimating the probability that a woman works, her labor and offered wage supply function, and the asking wage for a woman who does not work. He estimated a model for mature white women living with their spouses (NLS 1967 data) and compared his results to conventional estimates based on the subsample of working women. Conventional estimates appear to understate the effect of young children on labor supply (asking wage) and the effect of educational and work experience on offered wages. Heckman (1976) uses some alternative estimation techniques which show that the wage equation is only minimally affected by sample selectivity, but the supply equation is greatly affected by it. Fligstein and Wolf (1978) apply Heckman's technique to the same NLS data in order to determine whether sample selection biased the finding that occupational attainment equations of men and women are quite similar. However, the inclusion of women who did not find jobs commensurate with their training and background had only minimal effects.

While the technique for assessing subsample selectivity bias generalizes to other areas, Heckman's exposition within the context of a household decision-making model is particularly important for analyzing the labor market experiences of women. Failure to account for the effects of subsample selection on the decision to enter the labor force is a potential problem in virtually all existing research on the socioeconomic attainments of women. Heckman's technique, substantively grounded in a theory of household decision making, merits more attention in research on the labor market experiences of women.

Use of the NLS Data on Mature Women

The longitudinal nature of the NLS data should be more fully exploited by researchers. The longitudinal aspect has not been overlooked for lack of appropriate substantive conceptualization; life-cycle and developmental perspectives are central to economic, sociological, and psychological theories of individual labor market behavior. Rather analysts seem to lack (or be unaware of) the appropriate methodologies for analyzing panel data. Perhaps social scientists have become too comfortable interpreting cross-sectional differences among individuals as confirmation of longitudinal processes. The current availability of NLS data with observations at six points in time and the increased sophistication of structural equation representations of market theories should provide an incentive for the application of longitudinal analyses.

Of course, the substantive context of the analysis determines which specific variables are examined. For example, researchers using analytically powerful human-capital models emphasize data on schooling, ability, experience, and wages. Human-capital models that incorporate training other than schooling, labor market information, and socioeconomic origins have been empirically tested with NLS data. Similarly, variables relevant to family decision making have been well exploited in studies of household labor supply. But—surprisingly— detailed information quite relevant to contemporary economic and sociological theories of labor market behavior has been virtually ignored. We have seen no analyses that use the expanded information on health, available for the mature women cohort beginning in 1971, yet physical health would seem to be a crucial factor in determining the depreciation of human capital. Nor have we seen any analysis of determinants of individual or household demand for health care.

Although data are currently available for the cohort of mature women surveyed in 1967 and 1974, few researchers have examined aging as a developmental process. The longitudinal information on economic, physical, and social psychological well-being, future job plans, and financial assets all merit investigation.

The designers of the NLS included the mature women cohort because they anticipated that this group would have unique labor market problems in the 1960s and 1970s. While the extensive analyses conducted by the CHRR staff provide insights into the history of the cohort, other researchers have offered few analyses of the social demography of the cohort. The social policy concerns that shaped the design of the NLS surveys appear to have failed to motivate analysts to integrate those concerns in their research, although this is perhaps less true of the surveys of women than those of men. We agree that these areas have important implications for manpower and other social policy issues. Unfortunately, social scientists working within specific and well-developed research paradigms may not have the insight, incentive, or even ability to incorporate those areas into their empirical research.

As noted earlier, to analyze issues in labor demand and sex discrimination using social survey data on individuals is often difficult. This statement certainly applies to the NLS data, which seem deficient in certain respects. For example, in order to examine how individuals enter the labor force and move up authority hierarchies, analysts require information on job characteristics and the work setting, variables that the NLS does not measure. Longitudinal data on promotions, supervisory responsibilities, job autonomy, and decision-making capacities would allow researchers to empirically test some dual or segmented labor market hypotheses. Furthermore, such data might allow an empirical assessment of the degree to which occupational segregation by sex is attributable to individual occupational choice rather than to employer's or employee's decisions.

Even in research areas that are well defined and adequately covered by the NLS, some questionnaire items are at variance with corresponding substantive concepts. A particularly important example is the assessment of labor market experience. The measure of general labor market experience prior to the initial survey for the cohort of mature women has some undesirable properties. Respondents were asked to report the number of years in which they worked at least six months. If total weeks of experience is an appropriate indicator, then the NLS item will tend to have errors that are positively correlated with true experience. For example, women who consistently work between twenty-seven and fifty-one weeks a year will have their experience overstated, since they will be attributed a full year of experience, while those who consistently work between one and twenty-five weeks a year will have theirs understated, since they will be attributed no experience. A less serious problem is the measure of employer-specific experience or job tenure of the first job after leaving school. The first job for young men and women and mature men is defined as the first job after schooling that was held for at least a month. For never-married mature women with no children, it is the first job held at least six months. For women who did marry and for never-married women with children, the first job is not assessed.

Finally, users of the NLS data would benefit from a comprehensive review of the reliability of the most important and most frequently used measures. Although the data have been analyzed by many researchers over a span of nearly seven years, we have at best only impressionistic notions of the reliability of even the most basic items, such as years of schooling, job experience, and income.

What will be the research issues of the 1980s? One of the most important substantive topics for the 1980s, in our view, is the family. Research addressing the developing social forces that affect the family requires a greater understanding of its internal decision-making processes with respect to labor supply, allocation of resources, marriage, and divorce. Related policy issues concern public assistance, child care, and educational policy. A second important substantive topic is the institutional constraints on the demand for labor. Occupational segregation and labor market discrimination by race and sex, and the matching of individuals to jobs are still only vaguely understood by social scientists. Related policy issues are affirmative action, corporate promotion policies, unemployment, and the creation of public-sector jobs. Topics relevant to these issues include the social demography of successive cohorts over time, technological change, and institutional responses to these developments. The NLS provides vital information on all these issues, as shown in our review of research on the first five years of panel data.

Social programs to ameliorate the disadvantages faced by women entering the labor force and on the job can be better designed and evaluated when informed by sound research on the labor market experiences of women. Indeed, the kind of longitudinal analyses that can be conducted with the NLS data should be particularly useful. For example, we will better understand the demand for effective childcare programs if we disentangle the effects of familial constraints, spouse's income, and wage rates on labor supply. Research on the relative contributions of investments in human capital, occupational segregation, and wage discrimination to women's career and income opportunities will facilitate an assessment of the relative effectiveness of training programs for women compared to more direct intervention by employers. Some of the best social science research to date on labor supply and, to a lesser extent, labor demand has been based on analyses of the NLS data on mature women. However, as we noted earlier, the more substantive or theoretical research has not been applied to questions about the design and evaluation of social policy and programs. As the problems of women in the labor market become increasingly important to policy makers, they will almost certainly rely more heavily on the burgeoning social science research in program design and evaluation.

It would be presumptuous of us to prescribe the research that our colleagues should undertake in the next decade. However, our survey of an extensive body of research can form a basis for future investigations, and we hope that researchers consider the themes we have discussed as they pursue their investigations. We hope our report will encourage social scientists to give greater consideration to adopting the NLS in their empirical research.

References

Andrisani, P. J., and others. *Work Attitudes and Labor Market Experience: Evidence from the National Longitudinal Surveys.* Report No. DLMA 21-42-75-06. Unpublished final report, U.S. Department of Labor, 1977.

Bahr, S. J. "The Effects of Income and Age at Marriage on Marital Stability." Unpublished manuscript, Department of Child Development and Family Relations, Brigham Young University, n.d.a.

Bahr, S. J. "The Effects of Income and Assets on Marital Instability. A Longitudinal Analysis." Unpublished manuscript, Department of Child Development and Family Relations, Brigham Young University, n.d.b.

Becker, G. S. "A Theory of Marriage: Part I." *Journal of Political Economy*, 1973, *81*, 813–846.

Becker, G. S. "A Theory of Marriage: Part II." *Journal of Political Economy*, 1974, *82*, 511–527.

Becker, G. S., Landes, E. M., and Michael, R. T. "An Economic Analysis of Marital Instability." *Journal of Political Economy*, 1977, *85*, 1141–1187.

Becker, G. S., and Lewis, H. G. "On the Interaction Between the Quantity and Quality of Children." *Journal of Political Economy*, 1973, *81*, 279–288.

Benham, L. "Benefits of Women's Education Within Marriage." *Journal of Political Economy*, 1974, *82*, 557–571.

Bielby, W. T., Hawley, C. B., and Bills, D. *Research Uses of the National Longitudinal Surveys.* Manpower Research Monograph, U.S. Department of Labor. Washington, D.C.: U.S. Government Printing Office, 1979.

Blau, P. M., and Duncan, O. D. *The American Occupational Structure.* New York: Wiley, 1967.

Bonacich, E. "Advanced Capitalism and Black/White Race Relations in the United States: A Split Labor Market Interpretation." *American Sociology Review*, 1976, *41*, 34–51.

Bowen, G., and Finegan, T. A. *The Economics of Labor Force Participation.* Princeton, N.J.: Princeton University Press, 1969.

Bowles, S., and Gintis, H. *Schooling in Capitalist America.* New York: Basic Books, 1975.

Cain, G. G. *Married Women in the Labor Force.* Chicago: University of Chicago Press, 1976.

Cain, G. G., and Dooley, M. D. "Estimation of a Model of Labor Supply, Fertility, and Wages of Married Women." *Journal of Political Economy*, 1976, *84*, 1179–1199.

Center for Human Resource Research. *The National Longitudinal Surveys Handbook.* Columbus: Ohio State University, 1976.

Cherlin, A. *Economics, Social Roles, and Marital Separation.* Paper presented at the meeting of the American Sociological Association, New York City, September 1976a.

Cherlin, A. "Social and Economic Determinants of Marital Separation." Unpublished doctoral dissertation, Department of Sociology, University of California at Los Angeles, 1976b.

Cherlin, A. "The Effect of Children on Marital Dissolution." *Demography*, 1977, *14*, 265–272.

Cogan, J. F. *Labor Supply and the Value of the Housewife's Time.* Report Number R-1461. Santa Monica, Calif.: RAND Corporation, 1975.

DeTray, D. N. "Child Quality and the Demand for Children." *Journal of Political Economy*, 1973, *81*(2),170–195.

Director, S. M. "Underadjustment Bias in the Evaluation of Manpower Training." *Evaluation Quarterly*, 1979, *3*, 190–218.

Doeringer, P., and Piore, M. *Internal Labor Markets and Manpower Analysis.* Lexington, Mass.: Heath, 1971.

Edwards, R. C., Reich, M., and Gordon, D. M. (Eds.). *Labor Market Segmentation.* Lexington, Mass.: Heath, 1975.

Fleisher, B. M. "Mother's Home Time and the Production of Child Quality." *Demography*, 1977, *14*, 197–212.

Fleisher, B. M., Parsons, D. O., and Porter, R. D. "Assets Adjustment and Labor Supply of Older Workers." In G. G. Cain and H. W. Watts (Eds.), *Income Maintenance and Labor Supply.* Chicago: Rand McNally, 1973.

Fleisher, B. M., and Rhodes, G. F. "Fertility, Women's Wage Rates, and Labor Supply." *American Economic Review*, 1979, *69*, 14–24.

Fligstein, N., and Wolf, W. "Sex Similarities in Occupational Status Attainment: Are the Results Due to the Restriction of the Sample to Employed Women?" *Social Science Research*, 1978, *7*, 197–212.

Furstenberg, F. F., and Thrall, C. A. "Counting the Jobless: The Impact of Job Rationing on the Measurement of Unemployment." *Annals of the American Academy of Political and Social Sciences*, 1975, *418*, 45–59.

Gordon, D. M. *Theories of Poverty and Underemployment.* Lexington, Mass.: Heath, 1972.

Greenberg, D. H. *Problems of Model Specification and Measurement: The Labor Supply Function.* Report No. R-1085-EDA. Santa Monica, Calif.: RAND Corporation, 1972.

Heckman, J. R. "Effects of Child-Care Programs on Women's Work Effort." *Journal of Political Economy*, 1974a, *82*(2), 1136–1163.

Heckman, J. R. "Shadow Prices, Market Wages, and Labor Supply." *Econometrica*, 1974b, *42*, 679–694.

Heckman, J. R. "The Common Structure of Statistical Models of Truncation, Sample Selection, and Limited Dependent Variables and a Simple Estimator for Such Models." *Annals of Economic and Social Measurement,* 1976, 5, 475–492.

Heckman, J. R., and Willis, R. J. "Reply to Mincer and Ofek." *Journal of Political Economy,* 1979, 87, 203–211.

Hill, C. R., and Stafford, F. P. "Allocation of Time to Preschool Children and Educational Opportunity." *Journal of Human Resources,* 1974, 9, 323–341.

Hudis, P. M. "Commitment to Work and Wages." *Sociology of Work and Occupations,* 1977, 4, 123–146.

Hyman, H. H. *Secondary Analysis of Sample Surveys: Principles, Procedures, and Potentialities.* New York: Wiley, 1971.

Jusenius, C. L. "The Influence of Work Experience, Skill Requirement, and Occupational Segregation on Women's Earnings." *Journal of Economics and Business,* 1976, 29, 107–115.

Jusenius, C. L., and Shortlidge, R. *Dual Careers.* Vol. 3. Columbus: Center for Human Resource Research, Ohio State University, 1975.

Kim, S. *Determinants of Labor Force Participation of Married Women 30 to 44 Years of Age.* Columbus: Center for Human Resource Research, Ohio State University, 1972.

Kniesner, T. J. "Fertility, Marital Instability, and Alimony." Paper presented at the meeting of the Southern Economic Association, Atlanta, 1976a.

Kniesner, T. J. "An Indirect Test of Complementarity in Family Labor Supply Models." *Econometrica,* 1976b, 44(4), 651–669.

Lazear, E. "Academic Achievement and Job Performance: Note." *American Economic Review,* 1977, 67, 252–254.

Leibowitz, A. "Home Investments in Children." *Journal of Political Economy,* 1974, 82, 111–131.

Lewis, H. G. "Hours of Work and Hours of Leisure." *Proceedings of the Ninth Annual Meeting of the I.R.R.A.* Madison: University of Wisconsin-Madison, 1956.

Low, S., and Spindler, P. G. *Childcare Arrangements of Working Mothers in the United States.* Washington, D.C.: Children's Bureau, Department of Health, Education, and Welfare; and Women's Bureau, Department of Labor, 1968.

Meyer, J. A. "The Impact of Welfare Benefit Levels and Tax Rates on the Labor Supply of Poor Women." *Review of Economics and Statistics,* 1975, 57, 236–238.

Mincer, J. "Labor Force Participation of Married Women." In H. G. Lewis (Ed.), *Aspects of Labor Economics.* Princeton, N. J.: Princeton University Press, 1962.

Mincer, J., and Ofek, H. "The Distribution of Lifetime Labor Force Participation of Married Women: Comment." *Journal of Political Economy,* 1979, 87, 197–202.

Mincer, J., and Polachek, S. W. "Family Investments in Human Capital: Earnings of Women." *Journal of Political Economy,* 1974, *82,* 176–1108.

Parnes, H. S., and others. *Dual Careers.* Vol. 4. Columbus: Center for Human Resource Research, Ohio State University, 1975.

Polachek, S. W. "Occupational Segregation Among Women: An Alternative Hypothesis." *Journal of Contemporary Business,* 1976, *5,* 1–12.

Polachek, S. W. "Occupational Segregation Among Women: A Human Capital Approach." Unpublished manuscript, Department of Economics, University of North Carolina, 1977.

Rosen, H. S. "Tax Illusion and the Labor Supply of Married Women." *Review of Economics and Statistics,* 1976a, *58,* 167–172.

Rosen, H. S. "Taxes in a Labor Supply Model with Joint Wage-Hours Determination." *Econometrica,* 1976b, *44,* 485–507.

Rosenberg, H. M. *The Influence of Fertility Strategies on the Labor-Force Status of American Wives.* Columbus: Center for Human Resource Research, Ohio State University, 1972.

Rosenfeld, R. A. "Intergenerational Occupational Mobility of Women." *American Sociological Review,* 1978, *43,* 35–46.

Ross, H. L., and Sawhill, I. S. *Time of Transition: The Growth of Families Headed by Women.* Washington, D.C.: Urban Institute, 1975.

Sandell, S. H. "Attitudes Toward Market Work and the Effect of Wage Rates on the Lifetime Labor Supply of Married Women." *Journal of Human Resources,* 1977,*12,* 379–386.

Sandell, S. H., and Shapiro, D. *The Theory of Human Capital and the Earnings of Women: A Reexamination of the Evidence.* Columbus: Center for Human Resource Research, Ohio State University, 1976.

Sandell, S. H., and Shapiro, D. *Women's Incorrect Expectations and Their Labor Market Consequences.* Paper presented at the annual meeting of the Western Economic Association, Anaheim, Calif., 1977.

Schultz, T. W. (Ed.). *The Economics of the Family: Marriage, Children, and Human Capital.* Chicago: University of Chicago Press, 1974.

Sexton, P. C. *Women and Work.* Washington, D.C.: U.S. Department of Labor, 1977.

Shea, J. R. "Welfare Mothers: Barriers to Labor Force Entry." *Journal of Human Resources,* 1973, *8,* supplement, 90–102.

Shea, J. R., Kim, S., and Roderick, R. D. *Dual Careers.* Vol. 2. Washington, D.C.: U.S. Government Printing Office, 1973.

Shea, J. R., Spitz, R. S., and Zeller, F. A. *Dual Careers*. Vol. 1. Columbus: Center for Human Resource Research, Ohio State University, 1970.

Shortlidge, R. L., and Brito, P. *How Women Arrange for the Care of Their Children While They Work: A Study of Child Care Arrangements, Costs, and Preferences in 1971*. Columbus: Center for Human Resource Research, Ohio State University, 1977.

Shortlidge, R. L., Waite, L. J., and Suter, L. E. "Changes in Child Care Arrangements of Working Women: 1965–1971." *1974 Proceedings of the Business and Economics Statistics Section of the American Statistical Association*, Washington, D.C.: American Statistical Association, 1975.

Smith, J. P. *Assets, Savings, and Labor Supply*. Report No. P-5470-1. Santa Monica, Calif.: RAND Corporation, 1976.

Spence, M. A. "Job Market Signaling." *Quarterly Journal of Economics*, 1973, *87*, 355–374.

Starrett, D. "Social Institutions, Imperfect Information, and the Distribution of Income." *Quarterly Journal of Economics*, 1976, *90*, 261–284.

Suter, L. E., and Miller, H. P. "Income Differences Between Men and Career Women." *American Journal of Sociology*, 1973, *78*, 962–974.

Thrall, C. A., and Furstenberg, F. F. *The Rationing of Jobs: Consequences for Women Who Want to Work*. Paper presented at the 70th annual meeting of the American Sociological Association, San Francisco, August 1975.

Thurow, L. C. *Generating Inequality*. New York: Basic Books, 1975.

Treiman, D.J., and Terrell, K. "Sex and the Process of Status Attainment: A Comparison of Working Women and Men." *American Sociological Review*, 1975, *40*, 174–200.

Tyree, A., and Treas, J. J. "The Occupational and Marital Mobility of Women." *American Sociological Review*, 1974, *39*, 293–302.

U.S. Department of Labor. *Dual Careers: A Longitudinal Study of Labor Market Experience of Women*. Manpower Research Monograph Number 21. Washington, D.C.: U.S. Department of Labor.

Willis, R. J. "A New Approach to the Economic Theory of Fertility Behavior." *Journal of Political Economy*, 1973, *81*, 14–64.

Wortman, P. M., Reichardt, C. S., and St. Pierre, R. G. "The First Year of the Education Voucher Demonstration: A Secondary Analysis of Student Achievement Test Scores." *Evaluation Quarterly*, 1978, *2*, 193–214.

Wright, E. O., and Perrone, L. "Marxist Class Categories and Income Inequality." *American Sociological Review*, 1977, *42*, 32–55.

Name Index

A

Acton, J. P., 220, 222
Ahtola, O. T., 318, 321
Akers, R., 49
Alexander, L., 21n
Alvarez, H., III, 219, 223
Ambacher, B. I., 10, 34–42, 82
Andrews, F., 47
Andrisani, P. J., 365, 381
Antonoplos, D., x
Appelbaum, M. I., 326, 339–340
Atkin, C., 232, 235

B

Bahr, S. J., 372, 382
Bailey, J. S., 219, 224
Baird, L. L., 201, 210
Baldus, D. C., 15, 17, 145n, 154, 156–157, 161, 262, 263, 274–275, 276, 277, 278, 279n, 280, 281
Bargman, R. E., 165, 191
Barnow, B. S., 3, 17
Becker, G. S., 368, 371, 382
Bejar, I. I., 16, 294–308

Bell, A. G., 6
Bem, D. J., 330, 338
Benham, L., 382
Bentler, P. M., 15, 17, 165, 180, 191
Berger, D. E., 58, 66
Berk, R. A., 6, 20
Bernier, L., 97, 141
Bielby, W. T., 17, 364–386
Bills, D., 365, 382
Birnbaum, A., 289, 292
Blau, P. M., 137, 374, 382
Block, M., 48
Bloom, B. S., 196, 208
Bloom, H. S., 214, 222
Blumenthal, M., 47
Blumstein, A., 46, 49
Bock, R. D., 165, 191, 284, 285, 289, 292, 302, 307, 326, 327, 329, 338
Boeckmann, M. E., 17, 341–355
Bonacich, E., 373, 382
Bond, E., x
Bonnen, J., 10, 21n
Borchard, E. M., 4, 17
Borgatta, E. F., 137
Borko, H., 97, 141

Boruch, R. F., ix-x, 1-20, 34, 42, 57, 66, 70, 71, 82, 112, 123, 141, 163, 164, 191, 225, 235, 327, 329, 339, 353, 355, 357, 359, 362
Borus, M. E., 362
Bowen, G., 366, 382
Bowers, W. J., 15, 237-281
Bowker, R. R., 126
Bowles, S., 373, 382
Brehm, J. W., 330, 338
Brito, P., 369, 386
Brody, B. D., 310-311, 320
Brody, N., 310-311, 320
Broman, S. H., 311, 312, 320
Brophy, J. E., 69, 82, 196, 208
Brown, W., 201, 208
Bryant, F. B., 34, 41, 71, 82
Burstein, L., 14, 194-211
Buss, W. C., 144n, 157-158, 161

C

Cain, G. G., 3, 17, 18, 366, 368, 373, 376, 382
Campbell, D. T., 3, 18, 70, 163n, 164, 191-192, 225, 235, 324, 327, 328, 329, 339, 341n, 342, 352-353, 355, 357, 359, 362
Capell, F., 197, 201, 208
Caplan, N., 23, 32
Carr, A., 237n
Carr-Hill, R. A., 279, 281
Cautley, P. W., 137
Cecil, J. S., 2, 17
Chambers, E., 237n
Champagne, A. S., 47, 48
Charren, P., 232, 235
Chelimsky, E., 6, 18
Cherlin, A., 371, 382-383
Chibucos, T. R., 327, 340
Ciarlo, J. A., 218, 223
Clark, D. H., 312-314, 320-321
Clemence, T., 21n
Cline, M. D., 196, 209
Cobb, L. A., 219, 223
Cochran, W. G., 327, 339
Cogan, J. F., 383
Cohen, A. R., 330, 338
Cohen, J., 46, 49, 213, 216, 217, 223
Cohen, M. R., 149, 161

Cole, J. W. L., 15, 17, 145n, 154, 156-157, 161, 262, 263, 274-275, 276, 277, 278, 279n, 280, 281
Cole, N. S., 146, 161
Coleman, J. S., 41, 72, 81, 82, 195, 209, 337, 339
Comber, L. C., 209
Conlisk, J., 343, 355
Conolley, E. S., 337, 339
Conry, J., 311, 320
Cook, T. D., 3, 15, 16, 18, 77, 82, 324, 339, 341n
Cooley, T. F., 359, 363
Cooper, J., 264, 281
Cordray, D. S., ix-x, 1-20, 58, 66
Crick, F., 4, 6
Cronbach, L. J., 3, 14, 18, 195, 196, 197, 198, 203, 209, 288
Cuzzort, R. P., 197, 209

D

Datta, L., 4, 18
David, M., 114, 118, 122, 141
de Finetti, F., 145, 161
Del Bene, L., 6, 18
DeTray, D. N., 368, 383
Deutscher, I., 80, 82
Dever, R., 311, 320
Dickinson, P., 137
Director, S. M., 17, 356-363, 365, 383
Dodd, S. A., 84n, 89, 91, 94, 95, 125-126, 141
Doeringer, P., 373, 383
Dollar, C. M., 10, 34-42, 82
Dooley, M. D., 368, 382
Drabman, R. S., 231, 235
Duncan, B. D., 197, 209
Duncan, J. W., 85, 141
Duncan, O. D., 137, 165, 192, 197, 209, 374, 382
Dyer, J., 229-231, 236

E

Edwards, R. C., 373, 383
Ehrlich, I., 15, 18, 46, 47, 237-260, 262-282
Eimermann, T., 48
Elias, P. J., 202, 210
Emlet, H. E., 215, 223

Engelmann, S., 214, 221, 223
Erickson, E., 229–230, 235
Erlebacher, A., 3, 18, 164, 192

F

Fair, R. C., 264–265
Fawcett, S. B., 218, 221, 223
Featherman, D. L., 89, 137
Feige, E. L., 209
Feinberg, S., 49
Fellegi, I., 21n
Felson, M., 167, 192
Feshbach, S., 231–232, 235
Fifer, G., 312–314, 320–321
Figueroa, R. A., 314, 315, 317, 318, 319, 320
Finegan, T. A., 366, 382
Finn, J. D., 327, 339
Fischer, K., 195, 198, 208
Fishbein, M., 36, 42
Fleisher, B. M., 279, 281, 367–368, 383
Fligstein, N., 378, 383
Foster, B., 68n, 341n
Freedman, J., 219, 223
Freeman, J., 210
Furstenberg, F. F., 376, 377, 383, 386

G

Galileo, G., 4
Gallagher, L., x
Garner, J., 10, 43–49
Gates, W., 114, 141
Gerard, D. S., 323, 335, 339
Gerard, H. B., 12, 16, 18, 68, 69, 70, 71, 73, 74, 75, 76, 82, 83, 323, 324, 325, 326, 328, 336, 337, 339, 340
Gibbs, G., 279, 281
Gilbert, J. P., 225, 235
Gintis, H., 373, 382
Glass, G. V., 4, 14, 18–19, 20, 204, 205, 209, 210, 216, 224, 336, 339, 342, 347, 349, 350, 355
Glendening, L., 196, 204, 209
Gold, M., 47
Goldstein, M. J., 318, 321
Gomez, H., 16, 283–293, 295, 297, 302, 307, 322n
Good, T. L., 69, 82
Gordon, D. M., 373, 383

Gordon, N., 231, 236
Goulet, R. L., 287, 292
Graves, S., 231, 236
Green, C., 343, 355
Green, D., 323, 335, 339
Greenberg, D. H., 366, 383
Gruder, C. L., 15, 16, 18, 77, 82

H

Hagen, E., 310, 321
Hall, J. A., 213, 223
Haner, N., 49
Haney, W., 195, 196, 209
Hannon, M. T., 195, 210
Hanratty, M. A., 231, 235
Hauser, R. M., 89, 137
Havelock, R. G., 136, 141
Havens, H. S., 11, 50–56
Hawley, C. B., 17, 364–386
Hawley, W. D., 78, 82
Heber, R., 311, 320
Heckman, J. R., 369, 370, 378, 383–384
Heddesheimer, W. J., 36, 42
Hedrick, T. E., 34, 42, 57, 66, 70, 71, 82, 112, 123, 141
Henderson, R. D., 69, 82
Hendrick, I. G., 336, 339
Hendricks, M., 12, 68–83
Herner, S., 63, 66
Hill, C. R., 384
Holther, J., x
Hopkins, K. D., 204, 210
Hops, H., 217, 224
House, E. R., 3, 19
Hudis, P. M., 375, 384
Hyman, H. H., 364, 384

I

Ismael, Rabbi, 6

J

Jabine, T., 21n
Jackson, G., 3, 19
Jackson, T. D., 337, 339
Jeffrey, R. W., 216, 223
Jensen, A. R., 314, 315, 317, 318, 319, 320
Jipson, F. J., 314, 321

Johnson, D., 88, 141
Johnson, E. B., 74, 75, 76, 83, 336, 337, 339
Johnson, S., 57
Johnston, J., 249, 260, 267, 270, 281
Jones, H. G., 35, 42
Jöreskog, K. G., 76, 83, 165, 175, 176, 186, 192, 193, 284, 292
Jurs, S. G., 342, 347, 349, 350, 355
Jusenius, C. L., 365, 374, 384

K

Kahn, R., 47
Kaplan, B. J., 294, 306, 307
Karni, E., 259, 260
Kazarian, R., 237n
Keesling, J. W., 195, 210
Keeves, J. P., 209
Kelling, G. W., 221, 223
Kennedy, W. A., 311, 312, 320
Kenny, D. A., 327, 339
Kephart, C., 318, 320
Kerlinger, F. H., 165, 192
Kilo, C., 15, 19
Kim, S., 365, 367, 384, 385
Kirk, R. F., 349, 355
Klecka, W., 48, 49
Klitgaard, R. E., 200–201, 210
Kniesner, T. J., 368, 371, 384
Knudten, R., 49
Kobrin, S., 49
Koch, G., 49
Krislow, S., 45, 49
Kruzas, A. T., 60, 66
Kutscher, R., 21n

L

Lakin, P., 237n
Land, K. C., 167, 192
Landes, E. M., 371, 382
Lang, A. R., 222, 223
Lansing, J. B., 104–105, 112, 141
Lazear, E., 376, 384
Leibowitz, A., 384
Leifer, A., 231, 236
Lenihan, K. J., 6, 20
Lesser, C. S., 312–314, 320–321
Levin, B., 78, 82
Lewis, H. G., 368, 382, 384

Lewis, J., 11
Liefeld, J. P., 232, 236
Light, R. J., 4, 14, 19, 205, 210, 225–236
Lindley, D. V., 145, 148, 149, 151, 162
Lininger, A., 117, 143
Linn, R. L., 176, 192, 196, 197, 201, 202, 208, 210, 287, 292
Linsenmeier, J. A. W., 3, 12, 19, 68–83, 322, 339
Lipsey, M. W., 58, 66
Lipton, D., 221, 223
Loftin, C., 48
Lofton, J. D., Jr., 68, 83
Loftus, E. F., 4, 19
Lohnes, P., 200, 201, 210
Long, J. S., 165, 192
Lord, F. M., 151, 162, 289, 292, 310, 321
Low, S., 369, 384

M

McCall, R. B., 326, 339–340
McCoy, D. R., 35, 42
McDonald, F. J., 202, 210
McGuire, T. W., 359, 363
McKay, A., 295, 296, 307–308
McKay, H., 218, 223, 287, 289, 292, 295, 296, 297, 300, 307–308
McLaughlin, M. W., 19
McLean, J., 61, 67
McSweeney, A. J., 72, 83
Madden, N. A., 337, 340
Madison, J., 5
Magidson, J., 3, 15, 19, 163n, 175–176, 180, 181, 192, 335, 340
Mallar, C., 355
Mangum, G. L., 356, 357–359, 363
Marco, G. L., 210
Mark R., 262n, 264
Martinson, R., 221, 223
Maxwell, D., 279, 281
Mead, R. J., 287, 288, 293
Mednick, S. A., 49
Mercer, J., 71
Merrill, M. A., 310n, 321
Meyer, J. A., 370, 384
Meyer, J. W., 210
Michael, J., 214, 223
Michael, R. T., 371, 382
Milgram, S., 220, 223
Miller, H. P., 374, 386

Miller, J. P., 15, 19
Miller, L. B., 229-231, 236
Miller, L. K., 218, 221, 223
Miller, M. D., 14, 194-211
Miller, N., 12, 16, 18, 68, 69, 70, 71, 73
   74, 75, 76, 80-81, 82, 83, 323, 335,
   336, 337, 339, 340
Miller, R., 114, 141
Miller, W. B., 49
Mincer, J., 366, 367, 369, 373, 375,
   384-385
Minkin, N., 218, 223
Monkonnen, E., 48
Morgan, J. N., 104-105, 112, 141
Morrison, A., 23, 32
Moskowitz, J., 16, 322-340
Mosteller, F., 3, 19, 202, 210, 225, 235
Moynihan, D. P., 3, 19

N

Nagel, E., 149, 161
Nagel, S. S., 47, 48
Nagin, D., 46, 49
Neef, M., 48
Nichols, P. L., 311, 312, 320
Nickles, H., 68*n*
Novick, M. R., 13, 144-162, 310, 321

O

Ofek, H., 385
Orne, M. T., 221, 224

P

Palmer, A. M., 61, 66
Panchapakesan, N., 293
Parnes, H. S., 365, 385
Parsons, D. O., 383
Paskar, J., 61, 67
Passell, P., 279*n*, 281
Peck, J., 346, 355
Peckham, P. D., 204, 210
Pedhazur, E. J., 165, 192
Perline, R., 285, 292
Perrone, L., 373, 386
Phillips, L., 279, 281
Pierce, G. L., 15, 237-281
Pillemer, D. L., 14, 19, 225-236
Piore, M., 373, 383

Poirier, D., 355
Polachek, S. W., 369, 373, 374, 375,
   384, 385
Poor, D. D., 327, 340
Porter, A. C., 204, 209, 327, 340
Porter, R. D., 383
Prescott, E. C., 359, 363

R

Rasch, G., 284, 285, 286, 287, 289, 290,
   291, 292-293, 297, 308
Redfearn, D., 73, 83, 324, 325, 328, 340
Redner, R., 212, 224
Rees, A., 343, 344, 355
Reich, M., 373, 383
Reichardt, C. S., 3, 20, 77, 83, 322*n*,
   327, 329, 340, 362, 363, 365, 386
Reinbolt, K., 48
Reis, J., 57, 66
Reschly, J., 314, 317, 321
Rezmovic, V., 16, 163*n*, 288, 293,
   294-308
Rhodes, G. F., 368, 383
Riecken, H. W., 2, 19, 225, 236, 342,
   346, 355
Rindskopf, D. M., 5, 13, 14, 17, 19,
   163-193, 340
Robbin, A., 12, 84-143
Roberson, L. K., 21*n*
Robertson, T. S., 232, 236
Rock, D. A., 201, 210
Roderick, R. D., 365, 385
Roistacher, R. C., 44, 84*n*, 91, 94, 95,
   101, 105, 107, 108, 111, 112, 115,
   116, 117, 118, 120, 121, 142
Roos, L. L., 6, 19
Rosen, H. S., 371, 385
Rosenberg, H. M., 367, 385
Rosenfeld, R. A., 376, 385
Rosenshine, B. V., 203, 210
Rosenthal, R., 14, 20
Ross, H. L., 372, 385
Ross, J., 34, 42, 57, 66, 70, 71, 82, 112,
   123, 141, 163*n*
Rossi, P. H., 6, 20
Rossiter, J. R., 232, 236
Rottenberg, S., 279, 282
Rubin, D. B., 164, 192
Rubin, R. S., 232, 236

S

Sage, W., 69, 83
St. John, N. H., 68, 69, 83, 325–326, 335, 340
St. Pierre, R. G., 3, 20, 77, 83, 327, 329, 340, 362, 363, 365, 386
Saks, D. H., 201, 208
Samejima, F., 285–286, 289, 293
Sandell, S. H., 367, 369, 373–374, 377, 385
Sarson, E., 232, 235
Sawhill, I. S., 372, 385
Scheuerman, L., 49
Scheuren, F., 6, 18
Schmandt, J., 85, 142
Schoenfeldt, L. F., 58, 66
Schuessler, K. F., 239, 260, 274, 282
Schultz, T. W., 366, 368, 385
Sechrest, L., 14, 212–224, 225n
Sellin, T., 239, 260, 262, 271, 275–278, 280, 282
Settel, B., 91, 142
Sexton, P. C., 365, 385
Shapiro, D., 369, 373–374, 385
Shea, J. R., 365, 370–371, 385–386
Shortlidge, R. L., 365, 369–370, 384, 386
Silverstein, L., 48
Simpson, E. H., 149, 162
Singer, H., 324, 325, 328, 340
Singer, N. M., 214, 222
Singer, R. D., 231–232, 235
Sinisterra, L., 295, 296, 307–308
Skogan, W., 48
Slavin, R. E., 337, 340
Smigel-Leibowitz, A., 279, 282
Smith, C. P., 72, 83
Smith, I. D., 196, 209
Smith, J. P., 386
Smith, M. L., 4, 19, 20, 216, 224, 336, 339
Smith, P. V., 234, 236
Smith, W., 21n
Snow, R. E., 201, 210
Sörbom, D., 165, 176, 186, 192–193, 284, 292
Spence, M. A., 376, 386
Spindler, P. G., 369, 384
Spitz, R. S., 365, 386
Stafford, F. P., 384

Stalford, C., x
Stambaugh, R., 23, 32
Stanley, J. C., 204, 209, 324, 328, 339, 342, 352–353, 355
Starrett, D., 376, 386
Stebbins, L. B., 196, 203, 210
Stephan, W. G., 322, 326, 337, 340
Stern, N. H., 279, 281
Stufflebeam, D. L., 80, 83
Stunkard, A. J., 216, 223
Suppes, P., 3, 18
Suter, L. E., 369–370, 374, 386

T

Tatsuoka, M. M., 189, 193, 287, 292
Taylor, J., 279n, 281
Terman, L. M., 310n, 321
Terrell, K., 374–375, 386
Thomas, M. H., 231, 235
Thorndike, R. L., 310, 321
Thrall, C. A., 376, 377, 383, 386
Thurow, L. C., 373, 376, 386
Tirnan, T., 225n
Title, C. R., 279, 282
Treas, J. J., 376, 386
Treiman, D. J., 374–375, 386
Tribe, L. H., 158, 162
Trochim, W. M. K., 12, 57–67
Tuchfarber, A., 49
Tukey, J. W., 202, 210
Tyree, A., 376, 386

U

Unertl, K., 137
Useem, E., 68, 83

V

Vandaele, W., 267, 279, 282
Van De Riet, V., 311, 320
Van Dusen, R. A., 122, 143
Velluci, M. J., 63, 66
Votey, H. L., Jr., 279, 281

W

Wackman, D., 232, 236
Waite, C., 21n
Waite, L. J., 369–370, 386

Walker, H. M., 217, 224
Walsh, J. E., 204, 211
Ward, S., 232, 236
Warren, E., 322–323
Warren, N., 294, 308
Warwick, P., 117, 143
Wasserman, P., 61, 67
Watson, J., 4, 6
Watts, H. W., 3, 18, 112, 123, 143, 209, 343, 344, 347, 355
Webb, N., 203, 204, 205, 209, 211
Webb, W., 107
Weibull, M., 204, 211
Wells, W. D., 231, 236
Werts, C. E., 176, 192
White, J. C., Jr., 311, 320
White, S., 45, 49
Wice, P., 48
Wildt, A. R., 318, 321
Wiley, D. E., 195, 196, 201, 203, 210, 211
Wilks, J., 221, 223
Willerman, L., 310, 311, 321
Williamson, J. R., 15, 19
Williamson, J. W., 218, 224
Willis, R. J., 368, 384, 386
Winer, B. J., 302, 308, 326, 327, 340
Wing, R. R., 216, 223

Wittenberg, S., 237n
Wittrock, M. D., 195, 211
Wolf, W., 378, 383
Wolfgang, M., 48
Wolins, L., 16, 20, 163n, 164, 193, 309–321
Wonnacott, R., 249, 261
Wonnacott, T., 249, 261
Woodward, J. A., 15, 17, 180, 318, 321
Wortman, P. M., ix-x, 1–20, 34, 41, 71, 82, 322–340; 341, 355, 362, 363, 365, 386
Wright, B. D., 283n, 285, 287, 288, 289, 293, 297, 308
Wright, E. O., 373, 386

Y

Yates, P., 21n
Yeaton, W. H., 14, 212–224
Young, A., 195, 210
Yunker, J., 270–271, 273, 279, 282

Z

Zeisel, H., 145, 149, 162
Zeisset, P. T., 21n, 88, 143
Zeller, F. A., 365, 386
Zill, N., 122, 143

Subject Index

A

Abstract, guidelines for, 97–99

Access: adequacy of, 22; aids to, 23–25; concept of, 22; current problems in, 22–28; to federal data, 21–33; and machine-readable data files, guidelines for, 125–129; media for, 25–28; options on, 28–31; recommendations on, 31–32

Action for Children's Television, 232

Agencies: oversight, reanalysis in, 50–56; policies of, 9–12, 21–67

Aggregation: data bank on, 31; guidelines for, 123

Alternative models: documentation of, 80–81; and nonexperimental data, 191

American Bicentennial Commission, 41

American Institutes for Research, and bilingual education, 8

American Library Association, 94, 126, 141

American National Standards Institute, 97, 124, 125, 141

American Psychological Association, 215

American Statistical Association (ASA), secondary analyses by, 5

American Statistics Index, 24, 63

Analysis: multilevel, issues in, 205–208; and randomization absent, 144–162; statistical, 159–161; unit of, and between-group and within-group effects, 196–198; units of, choosing, 195–200; within-group dependency in, 203–205

Appendices, guidelines for, 111–114

Archives: facilities for, guidelines for, 127–129; issues and sources in, 57–60

Arrest and conviction rates: analysis of, 266–267, 272, 278; reanalysis of, 238, 239–241, 245, 247, 252–254

Association of Public Data Users (APDU), 11, 12, 64, 65

Association of the Bar of New York, 47

Attrition: impact of, 341–342; in New Jersey Negative Income Tax Experiment, 344–347, 354

Automatic data processing (ADP), 30

B

Bayesian statistics, 147, 148, 160–161
Beginning Teacher Evaluation Study (BTES), 40, 202
Bereiter-Engelmann (B-E) curriculum, immediate and follow-up effects of, 229–231
Between-group effects: and slopes, 200–203; and unit of analysis, 196–198
Bilingual education, reassessment of, 8–9
BLS Data Bank Files and Statistical Routines, 63
British Columbia, University of, Data Library at, 64
Budget Control Act of 1970, 11
Bureau of Justice Statistics (BJS), 45, 49
Bureau of the Census Catalog, 63

C

Cali, Colombia, nutritional and educational enrichment in, 16, 218, 283–308
California, University of, at Los Angeles, 194*n*
California, University of, at Riverside, 70
Campus Unrest survey, 40
Canada, data sources in, 64
Capital punishment research: challenge to reanalysis of, 262–282; corroborating evidence on, 263–265; and data inadequacies, 238–242, 265–267; data sources for replication of, 257–260; dependent variable in, 238–239; deterrence variables in, 239–242, 265, 276–278; evidence and inference in, 275–278; evidence sources in, 251–256; measurement proper to, 278–279; new evidence in, 279–281; and observations deleted, 267–271; reanalysis of, 237–261; regression analysis errors in, 242–251; and statistical errors, 273–275
Carnegie Corporation, 11

Case studies: aims and methods of, 15–17; in secondary analysis, 237–386
Catalog of Machine-Readable Records of the United States, 62
Census, problems with, 5, 6
Center for Human Resources Research (CHRR), 364–365, 379, 382
Center for Machine-Readable Records, 39
Central Statistical Office (CSO), recommended, 22, 28–29, 30, 31, 32
Characteristics of Households Receiving Food Stamps, 40
Civil Aeronautics Board (CAB), 39
Codebooks, guidelines for, 108–111
COFAMM, 176, 184, 186
College Locator Services Study, 40
Colombia, nutritional and educational enrichment in, 16, 218, 283–308
Commensurability, and educational effect, 285–286, 289–290
Commission on Federal Paperwork, 24, 30
Commission to Determine the National Policy Toward Gambling, 40
Comprehensive Employment Training Act (CETA), 356, 359–362
Computer tapes, for data access, 26–27
Congress, and General Accounting Office, 50–56
Congressional Budget and Impoundment Control Act of 1974, Title VII of, 50–51
Congressional Budget Office, 7
Congressional Information Service, 26, 63, 66
Consultants and Consulting Organizations Directory, 61
Continuous Longitudinal Manpower Survey (CLMS), 360–361
Cooperative Reading Project, 200
Cost-benefit and cost-effectiveness, effect size related to, 219–220
Council for European Social Science Data Archives, 11
Crime records, maintenance of, 6
Criminal Justice Archive and Information Network, 46–49
Current Population Survey, 369, 374, 377

Custom-made retrievals, for data access, 27–28

D

Data: access to, 5, 8–9; aggregate, on-line access to, 27; authority to release, 70–71; bases, characteristics of various, 58; code standardization guidelines for, 122; educational, multilevel character of, 195; federal, access and dissemination, 21–33; federal support for archive centers for, 135; inadequate, 238–242, 265–267; maintenance of, 6; microlevel, and public use, guidelines for, 134; missing, guidelines for, 121–122; multilevel educational, regression-based analyses of, 194–211; obtaining, for reanalysis, 70–72; quality 9, 117–125; replication of, and regression analysis, 242–247; research 39–41; resources for locating, 57–67; sufficient, concept of, 170; tools for locating, 24–25; transfer and storage of, 34–42, 123–125; types of, guidelines for, 120–121
Data acknowledgements, guidelines for, 96
Data Clearinghouse for the Social Sciences, 64, 65
Data dictionary, guidelines for, 108–111
Data File Directory, 64
Data resources, policies of, 9–12
Decision Making Information (DMI), 357, 359
Dependence, within-group, in multilevel analysis, 203–205
Desegregation, school: analyses of, reassessed, 328–329; appendix for reanalysis of, 337–338; cohort and attrition effects in, 330; conclusions about, 332, 335; design of study of, 328; parental attitudes toward, 329–330; and personality adjustment, 332, 333–334; problems for future research in, 335–337; and reading achievement, 330–331; reassessment of, 3, 68–83, 322–340; River-

side School Study analyses of, 324–326
Digit-span tests, racial and ethnic differences in, 314–318
Directory of Automatic Data Processing Systems in the Public Health Service, 63
Directory of Computerized Data Files and Related Software, 24, 62
Directory of Federal Agency Education Tapes, 63
Directory of Federal Statistics for Local Areas, 24
Directory of International Statistics, 64
Discrimination: intentional, proof of, 154–159; by sex, in labor market, 373–376
Dissemination: and access, and federal statistics, 21–33; guidelines for, 134–135
Distributor, defined, 95
Documentation: access key to, 25; of alternative data, 80–81; of analyses, 79–80; components of, 88–89, 90; of data sources, as access aid, 25; defined, 87–88; of evaluations, 12, 68–143; guidelines for, 87–117; in machine-readable form, 115–116; minimal, 116–117; need for better, 68–83, 88; organization and format of, guidelines for, 114–117; package, 37; and quality data, guidelines for, 117–125; recommendations for, 78–82; roles in, 129–135; on subprojects, 80; support for use of, guidelines for, 133–134; types of, 79
Domestic Information Display System, 27, 31
Drug Use and Abuse survey, 40
DUALabs, 64, 65
Dummy variables, approach of, 175–176, 177–184

E

Education: data on, in National Archives, 39–40; interactions between immediate and follow-up effects in, 229–231; reevaluating effects of, 283–293

Education Voucher Demonstration, 40

Educational effect: and commensurability, 285-286, 289-290; numerical example of, 287-291; reanalysis of, 297-301

Educational Testing Service (ETS), 165, 202

Effect: educational, 285-291, 297-301; perceived or actual, 220-221; program, 6, 229-231

Effect size: behavioral implications of, 217-218; cost-benefit and cost-effectiveness analyses of, 219-220; defined, 213; empirical bases for estimating, 212-224; evaluating, 214-219; judgmental approaches to, 214-215; and normalization, 218-219; normative approaches to, 215-218; relative or absolute measures of, 213-214; treatments integrated with, 220-222

Elementary and Secondary School Civil Rights Survey, 40

Encyclopedia of Information Systems and Services, 60-61

Environmental Protection Agency, 53

Equal Educational Opportunity Surveys, 3, 11, 38, 40

Equal Employment Opportunity Commission, 38

Errors of measurement, effects of, 267

Europe, data sources in, 64

European Association of Scientific Information Dissemination Centers (EUSIDIC), 64, 65

Evaluation: documentation of, 12, 68-143; program, 3

Evidence: and labeling, 152-154; sources of, 251-256

Execution risk: analysis of, 264, 268-270, 272, 274, 278; reanalysis of, 238, 241-242, 245-247, 248, 249-250, 251-257

Experimental Housing Allowance Program, 40, 52

F

Federal Bureau of Investigation (FBI), 251, 264, 265, 266, 267; Uniform Crime Reporting System (UCRS) of, 238, 239, 240, 255n, 257, 258, 260

Federal Data Locator Service (FDLS), recommended, 24-25, 29-31

Federal government: guides to statistics from, 62-63; use of statistics from, 84-86

Federal grants and contracts: access under, 43-44; dissemination and use under, 37-38

Federal Information Locator Service. *See* Federal Data Locator Service

Federal Information Processing Standards (FIPS), 122

Federal Information Sources and Systems, 62-63

Federal records, defined, 35

Federal Records Act of 1950, 35, 40

Federal Statistical Directory, 24, 63

Federal Statistical System Project, 10, 21-33, 58, 66

Federal Statistics Users' Conference, 58, 63, 65

Federal Trade Commission, 232

Field Corporation, 138

File processing history, guidelines for, 103-108

Follow Through, 3, 4, 195, 196

Ford Foundation, 283n, 295

Forsham v. *Califano*, and proprietary rights of investigator, 1, 6

Framework for Planning U.S. Federal Statistics, 62

G

Gain, relative: factors in, 228; in randomized experiments, 226-228

General Accounting Office. *See* U.S. General Accounting Office

George Washington University, 341n

Government Printing Office (GPO), 26, 127

Guide to Data Resources and Services, 64

Guidelines: conclusions on, 135-137; for data preparation and documentation, 84-143; for documentation, 87-117; index to, 138-141; need for, 86

H

Head Start: economical use of data
from, 4; immediate and follow-up
effects of, 229–231; reassessment of,
3, 15; structural equation model
reanalysis of, 176–190; Westinghouse study of, 3, 13, 149
Higher Education General Information Surveys, 40
Homicide rate, criminal: analysis of,
265–266, 268–270, 272, 274; reanalysis of, 238–239, 240, 241, 245, 248,
249–250, 251, 253–255, 257
Horatio factor, 151, 156, 160
Human Ecology Research Station
(HERS), 295

I

Identification problem, concept of,
171
Illinois, and capital punishment, 277
Illinois Test of Psycholinguistic Abil-
ities (ITPA), 176, 177n, 182, 184,
187
Indiana, and capital punishment, 277
Individuals, research on, 283–284
Information channels, guidelines for,
127
Inquiry service, as access aid, 23–24
Institute for Law and Social Research,
46
Intelligence: appendix on differences
in, 319–320; and digit-span tests,
314–318; discussion of differences
in, 318–319; racial differences in,
309–321; variability of, 310–314
International Association for Social
Science Information Service and
Technology (IASSIST), 11, 37, 58,
64, 65
International Classification of Diseases, 239
International Communication Agency, 40
International Educational Achievement (IEA), Six Subject Survey of,
198–200
International Educational Services,
165

International Federation of Data Organizations for the Social Sciences
(IFDO), 11, 64, 65
International Standards Organization,
122
Interuniversity Consortium of Political and Social Research (ICPSR),
41, 45, 46–49, 64, 133

J

Just-noticeable-difference approach,
217

L

Labeling: effects of, on prediction,
145–148; and evidence, 152–154;
and paradox, 150–152
Labor demand: and sex discrimination, 373–376; and structural factors, 376–377; and women, 372–377
Labor supply: Chicago model of, 368–
369; child care and welfare related
to, 369–371; and household decision making, 367–369; and marital
instability, 371–372; and women,
366–372
Lankershire milk experiments, 149
Latent trait theory, and educational
effect, 284, 285, 291–292
Law, reassessment in, 4
Law Enforcement Assistance Administration (LEAA), 10, 44, 45, 46, 47–
48, 49, 105, 107
Legislative Reorganization Act of
1970, 51
Leinwand Associates, 88, 142
Library of Congress, 126
LISREL computer program, 175, 176,
184
Logarithmic format, merits of, 271–
273
Longitudinal research: and continuity
in measurement, 286–287; external
validity of, 291; and factor composi-
tion, 288; and parameter estima-
tion, 288–289
Longitudinal Retirement History
Study, 40
Los Angeles, Police Department of,
and data access, 5

M

Machine-Readable Archives Division (MRAD), 36–38, 39, 41

Machine-readable data files (MRDF), guidelines for, 84–143

Manpower Development and Training Act (MDTA), 356, 357–359

Manpower training evaluations: bias potential in, 356–363; conclusions on, 362; and Department of Labor's evidence, 359–362; and Mangum's evidence, 357–359

Manpower Training Programs, 365

Massachusetts: and capital punishment, 276, 277; colonial data access in, 5

Measurement, errors of, effects of, 267

Medical records, maintenance of, 6

Meta-analysis: defined, 4; trend toward, 205

Metropolitan Readiness Test (MRT), 176, 177n, 182, 184, 187

Michigan, and capital punishment, 277

Michigan, University of: Center for Political Studies at, 107, 133; Institute for Social Research at, 23, 44, 46; Interuniversity Consortium for Political and Social Research (ICPSR) at, 41, 45, 46–49, 64, 133; Panel Study of Income Dynamics at, 372; Survey Research Center of, 137–138

Michigan State University: Institute for Research in Teaching at, 194n; and policy-data archive, 9

Microform, for data access, 26

Model misspecification, concept of, 13

Monitoring, sponsor's role in, 132–135

N

National Academy of Sciences, 45, 46

National Archives and Records Service. *See* U.S. National Archives and Records Service

National Center for Education Statistics, 63, 66, 137

National Center for Health Services Research, 9

National Center for Health Statistics, 48, 63, 66–67, 239, 260

National Center for State Courts, 48, 49

National Commission on Marijuana and Drug Abuse, 38

National Commission on the Causes and Prevention of Violence, 238, 260

National Commission on the Financing of Postsecondary Education, 39

National Institute of Education (NIE), x, 3, 40, 68n, 163n, 194n, 225n, 283n, 294n, 309n, 322n; and bilingual education, 8; policy of, 9

National Institute of Justice (NIJ): and access, 43–49; policies of, 9, 10–11, 43–45

National Institute of Mental Health, x, 163n

National Longitudinal Survey (NLS) of Labor Market Experience, 364–381

National Longitudinal Surveys (Employment and Training), 40

National Science Foundation, 37, 144n

National Technical Information Service (NTIS), 26, 58, 63, 127, 135; Information Documentation Center of, 64; Statistical Reference Service of, 24

National Testing Organization (NTO), 144n, 157–159, 160

Nebraska, capital punishment in, 276

Negative Income Tax Experiment. *See* New Jersey Negative Income Tax Experiment

New Hampshire, capital punishment in, 276

New Jersey: capital punishment in, 276; Negative Income Tax Experiment in, 17, 342–354, 366

New Jersey Negative Income Tax Experiment (NJE), 17, 366; analysis of, 342–354; attrition in, 344–347, 354; described, 343–347; discussion of, 353–354; reanalysis of, 347–350; results of reanalysis of, 350–354

New York, capital punishment in, 276
Nonexperimental data: approaches to, 175–190; structural equation models for, 163–193
Northeastern University, Computation Center of, 237n
Northwestern University, 341n; Conference on Solutions to Ethical and Legal Problems in Social Research at, 144n; Council for Intersocietal Studies at, 295; Project on Secondary Analysis at, 70–78
Nutrition research: findings from, 295–297; and height and weight, 301–306; implications of, 306–307; reanalysis of, 294–308

O

Occupational Changes in a Generation Survey, 374
Office of Economic Opportunity, 40
Office of Federal Statistical Policy and Standards. See U.S. Department of Commerce
Ohio State University. See Center for Human Resources Research
Organization for Economic Cooperation and Development, 122

P

Paradox, Simpson's, 13, 148–152
Pennsylvania, capital punishment in, 276
Performance Contracting Experiments, 40
Pittsburgh, University of, 48
Planning: researcher's role in, 130–132; sponsor's role in, 132–135
Police Foundation, 49
Policy Foundation, 11
Population Growth and the American Future, 40
President's Commission on Campus Unrest, 39
President's Commission on Law Enforcement and the Administration of Justice (PCL), 238, 260
President's Reorganization Project: background of, 21–22; Federal Sta-

tistical System Project of, 10, 21–33, 58, 66
Printed copy, for data access, 25–26
Prison records, maintenance of, 6
Privacy, in National Archives, 38–39
Privacy Act of 1974, 38
Producer, defined, 94
Program effects: immediate and follow-up, 229–231; probable rival hypotheses on, 6
Program evaluations, examples of secondary analysis of, 3
Project history, guidelines for, 99–103
PROMIS project, 46
Public Health Service, 63, 67
Public opinion polls, in National Archives, 40
Publicity, and marketing, as access aid, 23

R

Race: and differences in intelligence, 309–321; and digit-span test differences, 314–318
RAND Corporation, 49
Randomization: absence of, 144–162; advantages of, 225–226; and evidence, 152–154; and proof of discrimination, 154–159; proposal for, 159–161; and Simpson's paradox, 148–152
Randomized experiments: immediate and follow-up effects in, 229–231; and implementation issues, 233–235; and relative gain, 226–228; secondary analysis of, 225–236; time of implementation in, 231–233
Record and data item identification, guidelines for, 117–120
Records, appraisal of, 36
Regional Economic Information System, 40
Regression, as base for analysis of multilevel data, 194–211
Regression analysis: errors in, 242–251; and functional form, 248–251, 271–273; method upheld for, 264–265; and replication of data, 242–247; and temporal specification, 247–248

Replication, of primary analyses, 72–77
Research Centers Directory, 61
Research Microdata Files, 63
Researcher, planning role of, 130–132
Residual, concept of, 181
Review of Public Data Use, 63
Rhode Island, and capital punishment, 277
Riverside School Study (RSS), 12, 68–83, 323–338
Russell Sage Foundation, 11

S

Safe Schools surveys, 40
San Diego Police Department, 49
Scale dependent mistakes, analysis of, 309–321
School and College Achievement Test, 76
School Superintendents' Survey, and privacy, 38–39
Search for data: guidelines for, 59–60; issues and sources in, 57–60; narrowness of defining in, 58; organizations for, 64–65; resources for, 57–67; sources and guides for, 60–64
Seattle, mobile cardiac care units in, 219
Secondary analysis: additional analyses in, 77–78; benefits of, 34; case studies of, 237–386; clearinghouse for information on data for, 41; contemporary problems in, 5–6; and decision making, 54–55; decision to perform, 6–9; defined, 2, 51; as economical, 4: goals of, 4; improving, 13–14, 144–236; level of, 8; as meta-analysis, 4; overview of, 1–20; rationale for, 2–5, 7–8; replication in, 72–77; of social program evaluations, 54; time needed for, 81; value of, 81–82
Selected Federal Computer-Based Information Systems, 63
Sensitivity analysis, use of, 191
Separate-groups model, approach of, 176, 184–190

Sequential Tests of Educational Progress (STEP), 76, 331n
Sesame Street, 3, 11
Simpson's paradox, 13, 148–152
Slopes: and other group-level indices, 202–203; and school and class characteristics, 203; stability of, 202; within-group, and between-group analyses, 200–203
Social Science Citation Index, 91
Social Science Research Council, 132, 142; Committee on Evaluation Research of, 54; Committee on Social Experiments of, 2
Social sciences data, in National Archives, 40
Social Security Administration, 63, 67; Office of Research of, 9
Social security records, maintenance of, 6
Society of American Archivists Committee on Automation and Data Records, 37
Solution: interpreting, 181–184; standardized, 181
Some Statistical Research Resources Available at the Social Security Administration, 63
South Dakota, capital punishment in, 276
Southern California, University of, 46
Spencer Foundation, 194n, 225n
Sponsor, planning and monitoring role of, 132–135
Standardized Microdata Tape Transcripts, 63
Stanford Achievement Test (SAT), 331n
Stanford-Binet Intelligence Test, 229–231, 291, 297, 310, 311, 312
Statistical Abstract of the U.S., 24
Statistical analysis, proposal for, 159–161
Statistical Analysis System, 189, 193
Statistical Reporter, 63
Statistics Sources, 61
Structural equation models: approaches of, 175–190; concept of, 13–14; fit of, 180–181; identification of, 170–172; and interpreting the solution, 181–184; measurement models in,

Structural equation models: (cont.) 168–170; and nonexperimental data, 163–193; pitfalls in use of, 190–191; representation of, 170, 171; rules for writing, 167–170; steps in, 164; strategies for using, 165–175; writing, 165–167
Study overview, guidelines for documentation of, 89–108
Subject Access Project, 142
Survey of Income and Education, 40
Survey of Postsecondary Career Schools, 40
Sweden, educational effects models in, 198–200

T

Tax records, maintenance of, 6
Teacher bias: index of, 74; reanalysis of, 68–83
Telephone Contacts for Data Users, 24
Television: advertising on, 232–233; violence on, 231–232
Time, experimental treatments over, 231–233
Title I, 8
Title page, guidelines for preparing, 91–96
Toxic Substances Control Act, 53
Treatment, strength and integrity of, 212–213, 220–221

U

United Nations, 64, 66
United States, educational effects models in, 198–200, 203
U.S. Army, One Station Unit Training (OSUT) of, 51–52, 55
U.S. Bureau of Labor Statistics, 24, 258, 261; LABSTAT of, 27, 32
U.S. Bureau of Prisons, 258, 261
U.S. Bureau of the Census, 40, 107, 239, 255n, 257, 258, 259, 260, 261, 364–365; policies of, 9; publications of, 24, 26, 32, 63
U.S. Commission on Civil Rights, 38–39
U.S. Department of Commerce, 259, 261; National Bureau of Standards

of, 122; National Technical Information Service of, 62, 63; Office of Federal Statistical Policy and Standards of, 24, 25, 33, 37, 42, 58, 62, 63, 66, 132, 142
U.S. Department of Education, 9
U.S. Department of Health, Education, and Welfare, 12, 37, 39, 40, 63, 66–67, 237n
U.S. Department of Housing and Urban Development, 40
U.S. Department of Justice, 45
U.S. Department of Labor, 63, 67, 356, 359–362, 363, 386; Manpower Administration of, 365; Office of Manpower Research and Development of, 365
U.S. General Accounting Office, 4, 7, 12, 20, 67; and guidelines, 87, 126, 132, 133, 135; Institute for Program Evaluation of, 11; Program Analysis Division of, 11; publications of, 58, 62–63; and quality control, 11; role of, 50–56
U.S. National Archives and Records Service (NARS), 67, 85, 127, 134, 135; and data access, 9, 10; described 35–36; General Records Disposition Schedules of, 35; and Machine-Readable Archives, 36–38, 39, 41; policy of, 34–42; and privacy, 38–39; publications of, 24, 58, 62; and research data, 39–41
U.S. Office of Education, review of data quality by, 3
U.S. Office of Management and Budget, 29, 63, 67, 126, 132
U.S. Public Health Service, 239, 260, 261, 266, 282
U.S. Supreme Court, 322–323, 340
U.S. v. Youritan Construction Company, 154–157, 158, 159, 160, 162
University Group Diabetes Program Data, controversy over, 1, 15

V

Valle, Universidad del, 295
Variables: dependent and independent, 166; relating to one another,

165–167; three, and one factor, 174–175; two observed and one trait, 172–174

Vermont, capital punishment in, 276

Violence in America, 40

Virginia, University of, 41

Vital and Health Statistics Publications Series, 63

Vocational Education Directory Survey, 40

Voucher projects, reassessment of, 3

W

Wechsler Intelligence Scale for Children-Revised (WISC-R), 288, 296, 297–301, 306–307, 314, 315, 317

Wechsler Preschool and Primary Scale of Intelligence (WPPSI), 288

Westat, Inc., 359–360

Westinghouse study of Head Start, 3, 13, 149

Wisconsin, and capital punishment, 277

Wisconsin, University of: Institute for Research on Poverty Data Center at, 133, 342; New Jersey Maintenance Project study at, 133

Wisconsin, University of, at Madison, guideline testing at, 87

Within-group effects: and dependency, 203–205; and slopes, 200–203; and unit of analysis, 196–198

Women: analysis of survey data on, 364–386; intergenerational mobility of, 376; and labor demand, 372–377; and labor supply, 366–372; research issues on, 378–381; and subsample selectivity bias, 378

Y

Youritan case, 154–157, 158, 159, 160, 162